DISASTERS OF BIBLICAL PROPORTIONS

Disasters of Biblical Proportions

THE TEN PLAGUES THEN, NOW, AND AT THE END OF THE WORLD

STEVEN WEITZMAN

PRINCETON UNIVERSITY PRESS
PRINCETON & OXFORD

Published by Princeton University Press
41 William Street, Princeton, New Jersey 08540
99 Banbury Road, Oxford OX2 6JX

press.princeton.edu

GPSR Authorized Representative: Easy Access System Europe - Mustamäe tee 50, 10621 Tallinn, Estonia, gpsr.requests@easproject.com

ISBN 978-0-691-27046-3
ISBN (e-book) 978-0-691-28740-9
ISBN (Web PDF) 978-0-691-27051-7

Library of Congress Control Number: 2025946089

British Library Cataloging-in-Publication Data is available
Editorial: Fred Appel, Tara Dugan
Production Editorial: Elizabeth Byrd
Jacket: Chris Ferrante
Production: Erin Suydam
Publicity: Maria Whelan (US), Kathryn Stevens (UK)
Copyeditor: Ashley Moore

Jacket image: Hein Nouwens / iStock

Printed in the United States of America

10 9 8 7 6 5 4 3 2 1

Dedicated to the staff, fellows, and board members of
the Herbert D. Katz Center for Advanced Judaic Studies at
the University of Pennsylvania for all they have done to create,
and re-create, the Katz Center as a source of light and warmth.

Angel of death, pass over us all, turn back into the myth you used to be before you became the news.

—ALICIA JO RABINS

CONTENTS

FIGURES AND EPIGRAPH CREDITS

Figures

Epigraph Credits

ACKNOWLEDGMENTS

THE INITIAL idea for this book came to me during the opening month of the global shutdown caused by Covid-19, on the evening of April 8, 2020, to be exact, the first night of Passover that year. It is traditional for Jews to recall the ten plagues during Passover, and in the days before the holiday that year, so many Jews were connecting that custom to Covid, using the ten plagues to make sense of the pandemic or the pandemic to interpret the plagues, that I realized that it would make for a diverting research project to explore how people had used the story to find something edifying, redemptive, reassuring, or funny in the pandemic and other disasters. I was only intending to work on it until life returned to normal, but life never quite did that; I found myself with new motives to pursue the project, and it eventually developed into this book.

In the early months of the pandemic the project became an obsession, a kind of doomscrolling as it were, only instead of searching relentlessly for information about present-day disasters, I was hunting for insights into biblical disasters. As the project took shape, however, I found myself stymied by the quarantine. My university library was closed at the time; there were no colleagues around to speak with or bounce ideas off of; and there were only so many times that I could test my relationship with my learned and very patient wife, Mira Wasserman, by cajoling her into listening to the latest thing I had learned about frogs or locusts.

Beyond her love and support, three things sustained the project during this early period. The nonprofit HathiTrust, a digital library, made its resources freely available to everyone to the fullest extent that was legal, including older books not to be found online in any other way. Penn Libraries figured out a system for mailing books to people's homes.

And scholars—many of whom I did not know—were willing to respond to my out-of-the-blue email inquiries. I want to express heartfelt gratitude to and admiration for HathiTrust and Penn Libraries for all they did to provide treasured access to books, taking special note of Josef Gulka, Arthur Kiron, and Bruce Nielsen of the Katz Center's library at Penn, and I want to thank the following people for responding to my inquiries or for offering encouragement during this challenging period: Elisheva Baumgarten, Peter Decherney, Lucie Doležalová, John Efron, Hadar Feldman, Julie Anne Harris, Ron Hendel, Ikea Johnson, Ruth Kara-Ivanov Kaniel, Hartley Lachter, Jacob Morrow-Spitzer, Andrea Rapp (an archivist at the Shavzin-Carsch Collection of Historic Jewish Children's Literature), Dorothea Salzer, Adi Shiran, and John Wallis. I regret that I was not able to squeeze in every insight that I gleaned from these colleagues, and I should add that if I have accidentally omitted anyone, it is because the most intensive period of reaching out to scholars for guidance occurred during Covid, remotely, and my memory of that period is rather foggy.

I also want to thank another group of colleagues. During this same period, as another coping measure, I joined with a group of Jewish studies and religious studies colleagues to form an online poker group, a group that still meets weekly and now includes as regular or frequent participants Ofer Ashkenazi, Dustin Atlas, Hussein Banai, Zachary Berger, Jeremy Dauber, Reyhan Durmaz, Joshua Garoon, Marie Harf, Ruth Kara, John Penniman, Gabriel Raeburn, Joshua Shanes, and Jeff Veidlinger. Many of us were not very skilled at poker, but the game was an opportunity for weekly banter, jokes, and mutual support, and I mention it here not just because it helped me get through the pandemic but because the conversation generated some key ideas. An example is a gift mailed to me by John Penniman, a collection of toy ten plagues that focused my attention on the modern-day "playification" of the ten plagues, their transformation into toys, games and other kinds of play—a subject I treat in the chapter on the plague of frogs.

Of course, the pandemic was many years ago already, and the book has developed considerably since then. There were several points when I thought I was finished with it, only to realize—once others began to read it—that it needed to be substantially improved in content, organization, and the level of writing. This book has benefited immeasurably from the interventions and advice of editors whom I commissioned at different stages—Vanessa Davies at a very early stage; Alex Ramos; Angela Erisman; and Thomas LeBien, Amanda Moon, and James Brandt of Moon and Company. In retrospect, I am embarrassed by my earlier thinking and writing, and feel very indebted to what each of these individuals did to help the book mature.

In the summer of 2023, the pandemic having waned, I had the opportunity to try out some ideas in the context of a brief course on the ten plagues at the Hebrew University. I won't mention the students in that course by name, but I am very grateful to them as a group for allowing me to share some ideas with them; to Gilor Meshalum, a wonderful course assistant; and to Professor Noam Mizrachi for arranging the course—and supporting it despite a faculty strike at the time. I wasn't able to stay in touch with the students, but I think about them a lot, knowing their lives were transformed by October 7 and the war in Gaza that broke out a few months later. I also had a chance to try out some ideas in the context of a summer school for graduate students in Jewish studies that I codirect with Aaron Segal and Vivian Liska, and I want to thank those students and participating faculty as well. Almost none of the research presented here has been published before, and only a little of it has been presented in public, but I did present a version of the first plague chapter at a conference organized in October 2024 on justice in the Hebrew Bible, and I want to thank dear friends Leora Batnitzky, Ilana Pardes, and Vivian Liska for making that possible. The only section to have appeared in writing before, a brief discussion of the Haggadah that I have expanded on in chapter 10, was published as a post on the website TheTorah.com in 2024: https://thetorah.com/article/i-god-and-not-an-angel-the-haggadah-counters-jesus-and-the-arma-christi.

I am especially indebted to Fred Appel, publisher at Princeton University Press, who has been supportive of my research for more than a decade now, and whose contributions as an editor to scholarship are immeasurable. Fred recognized something worthwhile in the book but urged me to keep working on it; arranged and supported the revision process with

Moon and Company; and has been extraordinarily encouraging, patient, and helpful at every step of the way. The field of Jewish studies is exceedingly fortunate to have Fred working on its behalf.

I am also extremely thankful to others at Princeton University Press or working on its behalf for all they have done to bring the book into being: the anonymous reviewers of the manuscript for excellent feedback and suggestions for revision; editorial associate Tara Dugan, who was just beginning at Princeton University Press at the time and yet was so helpful as I prepared the manuscript for submission; John Donohue, editor at Westchester Publishing Services, expert at shepherding the book to completion; Elizabeth Byrd of Princeton University Press, manager of the production process; copyeditor Ashley Moore; and Enid Zafran, who prepared the index. I was only able to navigate the process of securing permissions for the illustrations because of the assistance of Charlotte Fletcher, an outstanding Penn student.

As I have mentioned, my ability to carry through with this project was made possible by the support of my wife, Mira Wasserman; we have been through our own personal plagues of frogs, hail, boils, locusts, and darkness, and her love makes it easier to brace for whatever happens next. I also want to express my gratitude for the forbearance of my four sons, Yosi, Hillel, Lev, and Or, who had to endure four-plus years of ten plagues–related musings, and for encouragement from my father, Gerald Weitzman, who passed away while I was writing this book; siblings Angie and Mark; mothers-in-law Judy Wortman and Ricki Wasserman; and a lifelong friend, Kevin Gerson. I know that I can only do what I do as a scholar because of the support of the University of Pennsylvania, especially the community at the Herbert D. Katz Center for Advanced Judaic Studies, which I have been privileged to direct since 2014. I dedicate this book in gratitude to the Katz Center community for all that its members have done to advance scholarship and continue to do so, even in this age of cascading disaster and hard-heartedness.

Introduction

A HISTORY OF SIGNS AND WONDERS

What happened to the ancestors is a sign for the children.

—*MIDRASH TANCHUMA*

THE BOOK of Exodus begins with the well-known story of Israel's departure from Egypt. As I suspect most readers will recall, God sends ten catastrophes in order to compel the Egyptians to liberate the Israelites—turning the waters of Egypt into blood; summoning frogs from the river to invade people's homes; afflicting the Egyptians with lice, flies, cattle plague, and boils; unleashing hail and locusts; causing three days of darkness; and finally striking down all the firstborn in Egypt, humans and animals. This is a very old story, and one that may seem like it was frozen in place by the canonization of the five books of Moses. Indeed, over its long history and through countless retellings, many of the core elements have remained more or less intact: the enslavement and suffering at the start of the story, the role of Pharaoh as the villain, the Passover sacrifice offered during the tenth plague, and the redemption of the Israelites at the end.

Yet throughout the centuries, as people have confronted their own plagues—wars, outbreaks, famines, and all manner of natural disaster—they have found ways to adjust this biblical story to reflect their situations, investing it with their own fears, trauma, and outrage and using it to figure out how to respond and to find a way forward. Even in our own time, there has been no shortage of occasions that have motivated people to imbue the plagues of the exodus with new meaning, as one can see from how the story has been connected to two recent crises: the Covid-19 pandemic and the Hamas attack against Israel on October 7, 2023, and the ensuing war in Gaza.

The global shutdown in 2020 occurred just a few weeks before Passover, a holiday that involves the recitation of the plagues, so it was inevitable that people would seek to connect them to the pandemic; and in fact, some reported feeling that the plagues were happening again.

There were also religious leaders at the time warning against interpreting the pandemic as a new ten plagues, remembering how damaging it had been when people interpreted AIDS as a biblical plague sent to punish people for their sins.[1] For many others, though, the pandemic did indeed feel like a repetition of the ten plagues, a divine chastisement sent to teach humanity a lesson. Google has a tool that allows one to identify trends in what people are searching for online, and a sudden and very sharp spike in searches for the phrase "ten plagues" in March and April of 2020—a surge of interest greater than what the tool revealed for Passovers of the last twenty years—suggests the pandemic led a lot of people to remember and look into the biblical story.

The relevance of the ten plagues for making sense of Covid was the result of a calendrical coincidence—the story might not have come to mind for as many people if the global shutdown had occurred over the summer or during the fall as opposed to just before Passover. But once introduced into people's consciousness in this way, the story resonated very powerfully as a way of transforming the pandemic into a meaningful and even beneficial experience. In a 1989 essay entitled "What Is an Epidemic?," the sociologist Charles Rosenberg observed that one way that people managed their fear of AIDS was to try to reassert control by narrating the epidemic as a story unfolding according to a discernible plotline.[2] Depictions of Covid-19 as a repetition of the ten plagues, or as an eleventh plague, emerged during the shutdown as such a story, tying the pandemic to Passover in a way that transformed a frightening and disorienting experience into a sign from God or the universe that it was time to free oneself from the enslavements of modern life, or to focus on those afflicted by present-day injustice and oppression and liberate them.[3]

A few years later, a different kind of disaster struck—the shocking Hamas attack that killed some 1,200 people and took 250 people hostage, along with Israel's ensuing counterattack against Gaza that killed tens of thousands and displaced its population. As Jews had done with Covid-19, when Passover came around in 2024, they turned to the story of the ten plagues as a way to draw some lessons from the events of October 7. Some invoked the ten plagues as a model for the violent retribution they wanted to see exacted against Hamas for its crimes: "Perhaps the most significant message of the [story] this year," wrote Rabbi Nolan Lebovitz, is "that an overwhelming punishing response is the only appropriate action against such villains."[4] In other versions of the story, it was the Israeli government that was cast in the role of the Egyptians. The journalist Anshel Pfeffer, for instance, published a list of the "self-inflicted ten plagues" imposed on Israel by Prime Minister Benjamin Netanyahu.[5] Some of the family members of the hostages, to express their outrage with Netanyahu for celebrating Passover during the ordeal, even staged a ten plagues–related protest outside his home, splashing red paint on a mock Seder table to recall the plague of blood against Pharaoh and then burning the table.[6]

At Passover time in 2020, the ten plagues story had been used to articulate the fear and disorientation caused by the pandemic, and to urge people to reflect on their shortcomings and embrace a need for a radical change of some sort. Three years later, the story took on a very different meaning, expressing—and sometimes enacting—people's anger with those they held responsible. In both crises, comparing an ongoing trauma to the ten plagues helped to impose a narrative structure on a chaotic present and offered guidance about how to respond. Yet how people were using the story—its significance and emotional tonality—was radically different in the two situations. During Covid-19, people had drawn on the story to interpret the pandemic as a call for personal or societal transformation. In the wake of October 7, people used the story to call for retribution, to denounce the Israeli government as Pharaoh-like, or to plead for empathy with the Palestinians devastated by the war—an adaptation of the Passover custom of using the recital of the plagues to acknowledge what the Egyptians had to suffer for Israel to go free.

As these examples demonstrate, the ten plagues, though often taken for granted as a vaguely remembered biblical story, can sometimes feel uncannily and urgently relevant. The biblical account was written in a far-off time and place, emerging from ancient Canaan more than 2,500 years ago in an ancient language unfamiliar to most people today, and yet it can be called back to mind as if it were a story about people's own personal circumstances intended as a guide for how to make sense of present-day catastrophe. Scientists can now explain disasters without reference to God, and theologians have come up with more sophisticated ways of interpreting catastrophe religiously, but the core idea of the ten plagues story—that disasters are a sign sent to punish the wicked, to warn people to repent of their sins, and to reestablish justice—continues to ring true for many people, and that view has kept the ten plagues story alive as a way to impose meaning on disaster, assign blame, and express the feelings of powerlessness, guilt, and outrage that the world's injustices can arouse.

What these examples also demonstrate, however, is that the retelling of the ten plagues story is a remarkably flexible and adaptive response to crisis. That too is part of the tale's ability to feel relevant for so long for so many people, and it is what motivates the central aim of this book, which is to understand how people have drawn on the biblical story of the ten plagues to make sense of their own lives. In what follows, we will be exploring what happened to the ten plagues story when people took creative ownership over it, working with details taken from the biblical story—Moses, Pharaoh, and the other characters of the story; the setting in Egypt; the character and sequence of the plagues; and the Passover sacrifice and exodus that follow in their wake—but adapting and expanding on this narrative foundation in light of their own experiences and goals as storytellers. The earliest examples of such retelling come from the Bible itself, from psalms and prophetic texts that retell the plagues, and it continues into our own era, as illustrated by how the story was applied to Covid-19 and the events of October 7. This is the history we will be exploring in this book, a history of people reimagining the signs and wonders of the exodus.

This aim, it is worth noting up front, means that our primary focus will not be on the biblical account of the plagues itself. For readers interested in the ten plagues as recounted in Exodus, there are many resources, including a good number of books that treat the ten plagues as historical events, proposing to have uncovered historical or scientific evidence that proves they really happened, as well as commentaries that explain what we know about the authorship of the Exodus account and the circumstances in which it was composed. Our focus, instead, will be the story as it has taken shape in people's imaginations, the story that combines elements from the biblical account with elements imported into it by those who are retelling it. The ten plagues story is, in this sense, not a single story at all but a multigenerational family of stories—thousands and thousands of descendent stories that expand on or reenact the biblical account.

One of the lessons I hope the reader takes away from our exploration of this material is a deeper appreciation of retelling as a way of making sense of life. Many of us have not had the experience of coming up with a completely new story, but we are all of us retellers of stories heard from others or encountered in a book, in an illustration, in a movie, or online, and the act of retelling that story involves its own distinctive form of creativity—repeating an already told story but in a way that injects a little of ourselves into it and that adapts it to new audiences and new circumstances.[7] Such a practice might seem more conservative than creative, an act of preservation and transmission rather than invention. However, as happens every time a joke or a rumor is retold, people always have some reason of their own for repeating the story, something of their own they are aiming to communicate to their audience, and they do not simply pass on what they receive from others without introducing changes in pursuit of those aims. One of my goals in this book, using the ten plagues as an example, is to show how this creative process of adaptation and personalization has reshaped—and is still reshaping—the meaning of the Bible.

Signs of the Times

This book is what scholars refer to as a reception history, a history of how people in different historical eras and social contexts have interpreted and retold the ten plagues story in light of their own experiences, but it is not organized as a conventional history. Books of this type usually begin with the earliest interpretations of the biblical story and move from there to later periods, and if we were following that model, we'd begin with the earliest known references to the ten plagues found in the Hebrew Bible—the book of Exodus, the Psalms, and the Prophets—move from biblical texts to the earliest known postbiblical interpretations in ancient texts like the Wisdom of Solomon and the writing of the first-century-CE philosopher Philo of Alexandria, and then move from those sources to later interpretations from the Middle Ages and modern times. My problem with a straightforwardly chronological approach is that the retelling of the ten plagues moves in too many directions simultaneously to fit into a single linear narrative.

What I have done instead is organize the book according to the ten plagues themselves, as laid out in Exodus. Each chapter zeros in on something odd or puzzling in the biblical account, some detail or question that distinguishes the plague in question from the other nine, and uses that element to launch an essay about how the plague has been understood, expanded on, visualized, or reenacted in later interpretive tradition. When I first undertook to write this book, I was influenced by recent study of the role of the Bible in giving meaning to disaster, especially books focused on that equally paradigmatic biblical disaster, the flood of Genesis, and tried to model myself methodologically on Lydia Barnett's *After the Flood: Imagining the Global Environment in Early Modern Europe* and *Noah's Arkive* by Jeffrey Cohen and Julian Yates. But as my research deepened, it became clearer and clearer that people retell the ten plagues for all kinds of reasons—to make sense of the disasters they experience, but also to keep children awake at Passover Seders, to envision the end of the world, and to protest injustice. The chapters grew more varied as a result, each one finding its own pathway through the story's history.

Before turning to the first plague, however, I want to use the rest of this chapter to introduce some background to help orient the reader. Since we won't be following a straight line from ancient to medieval to modern interpretations but moving back and forth between them, it will be helpful to sketch at the outset some history about how the plagues came to play such a central role in collective consciousness, and why people understand the story so differently.

The story owes its status and familiarity to its presence in the Bible as a part of the Exodus story, and for that reason, it will certainly enhance the reading of this book to review the biblical account in Exodus 1–12—the narrative of the Israelites' enslavement in Egypt under the harsh Pharaoh, Moses's encounter with God at the burning bush, the signs and wonders that follow when Moses and his brother Aaron confront Pharaoh in Egypt, and the divine intervention of the last plague, the slaying of the firstborn, that finally compels the Egyptians to let the Israelites go from their bondage and embark for the land promised to their ancestors in Canaan.

But reading, or rereading, the biblical account will not suffice as background. When a person today recalls the ten plagues, they usually aren't simply remembering the story as it is told in Exodus but are recalling the story in some mediated form. They may have first heard it told to them by a parent or read about it in a children's book. They might know the story as recounted in a Passover Seder. They may have first experienced it through a movie or a painting. Even if a person's first encounter with the plagues is the narrative in Exodus, there is a good chance that they know the story from some translation, and different translations, retellings in their own right, can change the meaning of the biblical story in small but important ways.

Consider, for instance, the English expression "signs and wonders," taken from Exodus 7:3, where the phrase is used in reference to the plagues. One consequence of this translation is that the plagues came to be associated in the minds of those reading the English Bible with the emotion of wonder, the feeling of amazement in the presence of a miracle, and an association with miracles was further encouraged by the use of "signs and wonders" in the New Testament to refer to the miracles of

Jesus and the early church. However, this is not the only way to understand the underlying Hebrew word translated here as "wonders," *mophetim*. The ancient Greek translation of the Torah known as the Septuagint ascribes to it a somewhat different meaning by rendering it as *terata*, portents, a term used in reference to rare and strange events signaling future change and calamity. Both "wonders" and "portents" denote the plagues as extraordinary events, but they have different shades of meaning: one has an association with spectacle—"wonders" are events to behold and be astounded by—while "portents" foreshadow doom, and this small variation in translation encouraged different understandings of the overall story. Reading the word as "wonders," suggesting the plagues were visually arresting, helped to focus people's attention on what it was like to witness them. Reading the word as "portents" associated the plagues with omens, turning them into warnings of a greater disaster to come.

What is true of how we understand a particular biblical phrase like "signs and wonders" is true of the whole ten plagues story. The core of the biblical story comes from the book of Exodus, but what we remember about the story has been filtered through intervening interpretations—translations into Greek, Latin, English, and other languages; biblical commentaries; religious events where the story is retold, such as the Seder or the Sunday sermon; and retellings and expansions of the story in different media like painting and film. In truth, the biblical story can only be encountered these days in a mediated way—even the Hebrew text read in synagogues by Jews today is only known in a medieval form bequeathed to Jews by ancient scribes known as the Masoretes who added vowels and punctuation to make the text more readable. Each intervention in how the story was presented—each translation, each physical reformatting of the biblical text; even a shift in meaning or emotional resonance of a single word—had the potential to change how it was experienced, understood, and remembered.

This kind of modification of the story is even reflected in the expression "the ten plagues" itself, an English translation of the Hebrew *'eser makkot* introduced in ancient rabbinic sources. The phrase itself does not appear in the Hebrew Bible, which never counts up the plagues or distinguishes them as a set of ten distinct from other signs and wonders recorded in Exodus, and the fact that Psalms 78 and 105, in brief summaries of the exodus story, only refer to six or seven calamities in a different order from Exodus suggests that the exact number and sequence of plagues did not even register as significant at this very early point in the story's history. Jews only began to refer to ten plagues in the Hellenistic age, and it is only from that point forward that the number ten became important to how people interpreted them.

The translation of *makkot* as "plagues" triggered yet other changes in the understanding of the story. Originally, the two terms meant the same thing—"blows" or "wounds"—and could be applied to any kind of calamity, but by the sixteenth century, the English word "plague" had come to be used as a synonym for "pestilence," a fatal disease that can spread to large groups of people, and that shift in the word's meaning made the ten plagues feel newly relevant for understanding present-day epidemics and pandemics—this is part of the background of why the ten plagues came to mind for so many people during the opening months of Covid-19. We need to factor in the shifting understanding of what the Bible is, and what its language denotes and connotes, to understand why people recount the plagues in such different ways.

We also need to factor in how the biblical account in Exodus was supplemented by other sacred texts. When Jews, Christians, and Muslims retold the story, they were not basing it on Exodus alone, or at all in the case of Muslims, but following the story as recounted in other sources. As a Jew, my understanding of the plagues has been influenced by how they are treated in a booklet known as the Haggadah that is read during the Passover Seder, while a Christian or Muslim reader will know the story not from the Haggadah but in light of the New Testament or from the account of Moses's confrontation with Pharaoh in the Qur'an. All of these sources draw on information that ultimately goes back to the Hebrew Bible, but they present the plagues in different ways, reframing them in different literary and religious contexts, and interpreting them in light of different ideas and beliefs, and as a result of their influence, the story has developed in very different directions within Jewish, Christian, and Islamic tradition.

The differences in how these sources refer to the plagues is important enough to the history I aim to relate that it is worth looking briefly at what each one says about the plagues and how its influence subsequently affected the way later people understood and related to the story.

Warning Signs and Wake-Up Calls: The Plagues in Christian Tradition

Christian interpretation of the ten plagues goes back to the very beginning of Christianity in the first few centuries of the common era and has been heavily influenced by the writings collected in the New Testament. Verses from Exodus 7–12 come up throughout New Testament writings, but I will mention just two examples that illustrate how the New Testament influenced the way Christians recounted the ten plagues, encouraging them to tie the story to the story of Jesus.

The first example comes from the Gospel of John and its "seven signs," a series of miracles performed by Jesus that begin with a miracle, the turning of water into wine in John 2:1–12, redolent of the first plague, where Moses turns the waters of Egypt into blood. The Jesus of John questions why people need "signs and wonders" in order to believe (see John 4:43–54), but the fact that the gospel adopts the language of signs and wonders, used to refer to the plagues in Exodus 7:3, shows that its author, a Christian at the end of the first century, detected and wanted his readers to see a correspondence between Jesus's miracles and Moses's wonders.

Another early Christian who saw a connection between the ten plagues and Jesus was the author of Revelation, also known as the Apocalypse of John. The last and most cryptic book in the New Testament, Revelation includes a vision of God's final judgment of humanity, the return of Christ, and the establishment of a new heaven and earth. Among the events envisioned, addressed in chapter 16, is a series of seven apocalyptic plagues that were clearly modeled on the plague narrative in Exodus, including plagues that involve water turning to blood, painful sores, darkness, and a terrible hailstorm (figure 1). The correspondence with the ten plagues is not exact, but the resemblance was close enough that later Christians sometimes conflated the two sets of

FIGURE 1. Angels pouring out the apocalyptic plagues described in Revelation 16, from an illustrated version of the New Testament completed in 1531. The Ottheinrich Bible, p. 298. Alamy.

plagues, seeing the ten plagues in Egypt as an anticipation of the disasters that would devastate humanity at the time of Christ's return. A fifth-century text known as the Apocalypse of Thomas, for instance, elaborated on Revelation with a description of a series of disasters expected to come before the end of the world, and in turn, its influence spawned the widely circulated medieval tradition known as the "Fifteen Signs before Doomsday," a cataloging of apocalyptic ecological catastrophes expected to occur in the weeks leading to the Day of Judgment and Christ's return, including the rising of the sea, the bleeding of trees and other plants, storms, and falling stars.[8]

Apocalyptic narrative gave Christians a way to develop the correspondence between the ten plagues and the story of Christ, but another, equally important way to expand on the story was the sermon, a genre perhaps inherited from earlier Jewish tradition but developed by early Christians into a highly effective form of spiritual and moral instruction performed in church-related and educational settings. Delivered during Sunday worship gatherings or in the context of holidays and festivals like Easter, the sermon was used not only to develop the connection between the ten plagues and the story of Christ and the Crucifixion but to urge Christians to repent of their sins lest they suffer the same fate as the Egyptians in the story.

A third-century example comes from Origen, a highly prolific writer considered the greatest Christian philosopher before Augustine, a long sermon that aims to uncover a logic behind the progression from one plague to the next.[9] Origen developed many of his sermons for public gatherings and worship, but this sermon seems to have been meant for students of the school that Origen established in Caesarea in 232 CE after being expelled from Alexandria. Using allegorical biblical interpretation to detect hidden meaning in the plagues, he asserted that each one symbolized a field of pagan learning that Christians need to reject for the sake of their soul. The waters of Egypt turned into blood represent the slippery teachings of the philosophers; the frogs of the second plague (which Origen understood to be very noisy) manifest the puffed-up melodies and stories of the poets; the gnats symbolize the stinging words of philosophical argument; and so on for each of the plagues. Origen's point was that Christians should reject the folly of these different kinds of pagan education in favor of a scripture-centered Christian education, and by reading the plagues in light of Christ's sacrifice on the cross, he also discovered in them a ten-step method that would help Christians see through the illusion of material reality, overcome their sins, and develop their souls to more fully appreciate Christ.

An important sermon imputed to Augustine himself was inspired by the New Testament's description of Jesus as a physician who has come to heal the sick (Mark 2:17). The idea was important to Augustine, who emphasized Christ's role as a healer of humankind, and the sermon in question, though probably not written by the bishop, was circulated in his name, and it may be that what suggested him as the author was how it built its interpretation of the ten plagues on the concept of sin as a sickness that God seeks to heal.[10] Here, each plague is said to have exposed a spiritual "wound" in humanity, and the cure was to be found in the corresponding commandment in the Ten Commandments. Thus, the first plague, darkening the waters into blood, revealed the murkiness of a mind that refuses to recognize that God, like water, is the source of everything, and the remedy is the first commandment in Exodus 20—"You shall have no other gods beside me." The loquacious frogs of the second plague symbolize the empty prattling of philosophers and heretics who deny the truth of Christ, and the cure for their nonsense is the second commandment—"You shall not take the name of the Lord in vain." The sermon develops similar correspondences for all the remaining plagues and commandments.

Thanks to its association with Augustine, the sermon's effort to establish correspondences between the ten plagues and the Ten Commandments had a major impact on how later Christians understood the plagues. Out of the fifty-seven illustrated Ten Commandment cycles known from Europe from before the sixteenth century—these were listings of the commandments in various forms meant to help Christians learn and remember them—twenty-two connect the commandments and the plagues, listing them side by side or interrelating them in other ways. The resulting list of sins and their punishments offered an alternative to the seven deadly sins that Christians had been using to teach what vices to avoid and helped to establish the Ten Commandments as the spiritual and moral code they remain for many Christians to this day.[11]

Yet another example of how Christians used the sermon to fuse together the story of the plagues with the story of Jesus is a sermon known as "On the Plague of Hail and His Father's Silence," delivered by the bishop Gregory of Nazianzus in 373.[12] This is, as far as I am aware, the earliest example where the ten plagues were used to make sense of a present-day disaster. The town of Nazianzus had recently been devastated by a succession of catastrophes that recalled the biblical plagues—hailstorm, a cattle plague, and a drought—and Gregory's sermon explained these events as divine punishment for the community's sins, especially its mistreatment of the poor. In contrast to the Origen and Augustinian sermons, this sermon does not focus on the ten plagues, but Gregory did make reference to them, warning that the calamities that had occurred so far were relatively mild and that God had it in his power to send more devastating plagues—the boils, the locusts, the darkness, and the slaying of the firstborn—if people persisted in their sins. Rather than suffer the full extent of God's wrath, the sermon continues, the sinful ought to recall what the Israelites did to save themselves when they sprinkled the blood of the Passover sacrifice on the doorposts of their homes and train their thoughts on the saving power of Christ's blood.

In some Christian retellings of the story, the ten plagues exemplify a conception of divine justice associated with the Old Testament as opposed to the New Testament and its focus on divine mercy. This is the meaning of the ten plagues in Albert Camus's 1947 novel *The Plague*, where a Jesuit priest named Paneloux, a scholar of Augustine, delivers two sermons over the course of the story.[13] In the first sermon, the priest warns his congregation that the epidemic that has hit their city is divine punishment for turning away from God, and that they need to repent before the death angel comes for them too. In the second sermon, delivered a few months later after the priest's confidence in God is shaken by witnessing the excruciating death of a child named Philippe, Paneloux gives up on explaining God's will in the way he does in the first sermon, but he nonetheless demands absolute faith even in the face of suffering that cannot be understood. As an atheist, Camus was not endorsing either theological explanation—in fact, the novel's narrator doubts that anyone really believes in Paneloux's God—but he was being true to Christian homiletical tradition in imagining a sermon that uses the ten plagues to interpret a present-day disaster as a warning against sin and a call to repentance, and there is also something authentically Christian about the succession of the two sermons, the first inspired by the Old Testament, the second by the New. Paneloux never renounces the concept of divine justice he illustrates with the ten plagues, but he subordinates the story to the story of Christ's suffering through the second sermon and its call on the faithful to embrace such suffering themselves. Whether Camus was basing the story on a sermon he heard we do not know, but his novel is true to the deeply rooted Christian tradition of using the sermon to retell the ten plagues in relation to the Crucifixion as a signifier of Old Testament justice as opposed to New Testament mercy.

Dinner-Table Deliverance: The Plagues in Jewish Tradition

To understand Jewish interpretations of the plagues story, it helps to know something about the history of reciting the plagues during the Seder, the ritualized dinner used to celebrate Passover. The term "Passover" and the core elements of the Passover ritual—the sacrifice of a lamb and the consumption of unleavened bread or matzah—come from the ten plagues story itself, from Exodus 12, but other elements of the Seder come from the Mishnah, the earliest authoritative collection of rabbinic teachings that was produced in the third century CE.

The Mishnaic tractate that discusses the laws of Passover, known as Pesahim, does not mention the practice of reciting the ten plagues, but it laid the groundwork for the practice by requiring the leader of the Seder to explain to his son the meaning of a passage in Deuteronomy 26:5–8, a summary of the exodus that, according to early rabbinic interpretation, referred to the plagues in verse 8 (here placed in italics): "A wandering Aramean was my father, and he went down into Egypt and dwelled there, few in number, and he became there a great nation, strong and populous. And the Egyptians abused us, oppressed us, and forced hard labor on us, and we cried to the Lord, the God of our fathers, and he heard our voice and saw our oppression, and our toil, and the strain we were under. *And the Lord brought us out of Egypt with a mighty hand and an outstretched arm, with great terror, and with signs and wonders*" (Deuteronomy 26:5–8). The Haggadah, which emerged centuries later in Palestine and Babylonia sometime after the seventh century, is an attempt to fulfill the Mishnah's directive to explain Deuteronomy 26:5–8 to one's son, drawing on the mode of rabbinic interpretation known as midrash to develop its interpretation.

The Deuteronomy passage does not mention the plagues, but in verse 8, it does echo how they are referred to in Exodus—"a mighty hand and an outstretched arm" echoes a description of the plagues in Exodus 6:6; "signs and wonders," Exodus 7:3—and that suggested this verse as a kind of summary of the plagues part of the story. At some early point, someone thought to make the connection between the verse and the plagues more explicit, incorporating into the Haggadah a midrash that construed Deuteronomy 26:8 as a concise reference to all ten plagues: "With a mighty hand" was understood as a reference to two of the plagues; "and with an outstretched arm" the next two; "with great terror" two more; "with signs" two more; "and with wonders" the last two, squeezing all ten plagues of Exodus into five brief phrases.

This midrash is very terse, but it reflects an approach to the Bible that is very typical of midrash. God, as the early rabbis imagined him, does not create anything superfluous in the world: he operates on a grand scale but also, in a surgical way, on a very small scale, investing the tiniest elements of creation with purpose. As it happens, in fact, rabbinic interpreters of the Bible found evidence that God operated in this way in the ten plagues themselves. His attention to detail is precisely why he chose plagues that involved small creatures like frogs and flies:

> Even those things that you perceive to have no purpose in the world, like flies, fleas, and mosquitoes, are a part of God's plan for creation, as it says [in Genesis 1:31]: "And God saw everything that he made, and behold, it was very good." Rabbi Aha son of Rabbi Hanina said, "Even those creatures that you perceive to be superfluous in the world, like serpents and scorpions, have their place as a part of creation. . . . And you can know this from the fact that . . . had it not been for the frog, how would [God] have punished the Egyptians." (Exodus Rabbah 10.1)[14]

The rabbis applied the same idea to the Torah itself: nothing there was superfluous or purposeless either, not the smallest phrase or word. Even when its language seemed redundant or verbose, as when Deuteronomy 26:8 piles on a series of terms that all refer to the power God displayed in Egypt, midrash asserts that the Torah was not simply repeating itself but was using each term to refer to discrete events. In the case of the brief midrash about Deuteronomy 26:8, the midrashist reads the verse as if each phrase within it—"a mighty hand," "an outstretched arm," and so on—had its own distinct meaning, referring not to the plagues in general but to a subset of two plagues. Why two per phrase? The terse passage does not explain itself, but it is probably relevant that the Hebrew for "with a mighty hand," "with an outstretched arm," and "with great terror" involves two words each, while "signs" and "wonders" are in the plural. Treating the tiniest of scriptural details as significant, the midrashic author understood the doubling and pluralization of words as hints that each expression referred to more than one plague, and then deduced from the use of five expressions that each referred to two plagues.

This is the oldest part of what the Haggadah has to say about the ten plagues, attested in the earliest known versions, but the Haggadah was not static, growing over the centuries, and its treatment of the ten plagues expanded accordingly. A second, longer midrash on Deuteronomy 26:8 was added later on, as was a mnemonic acronym formed from the first letter of each of the plagues to remind people of the order of the plagues. At some point before the tenth century, it became customary to recite the ten plagues themselves during the Seder one by one, and there also arose a supplementary tradition, a kind of epilogue inserted into the Haggadah after the recitation of the plagues in which Akiba and other rabbinic sages use midrash to uncover greater numbers of plagues in Egypt and at the Red Sea. We will have occasion to further explore the Haggadah's treatment of the ten plagues later in the book, but what I want to do now is offer a few illustrations of how it has influenced Jewish interpretation and retelling of the story.

One example of that influence involves the mnemonic incorporated into the Haggadah—what appear to be three Hebrew words formed from the first letters of each of the plagues—*detsakh adash be'ahav* (the *d* is for *dam,* "blood"; *ts* for *tsefarde'a,* "frogs"; *k* for *kinnim,* "lice"; etc.). The mnemonic was attributed to Judah, not the Judah the Patriarch credited with creating the Mishnah but a sage from the preceding generation, a student of Akiba and a teacher of Judah the Patriarch known for his use of mnemonics; and it was only added to the Haggadah long after the midrash on Deuteronomy 26:8 mentioned earlier (it does not appear in the earliest manuscripts from Palestine, only in a later version from Babylonia).

Why Judah felt the need to develop the acronym is unclear. Perhaps he was simply trying to make sure the plagues were recited in the order in which they appear in Exodus—we know of other ancient enumerations of the plagues that scramble their order, such as the previously mentioned sermon imputed to Augustine, which reverses the fifth and sixth plagues, and the Qur'an has the plagues in a different order too. Perhaps all that Judah was seeking to accomplish was pedagogical—to help people remember the order of the plagues correctly, in the way they had to be reminded of the order of the Passover meal itself. However, there may have been something else at stake in the mnemonic. According to another teaching attributed to Judah, when God instructed Moses to perform the plagues, he ordered him to inscribe the acronym into the staff to ensure that they would occur in that order (Exodus Rabbah 8.3). The plagues were not haphazardly arranged, the midrash suggests; their exact sequence was planned out in advance and was essential to the outcome that God sought to achieve. Perhaps then Judah's acronym as presented in the Haggadah was also a way of suggesting something powerful about reciting the plagues in a particular sequence, just as reciting the words in a spell in the right order can be essential to their ability to produce an effect.

Whatever the original purpose of the acronym, the way it organized the plagues into three mysterious words—*detsakh adash be'ahav*—had an impact on medieval and modern Jewish interpreters of the plagues, who saw the mnemonic as a key to understanding the sequence of the plagues. In this kind of interpretation, there was a logic to the order of the plagues—God chose the plagues and placed them in the sequence in which they occur in Exodus in order to communicate a hidden message to Israel about the nature of his power—and the first letters of each of the plagues revealed this message to those who knew how to interpret them. One example of this approach appears in an eleventh-century commentary called Midrash Leqah Tov, composed by a scholar named

Tobiah ben Eliezer.[15] In a comment on Exodus 8:13, Tobiah suggests that the plagues were divided into three groups of three because God was following a judicial principle that requires two warnings before someone can be punished for a capital offense: the first two plagues of each unit were preceded by a warning from Moses, while there was no warning for the third plague in each unit—the third, sixth, and ninth plagues.[16] Another ingenious explanation for the alleged tripartite structure of the plagues was suggested by the eleventh-century Isaac ben Asher Halevi of Speyer, who discerned that if one writes the first letters of the third, sixth, and ninth plagues on top of each other, they appear twice, one time by reading horizontally, the other by reading vertically:[17]

ח ש כ

ש ח נ

כ נ מ

Other interpreters who detected messages encoded into what appeared to them as the plagues' three-unit structure include Yehuda ben Eliezer (fourteenth century), Bahya ben Asher (1255–1340), Isaac Abarbanel (1437–1508), the Maharal of Prague (1520–1609), the Malbim (1809–1879), and Samuel Raphael Hirsch (1808–1888), and even Jewish scholars trained in the methods of modern secular scholarship could discern hidden meaning in the plagues under the influence of this tradition: in a modern scholarly commentary by Moshe Greenberg, for example—a predecessor of mine at the University of Pennsylvania—the plagues are structured almost like a three-stanza poem, each of the three sets of plagues revealing something distinct about God's rule of the world.[18] Exodus never claims that the plagues were meant to be bunched into three units, nor does it indicate that there was a message encoded into their number and sequence, but this way of reading them was strongly encouraged by the three-word acronym in the Haggadah.

Another element of the Seder that had a strong influence on how Jews retold the plagues was the recital of the plagues during the Passover meal, a very memorable part of the experience. By the eleventh century, rabbinic culture had extended its influence from its base in the Islamic world into Ashkenaz, a biblical term for the region of Germany and France, and there another ten plagues–related Passover custom emerged: spilling drops of wine as each of the ten plagues is recited. Although the custom originated among Ashkenazic communities in Europe, it spread to Sephardic Jews as well, and it is now a part of Passover observance for Jews throughout the world. The original form of the Haggadah as we know it from early manuscripts may not have even included a list of the ten plagues, but thanks in part to the custom of spilling a drop of wine for each plague, an act which recalls the blood of the first plague, reciting them is now one of the most dramatic moments of the Seder, and Jews in different families and communities have come up with various ways of enacting the custom and can supplement it with their own commentary.

Today, among many American Jews, the custom is often explained as an act of empathy for the Egyptians who had to perish during the plagues so that the Israelites could go free. Spilling a drop of wine for each of the plagues is understood as a way of symbolically subtracting from the joy of the holiday in acknowledgment of what the Egyptians suffered. Yet this is not the original meaning of the custom. As the scholar Zvi Ron has demonstrated, this interpretation developed only in the twentieth century in response to an anti-Semitic caricature of the Jews as punitive and vengeful. In earlier eras, the custom was ascribed other meanings.[19]

The earliest known explanation comes from Eleazar of Worms (1176–1238), also known as Eleazar Rokeach, the leader of a movement of pietistic scholars known as Hasidei Ashkenaz. Eleazar, who traced the practice back to his predecessors, suggests a numerological explanation for the custom that ascribed esoteric significance to Hebrew words by assigning numerical values to specific letters (a mode of interpretation known as gematria in Hebrew).[20] Applying this approach to the custom—sixteen drops as he practiced it rather than ten—Eleazar claimed that each drop corresponded to one of the sixteen edges of God's sword, the sixteen mentions of the word "plague" in the book of Jeremiah, the sixteen appearances of the word "life" in Psalm 119, the sixteen times that Jews read the Torah publicly each week, and the sixteen lambs sacrificed in the temple each week, as well as to the numerical value of a pronoun used in Proverbs in reference to Wisdom—

identified with the Torah in Jewish tradition—which also adds up to sixteen.

The purpose of the custom, according to Eleazar's explanation, was not to express empathy for the Egyptians but to provide Jews with reassurance by evoking God's power—the destructive power of God's sword and of divine plagues, and also the protective, life-sustaining power of the Torah. As Eliezer puts it, the custom teaches "that we will not be injured." Injured by what, he does not explain, but later medieval and early modern references to the custom claim that its purpose was to protect Jews from the plagues being called to mind at that point in the Seder, and to redirect them against those trying to harm the Jews, especially hostile Christians.[21] It may not be a coincidence that in the same period in medieval Europe, the wine consumed during the medieval rite of the Eucharist was similarly double-edged: the wine was thought to transform during the ceremony into the life-saving power of Christ's blood, but when Christ or God wanted to punish a sinner, it could also become a "cup of wrath" that destroyed them.[22] Perhaps the Seder custom developed on the model of this practice, also drawing on the biblical image of the cup of wrath to conjure the power of God's fury against present-day oppressors and enemies.

By the twentieth century, this way of understanding the custom had become an embarrassment for Jews who wanted to integrate into non-Jewish society, and they sought to distance themselves from it. Some, like members of the American Reform movement, tried to eliminate the custom altogether on the grounds that it smacked of superstitiousness and animus against non-Jews. In 1905, the movement produced a version of the Haggadah where the plagues were not recited at all because the practice was deemed "unworthy of enlightened sensitivities."[23] This effort to remove the plagues did not succeed—the custom of reciting them was restored in the Reform movement through an edition of the Haggadah published in the 1970s—but what did take root was the reinterpretation of the custom as an expression of empathy for non-Jews.

Building on this custom, some modern-day Jews have repurposed the recital of the ten plagues as a way of speaking out against forms of injustice that affect Jews and non-Jews alike. In this version of the custom, Jews use the plagues to enumerate a list of ten "modern plagues," not natural disasters but forms of human cruelty, inequality, and abuse like poverty, racism, misogyny, and climate change that the Passover participants acknowledge by reciting them out loud and resolve to address. This way of retelling the ten plagues story has particular appeal to Jews on the left end of the political spectrum, and its influence reaches beyond the Seder itself. An example appears in a 1993 book entitled *Specters of Marx*, by the philosopher Jacques Derrida (1930–2004), which presents a version of the ten plagues as a litany of injustices caused by capitalism.[24]

This way of retelling the ten plagues has its origins among socialist Jews in Russia and eastern Europe, and it came to the United States when Jews from these regions migrated there in large numbers in the early part of the twentieth century and initiated practices like the Third Seder, an alternative Seder celebrated on the third night of the holiday by the Workmen's Circle, an immigrant mutual aid society that developed a focus on Yiddish culture and social-justice activism.[25] The Third Seder became very popular, sometimes filling up hotel banquet halls, and by the 1950s the custom inspired its own versions of the Haggadah, which included reciting a list of modern plagues such as war, totalitarianism, and racism.[26] While the Third Seder itself is no longer widely celebrated, the practice of reciting the plagues as a way of calling attention to injustice came to be incorporated into the first night of Passover and shapes how the ten plagues are recited by Jews of a liberal or progressive orientation to this day. It has also inspired Passover-inspired protests that deploy the recitation of the plagues as a form of protest theater.

In 1975, for example, a Zionist group known as Betar splattered blood on the floor and dumped live frogs, locusts, and mice at the Pan American World Airways building in New York to decry the plight of Syrian Jews. (Pan Am was the only American airline with service to Syria.) By the 2000s, the practice had also been embraced by environmentalists. In April 2019, for example, the movement Extinction Rebellion, known for nonviolent but disruptive protest, staged a recitation of the plagues to dramatize the threat posed by climate change, linking each one to one of the destructive effects of greenhouse gas emissions.[27] The practice has also inspired socially conscious artists, yielding visualizations of the

FIGURE 2. The ten plagues as a cell phone display, from Eli Kaplan-Wildmann's *The Recreated Haggadah*. Image reproduced with permission from Eli Kaplan-Wildmann.

ten plagues in various media. Examples include Harriete Estel Berman's "10 Modern Plagues," which uses each plague to highlight a global problem; the "X Plagues" project by Polish artist Natalia Romik, which encloses various objects in socialist-era crystal ware to symbolize the plagues unleashed by capitalism; and a Haggadah from designer Eli Kaplan-Wildmann that presents the plagues as icons on a cell phone display, with each icon symbolizing a "modern plague" such as increasing social disconnection, symbolized by the Delete Contact icon, and the world's depletion of its energy supply, represented as a low-battery bar (figure 2).[28]

The most recent examples of ten plagues–related activism come from anti-Israel campus protests in 2024 when people on both sides of that political divide adapted the practice to make their point. At Columbia University, Jewish pro-Palestinian protesters staged a Seder where the leader asked participants to call out the plagues that were afflicting the university (answers included policing, misinformation, and capitalism), while in an incident at New York University born of an opposing political perspective, a comedian dressed as Moses asked anti-Israel protesters if Hamas should let its hostages ago, and gifted them a mock plague when they said no. Although it did not occur during Passover, another example from that year is an incident where vandals set crickets loose in the lobby of an apartment building inhabited by a Columbia University executive and splattered red paint around its front door.[29]

The practice of reciting the ten plagues began as a way of explaining Deuteronomy 26:8 to one's children, but already during the Middle Ages, the practice served as a way for Jews to symbolically push back against present-day oppressors; and as the Seder developed in the twentieth century, the custom was repurposed yet again as a call to think beyond one's own redemption and acknowledge the suffering of others. Reenacting the plagues as vandalism is obviously different from recalling them during a Seder, turning the ritual spilling of wine into violence, but it counts as an extension of this tradition, and as such, it too attests to the Haggadah's continued impact on how Jews—and others influenced by Jewish tradition—understand, retell, and reenact the plagues.

Signs Self-Evident Yet Misunderstood: The Plagues in Islamic Tradition

Muslims know the story of the exodus and the plagues not from the Bible but from the Qur'an, the 114-chapter record of what God revealed to the prophet Muhammad between roughly 610 and 632 CE. Although the Qur'an records the experience of Muhammad himself, a good portion of it concerns figures known from the Jewish and Christian Bibles, including Moses, who is mentioned 136 times. There now exists a fair amount of scholarship devoted to the Qur'anic version of the exodus, and one central insight from this work is that the Qur'an's depiction of Moses's birth, his effort to deliver signs to the Egyptians, the opposition he faced, and his role in receiving a divine text corresponds to the life of Muhammad as portrayed in the Qur'an. Muhammad is understood by Muslims not just as a successor to the prophet Moses but as a new Moses in his own right, following the same calling, coming up against the same closed-mindedness, and producing his own miraculous signs, and the correspondence between the two prophets is grounded in the distinctive version of the exodus story recounted in the Qur'an.[30]

For all the attention given to Moses and the exodus, however, the plagues are scarcely mentioned, with the notable exception of a verse here and there. The only mention that refers to specific plagues appears in the seventh chapter (or sura) of the Qur'an, known as "The Heights" (al-ʿAraf): "So we plagued them with floods, locusts, lice, frogs, and blood—all as clear signs, but they persisted in arrogance and were a wicked people" (verse 133). The "we" here is spoken by the angel Gabriel as a representative of all the angels, the narrator of the Qur'an, who, according to later Islamic tradition, revealed its content to Muhammad over twenty-three years.

Why does the Qur'an refer to only five plagues, and why in a different order from in Exodus? We will return to these questions later in the book, so suffice it to say for now that the author of the Qur'an, though showing familiarity with the Bible elsewhere in the chapter, was not necessarily basing his understanding of the plagues on Exodus. According to some commentators, for example, the verse's mention of blood does not refer to the waters of Egypt turning into blood or to the blood of the Passover sacrifice, but to a plague of nosebleeds.[31]

Another significant difference from the biblical account concerns how the Qur'an frames the plagues. Its author seems more interested in the episode where Pharaoh's magicians try to match the miracles of Moses by turning their staffs into serpents, referring to it several times, and it treats all the signs of the Exodus story—those performed by Moses before the plagues, the plagues themselves, and events at the sea—as part of a larger history in which God sends various signs to human beings to warn them to submit to God and change their ways.

As Sura 7 makes clear, humans are prone to disbelieve these signs and to reject the prophets who send them, a pattern that has been repeated since the time of Noah. If anything distinguishes the signs mentioned in verse 133 from earlier signs, it is that they were especially clear or self-evident, designed to be difficult to misinterpret, but even so, Pharaoh and his nobles rejected them just as earlier leaders had scoffed at the signs offered to them by other prophets. The Qur'an's version of the story thus suggests that the opposition Muhammad faced from leaders rejecting his claim to be God's messenger was a repetition of the Egyptians' rejection of Moses and his signs.

Just as the New Testament shaped subsequent Christian retellings of the ten plagues, and the Haggadah determined the course of the story in Jewish tradition, the Qur'an's version of the story, as brief as it is, has left an enduring imprint on how Muslims retell what happened. An example involves the staff that Moses uses to perform the plagues and other miracles of the story. In the biblical account, Moses carries a staff that turns into a snake at the burning bush (Exodus 4:1–3), but it is actually his brother Aaron who handles the wonder-working staff during the confrontation with Pharaoh, turning it into a serpent in Pharaoh's court and using it to bring about the first three plagues. In Sura 7 and other Qur'anic chapters that refer to the confrontation with Pharaoh, it is always Moses, not Aaron, who wields the staff against Pharaoh and his magicians, and that is the version of the story that has been recounted by Muslims ever since.

Beyond what Muslims can glean from the Qur'an about the plagues, they also have another source of information about what happened, a kind of Scripture-centered lore known as Israʾiliyyat, or "Israelisms" in English. Although such material can include stories originating from Christian or Zoroastrian sources, the term, first used in the tenth century, suggests a connection to the Jews, and many of the stories in question came from Jewish sources such as Abdallan b. Salam, a rabbi in Medina and early convert to Islam; Ka'b al-Ahbar, a rabbi from Yemen who converted not long after the death of Muhammad; and Wahb b. Munabbih, another Yemeni convert, perhaps a Jew, who is credited with writing the first book of Israʾiliyyat.[32] Although some

Muslim scholars regarded these traditions with suspicion, others treated them as a reliable source about the history of God and his prophets in the period before the revelations to Muhammad, and Qur'anic commentators, historians, and poets regularly drew on them.

In the exodus story as presented in Isra᾿iliyyat, the confrontation with Pharaoh grows more and more elaborate—the serpent in Exodus becomes a great dragon that swallows one of the magicians, for example, and Moses wields the staff against other enemies as well, such as a giant named Og or ʿUj in Arabic. Such was the stature of the staff that, as happened in Christianity, the staff became an important religious relic in Islam, thought to generate blessings and protection for those who gained access to it.[33] But it is always Moses who wields the staff in Islamic tradition, and that idea persists to this day. In 1970 Ayatollah Khomeini called on supporters to wield the staff of Moses against their Pharaonic enemies, one of several ways in which he used Moses's story to symbolize his conflict with the shah of Iran and the West.[34] Fifty years later, inspired by Khomeini's call, an Iranian hacker group decided to call itself Moses' Staff, using as its logo a fist clenching the staff like a dagger to cast its attacks against Israel as a repeat of the plagues that Moses sent against Pharaoh (figure 3).[35]

Lest one think that the staff's use as a weapon is the only role ascribed to it in Islam, I hasten to add that it has been ascribed other meanings and roles as well. In medieval magical tradition, the staff, or divine names thought to have been inscribed into the staff, became important as a source of magical language.[36] In the poem "Masnavi," the thirteenth-century mystic Rumi describes himself as a staff of a hidden Moses, as if his writing were a similar wonder-working instrument.[37] "The Rod of Moses" is also the name of an important poetic-political manifesto published in 1936 by the South Asian philosopher Muhammad Iqbal, and more recently, the Indonesian children's writer Muhammad Vandestra has turned the staff into the narrator of a Harry Potter–esque story about Moses.[38] For all their differences, however, what these portrayals of the staff all share is that they have been influenced by the Qur'an's distinctive version of the exodus where it is Moses, not Aaron, who wields the staff that defeats Pharaoh.

FIGURE 3. Logo of the Iranian hacker group Moses' Staff.

Wonders to Behold

Almost all of the versions of the ten plagues story that we will consider in this book developed out of or in response to one of these religious traditions. There are some exceptions—such as a few surviving ancient retellings of the story that predate the emergence of Christianity and rabbinic Judaism—but for the most part, we will be focused on Christian, Jewish, and Muslim retellings of the story that build on the story as it was reimagined by early readers of the Bible or the Qur'an. For this reason, it has been a little misleading to refer to the ten plagues story as if it were a single story. The various iterations can all be traced back to a single literary ancestor, but we are really talking about a large, globally dispersed, multibranched tree of related stories that have grown, and are still growing, from narrative seeds planted by the account in Exodus.

For all their differences from one another, however, what unites all the examples we will be looking at in this book is how, in one way or another, every retelling injects its author's personality, beliefs, emotions, self-interest, and hopes for the future into the biblical story in a way that mixes together the biblical "then" with the now. Mainstream academic biblical scholars seek to correct such anachronism in how they interpret and explain the Bible, trying to avoid reading themselves into the story of the exodus so that they can understand it on its own terms as the product of minds different from their own, but that is not the kind of insight we are after in this book: the interpreters, storytellers, and artists we will be surveying in the following pages treat the Bible not as an artifact of a bygone age but as a story about their own circumstances, struggles, and futures. In this book, retelling the Bible anachronistically is not a mistake that needs to be corrected but a mode of creativity worthy of study in its own right as the very practice that has kept the Bible alive in people's imaginations for more than two thousand years.

1

The First Plague

BLOOD JUSTICE

ON OCTOBER 11, 2023, during a press conference about the Hamas attack four days earlier, the Israeli political leader Benny Gantz, a retired army general newly appointed to an emergency war cabinet, briefly invoked biblical language to telegraph the harshness of Israel's retribution against the attackers, predicting that "the rewards of our enemies will be blood, fire and pillars of smoke."[1] The line, which echoes language from the biblical book of Joel, does not in its original context refer to the ten plagues but instead to a future act of divine retribution against Israel's enemies: "it shall come to pass afterwards . . . that I will perform wonders (*mophetim*) in the heavens and the earth, blood, fire, and pillars of smoke" (Joel 3:1–3 in the Masoretic text). Nevertheless, Jews familiar with the Seder would recognize an allusion to the plagues, especially the first one. The verse is cited in the Haggadah's midrashic lead-up to their recitation and in the version of the wine spilling custom that involves sixteen drops of wine rather than ten; three of the extra drops are spilled at the mention of the words "blood, fire, and pillars of smoke."

Gantz's use of the verse was a way to convey to Jewish Israelis the immense scale of the retribution to come; the overwhelming force the state would bring to bear; and the justness of its cause. Hamas was akin to the biblical Egyptians, and Israel's retribution would be like that of the ten plagues, as if coming not from the Israel Defense Forces (IDF) but from God.

Gantz's allusion to the ten plagues illustrates the role that the story has played in how people think about justice as an archetype of retributive justice, the kind of justice that uses violence to rectify a wrong. While Exodus makes clear that the main purpose of the plagues was to force the Egyptians to free the Hebrews, rather than to punish the Egyptians for their crimes, many Jews and Christians came to understand the plagues as a manifestation of justice in a perfectly realized form—a punishment that was terrible but fully deserved and rightly imposed.

The biblical account itself, however, does not explain how this justice works. What was God punishing? And why did he choose these specific punishments? These questions led later Jews and Christians to retell the story in ways that reflected different conceptions of retributive justice. Taking the first plague, the plague of blood, as our focus, I want to use this chapter to examine some of these retellings and show how they are tied to the evolving character of justice itself, an ideal that has been conceived differently in different legal, moral, and cultural contexts. As this chapter moves from ancient to modern retellings of the plague of blood, we will be tracing how the biblical story has changed in tandem with changes in the conception of justice.

My reason for using the plague of blood to explore this dimension of the story's reception is the strong association between blood and justice found in the Bible. In Genesis 9:6, God establishes the principle that the only way to punish an act of murder is to shed the blood of the perpetrator—"Whoever sheds the blood of a human, by a human his blood will be spilt"—and the Bible also inspired the figure known in Jewish tradition as "the redeemer of blood," a person authorized by God to kill a family member's murderer as a way of compensating for the victim's blood. In these and other passages, the Bible establishes a link between blood and justice, but it never explains the connection between them. As once observed by Bertha von Suttner, the first woman to win a Noble Peace Prize, "No reasonable creature would conceive of the idea of obliterating ink stains with ink, or spots of oil with oil. It is only blood which has always to be washed out with new blood."[2] The Hebrew Bible helped to introduce this principle, but it never explains why an exchange of blood for blood is necessary to right the wrong of bloodshed, and this includes the first plague, yet another episode where the Bible brings the themes of justice and blood together without clear explanation. As we will see, the visceral but vague connection between justice and blood in the Bible opened a door for later retellers of the episode to inject into the first plague different ideas about why God chose to punish the Egyptians with blood.

The plague of blood as people recall and imagine it retains its status as a biblical archetype of poetic justice—justice deeply satisfying at a moral and emotional level because the punishment it inflicts feels so deserved and fitting—but it only achieved this status through many generations of retelling. The examples highlighted in this chapter from ancient, medieval, and modern elaborations of the first plague are meant as glimpses of that history, capturing the biblical story retold and transformed in light of different conceptions of what justice looks like when it has the power at its disposal to impose a punishment that exactly fits the crime.

Bleeding between the Lines

Before we turn to the first plague, however, we need to learn a little about divine justice as depicted in the Bible and as understood by later interpreters. Since I will be focusing in this chapter on Jewish retellings of the first plague, the interpreters of most relevance are the ancient rabbinic authors of midrash along with later Jews who approached the episode under the influence of midrashic interpretation. Although the rabbis drew on the Bible for their conception of divine justice, they had their own ideas about how it worked, and I want to begin this history of the first plague by introducing the rabbis' distinctive conception of divine justice, exploring where it came from, and illustrating how it transformed the meaning of the ten plagues.

Of particular relevance in this context is a rabbinic concept of divine justice referred to as *middah keneged middah* (measure for measure)—the idea that God punishes sin in a way that mirrors the nature of the offense. To bring out what is distinctive about this conception of justice, it may help to contrast it with a more familiar principle of justice known from the book of Exodus: that of "an eye for an eye." The biblical and rabbinic conceptions of justice both involve a kind of symmetry between crime and punishment, a restoring of balance by making the perpetrator suffer in an equivalent way, but there are important differences between them. The idea of taking an eye for an eye involves tit-for-tat equivalences: a perpetrator is to lose an eye if he has injured an eye, or forfeit his life if he has taken a life (Exodus 21:23–27). Whereas eye-for-an-eye justice involves punishments meant to equal the crime, measure-for-measure punishment, enforced by God when a culprit is beyond human justice, involves punishments that rhyme with the offense, echoing it in a way that only reveals itself with time and requires subtle interpretation to appreciate, an ability to discern the resemblance between the offense and the offender's fate.[3] A midrashic example involves the biblical Samson: God permitted the Philistines to put out his eyes because he sinned with his eyes by straying after the beautiful Delilah (Mishnah Sota 1.8). Both kinds of justice involve a mirroring of the sin in the punishment, but measure-for-measure justice is not proportionate, usually much more injurious than what it was punishing, and the same principle also worked to reward righteousness.

Another important difference between the principles concerns the agent responsible for meting out the punishment. "Eye for an eye" is an operating principle in the justice system that God imposes on the Israelites through the Torah—it is something for the Israelites to execute on God's behalf—whereas measure-for-measure justice is implemented by God without human intervention. It involves an act of divine intervention in the created world so that people get the exact punishment they deserve without other humans needing to detect the perpetrator, try him or her, and impose a punishment. Even when the culprit is too powerful to be held to account through the laws and institutions of human justice, God's measure-for-measure punishment makes sure that there will always be the retribution needed to restore the world to moral balance.

It is not clear that the plagues as depicted in Exodus consistently follow either principle of justice. Near the end of the scene where God is speaking to Moses out of the burning bush, he instructs the prophet to tell Pharaoh, "Israel is my son, my first born. I told you, 'let my son go so that he can serve me' but you refused to let him go. Look, I am slaying your son, your first born" (Exodus 4:22–23). The passage seems to explain the last plague, the slaying of the firstborn, as an eye-for-an-eye punishment for what Pharaoh did to God's firstborn, the Israelites, but it is the exception that proves the rule: nowhere else does the Exodus account suggest any juridical logic to the plagues, nor does it suggest that God has chosen any of the other plagues to match specific crimes. Even in the case of the slaying of the firstborn, it never explains why, if the plague was an eye-for-an-eye punishment for sin, so many bystanders were afflicted when they had no role in Pharaoh's sin against the Israelites: the handmaids of the Egyptians, the prisoners held captive in their dungeons, the firstborn not just of the Egyptians themselves but of their animals as well.

It is only in the much later Hellenistic period that we find a logical principle laid out explicitly, something akin to the measure-for-measure principle of later rabbinic Judaism, and the catalyst are the Greeks who ruled the Jews in this period and their transformative impact on Jewish culture and thought. Justice, including divine justice, was a central theme in Greek poetry and philosophy—it was Plato and his students who introduced justice as a subject of philosophical inquiry, laying the foundations for how justice is theorized today in Western societies.[4] In the centuries following the conquest of the Near East by Alexander the Great in the fourth century BCE, Jews were exposed to Plato's theory of justice along with other Greek ideas about justice and incorporated them into how they understood the biblical text. Under the influence of such ideas, new interpretations and retellings of the ten plagues were developed that emphasized them as following a consistent logic that sustains society and the cosmos as an orderly and harmonious place. On this view, the plagues were not a merely a series of harsh punishments but followed a rational system of justice that governs the cosmos in general, in biblical times and after, sustaining it as a just place. Mortals may not recognize this justice at work in their own lives, but it is always operative in the world as a kind of invisible law of cause and effect, and the clearest example of this kind of justice were the plagues sent against Egypt.

Evidence of this kind of interpretation comes from an early Jewish text known as the Wisdom of Solomon, which is included within the Catholic Bible as Scripture but not in the canons of Jews or Protestants. As its title suggests, the Wisdom of Solomon has been attributed to Solomon, a ruler famous for his association with justice. It was, however, written in Greek and composed during the Hellenistic period, when Jews were under the sway of Greek rule and culture. In one long section, the author offers a retelling of the ten plagues that serves to illustrate his philosophically informed view of divine justice. The Wisdom of Solomon is the earliest known text to try to fill in an explanation for why God sent the specific plagues that he did.

Consider, for example, how the Wisdom of Solomon accounts for the plagues that involve noxious animals like the plague of frogs. Philo of Alexandria, a Jewish philosopher from a little after the time of the Wisdom of Solomon, claimed that the Egyptians' worst sin—worse even than the enslavement of the Israelites—was their worship of animals: crocodiles, cattle, and other creatures that the Egyptians treated as divine beings. For its part, the Wisdom of Solomon cites this worship as the reason that God sent serpents and other verminous creatures to punish the Egyptians; the animal-related plagues were mirroring back the Egyptians' sin in worshiping irrational creatures: "In return for their foolish and wicked thoughts, which led them astray to worship irrational and worthless animals, you sent against them a multitude of irrational creatures to punish them, so that they might learn that one is punished by the very things by which one sins" (11:15–16). This is not exactly the measure-for-measure principle as articulated in rabbinic sources. As the biblical scholar Yehoshua Amir has pointed out, the Wisdom of Solomon claims that God sent the plagues not just to punish the Egyptians but to educate them, to make them conscious of the divine justice at work in the world, and no such intention to enlighten the Egyptians is ascribed to the plagues in ancient midrashic interpretation.[5] What the two approaches to the story do share is the idea that the plagues were following a consistent principle of justice manifest in the way each plague mirrored the sin that it was punishing.

Notably, however, the Wisdom of Solomon does not apply this approach to the first plague, and it is only in later rabbinic interpretation that this plague is explained as a response to a particular sin. The key to this kind of interpretation was the blood of the plague. In the original biblical account, it would seem that God's motive in turning the rivers, streams, and ponds of Egypt into blood was simply to cut off the Egyptians' water supply, to create what amounted to a weeklong drought in order to pressure them into letting the Israelites go. So understood, the fact that the water of Egypt was turned into blood is incidental to the plague; if it had simply dried up, the effect on the Egyptians would have been the same. Later midrashic readings, however, detected significance in the blood of the plague, inferring that it must have been a measure-for-measure punishment for some hidden Egyptian crime that involved blood. The biblical account does not connect the blood of the plague to any particular sin, but such a connection could be detected between the lines of the episode in the light of the rabbinic principle of measure for measure and its idea that divine justice always involves a mirroring of the sin in the punishment.

In one such midrash, the Egyptians, threatened by how the Israelites kept multiplying, sought to completely wipe them out by preventing them from having children. In Exodus, Pharaoh tries to stop the growth of the Israelite population by ordering their newborn babies thrown into the Nile. In the midrash, the Egyptians come up with another even more dastardly plan to exterminate the Israelites completely, a plan that was less obviously brutal but would have eliminated the Israelites completely by using their own law against them. Blood as the Torah represents it is a source of pollution that needs to be cleansed when a person comes into contact with it. This is why, according to Leviticus 15, a woman is considered unclean during her menstruation and is only permitted to have sex with her husband after she immerses herself in the ritual bath. Seeking to exploit this requirement to their advantage, the scheming Egyptians prohibited Israelite women from purifying themselves after their menstruation, thus preventing them from having sex with their husbands and bearing any more children. This was the crime that God was punishing by turning the waters of Egypt into blood, and the plague followed the principle of measure for measure, forcing the Egyptians to wallow in blood just as they had forced the women of Israel to wallow in the blood of their periods (Exodus Rabbah 9.10).

The rabbis acknowledged that it was not always easy to recognize the measure-for-measure principle at work in a world where evildoing often seem to go unpunished. It required perceptiveness to discern divine justice at work, an ability to spot a subtle correspondence between sin and a punishment that is not obvious and can take time to reveal itself. But when it became apparent, the experience not only showed how God holds the wicked accountable but revealed a kind of artistry in divine justice—an ingenious ability to create symmetry and irony. According to another midrashic commentary on Exodus, when Jethro, the father-in-law of Moses, recognizes the measure-for-measure correspondence between the Egyptians' sin in throwing the Israelite babies into the water (Exodus 1) and their eventual measure-for-measure comeuppance when they are drowned in the sea in turn (Exodus 14), he is so amazed that he feels compelled to declare God's praises (Mekhilta de-Rabbi Ishmael, parashah 6). For the rabbis, detecting measure-for-measure justice at work in the plagues was akin to seeing a miracle with one's own eyes in its revelation of the awesomeness and artfulness of divine justice.

Blood Baths

Jews during the Middle Ages and early modern period built on the midrashic reading of the first plague as a case of measure for measure, but they developed this tradition in light of ideas about divine justice—and about blood—absorbed from the Christian world. To illustrate this point, let us now turn to how the first plague is represented in a seventeenth-century Haggadah that includes the illustration shown in figure 4, a depiction not of the plague but of the sin it was believed to be punishing.

We see here the murder of Israelite babies—not the drowning of Hebrew children depicted in Exodus 1 but a crime not mentioned in the Bible: the brutal slaughter of children in order to drain their blood into

FIGURE 4. A leprous Pharaoh bathing in the blood of murdered Israelite infants, as illustrated in the Venice Haggadah from 1609. Reproduced with permission from the Bodleian Libraries, University of Oxford, Opp.add.fol.III.468, p. 19.

Pharaoh's bath. On the left, soldiers are wresting the babies from their grieving mothers; on the right, a soldier is stabbing a baby in the neck to drain its blood into a basin. Pharaoh, covered in marks that indicate he is suffering from leprosy, is soaking in the blood.

This image comes from a printed edition of the Haggadah prepared in Venice in 1609 through a collaboration between the printer Israel ben Daniel Zifroni and the rabbi Leon Modena (1571–1648)—the latter so proud of his role in its production that he added a poem at the end where the first letters of each line spelled out his Hebrew name, as if to put his signature on the work. The Venice Haggadah was published in the three languages used by the Jews of Venice—Judeo-Italian, Ladino, and Yiddish—and it proved so successful that it was reissued in a new edition in 1624 that included an abridged commentary by Isaac Abarbanel. The illustrations, evidently selected by Modena, are very striking, as is the case with a scene that shows demons tormenting the Egyptians with the plagues, and one of its illustrations has left an enduring mark on how the ten plagues appear in many printed Haggadot to this day, presenting all ten plagues together on a single page so that they could be taken in all at once. The format calls to mind how early printed versions of Dante's *Divine Comedy* from the same period used cleverly designed diagrams and maps to show the punishments of hell in a single graphic, and it is but one example of how the Venice Haggadah broke new ground in its representation of the plagues, even as it also drew on ideas and motifs inherited from earlier midrash and Haggadah illustration.

The Venice Haggadah is not the first Haggadah to show Pharaoh bathing in the blood of murdered Israelite children. Such illustrations appear as early as the fifteenth century in manuscripts like the Yahuda Haggadah from around 1470, and they were based in turn on a midrash that went back to at least the thirteenth century.[6] Part of what distinguishes it from these earlier examples, however, is that it adds a caption to the illustration connecting the blood bath to the plague of blood as a measure-for-measure punishment: "Pharaoh washes with blood to cure leprosy, but eventually, water turns into blood and makes him suffer." Like the other explanatory captions included in the Venice Haggadah, this one was likely introduced by Modena himself, and it reasserts the idea that the plague of blood was a measure-for-measure punishment for the sins of Egyptians—now a brutal campaign of infanticide to cure Pharaoh of leprosy.

On the surface, the Venice Haggadah would appear to be merely continuing the midrashic understanding of the plague of blood. Jews at the time not only continued to recognize this principle between the lines of the Bible but detected it at work in the present. Thus, for example, the Italian Jewish writer Abraham Yagel (1553–1623), in a Hebrew work known as *A Valley of Vision*, composed in Italy just a decade or two before the Venice Haggadah, noted that while the human-mediated justice of rabbinic courts was no longer enforced in his day, the measure-for-measure principle of divine justice was still operative, and Modena himself, as he later remarked in his autobiography, detected this kind of justice at work in his own life.[7]

This kind of continued belief in measure-for-measure justice has clearly shaped the Venice Haggadah's version of the plagues. The commentary added to the 1624 edition explicitly asserts it as the principle governing all the plagues, explaining that the blood was punishment for shedding the blood of Israelite children, the cries of the frogs were punishment for the cries of the mothers who lost their children, and so on. The caption used in the earlier edition for the blood bath scene worked similarly by making sure Seder attendees did not miss the measure-for-measure correspondence between Pharaoh's infanticide and the first plague's river of blood.

If one looks a little closer at the illustration, however, it is possible to recognize some ways in which it differs from earlier midrashic tradition, and to bring out that difference, it is instructive to compare the illustration with the earlier midrashic legend on which it is based, a story told in slightly different ways in midrashic collections that are relatively late in date but were composed before the Venice Haggadah. In the midrash as it appears in Exodus Rabbah (1.34), the blood bath episode is connected not to the blood plague but to another moment in the exodus story in Exodus 2:23: "After a long time the Pharaoh of Egypt died, and the Israelites groaned." The Pharaoh mentioned in this verse is the predecessor of the one who faces off with Moses during the plagues, the one who orders the male children of the Israelites thrown into the Nile. What puzzled the author of the midrash is the Israelites' response to the death of this Pharaoh: Shouldn't they have cheered at the news of his death? The reason that the Israelites were still miserable, according to this midrash, is that this Pharaoh wasn't quite dead yet but only on the verge of death, and he had become all the more dangerous as he desperately sought a cure.

The sickened Pharaoh had learned from his advisers that there was only one way to treat the disease; he must bathe in blood. While such a treatment may sound outlandish to modern ears, it was, in fact, a therapy recommended by premodern medicine, which diagnosed leprosy as an effect of poisoned or corrupted blood, and especially effective was the blood of innocent children, considered purer and more efficacious than that of adults. To generate the quantity of blood needed for a twice-daily bath, Pharaoh's advisers recommended that 150 Hebrew children be killed every morning and another 150 every evening—this according to Exodus Rabbah. In another midrashic work known as Sefer Hayashar, published in Venice in 1544, the babies were slaughtered one per day, God intervening only after the death toll reached 375.

Although we cannot pin down when this midrashic tradition first emerged, we do know that it was modeled on a widely circulated legend about Constantine the Great (272–337 CE), the first Roman emperor to convert to Christianity.[8] Like the Pharaoh of the midrash, Constantine in this legend contracts leprosy and is advised to bathe in the blood of children. He proceeds to order their slaughter, but as the priests begin to wrest the babies from their mothers, he is so moved by their tears that he decides to restore their sons to them. He then converts to Christianity and finds the cure he seeks by undergoing baptism as administered by the bishop of Rome, Sylvester I. This was not just any story. For many centuries, its account of how Sylvester miraculously cured Constantine of leprosy through baptism was seen as a founding story of the papacy itself, thought to explain what motivated the emperor to confer supreme religious authority over the Western Roman Empire on Sylvester and his successor bishops in Rome.[9]

This background reveals that the midrashic blood bath originated in response to, and as an inversion of, baptism and its salvific power, and it is possible, as Jeremy Glatstein has argued, that the Venice Haggadah illustration was likewise intended as a critique or parody of baptism, perhaps responding to the forced baptism of Jewish babies in Venice itself in earlier decades.[10] What nonetheless distinguishes its version of the blood bath from earlier midrashic tradition, however, is its intensification of the violence. In the earlier form of the midrash in Exodus Rabbah, Pharaoh fails to carry through with the murder of the Israelite children because God intervenes to stop him. In the Venice Haggadah and other early modern Haggadot, however, the children are shown being murdered in grisly ways. A 1526 Haggadah from Prague shows soldiers impaling babies on their spears. In a 1560 Haggadah from Mantua, the central image is an Egyptian sticking a knife into the neck of a child, while another Haggadah from Prague later in the century shows soldiers wielding their swords against a baby still in the arms of its mother. The Venice Haggadah follows this tradition, showing a soldier stabbing a baby in its neck.

What was it that led the authors of early modern Haggadot to intensify the violence and horror of the midrashic story? One answer, suggested by the historian David Malkiel, is that the earlier midrashic story was transformed by the violence suffered by Jewish communities during the Middle Ages.[11] Following anti-Jewish massacres in the Rhineland during the First Crusade in 1096, Jewish chroniclers and poets memorialized the victims as martyrs in ways that emphasized the gruesome and heartrending deaths of children in particular. Malkiel suggests that the trauma generated by this violence, kept alive in Jewish memory through liturgical poetry recited in the synagogue, was what moved illustrators to heighten the brutality of the blood bath episode.

Another important influence, noted by the historian Ephraim Shoham-Steiner, was the rise of the blood libel in medieval Europe after the thirteenth century.[12] Based on the idea that the blood of the innocent had a curative power, Christians accused Jews of killing Christian children in order to mix their blood into the wine and food they consumed during Passover and thereby heal themselves from disease, including leprosy. In the city of Trent in 1475, for instance, an especially notorious blood libel case was incited by the death of a toddler named Simon who was subsequently venerated as a Christlike martyr. According to the account provided by the Italian scholar Ubertino Puscolo (1430–1507), after kidnapping and torturing the child, the Jews of the city laced matzah and wine with his blood in order to consume it during the Passover meal. Puscolo's account, it should be noted, depicts the Jews using their recital of the plagues during the Seder to call for God to send such punishments against Christians: "Destroy the Christ-worshipping people; inflict on them the ten bitter scourges that Pharaoh, king of Egypt, once saw loosed upon his people. May the Christ-worshippers have an over-flowing stream of blood; may they have frogs, leprosy and famine; may they have fleas, darkness, all-destroying locusts." His account of the wine spilling part of the ritual is equally grotesque and horrifying, turning it into a twisted version of the Eucharist by imagining the Jews pouring out the blood of Simon as an offering to God: "Here is the body that we have sacrificed to you, Holy Father, and here now is the liquid we pour out to you, shed from the body of the still-living Christian infant."[13]

As Shoham-Steiner suggests, the illustrator of the Venice Haggadah was likely responding to the blood libel. Such accusations were frequent in the period before the creation of the Venice Haggadah. Between 1401 and 1543, there were at least thirty-seven cases that led to the incarceration and death of Jews; and in Venice alone, such episodes occurred three times—in 1480, 1485, and 1506.[14] Of particular interest for understanding the blood bath scene as a response to such accusation is a version of the blood libel mentioned briefly in fifteenth- and sixteenth-century sources that tell of how a Jewish physician tapped the blood of three ten-year-old Jewish boys in order to cure Pope Innocent VIII from a disease, killing the boys in the process. In later nineteenth-century scholarship, this episode was taken as a real-life incident—in fact, it is still cited in medical literature as the first known case of an attempted blood transfusion—but it originated as a blood libel, imputing the cure to a Jewish physician whom Pope Innocent subsequently seeks to punish after the boys die and the cure fails.[15] This particular variation of the blood libel, circulating in Italy in the sixteenth century, might be part of what the Venice Haggadah was responding to—and turning back against its Christian authors—through its image of a non-Jewish ruler killing children for their blood in order to heal himself.

When viewed in this context, the illustration of Pharaoh's blood bath in the Venice Haggadah appears as what we might consider a "counter–blood libel," in which Jewish children are the victims and their non-Jewish rulers are the ones murdering them for their blood. To get a sense of how precisely the Venice Haggadah blood bath illustration mirrors the blood libel, compare it with Simon's martyrdom as visualized in a work known as the *Nuremberg Chronicle* from 1493 (figure 5)—and pay particular attention to the blood that flows in the two scenes.

The scene shows Simon being mutilated by a cabal of Jews, with wounds that include the mutilation of his penis in a way that both calls circumcision to mind and evokes the bleeding wounds of Christ on the cross. Of particular significance in this context is the blood streaming out of Simon's body into a bowl below, which has a counterpart in the Venice Haggadah in the part of the scene where a soldier is pouring the blood of a murdered child into Pharaoh's bath.[16]

The Venice Haggadah illustration is not, then, simply a rendering of a midrashic measure-for-measure reading of the plague of blood but an effort to use the episode to exact a kind of virtual retribution against

FIGURE 5. The martyrdom of Simon as illustrated in Hartmann Schedel's *Liber Chronicarum* (or *Nuremberg Chronicle*, 1493), fol. 254v. Alamy.

present-day enemies. Venice in the early seventeenth century was not a place where Jews could expect justice from the Christians among whom they lived, as Shylock, Shakespeare's retribution-obsessed merchant of Venice, is made to learn the hard way when he tries and fails to secure justice against a Christian enemy only to be forced to give up a pound of flesh. The Venice Haggadah shows that real-life Jews in Venice at the time did imagine themselves getting even, however, and one of the ways they did so was through the recounting of the plagues during the Seder, a moment used to voice—and to visualize—a desire for retribution that could not be achieved directly. This is what has been preserved in its version of the plague of blood, a kind of revenge fantasy that adapted midrashic tradition to express in biblical guise a yearning for retributive justice impossible to act on directly in a society controlled by Christians.

"The Blood of Israel Avenges"

The ten plagues continued to resonate as an archetype of divine justice well into the twentieth century, but people's faith in divine justice itself was greatly shaken by two major events in modern Jewish experience: the Holocaust and the establishment of the State of Israel. The Holocaust destabilized beliefs about God as an agent of justice, while the emergence of the Israeli state with its own military empowered Jews to seek justice through their own efforts. Both of these changes in how Jews related to justice had an impact on how they retold the ten plagues.

An important example of this evolution involves the role of the ten plagues in the military rhetoric of the IDF, which was formed following Israel's Declaration of Independence in May 1948 and immediately found itself in a war against Egypt and other enemy states that lasted until 1949. On October 15, 1948, the Givati brigade, an infantry brigade embarked on a campaign to break the Egyptian army's hold over the Negev, a campaign referred to by the code name Operation Yoav but initially known as Operation Ten Plagues.[17] The idea that the operation was in some sense a reenactment of the ten plagues was activity promoted by one of the brigade's officers, thirty-year-old Abba Kovner, who sought to help build morale and motivate the troops by distributing a series of missives that made connections between the present-day fighting and the biblical story. The battle missive was a short text composed and distributed by military commanders in order to prepare troops to risk their lives during battle, and such messages are used to this day in the Israeli military.[18] Kovner dispatched more than thirty such missives as an education officer during the 1948 war, circulated in about seven thousand copies to the members of the Givati brigade. These made frequent references to the Bible in order to inspire soldiers, and these included references or allusions to the plagues—and especially the plague of blood—as a way of adding an emotional charge and religious-moral resonance to their exhortations.

Although honored for his heroism as a resistance fighter during the Holocaust and later celebrated for his poetry, Kovner remains an extremely controversial figure in Israel to this day in large part because of his efforts to exact revenge for the Holocaust but also because of the battle letters he sent, which were so inflammatory that they drew a rebuke at the time from the Zionist leader Meir Ya'ari, who described them as "Fascist horror propaganda."[19] One of the scholars I have relied on for understanding these letters, Reuven Shoham, was so disturbed by them that he felt the need to apologize for merely discussing them in an academic study.[20] Kovner's superiors permitted him to send the letters because they recognized how effective they were in motivating the soldiers. Still, the letters drew protests from some of Kovner's fellow officers, who feared what unleashing such violent retribution would do to the new state.

One such letter from July 14 carried the subheading "The Plague of Darkness—the Plague of Blood." Another letter from two days later, after referring to fallen Egyptian officers as "Pharaoh's great-grandsons," promises that if the enemy rises again, "the canyon too will rise and gush with blood." Yet another reference appears in a letter sent the following day, entitled "The Plague of Stench," that tauntingly recounts all the plagues that have beset and humiliated the Egyptian king Farouk, and then relishes the arrival of a final plague—the plague of blood, here mentioned as a scarcely veiled reference to a threatened slaughter of the enemy:

> He has become accustomed to LICE and feels good about it.
> He has become accustomed to BOILS and feels good about it.
> He has become accustomed to PESTILENCE and feels good about it.
> And to WILD BEASTS he has become accustomed, and to FROGS and LOCUSTS—his royal chariot is harnessed by these. Only the plague of blood remains to be learned! And it will come.[21]

Kovner's invocation of the plagues is recognizable as an adaptation of the Passover custom of reciting the ten plagues as a way of calling for retribution against present-day enemies. In the medieval and early modern period, Jews used the recitation of the ten plagues to appeal to God to exact vengeance against their enemies as he did to the Egyptians—this was the practice that Puscolo was basing himself on when accusing the Jews of murdering Simon—and Kovner converted this practice into a battlefield exhortation that called on the IDF rather than God as the agent of retribution. Kovner's role as an education officer was to help motivate and unify soldiers from various backgrounds, some knowledgeable in scripture and rabbinic literature but many not, and part of what made the ten plagues so useful from this perspective was their familiarity from the Passover Haggadah. Jews from all manner of backgrounds, religious and secular, were accustomed by the Seder to the idea of the ten plagues as the model of righteous retribution against present-day oppressors. Although not composed during or in anticipation of Passover, Kovner's letters drew on the story's role in that context to frame the battle against the Egyptian army as a reenactment of the divine violence used to deliver Israel from biblical Egypt.

But Kovner's use of the plagues reflects another influence as well: Soviet calls to exact revenge against the Nazis during World War II, concluded just three years earlier. Blood is often mentioned in Soviet exhortations to fight the Nazis—an example taken from an article published in the partisan newspaper *Za Rodinu* in May 1942 reads, "Our people will never forgive the fascists for their bloody crimes. The blood of tortured Soviet people calls for merciless revenge."[22] Another example involves a 1941 newsreel entitled *Blood for Blood, Death for Death* by the famed documentary director Dziga Vertov. In a poster for the film, a giant Soviet fighter dressed in red towers over German soldiers that he is about to strike, and stretching over the scene, in large red letters, are the words *krov za krov* (blood for blood). Soviet propaganda stressed the imperative to exact retribution from the Nazis for fallen comrades, and such calls often used the language of blood for blood revenge to describe such retribution, a motif that also tapped into the symbolic power of the color red as a symbol of revolution and the Soviet Union.

The use of blood and blood imagery in calls for retribution had an influence on Jews in the period. Consider a story set in the time of a pogrom against the ghetto of the Lithuanian city of Kovno in the early 1940s, a story that tells of how, in his final moments, a Jew murdered by the Lithuanians is said to have used his blood to write the words "Jews, revenge!" (*Yiden, nekoma* in Yiddish) on a wall and floor of his house. Although the incident is seemingly corroborated by a photograph of the blood inscription, it is far from clear that the incident took place, and the photograph may have been staged.[23] Even if the episode (first recorded in 1948) is a fiction, however, it accurately reflects the importance of the blood revenge theme in the effort to mobilize Soviet Jews to fight, as reflected in other Jewish-Soviet writing from the period. An example is the blood-related imagery of the 1943 essay "To the Jewish Warrior," by the Yiddish poet Peretz Markish, which depicts blood-soaked streets and cities crying out for revenge.[24]

This was the world that Kovner came from—during the war, he had served as an anti-Nazi partisan leader in Vilna, the Soviet capital of Lithuania at the start of World War II—and the vengefulness of Soviet antifascist rhetoric had a profound impact on his style. When the IDF was formed in May 1948, it was not starting from scratch, as it drew on the structure and practices of the earlier paramilitary organization known as the Haganah, and some of its techniques for building the esprit de corps of soldiers drew from Soviet military culture—in fact, education officers like Kovner were sometimes referred to by the Soviet term *politruk*.[25] The battle missive itself was imported by Kovner from the Soviet Union, and as was recognized at the time by Arnan Azaryahu, another officer who called Kovner to task for the letters, their Soviet-style rhetoric indicated that Kovner was treating the war as if it were World War II.[26] A letter from July 13, 1948, shows the transference involved, describing a battle with Egypt as "Negevgrad" in order to liken it to the heroic Soviet battle against the Germans at Leningrad.

Kovner's evocation of the plague of blood is an example of how he repurposed Soviet antifascist sloganeering, evoking the role of the plagues during the Seder but also putting a biblical spin on Soviet calls for "blood for blood" revenge. In his melding of a Soviet-style call for retribution with the biblical language of divine justice, he was preceded by the poet Markish, mentioned earlier, who used biblical examples to frame his calls for revenge against the Germans as a continuation of Jewish heroic tradition. Markish even invoked the ten plagues, comparing the Dnepr River in Ukraine, witness to the murder of Jews, to the bloody Nile. The rhetoric of Kovner's missives came out of this Soviet-biblical fusion, adapting it to Israel's war with Egypt. The river of blood signified not the blood of Jews murdered by the Nazis but the blood of

Egyptian soldiers spilled on the battlefields of the Negev, but the idea to use the biblical story to biblicize a call for retribution was one Kovner inherited from earlier Soviet Yiddish writing.

What also distinguishes Kovner's ten plagues from those of earlier Jewish tradition was their secularization of divine justice. Kovner was not antireligious, but he felt that God had been absent during the Holocaust, and that it fell to humans to restore justice in the world.[27] This view shaped and was shaped by his efforts following World War II to hold Germans to account for the Holocaust. Along with about fifty other Holocaust survivors, Kovner created an organization that they called Dam Israel Noter (the Blood of Israel Avenges), which sought to kill six million Germans in retribution for the Nazi murder of six million Jews. The organization was not able to execute this plot, something that Kovner greatly regretted, but it did find a way to lace the bread supply of a German prisoner-of-war camp with arsenic, leaving two thousand prisoners sick. The conviction that motivated this revenge plot, Kovner's belief that humans had the right, the responsibility, and the power to act in place of God as agents of ultimate justice, also motivated the battle letters and their call on soldiers to exact ten plagues–like retribution against the enemy.

To some at the time, finding a punishment equivalent to a crime as massive as the Holocaust was simply impossible: in the words of one survivor, "Bloody revenge appears worthless to us when measured against the magnitude of our sacrifices."[28] But to Kovner it was still possible to achieve something like divine justice even in the absence of God, not the measure-for-measure justice of rabbinic lore but the eye-for-an-eye justice that God had delegated to humans according to the book of Exodus, and the example of World War II itself, the industrial-scale killing and the immense destructive power of the atomic bomb, made it feel newly realistic to enact the massively scaled punishment that would be necessary to equal Nazi atrocities.[29] This secularized biblical justice was what Kovner was seeking through his revenge plot, not collective punishment that sweeps away the innocent along with the wicked but an act of eye-for-an-eye justice large enough to match and balance out the scale of the Nazis' crimes.

This same drive to see justice done for the Holocaust permeated Kovner's thinking about the war with Egypt. To him, there was no moral distinction between retribution against the Arab enemy and retribution for the Holocaust, a point he made explicit in the first of his missives, from June 11, 1948, in which he framed the war against Egypt as vengeance for "the souls of the six million." There are indications in his writing from the time that Kovner was more empathetic toward Palestinians killed or displaced by the war.[30] But he did not muster any empathy for his Egyptian enemies, whom he conflated with both the biblical Egyptians and the Nazis, and his references to the plagues can be understood as a part of this effort to present the fighting as eye-for-an-eye justice for Nazi crimes. By invoking a plague of blood against the enemy, Kovner was not merely restating in biblical form the calls for blood-for-blood retribution learned from the Soviets; he was asserting such retribution as the ultimate justice that God himself would have exacted were he to have intervened to punish the perpetrators and accomplices of the Holocaust.

The reader who recalls how we began this chapter may have figured out where this history is headed: Kovner's battle letters show that Benny Gantz's implicit call for ten plagues against Hamas did not come out of nowhere but was following the role ascribed to the plagues in earlier Israeli military culture. By the 1980s, the rhetoric of battlefield missives had been toned down, and the biblical allusions cut back, but there had been another way that the comparison with the ten plagues reached soldiers—Passover observance as guided by a version of the Haggadah produced in the 1950s by the military rabbinate of the IDF under Rabbi Shlomo Goren.

I had the opportunity to examine an edition of the Haggadah published by the military rabbinate in 1953, and it is hard to miss its effort to associate the ten plagues with the army's military might. In its illustration of the words "blood, fire and pillars of smoke," printed in large letters (figure 6), a combat plane is shown flying over an Arab city that appears to have just been bombed.[31]

The illustration reflects the critical role that combat planes had played during the 1948 war—early in the war, in Israel's first use of such aircraft

FIGURE 6. From the ten plagues–related section of the Passover Haggadah that includes the Hebrew "blood, fire and pillars of smoke" in enlarged Hebrew lettering, from a Haggadah published by the military rabbinate in 1953, p. 20. Courtesy of the Library at the Herbert D. Katz Center for Advanced Judaic Studies, University of Pennsylvania.

to attack the enemy, they had helped stop the advance of an Egyptian column headed toward Tel Aviv—and this particular illustration may refer more specifically to the role of such aircraft during the period of Operation Ten Plagues when they were used to take out an important Egyptian airbase. In front of the plane, as if guiding it, there appears a long sword, implying that the damage it did to the enemy was a projection of divine power. Later editions of the Haggadah published by the IDF dropped the image, but this example suggests how it is that the weaponized retelling of the plagues was further instilled into the consciousness of soldiers in the early years of Israeli military culture: it was rendered in visual form and distributed through the IDF's version of the Passover Haggadah.

Poetic Injustice

Although Kovner sought to adapt the concept of biblical justice in the wake of the Holocaust, others found it impossible to do so. There were so many victims and so many perpetrators, and the extent of the suffering and loss was so great, that there was simply no way to balance out the crime with some corresponding punishment as envisioned in Exodus and its midrashic elaboration. In the words of one theologian, "If the Holocaust accomplished anything, it effectively killed the doctrine of retribution"—that is, the idea that God (or anyone) can rectify injustice by causing pain and loss that reciprocates and equals out the injustice.[32]

What further discredited the Bible's concept of retributionist justice was the way the biblical language of "an eye for an eye" had been co-opted by fascist propaganda. Adolf Hitler, disgusted by Christianity's turn-the-other-cheek approach, embraced the eye-for-an-eye principle as the core of his own concept of justice—the one part of the Jewish Bible that he was willing to embrace. In fact, Nazi propagandists stressed retribution as the reigning principle of justice: the *V* in V-1, the designation of the flying bomb used to terrorize England, stood for *Vergeltung*, or "retribution," which framed the air attacks as a moral act of requital in which each and every air raid on Germany required a correspondingly destructive raid on England.[33] The propagandist Joseph Goebbels went so far as to use the biblical concept of an eye for an eye to justify the extermination of the Jews, as did Hitler himself in a speech delivered in the Berlin Sports Palace on January 30, 1942: "Now for the first time they will not bleed other people to death, but for the first time the old Jewish law of 'an eye for an eye, a tooth for a tooth' will be applied."[34]

The fascist appropriation of biblical justice made it all the more objectionable to those in the period who questioned the morality of retribution, or the role of violence as a way of achieving it, which brings me to the last treatment of the blood plague that I want to consider in this chapter, a retelling of the story composed by the Hebrew poet Natan Alterman over the course of World War II entitled *Songs of the Plagues of Egypt*. Structured as a three-part cycle of songs, the work recounts the story of the plagues from the perspective of an Egyptian father and son caught up in them, using the first part to introduce the Egyptian city of No-Amon where the story takes place, narrating the plagues with a succession of songs in the second part, and concluding with an epilogue entitled "Ayelet," Hebrew for the morning star that appears just before dawn. The song is allegorical, using the city of No-Amon as a symbol for Europe or the world in general during World War II, but its message is not easily decoded, and it has been interpreted in different ways. Alterman took several years to compose the work, beginning to write it in 1939 and only concluding it in 1944; and its final form, though couched in the rhyme scheme of a child's poem, is a tragic account of apocalyptic violence, cultural unraveling, and dehumanization and a searing indictment of the world for having embraced war and fascism.[35]

The songs about the plagues all share a common structure. Each begins with a description of the plague and its impact on the city, followed by a conversation between the Egyptian father and his firstborn son during which they respond to what has happened. In the plague of blood, for instance, there is no mention of God, Moses, or Pharaoh in the poem, just an oblique reference to the Hebrews as "strangers." The only other human figure featured in the poem apart from the father and son is a maiden who comes to a well to draw water. She is not a villain but an innocent bystander, and she is so startled by the blood she draws out of the well that she drops the pail into the darkness as she is scorched by the blood-red fire of the plague. The maiden seems to have been intended as a symbol of beauty or of art itself, and the pail that she lets drop into the well, ringing out as it falls into the darkness, may be Alterman's way of alluding to the abyss into which poetry fell because of the war. The other plagues are similarly cryptic, with flashes of nightmarish and bewildering imagery that is deeply symbolic but difficult to decode.

A reader steeped in the Hebrew poetic tradition might recognize *Songs of the Plagues of Egypt* as an evocation of the role of the ten plagues in Jewish liturgical poetry, or *piyyut* as this genre is known in Hebrew, the first poetic genre in Hebrew literature to introduce rhyme as a structuring device. The theme of divine retribution against the nations of the world comes up in many such poems, as do references to the ten plagues as the biblical exemplum of such retribution.[36] While Alterman's poem evokes this tradition, however, it is not itself a liturgical poem, never mentioning God, nor is it calling for violence against Israel's enemies. The Egyptian father and son featured in the poem are not perpetrators but collateral damage, or at least the son is. They are never depicted oppressing the Israelites, and in recounting the plagues from their perspective, the songs draw the reader into feeling empathy for their suffering.

The story that Alterman tells through the poems was modeled in part on an earlier and rather famous poem: Goethe's ballad "Der Erlkönig" (The elfin king), which was subsequently set to music by Franz Schubert and many other composers.[37] Alterman knew the poem from having translated it, and the *Songs of the Plagues of Egypt* emulates its structure, which was also built around a dialogue between a father and a son. The son in "Der Erlkönig" feels that he is being stalked by an invisible force, the elfin king, and appeals to the father to help him. While the father tries to reassure him that they will get home soon, he also dismisses the son's fears, telling him that what he sees is just the mist or the wind. As they ride home, the son cries out that the elfin king has begun to hurt him, but the father still does not believe him, and by the time they arrive home, the father discovers that his son has died. Alterman's version of the ten plagues follows a very similar plotline. There, too, the poem is constructed around a dialogue between father and son; the son is stalked by a terrifying invisible force, repeatedly crying out to his father for help; the father, though initially responding tenderly to the son's pleas, becomes dismissive; and the son dies in the end, betrayed by the father who was supposed to protect him.

What I want to call attention to is how Alterman's version of the ten plagues fits, or does not fit, into the history of retelling the first plague that we have been tracing in this chapter, and his treatment of the plague of blood is especially instructive. It would appear at first glance that the plague is following the reciprocal logic of biblical justice, eye for an eye or measure for measure, implying that the blood of the plague was a punishment for an act of bloodshed committed in the Egyptian city of No-Amon, where the father and son live. A problem with this interpretation, however, is that we learn what happens from the father, who proves a rather unheroic figure, and a close reading of his response reveals something sinister between the lines:

My firstborn son, my firstborn son, the water has become blood,
for the blood is pure, my son, for the blood is poured like water.
The depths of the well have grown dark, the eyes of the beast
  have grown red.
The blood was in the city, and the city did not tremble.

In an effort to shed light on the meaning of these lines, the literary scholar Uzi Shavit has suggested that they are alluding to a midrash in the eleventh-century midrashic commentary Leqah Tov: "Because they poured the blood of Israel like water, their rivers were turned into blood and their streams became undrinkable."[38] It is conceivable that the father is simply repeating such a view, explaining the plague as a measure-for-measure punishment for the city's toleration of bloodshed, but when one factors in the larger context in which Alterman was writing, the father's language resonates in a more sinister way: an example is his declaration that 'the blood is pure," which brings to mind Hitler's idea that the preservation of blood purity was of utmost importance to the survival of the Aryan nation.[39] The father's explanation for the first plague sounds biblical at first, but the language of blood purity has a Nazi ring to it, and so too does a line in the next stanza—"The star of strangers gleams over the city," referring to the Hebrews' ascendancy within Egypt but also echoing Hitler's complaint in *Mein Kampf* that "the Star of David" had ascended even as the Germans' will to live declined. Like the father in Goethe's poem, the Egyptian father loses the reader's sympathy as he fails again and again to help his son, but the echoes of *Mein Kampf* intimate the even darker possibility that the father is a fascist, embracing Hitlerian ideas to justify the violence destroying the city around him.

This holds true for the father's understanding of justice as well. Later on in the poem, during the third plague, the father offers what seems to be an eye-for-an-eye explanation for the plagues, echoing the language of Exodus, but here too, he puts a fascistic spin on the idea as Hitler and Goebbels did, pushing the biblical language to a brutal extreme:

> A life for a life is not enough, my firstborn son
> Skin for skin must be taken,
> An eyelash for an eyelash
> Every finger must be collected, every tooth, every strand of hair.

The kind of retribution at work in the plagues, as the father explains them to his son, follows the logic of a life for a life, but it does not stop there. The entire body must be disassembled, broken down into parts and then collected in the way that the Nazis collected dental fillings and even the skin of concentration camp victims as artifacts. Here too, Alterman has transformed the ten plagues into a fascistic travesty, having the father describe it as if it was biblical justice but implying that such language was really just a justification for annihilatory violence.

Eventually, during the final plague, the father ends up sacrificing the son himself, a self-imposed tenth plague that also follows the plotline of Goethe's poem, where the son dies at the end as a tragic consequence of the father's dismissive rationalizations, but here too Alterman adapted the story to register the destructive impact of fascism—in this case, the Hitlerian/Nazi ideal of the parent as ready even to sacrifice beloved children out of a sense of duty to a higher cause.[40] Among its other meanings, *Songs of the Plagues of Egypt* documents in poetic form the various ways that fascism ruined civilization—its destruction of poetry, beauty, even parent-children relationships—and the damage it did includes the fascization of the notion of justice associated with the Bible, its perversion into sadistic and ultimately self-annihilating brutality.

I would situate Alterman's poem in the context of the moral and theological crisis that followed in the wake of fascism's rise and World War II when some came to realize that retributionist justice could not accommodate the magnitude of the era's violence and guilt. There were people like Kovner who remained committed to eye-for-an-eye justice as a way of rectifying the crimes of the Holocaust, but others were ready to abandon the concept: in biblical studies, for example, there was effort in the 1950s to argue that such retribution was not even a genuinely biblical concept.[41] Alterman's response to the apocalyptic retributionism of World War II was not to excise retributionist justice from the Bible but to use the Bible to dramatize its devastating impact, and he did so by fusing the ten plagues with "Der Erlkönig" into a tragedy.

Alterman's poem is now recognized as a classic of modern Hebrew literature, but we live in a different age now, an age when revenge and violent retribution have been revived as legitimate modes of justice, and in that context, the ten plagues story as a model of blood-for-blood retributionist justice has also made a comeback. In Israel, Gantz was the first to invoke the ten plagues in his response to the October 7 attack, but others have followed. In early 2024, a soldier and rabbi named

Abraham Zerbiv posted a video where he compared Israel's military operations in Gaza to the ten plagues.[42] As Passover approached a few months later, Oren Zini, a former commander of an IDF brigade in the West Bank, gave an interview where he called on the country to strike the enemy with a ten plagues.[43] When Passover arrived, Netanyahu himself gave a speech where he compared Hamas' refusal to release the hostages to the Egyptians' refusal to let the Israelites go, and then promised to unleash additional plagues against it soon.[44]

The point I am making is that the kind of justice at work in these calls and invocations of a ten plagues against Gaza, though expressed in biblical language, comes not from the Bible itself but from how people have retold it. The very idea that the plagues were following a judicial logic was only introduced retroactively in retellings of the story from the Hellenistic period, and later retellings of the story, as we have been learning in this chapter, introduced yet other conceptions of justice—the measure-for-measure justice of the rabbis or the blood-for-blood retributive justice of Soviet wartime propaganda. Something like this is also true for the use of the ten plagues as a way of framing military action against Hamas: it emerged from a way of telling the story that comes not from the Bible or midrash but from the story as recounted in Kovner's battle missives and in the ten plagues imagery of the IDF's early Haggadot. The conception of justice at work may seem grounded in the ancient eye-for-an-eye justice of the book of Exodus, but it actually comes from twentieth-century sources and has now been further shaped by our own era's re-embrace of retribution and by its power to unleash devastation on a scale once within reach of God alone.

2

The Second Plague

WHO LET THE FROGS OUT?

ONE OF the most influential retellings of the ten plagues story comes from Cecil B. DeMille's *The Ten Commandments,* an epic movie released in 1956. Because of its limited budget and running time, DeMille featured only four of the plagues—the turning of the Nile into blood, the hail, the darkness, and the slaying of the firstborn. There is a story to tell about the film's depiction of each of these four plagues, but my focus here is on an additional plague that was shot but cut from the film: the plague of frogs.

According to the screenwriter Jesse Lasky Jr., the decision of which plagues to exclude from the film was mostly driven by practical considerations. The boils, the lice, and the flies were all thought to be too revulsive for audiences to bear, while earlier films such as *The Good Earth* had already dramatized the dying animals and locusts. That left five possible candidates, and the original plan had been to depict them all, including the frogs of the second plague. Here is how the episode was to play out according to the script:

> *E-31 Ext. River's Edge—Full Shot—Reeds—(Night)*
>
> Dimly seen amid the reeds and mud, there is a stirring of formless reptiles. Though they are frogs, they more resemble the indistinct shapes of a nightmare. Their hoarse voices blend into a symphony of sound and music, as they ooze up by hundreds out of the murky slime.

*E-32 Int. Nefretiri's Bedchamber—Medium Shot—
Nefretiri—(Night) (A. D. 519)*

> She is sleeping. The blend of music and croaking heard on the riverbank now is growing in volume to fill the chamber. Nefretiri, awakened, sits up—pressing back in terror from what she sees, coverlet clutched to her throat. CAMERA PULLS BACK to reveal the swarm of dimly seen frogs invading the bedchamber. Some are even slithering up between the ibex bedposts of Nefretiri's couch. Her maidservant cowers against the wall, frozen with horror, as Nefretiri leans back further against the bed curtains.[1]

The scene was set at night, so that the frogs could ooze out of the darkness, and the croaking and the musical score would grow louder as the creatures slithered into the bedroom of the Egyptian queen Nefretiri, played by Anne Baxter. Since it was not feasible to use real frogs, the prop team manufactured a hundred rubber frogs with mechanical attachments connected by a wire to an electrical board that moved their legs. The scene as scripted—and as visualized in a sketch by the Academy Award–winning designer John Jensen (figure 7)—was supposed to play out like a nightmare: the frogs emerged from out of the darkness; their croaking got louder and louder; and while the film was meant to be G-rated, the bedroom setting implied a threat of sexual violation.

For all the ingenuity and effort invested in the scene, however, DeMille ultimately decided that he could not use the footage for one simple reason—it was too funny. When people on the studio lot previewed the footage that summer, the response was not horror but laughter. Baxter's reaction to the latex frogs was over the top and, as Lasky recalled, another source of mirth was the jumping of the frogs, the "hippity-hopping along. Hop-hop-hop-hopping along."

DeMille's team were not the only filmmakers in Hollywood to struggle with the challenge of how to make frogs frightening. Alfred Hitchcock made birds terrifying, and the household fly inspired its own classic horror movie. Yet when directors try to do the same for frogs, they often fail. *The Maze* (1953) features a man-size frog; *The Frogs* (1972) focuses on a family that is attacked by an army of vengeful swamp

FIGURE 7. John Jensen's concept for the frog plague in Cecil B. DeMille's *The Ten Commandments* (1956), an episode filmed but eventually cut from the movie. Image courtesy of Heritage Auctions / HA.com.

critters; and *Rana: The Legend of Shadow Lake* (1981) involves a team of loggers attacked by a mutant frog creature. These films and others like them owe their cult status in part to the ludicrousness of the frog as a monster or a murderer. In the words of William Sapp, DeMille's special effects coordinator, "Frogs just aren't that scary."

Some earlier retellings of the second plague solved this problem by displacing the frogs of the episode with a more terrifying creature. In medieval Jewish biblical interpretation, there emerged the idea that the Hebrew term translated in English as "frogs" (*tsefarde'im*, singular *tsefarde'a'*) referred to a far more dangerous creature known in Arabic as *al-timhas*—the crocodile.[2] In a legend that goes back to the Greek historian Herodotus, the crocodile was thought to exist in a symbiotic relationship with a bird known as the trochilus (an Egyptian plover, scholars believe), which would use its song to alert the crocodile to the presence of prey in exchange for being allowed to safely eat the food left behind in its mouth. According to the biblical commentator Nachmanides and other medieval Jewish scholars, the word *tsefarde'a*, explained as a combination of the Hebrew terms for "bird" (*tsippor*) and "knowledge" (*de'a*), originally referred to the bird allied with the crocodile, and then was applied to the crocodile itself. In this way of understanding the episode, there was nothing funny about the second plague because it involved an attack not of hapless frogs but of monstrous man-eating crocodiles.

In fairness, this way of understanding the story had some advantages. Psalm 78, in a brief recounting of the plagues, refers to the frogs as menacing creatures—"frogs that destroyed them" (verse 45)—and it is easier to understand how the creatures of the second plague could have "destroyed" the Egyptians if *tsefarde'a*ʿ is taken to refer to crocodiles. Frogs are not very intimidating, small and nearly or completely toothless, whereas an adult male Nile crocodile can grow up to sixteen feet long and can easily kill a human being. A particularly terrifying Nile crocodile named Gustave, likely dead but possibly not, is rumored to have killed up to three hundred people. An invasion of crocodiles would be as deadly as any of the other plagues.

If the crocodile reading had won out, the second plague would have become another in a series of the biblical story's terrible catastrophes, but because the frog reading prevailed, the episode took a different direction, yielding retellings where the frogs play some comical role. How did it come about that a plague that Exodus treats in a serious manner and that Psalm 78 describes as deadly became a joke, a story that makes people laugh, smile, or giggle? This is the main question that we will be investigating in this chapter, and to do so we will have to wrestle with challenging questions about what makes something funny and what humor itself is.

From the Sublime to the Amphibious

Humor remains an imperfectly understood phenomenon, and one measure of that is how difficult it is to explain why we laugh at frogs. In a cultural history of the frog, Charlotte Sleigh notes that only one serious research paper has addressed the question of the frog's humorousness—a 2007 study that considers why so many experiments involving frogs have won the Ig Nobel Prize, a mock Nobel Prize awarded to research that makes you laugh. (One prize went to an actual Nobel Prize winner who figured out how to levitate a frog.)[3] The authors of this study were able to identify qualities that make frogs funny—their squat bodies, their saltatory gait, their large eyes—but they were unable to develop an explanation for why humans find these traits funny.

In truth, it is not yet fully understood what makes anything funny, though there are many theories that offer a partial explanation.[4] One influential theory, known as the incongruity theory, argues that humor developed as a response to experiences that are puzzling, the mind deriving a certain kind of pleasure by making sense of situations or words that do not make sense logically.[5] Another theory explains humor as a way of channeling aggression, an approach that explains why humor so often involves mockery and other kinds of playful attack.[6] Drawing on disciplines that include psychology, philosophy, cognitive science, linguistics, and evolutionary biology, researchers have come up with many theories, but there is no unified theory that integrates them all into a single explanation for all the facets of humor—why some things make us smile and others makes us laugh, why people find it funny when someone falls on their face, what makes something ironic, etc.[7] I have found that different approaches to humor have different insights to offer, and for this reason I do not commit myself in what follows to any one theory, preferring—in the spirit of the creatures at the center of this chapter—to leap from one to the other.

I want to begin our exploration by looking at a midrashic retelling of the frog plague that appears in the Babylonian Talmud, in a tractate about the laws of Passover called Pesahim (53b). In this retelling of the second plague, the frogs are depicted as martyrs—not passive, irrational creatures as they are depicted in a pre-rabbinic work like the Wisdom of Solomon but intelligent and even pious beings who *chose* to throw themselves into the Egyptian ovens out of a sense of religious obligation. The figure of a martyr is, of course, a very serious one, an embodiment of high-minded piety, but a frog martyr is a different story. Among the many frog-related memes circulating on the internet are images of frogs with their hands clasped in prayer or dressed up like priests, and what makes such images funny is their incongruous mixture of the creaturely and the sublime. The frog martyrs of the Talmud also present an incongruous mix of the low and the high, but to fully understand the humor of the story we will need to know more about the rabbis.

The midrash in question is focused not on the book of Exodus but on an episode in the biblical book of Daniel where three companions of Daniel—Hananiah, Mishael, and Azariah—find themselves in trouble after refusing to bow down to a statue.

> What did Hananiah, Mishael, and Azariah see that led them to send themselves to the fiery furnace for the sanctification of the name of God [that is, to willingly accept death as martyrs] during the rule of Nebuchadnezzar rather than worship idols under duress?
>
> They drew an inference from the plague of frogs in Egypt. With regard to frogs, which are not commanded concerning the sanctification of the name of God, it is written: "And the river shall swarm with frogs, which shall go up and come into your house, and into your bedchamber, and onto your bed, and into the houses of your servants, and upon your people, and into their ovens and kneading bowls" (Exodus 7:28). When are kneading bowls found near the oven? You must say that it is when the oven is hot. If in fulfilling the command to harass the Egyptians, the frogs entered burning ovens, all the more so, we, who are commanded concerning the sanctification of the name of God, should deliver ourselves to be killed in the fiery furnace for that purpose. (Babylonian Talmud, Pesachim 53b)

To appreciate what is funny about this passage, we need to know something about the three heroes mentioned in the story, Hananiah, Mishael, and Azariah, figures introduced in the biblical book of Daniel. We also need to know something about the rabbinic concept of martyrdom—"the sanctification of God's name." The Talmud's take on the second plague as a story of zealous frogs throwing themselves into burning ovens is funny not just because frogs are inherently comical or because it is amusing to imagine animals acting like humans. Something more comes into view when one recognizes the distinctive sense of humor that has shaped the Talmud.

The three characters at the center of this story, it should be noted, were prototypical martyrs. In Christian tradition, Hananiah, Mishael, and Azariah are known as Shadrach, Meshach, and Abednego, Babylonian names given to them by King Nebuchadnezzar after carrying them off to exile in Babylonia. In the story told about them in Daniel 3, the king forces them to choose between bowing down to an idol, a violation of the Torah's prohibition of idolatry, and being thrown into a fiery furnace. In early Christianity, their decision to accept death made them heroes, models for later Christians who, during periods of Roman persecution, chose to die for their faith.[8] The three are also venerated in Jewish tradition for their willingness to martyr themselves alongside rabbinic heroes like Rabbi Akiba, who likewise accepted execution at the hands of the Romans rather than submit to a decree forbidding him to publicly teach the Torah.

For all the adulation heaped on Hananiah, Mishael, and Azariah, however, some rabbinic interpreters noticed something slightly off in the biblical account of their martyrdom. To be sure, Daniel's companions were ready to die out of allegiance to God, but some early interpreters detected a moment of indecision about whether it was actually obligatory in the particular circumstances depicted in Daniel 3 to sacrifice one's life for God. Martyrdom as the rabbis understood it was not obligatory in every single situation where a Jew was being forced or pressured to defame God's name by violating the Torah. Some divine commands were so essential that it was always obligatory to accept death rather than violate them, but that wasn't the case for most of the laws of the Torah according to the rabbis—preserving one's life was a religious value as well—and the Talmud records debate among the rabbis about when the duty to honor God's name *required* the sacrifice of one's life. This is the issue for Hananiah, Mishael, and Azariah; before they let themselves be thrown into a fiery oven, they evidently asked themselves what the Torah required in that kind of situation, only confirming that they did indeed have an obligation to accept death when they came across the example of the frogs who threw themselves into ovens out of devotion to God.

The frog story is not the only midrashic retelling of Daniel 3 where the three hesitate in this way, and in those other versions too, they pause long enough to investigate the question. In a midrash recorded in the rabbinic commentary Song of Songs Rabbah (7.8.1), the companions turn to the prophet Daniel to ask him whether they should bow down to the idol, but Daniel does not know the answer either, so he refers them to Ezekiel, who tells them to run away. The three decide to accept death even though a prophet had advised against doing so, and precisely because they were ready to die despite not knowing whether they were obligated to do so, God intervenes to rescue them from the fire. The whole episode had been staged by God to demonstrate to the world that his people were ready to martyr themselves on his behalf even when they were not required to do so and had no assurance of divine deliverance.

In the frogs midrash, Hananiah, Mishael, and Azariah turn not to biblical prophets but to the Torah, and they find the guidance they seek in the verse where the frogs climb into the ovens of the Egyptians. In a mode of rabbinic legal reasoning known as *qal vehomer* (light and serious), the rabbis would apply the legal implications of a lighter and less important case to a heavier and more important case. Using this mode of argumentation, Daniel's companions reason that if the frogs, non-Israelites with no obligation at all to follow the Torah, nonetheless chose to martyr themselves on God's behalf, how much more should they, as Torah-bound Israelites, be willing to do so?

The Talmud attributes the midrash to a sage named Todos, a leader of the Jewish community in Rome. The rabbis did not accept Todos as one of their own, even considering excommunicating him because he allowed for the eating of Passover sacrifices outside the Jerusalem temple, but they stopped short of that, acknowledging him as a "great master" because of his ability to interpret the Torah, and the Talmud cites the frog midrash as an example.[9] The thought has occurred to me that Todos might have been sympathetic to Christians, telling this story about the frog martyrs as a way of teaching that one did not have to be Jewish to sanctify God's name. In Todos's day, Christians in Egypt decorated lamps with images of frogs as a symbol of their faith in resurrection, including one with a cross on its back and accompanied by the words "I am the Resurrection," from John 11:25 (when the Nile used to overflow its banks every summer, the river would swarm with frogs, a phenomenon interpreted as a kind of rebirth even before the rise of Christianity).[10] I have wondered whether Todos's story, composed when Christians in Rome and elsewhere were being martyred, was playing sympathetically on the frog's association with the Christian faith to imply that Jews had something to learn from non-Jews ready to sacrifice themselves for God despite not being obligated by the Torah to do so.

Another way to understand the frog midrash is to read it as a parody of a kind of story that the rabbis told about themselves, a story where a pious rabbi, forced by the Romans to choose between staying true to God or suffering execution, looks to the Torah to confirm whether he has an obligation to die or not. The most famous example is the martyrdom of Akiba as recounted in the Talmudic tractate Berakhot (61b), set at the time of Akiba's arrest for publicly teaching the Torah in violation of a Roman decree. The execution was set to occur at the time of day when it was required for Jews to say the Shema, rabbinic shorthand for Deuteronomy 6:4–5—"You shall love the Lord your God with all your heart and all your life"—which Jews were supposed to recite daily as an affirmation of their faith in God. Seeing that their master was reciting these words even as his executioners were raking his flesh with iron combs, Akiba's disciples asked him why he was still willing to express such devotion to a God that was letting him die, and the sage explained: "All my days I have been disturbed by this verse 'You shall love the Lord your God with . . . *all your life.*' [Now I understood that to mean that] one must love God even if he takes your life. I have thought to myself, when will I get the chance to fulfill this command, and now that I have such an opportunity, shall I not fulfill it?" In his final hours, facing an injustice that would normally shatter a person's faith in God, Akiba turns back to the Torah for guidance, and what he discovers there is that martyrdom—expressing one's love of God by submitting to death—is indeed an act that the Torah requires him to accept.[11]

The frog story is another example of this same kind of story, and in fact, in variant forms of the midrash found in a text known as Midrash Tehillim, a commentary on Psalms, Daniel's companions find the scripture they are looking for in verses similar in phrasing to the verse that Akiba focuses on: Deuteronomy 4:29 ("You will seek from there the Lord your God, and you will find him if you seek him with all your heart and *with all your life*") and Jeremiah 29:13 ("You will seek me and you will find me when you search for me *with all your heart*").[12] What stands out about the Talmudic version of this story is that the companions find the scriptural support they are looking for not in a verse similar to the one featured in the Akiba martyrdom story but in a far less expected place, a verse about frogs jumping into ovens. In our own day and age, making a character a frog signals that the story is meant to be light-hearted, and I suspect something similar is happening in this story in a comic twist on the rabbinic martyrdom tale.

We cannot say for certain that the author was trying to be funny, but there is reason to think so, for there is evidence that the rabbis were familiar with the comic role of the frog in Greek culture at the time. The most famous example is the frog chorus in *The Frogs*, a comedy written by Aristophanes in 405 BCE, and frog-related humor also surfaces in a mock Homeric epic poem known as *The War of the Frogs and the Mice* (*Batrachomyomachia* in Greek), where frog warriors with names like Craugasides (derived from the Greek for "croak") fight a mini-battle with mice.[13] One can point to midrashic stories that borrow from Greek frog comedy. In a midrash that resembles a sing-off between a frog chorus and the god Dionysius in Aristophanes's comedy, King David, proud of himself for having composed so many psalms, is humbled by a frog who outsings him. In another midrash recorded in Exodus Rabbah 10.6, a story where Pharaoh begs Moses to stop the noise the frogs are making, the author was borrowing from another comic moment in *The Frogs* when Dionysius begs the frogs to stop singing.[14]

There is no exact counterpart to the frog martyr midrash in Greek comedy, but the connections between midrash and Greek comedy do suggest a way to understand the kind of humor at work in the Talmudic story. The role of frogs in ancient Greek comedy was often deflationary—to let the air out of solemnity, grandiosity, pretension, and pomposity. In Aristophanes's play, the target is the god Dionysius, a pretentious character who dresses up as Hercules, and the frogs put him in his place. In *The War of the Frogs and the Mice*, the comedy comes from reducing the grandness of the epic genre to a miniature scale, and its diminutive frog heroes make for a belittling caricature of the imposing warriors of Homeric legend. The frogs of the midrash can be understood as a similar deflationary device, only the intended effect in that case is not to deflate the high seriousness of tragedy and epic but to put a subversive comic spin on the most serious and profound of rabbinic stories, the martyrdom tale.

Like Akiba, Daniel's companions must choose between desecrating God's name and death, and like him, they turn to the Torah to understand what they ought to do. In an ironic twist, however, what they discover there is that it does not require a sage's deep knowledge of the Torah to fulfill the obligation to sanctify God's name; the frogs acted to sanctify God's name even without having studied a single word of the Torah. The thrust of the story in this reading is similar to the midrash about David and the frog: humans might think highly of themselves for what they do to express their devotion to God, but they should keep their egos in check because they are not the only ones to act in this way; even very lowly creatures do so.

It might seem strange that rabbinic editors would incorporate into the Talmud a story that seeks to deflate their own understanding of martyrdom, but not if one recognizes the distinctive sense of humor that animated those editors, a kind of self-deprecating humor willing to make fun of its own scholarly pretensions. In a book called *Socrates and the Fat Rabbis*, Talmudist Daniel Boyarin argues that this mode of comic self-criticism is adopted from a Greek philosophical practice known as *spoudaiogeloion* (serious comedy), a paradoxical kind of discourse used to make light of intellectual pretention by treating serious philosophical and scholarly topics in a playfully subversive and self-satirizing way.[15] The genre, which aims to entertain but also to induce a self-consciousness about the limits of what humans can know, was inspired by Socrates as imagined in the Hellenistic and Roman periods, a serious philosopher but also a joker who famously used humor to make fun of others and himself. This kind of self-subverting discourse, Boyarin contends, had an impact on the formation of the Babylonian Talmud and its juxtapositions of serious discussion with comical stories about rabbinic foibles. Not every scholar is convinced by the comparison with *spoudaiogeloion*, but Boyarin's recognition of a similarly self-subverting humor in the Talmud gives us a way to understand why its editors were open to a story that has some fun with the rabbinic martyr story: light-hearted self-parody is in line with the Talmud's efforts to undercut the pretentiousness of its own scholarly culture.

It is never easy under any circumstance to pin down what makes something funny or to explain how the humor works—as E. B. White's famous saying goes, analyzing humor is like dissecting a frog: few people are interested, and the frog dies of it. Whether or not one finds this particular midrash as amusing as I do, however, there are other midrashic retellings of the second plague even more clearly meant to be funny, such as one where the frogs convince the floors of the Egyptians' houses to open up so that they can sneak into privy chambers and emasculate their occupants, or another where the frogs get inside the Egyptians' bodies and start making shrieks from inside that drive them to distraction (Exodus Rabbah 10.3–6). The humor at work in these examples is different from that of the frog martyr story—it is the humor of "punching up," getting the last laugh against oppressors by putting them in humiliating situations—but they generated comedy from the biblical story in a similar way, finding some detail that could be twisted into a laughable absurdity, as Todos did by seizing on the mention of ovens in Exodus 7:28 to develop a martyrdom story modeled on Daniel 3 with frogs as the heroes. There were serious-minded Christians at the time who regarded frivolity as incompatible with piety, but not so the rabbinic authors of midrash who loved to find puns in the biblical text, read into it various farcical situations, turned the Egyptians into buffoons, and even ascribed bathroom humor to the Torah. They found humor in all ten plagues, but none yielded more laughs than the frog plague.[16]

The enduring impact of midrashic humor can be demonstrated with an illustration of the frog plague in the fourteenth-century Spanish Haggadah known as the Golden Haggadah (figure 8).[17] The scene is a rendering of Exodus 8:2—"Aaron stretched out his hand over the waters of Egypt, and a frog came up and covered the land of Egypt"—and its illustrator used the opportunity to inject visual humor into the scene, adding amusing details like a frog in the top left corner peeking its head out of a window to stare down an Egyptian. The startled Pharaoh in the illustration may have been intended as a stand-in for Christian rule,

FIGURE 8. Medieval illustration of "and a frog came up" (Exodus 8:2) from the Golden Haggadah. From the archive of the British Library, MS 27210, folio 12v. British Library / Granger Historical Archive.

wearing the crown of a European king, and in another funny embellishment the illustrator knocks him down a peg by sending frogs catapulting at his head. While the illustrator added his own mischievous touches to the episode, however, he was building on a comic tradition established by earlier midrash.

There were two aspects of Exodus 8:2 that struck the rabbis as odd—Why does the verse use a singular "frog" when later on it becomes clear that a whole army of frogs is involved? And if the plague only involved a single frog originally, where did the other frogs come from that are mentioned later in the narrative? The Talmudic passage in question features none other than Akiba, who explains the switch from the single frog of Exodus 8:2 to multiple frogs by claiming that there was one frog originally who gave birth to the other frogs (Babylonian Talmud, Sanhedrin 67b). Akiba's explanation did not impress his colleague Elazar, who dismissed it, but it won over the illustrator of the Golden Haggadah, who visualized it by showing a volley of frogs launched at Pharaoh from out of the butt of the frog in the river.[18]

The creator of this scene had his own reasons for making the episode funny—it has always been a challenge to keep young people awake and engaged in the Seder, and butt jokes are especially effective with children of a certain age. But what first opened the door to retelling the second plague as a joke was midrash. The rabbis who produced the Talmud were devoted to the Torah, honoring sages like Akiba for being ready to give up their lives in fulfillment of its commands, but that did not stop them from finding comedy in the Torah, including gross-out humor and amusing pokes at the powerful. The second plague gave the rabbis an excuse to import frog jokes into the biblical story, and the resulting retellings, modulating the seriousness of scripture into a farcical register, left a lasting mark on how later Jews recalled the episode.

Playing with Frogs

Having explored how the rabbis found humor in the second plague, I now want to turn to a later tradition of retelling the episode. This interpretation is also based on midrash, but it exemplifies a different, wilder kind of humor that scholars refer to as the carnivalesque. Carnivalesque humor, so named because it was acted out in the context of carnivals in Christian Europe, involved dressing up in funny ways, getting drunk, playing games and pranks, making fun of the authorities, and acting unruly. It also refers more generally to humor associated with raucousness and the transgression of boundaries.[19] The frogs of classical midrash were deflationary. In some more recent retellings, the frog plague is transformed into a carnivalesque performance.

In 1992, members of the Bobover community, a Hasidic community in Brooklyn, New York, staged precisely this kind of reenactment as part of a comic reenactment of the exodus story entitled *Me ʿavus leHeirus* (From slavery to freedom). The occasion was the festival of Purim, a time when Jews have traditionally performed a kind of folk theater known as the Purim *Spiel*, and for the strictly observant and self-isolating Bobover community, the holiday offered a rare opportunity to attend a theatrical performance, an entertainment normally off-limits.

Much of the performance may have been improvised, but it did follow a kind of plot formed from the biblical account and its midrashic expansion. After Aaron warns Pharaoh of the coming plague, the actor playing Pharaoh laughs derisively as he points toward a green plastic statuette of a frog god that has been placed on the stage. Within moments, live frogs emerge from the mouth of the statuette and are picked up by an actor and thrown about the stage. While another actor chases the jumping frogs around the stage, Pharaoh picks up a challah sandwich, and, after biting into the sandwich, he realizes that there is a live frog inside. He makes a show of spitting it out, but the audience is meant to understand that he swallowed it, for a few moments later, he begins to burp and gesture as if he has flatulence. The king's humiliation culminates with a kind of dethronement: he lifts up his royal headdress to reveal a live, three-pound bullfrog perched on his head even as another frog, the plastic frog statue, takes his place on his throne.[20]

All the bedlam, especially the ten or so live frogs featured as comic props in the play, had an exhilarating effect on the audience, and especially the children. One group of little boys, playing with the frogs at the edge of the stage, became so excited that they began shouting. The ecstatic reaction of the audience was so intense that the theater historian Shari Troy, who was able to view a video of the performance, was moved to observe that while the occasion for the performance was Purim, the exhilaration and sense of release experienced by the audience was akin to the exodus—a breaking free from restriction and a sublime feeling of freedom.[21]

The performance offers another example of the enduring impact of midrashic humor on how Jews understand the second plague. One key verse was Exodus 7:29: "And the frogs shall come against you and upon your people and upon your servants." The Hebrew preposition *b-*, added to the front of words, is usually translated in English versions of this verse as "against" or "upon," but it can also mean "in," and that is how classical midrash understood it, spinning the verse into the story where the frogs enter into the bodies of the Egyptians and start crying out from inside them. In the Bobover play, this midrash spawned the moment when Pharaoh swallows a frog and begins to burp and fart. Another antic inspired by midrash was the bullfrog under Pharaoh's headdress, the largest of the frogs on the stage. This detail sprang from a midrash in Exodus Rabbah 10.2, where the most exalted of the frogs, the one with the highest status, is said to be the one who enters the house of Pharaoh. And the green frog statuette with the live frogs coming out of its mouth was born of the Akiban midrash illustrated by the Golden Haggadah, another laughable way of showing how a single large frog spawned the others.

Many of the classic characteristics of the carnivalesque were on display during the Bobovers' mock second plague. Pharaoh seemed to violate Jewish law by pretending to swallow an unkosher animal, an act that a kosher-keeping Hasidic audience would have recognized as deeply transgressive. The subversion of hierarchy occurs in the scene when Pharaoh is displaced on the throne by a frog, similar to the mock dethroning of the carnival king. The scatological humor is hard to miss when the actor playing Pharaoh pretends to fart after swallowing the frog. Perhaps most importantly, the audience's reaction to the frolicsome frogs involved throwing off the restraints of decorum and acting on primal animalistic impulses—the heart of the carnivalesque. Purim, like carnival, brings momentary release from the restrictions of everyday existence, and all the more so for a community like the Bobover Hasidim, who lead a highly regulated life. In keeping with the spirit of the carnivalesque, the play offered liberation from religious restriction and the license to have fun at the expense of an authority figure.

Purim is the most carnival-like of Jewish holidays, but there are elements of the carnivalesque in other Jewish holidays as well, including Passover, and there, too, one can find examples of how the story of the second plague has been infused with a carnivalesque spirit—nothing as unruly as the Bobover play and its live frogs but reflecting a similar kind of humor.

A G-rated example of what I have in mind is a well-known Passover song for children first recorded in 1951 by a Canadian Hebrew school teacher named Shirley Cohen Steinberg: "One Morning," better known as the "Frog Song." For American Jews, this little ditty is one of the most recognizable Passover songs outside of those included in the Haggadah, and it too reflects a carnivalesque retelling of the frog plague, albeit at a preschool level:

> One morning when Pharaoh woke in his bed
> There were frogs in his bed and frogs on his head.
> Frogs on his nose and frogs on his toes
> Frogs here, frogs there,
> Frogs were jumping everywhere.[22]

Although the singing of this song is a much tamer experience than the frog-triggered frenzy that erupted during the Bobover play, it too injects mischief-making into the frog plague, portraying the frogs as if they were impish children jumping all over a dad waking up in the morning.

The frogs play a similar role in children's books for Passover. Osher Werner's *Pharaoh and the Fabulous Frog Invasion* (2007) draws on midrashic tradition to tell a story in which the frogs create mayhem for the Egyptians—sitting on people's heads, croaking inside their bellies, and singing a loud song "until every Egyptian's ear drums rang."[23] Even after Moses prays to quiet the frogs down, they have one last surprise: the ones that had leapt into the ovens burst out at the end of the story still alive to renew their song. Frogs also introduce mayhem into the Passover episode of *Shalom Sesame*, an American Israeli version of *Sesame Street*. Kermit himself, not a frog of the chaos-making variety, makes only a brief appearance, but the final scene involves a veritable riot of jumping frogs, which creates so much of a ruckus that the episode has to end.[24] Many of the Passover-related frog knickknacks that can be purchased online have a mischievous, carnivalesque quality as well: sticky rubber frogs meant to be thrown at a wall, frogs meant to be whacked, frogs designed to be used as slingshots, and silly, irreverent frog-related ties and T-shirts like one that reads, "Who let the frogs out?"

The rise of the mischief-making Passover frog as a part of the Seder experience reflects a modern development—a heightened attention to the perspective (and impatience) of children.[25] Children have always been participants in the Seder from its earlier origins, and keeping them entertained during the service has always been a part of the Passover experience, as we observed in connection to the Golden Haggadah. It was only in the nineteenth and twentieth centuries, however, that people began to publish versions of the Haggadah specifically designed for and addressed to children. Dorothea Salzer, an expert in Jewish children's Bibles, told me that the earliest one she has come across was published in Berlin in 1830 by Rabbi Shlomo ben Menachem for his children, but the genre of the children's Haggadah, and the related genre of the children's Passover book, really took off in the twentieth century in the wake of the success of Jewish children's literature like *The Adventures of K'tonton* from 1935, centered on a tiny Jewish boy modeled on Tom Thumb who gets into various kinds of trouble as a result of his small size. One of these misadventures was Passover related, in fact. K'tonton finds himself trapped when he is accidentally carried off in a basket of dishes put away in preparation for Passover and only finds his way out with information gleaned from a mouse.

One reflection of this effort to appeal to children was the "playification" of the Seder experience, an effort to introduce an element of spontaneity and game playing into the evening's otherwise highly structured and predictable proceedings. An early effort in this regard is a children's Haggadah published in London in 1933 by Rabbi Abraham Silbermann, which includes illustrations of the plagues (by Erwin Singer) on a wheel inserted into a fold of the page. Turning the wheel showed each plague through a viewer cut into the page, as shown in figure 9. While there is nothing humorous about the illustrations themselves, what makes Silbermann's Passover wheel a sign of things to come is its interactivity, a harbinger of the games, puppets, pop-up books, and other gimmicks used by parents today to make Passover fun for their children.

The effort to create a Seder for children recruited the frog of the second plague as an ally. This has been particularly so in American Jewish Passover Seders, a development likely reflecting the influence of the Easter Bunny, another small, cute, and hoppity animal that makes his

FIGURE 9. The plague of frogs as glimpsed through a rotating wheel included in Abraham Silbermann, *The Children's Haggadah*, 3rd ed. (London: Shapiro, Vallentine, 1942), 13. Courtesy of the Library at the Herbert D. Katz Center for Advanced Judaic Studies, University of Pennsylvania.

appearance at exactly that time of year, but another contributing factor was the frog's role as a comic figure in modern children's entertainment from the 1950s onward. The long-suffering but wry and witty Kermit, the vaudevillian Michigan J. Frog from Warner Brothers cartoons, and other frogs featured in children's television no doubt also encouraged the use of frogs as a way of keeping children entertained during Passover. The origin of this tradition goes back to midrashic readings of the second plague as farce, but it has been transmuted into modern, child-centered humor, a juvenile version of the carnivalesque that takes delight in being very noisy, jumping, throwing things, making authority figures look ridiculous, and creating chaos.

A Postmodern Punchline

For one last example, I want to turn from midrash back to the movies, a reenactment of the frog plague in the movie *Magnolia*, written and directed by Paul Thomas Anderson, where the episode has been detached from its setting in the exodus story and transplanted to a narrative about modern Los Angeles. While the makers of *The Ten Commandments* were forced to delete the frog plague because it was too funny, Anderson's film embraces the comic potential of the frog and uses it to create something like a resolution to a contradiction that the film introduces in its prologue and keeps returning to over the course of its 188 minutes.[26] The earlier examples we have looked at enlist the frogs of the second plague to help generate deflationary and carnivalesque humor. *Magnolia* taps into the comic power of the frog in a different way—not to subvert or to release people from inhibition but to manage a contradiction at the core of life, the dissonance between its indifferent randomness and the human need to believe that some invisible force is watching out for our best interests and intervening to steer us in the right direction.

The film is focused on a day in the life of several disparate characters who are all deeply flawed and rather pathetic, trapped in some kind of self-created emotional prison: an insecure police officer who becomes obsessed with finding a gun he loses while chasing a suspect; a traumatized and miserable woman he meets during an investigation; a quiz show host dying of cancer who happens to be the woman's father and also her abuser; the show's producer, also dying of cancer; his estranged, angry, and misogynist son; and a former child champion of the quiz show named Donnie Smith who was struck by lightning as a child and is now obsessed with getting his teeth fixed so that he can impress a bartender he has a crush on.

I won't attempt to summarize the movie's various subplots here, but what is relevant for our purposes is that they all intersect in a surprising climax involving a rain of frogs. Dropping like hail on Magnolia Boulevard, the frogs have an impact on every one of the film's main characters, sometimes harmful, but often helpful. The quiz show host, unable to deal with his guilt, is poised to shoot himself when a frog lands on his head, sending the bullet ricocheting into his television instead and saving his life, while yet another frog causes his wife to crash her car in front of their daughter's apartment, forcing her to seek shelter there and for the two to reunite. Donnie Smith, while climbing down a pole after stealing the money he needs for his braces, is hit by a frog, falls to the ground, and smashes his teeth, but he is saved by the policeman. As a result, the latter regains his confidence and sense of purpose—he even gets his lost gun back when it, too, falls from the sky—and he goes on to help Donnie return the stolen money and connect him to a dentist. Meanwhile, the loud thud of frogs hitting the ground wakes up the dying producer in time to see his estranged son beside him just before he passes. The episode is a deus ex machina, an ending that resolves all the problems of the film's characters in an abrupt and highly improbable way that the audience is meant to recognize as purposely contrived, only it is not clear that there was a deus involved: the frogs appear out of nowhere, and it is never made clear whether their appearance is divine intervention or a strange but random accident.

Beyond being a mere slapstick cascade of mishaps and accidents, the comedy of the frogs also plays a deeper role in the movie. The contradiction at the heart of *Magnolia* arises from the incompatibility between the haphazardness of life and our wish to believe that everything that happens to us happens for a reason, that our life has some purpose. The rain of frogs does not resolve this contradiction, but there is something about the comic absurdity of the episode, something about the ludicrousness of its frogs, that makes it work as an ending in another way.

Anderson has claimed that he got the idea for the movie's ending not from the Bible but from real cases of raining frogs as documented in a 1919 work entitled *The Book of the Damned* by Charles Fort (1874–1932).[27] The book introduced a field of inquiry that has come to be known as anomalistics, the use of science to search for a natural explanation for freakish events like frogs suddenly falling from the sky (which

Fort attributed to whirlwinds or hurricanes that suck up frogs from lakes or ponds and deposit them many miles away). In interviews, Anderson has insisted that the falling frogs of *Magnolia* were inspired by such phenomena, and that the connection to the biblical plague only emerged later in the writing process as an afterthought.

But even if we take him at his word about the initial inspiration, the final version of the story also accentuates the connection to the frog plague, making numerous visual references to Exodus 8:2, the verse in English translations of the Bible in which Moses warns Pharaoh that he will send a plague of frogs against him if he does not let the Israelites go free. Apart from quick flashes of "Exodus 8:2" itself, the numbers eight and two appear repeatedly throughout the movie—a weather forecast predicting an 82 percent chance of rain, a mug shot of a character taken with the record number 82082082082, a shot of a blackjack player in the movie's prologue needing a two to win and getting an eight, and the numbers eight and two appearing on the side of an airplane, on a poster at a bus stop, as an apartment number, as the score of a game written on a chalkboard, and on and on. According to one count, the verse is referred to over a hundred times, including, incredibly, through the film's 188-minute running time and its two eights.[28]

If the frogs of the film symbolize the anomaly, the randomness of life, why would the story work so hard to also associate them with the biblical miracle, the sign that nothing happens by accident? Not only does the film never resolve the contradiction between these possibilities, it actually heightens it in various ways. In one scene, for instance, a man sitting in the studio audience of the quiz show is glimpsed holding a sign with "Exodus 8:2" written on it, only to have it yanked from his hands by a stagehand played by Anderson himself. The struggle is easy to miss, unfolding in the background for just a second or two, but it dramatizes the tug-of-war at the center of the entire movie as it pulls back and forth between the anomalistic and the miraculous. The film does not fully align itself with one or the other of these perspectives, dangling the possibility of some deeper purpose at work in the strange coincidences of life while also underscoring the fate-changing impact of chance encounters and random occurrences.

While *Magnolia* does not resolve the contradiction between these two ways of viewing reality, it does suggest that it is possible to live with the contradiction, to act as if both were true, and this is where the funniness of the frogs proves essential. Many jokes begin with an incongruity, combining things that do not cohere in real life, and while the punch line feels like a resolution, it is not the kind of resolution that fits things together in a logical or realistic way. Consider a frog joke as an example: "What did the frog order at McDonald's?" The setup introduces an absurd situation that defies reality, while the punch line illustrates how humor makes it possible to assimilate incongruity without solving it: "French flies and a diet croak." The listener's initial frustration at not being able to account for an incongruous, impossible scenario is supplanted—transcended, really—when the punch line reveals another kind of coherence in the situation, an amusing double pun that creates its own kind of "Aha!" moment.

Like the frog joke, *Magnolia* presents the audience with an incongruous scenario, a set of circumstances that seem like fluke coincidences and miraculous interventions at the same time. It keeps reminding us of this contradiction, and in this way it builds up a kind of suspense and anticipation akin to what a person hears when presented with a riddle or an absurd scenario like the McDonald's frog joke—the riddle in this case, in the words of the narrator, is how life can be this and that, how it can be a "matter of chance" and yet seem at times like it is governed by an invisible force looking to sustain the world as a just place and to give people a chance to redeem themselves. The frog finale, like a punch line, addresses this question with something like a pun, a blending of things that don't fit together logically. In Exodus, the frogs' appearance is a miracle from God; in Fort's *Book of the Damned*, the rain of frogs is a fluke occurrence. *Magnolia*'s ending is joke-like not just because it is funny but because it resolves life's incongruousness by fusing together the random and the miraculous into a single event.

The difference between *Magnolia*'s frog plague and the deleted frog plague of DeMille's version of the exodus story says a lot about the difference between cinema in the 1950s and the 1990s. For DeMille, the humorousness of the episode was accidental and simply did not fit into the earnest film he was trying to create. Anderson's version of the frog plague makes conscious use of the comic association of the frog, and the humor is essential to what the film is trying to convey in asking the viewer to accept a contradiction—that life is random and miraculous at the same time. The punch line of a joke does not solve the incongruity of its setup in a rational sense, but it makes sense of it in another way that we were not expecting, and somehow the results make us feel better. This is how Anderson's frog finale works: as a signal that the ending is a punchline, it takes us beyond our inability to reconcile life's contradictions in a logical way.

Anderson's version of the frog plague is distinctively postmodern, resisting a binary approach to life as either this or that, but we are now in a position to appreciate what it shares with earlier comic retellings of the second plague like that of midrash that also exploited the contrast between the seriousness of the Bible and the funniness of frogs. There are different senses of humor at work in these examples, but they all originate from the insight that the laughter triggered by the frogs did not need to be excised or suppressed but could enliven the story and expand its meaning in ways that only humor and playfulness could accomplish.

As we have seen over the course of this chapter, the funniness of the frog plague was an accident of history. The biblical account in Exodus was not meant to be laughed at, and the story only inadvertently developed humorous associations as a result of a later event—the conquest of Alexander the Great, which exposed ancient Jews to Greek culture, including Greek comedy and the frog as a stock comic character. But some accidents are happy ones, and the accidental comedy of the second plague has had many felicitously funny consequences, including midrash that transmute the memory of persecution and martyrdom into lighthearted wit; mischievous illustrations, songs and toys bringing chaos and comic relief to Passover; and a 188-minute Hollywood movie that uses the frogs to create something miraculous out of life's randomness.

3

The Third Plague

MAGIC MEETS ITS MATCH

BY THE end of the second plague, Pharaoh is so desperate for the suffering to stop that he offers to let the Israelites go if Moses will pray to God to remove the frogs. The story might have come to a happy ending right then, but Pharaoh proves stubborn, backtracking as soon as the plague is over, and God must try again with a third plague, sending another noxious creature, the *kinnim*—a term interpreted by some as lice and by others as gnats—to torment the Egyptians yet again.

One of the reasons for Pharaoh's obstinacy is that he was not yet convinced that God was truly more powerful than he was. His own magicians had been able to replicate Aaron's feat in turning his staff into a serpent, and similarly replicated his feats with the first two plagues, and the wonderous power of his sorcerers, matching God's power point for point, seems to have convinced Pharaoh that there was nothing about Moses's power that he couldn't at least neutralize. The third plague undercut this confidence as a manifestation of divine power that magic failed to replicate.

Exodus 8 tells of how Aaron used his staff to strike the earth and summon the *kinnim* out of its dust to spread to all Egypt, but this time, the magicians are unable to do likewise, acknowledging a force at work greater than their own when they declare, "This is the finger of God" (Exodus 8:15 in the Hebrew text of Exodus; 8:19 in English translations).

Pharaoh remains defiant for seven more plagues and beyond, but the magicians never again try to replicate them, only appearing once more, during the sixth plague of boils in Exodus 9:9–11, which reports that they were no longer able even to stand before Moses, never mind trying again to counter the plague.

The defeat of Pharaoh's magicians is a minor subplot in the Exodus account, but it developed a life of its own over the course of the Hellenistic-Roman period, and a possible trigger for its development was Egyptian storytelling at the time. Egyptians in the Roman period, building on a native tradition of magical lore that went back to the time of the ancient pharaohs, told their own stories about magical duels, narratives where an Egyptian magician gets into a wonder-working battle with a foreign sorcerer.[1] Each side in these contests would use its magical power to try to overcome the other, using spells and other magical techniques to conjure various kinds of supernatural attack—very similar to the biblical story of Moses's contest with the Egyptians, except that it would always be the Egyptian magician who prevailed in the contest.

In one such story, a magician even performs a wonder similar to the ninth plague, a darkness that makes it impossible for people to see each other.[2] This kind of story drew on earlier Egyptian magical lore, but it only seems to have crystallized as a genre in the Roman period, around the first century BCE, and its popularity might have been what initially inspired Jews and Christians at the time to develop the magician subplot in Exodus into full-fledged stories where the Egyptian magicians in the narrative are not the victors but villains, fools, or tragic figures.

In this chapter we will be tracing the history of the magician subplot as it grew and changed over the course of antiquity, the Middle Ages, and modernity. Jews, Christians, and Muslims all elaborated on the subplot, but we will mostly be focused on Christian retellings, which are fascinating for, among other reasons, how they account for the magical power of the magicians and distinguish it from the power of God. The two kinds of power clearly resembled each other—at first, it seems as if the magicians can do exactly what God is able to do—but in the end, the magic of the magicians falls short, failing to produce the third plague. Early Jews and Christians retold the story in ways meant to account for this failure—and in the process clarify the difference between magic and miracles—how magic is able to produce miracle-like effects and what makes it different from divine power. What makes the history of retelling the third plague interesting is the insight it offers into the ten plagues story as a part of the history of magic. The characters of Pharaoh's magicians, the kind of magic they were thought to have practiced, and the reason that magic failed during the third plague were all transformed as the concept of magic itself developed over the course of antiquity, the Middle Ages, and modernity.

In following this history, I will be surveying different explanations for why the magicians' magic did not work against the third plague, and I will also be exploring different understandings of what the magicians say when they realize its failure: "It is the finger of God." Fingers play an important part in magic because of their role in manipulating small objects. For some, the mention of God's finger suggested that God was acting with this kind of finesse, choosing the creatures involved not because they were noxious pests but because they were tiny. Philo of Alexandria, a Jewish biblical commentator from the first century CE, was the first known person to emphasize the smallness of the plague as the key to its meaning.[3] For others, what stood out about the phrase was the word *elohim* (god). The Hebrew can be read as "This is a finger of a god"—that is, what the magicians recognized was a divine power at work without identifying the god involved as the god of Moses. However, many interpreters have understood it as an acknowledgment of *the* God, a conversion from paganism to monotheism, as in the Qur'an's depiction of this moment. The vagueness allowed the phrase to be construed in various ways, and a second goal of this chapter is to explore how interpreters at different points in the history of magic filled in its meaning. The words "This is the finger of God" took on special meaning in the context of stories that people told about magic, resonating in that way into the age of modern magic, but their significance has also changed in tandem with evolving attitudes toward magic.

Confessions of a Sorcerer

Although Pharaoh's magicians make only a few brief appearances in the biblical plague narrative, they manage to introduce a number of questions that drew the attention of early interpreters. On three different occasions—after Aaron turns his staff into a serpent, after he turns the water into blood, and after he brings the frogs out of the river—the text reports that the magicians "did in like matter." But what exactly did that mean? Did they produce the same effects in the same exact way? The text attributes this ability to what English translations render as "secret arts," but the underlying Hebrew word is enigmatic: What were these secret arts? Did their magic involve supernatural power or sleight of hand? One always wants to know how a magic trick works, and Exodus offers absolutely no information to address such curiosity.

The magicians' role in the story raised still other questions for interpreters. How were they able to turn water into blood if Aaron had already turned all the waters of Egypt into blood? Where did they get this water from? Why would they have added more frogs to the second plague if Egypt was already covered with them? Since the Egyptians were desperate to get rid of the frogs, why add more? Why doesn't the biblical text mention anything about the magicians bringing their versions of the plagues to an end, as it does for the plagues performed by Moses and Aaron? And what was it about the third plague that proved too difficult for them to replicate? If they could turn water into blood and conjure frogs, why couldn't they conjure the *kinnim* as well? What was it about this particular plague that proved impossible to replicate?

One of the ways that Jews and Christians addressed these questions was to retell the episode, and the earliest known examples came up with a way to answer at least some of them. The Hebrew Bible refers to various sorts of demonic creatures here and there, and from those hints early Jews and Christians developed elaborate demonologies that accounted for the origin of demons, gave them names, assigned them characteristics and roles, and organized them under the command of a supreme demon referred to variously as Mastema, Belial, or Satan.[4]

Both Jews and Christians came to believe that the magic of Pharaoh's magicians was powered by these demons, and that idea gave them a way to clear up some of the mysteries of the biblical text. Why were the magicians able to reproduce the miracles of God? Because they also had access to supernatural power. Why did their magic fail to keep up with God's miracles? Because the demons they were allied with, as dangerous as they were, could not match God's supreme power.

The earliest known text to offer this kind of explanation is the book of Jubilees from the second century BCE, which can also claim the distinction of being the earliest known text to specify the number of plagues as ten. In its version of the story, recounted in chapter 48, the demon responsible for the plagues is known as Mastema, a figure very similar to Satan but known by a name derived from a biblical word that means "enmity," which is its chief characteristic, enmity toward God. Mastema was driven by a desire to harm the children of Israel, a mission that led him to empower the magicians to perform the plagues, but what he did not realize is that God was in control the whole time. The magicians were able to reproduce the first two plagues according to Jubilees because God's angels permitted Mastema to help them, and those angels remained in control throughout: they did not permit the magicians to halt the plagues they created, as God allowed Moses and Aaron to do; and then during the plague of boils, the angels stepped in to stop the magicians altogether—Jubilees' way of explaining why the magicians disappear from the story after this point. Mastema was not deterred, encouraging the Egyptians to chase after the Israelites to the Red Sea, but angelic intervention thwarted him yet again. The author was able to address many of the foregoing questions about the source of the magicians' power and its limits by adding angels and demons to the story.

The rabbis of the Talmud also embraced the demonic explanation for the magicians' power, but they put their own midrashic twists on it. In one teaching recorded in the Babylonian Talmud (Sanhedrin 67b), Rabbi Hiyya bar Abba builds a distinctive account of the contest from a discrepancy in how the biblical word for "secret arts" is spelled in the Hebrew: *belahatehem* in Exodus 7:11 (the scene where the magicians turn their staffs into serpents) but *belatehem* in Exodus 7:22 and 8:3 (the first two plagues). The difference between the two forms of the word comes down to a single consonant, a missing letter *hey* in the second instance. What the omission of the *hey* was meant to signify, if anything, is not made clear, but since the rabbis regarded it as an abbreviation for the divine name, Hiyya likely understood its erasure as a sign that Exodus 7:11 was referring to a different kind of magic than the sorcery mentioned in verses 7:22 and 8:3. The first kind of magic in this account involved optical illusion, referred to in the Talmud as "the seizing of the eyes," a kind of magic prohibited by the rabbis but not considered bad enough to merit punishment. When the magicians lost that first contest, however, they turned to a more powerful and truly godless form of magic, demonic sorcery, which gave them the ability to turn water into blood and create frogs. Demonic magic was a far worse offense than using optical illusion to trick someone because it involved acting like God in his role as creator, enlisting demons to create living beings, and this is why it was considered a death-penalty-level crime.

But if demonic magic was so powerful, why didn't it work against the third plague? Shouldn't a small creature have been easier for a demon to create than blood or a frog? Rabbi Eleazer chimes in with a solution. A magician relying on illusory magic might have been able to make it appear that he had creating something small, in the way that a magician today can produce a coin out of the air, but according to the rabbis, a magician using demonic power would have an easier time creating a camel than a mosquito because of the limits of demonic power, which can generate something large but is unable to create something that is very small: as Eleazar puts it in the same Talmudic passage from Sanhedrin 67b, "A demon cannot create something smaller than a barley grain." Knowing this about demons, God seeks to outsmart the magicians by sending a tiny plague that their "secret arts" would not be able to reproduce, and that, according to the Talmud, is why they fail during the third plague. When the magicians then declare "This is the finger of God," what they are acknowledging is that God has a lot more power than demons do, and more finesse as well, able to create on a smaller scale.

The most influential ancient retelling of the episode appears in a work known as the Apocryphon of Jannes and Jambres, a kind of novel that describes the magicians as brothers like Moses and Aaron. Jannes and Jambres were already well-known characters even before the rise of Christianity, mentioned in a Dead Sea Scroll known as the Damascus Document, and by the first century CE, the story was circulated broadly enough that it was familiar in some form to Roman scholars like Pliny the Elder.[5] Early Christians knew of Jannes and Jambres as well. There is a possible allusion to Exodus 8:15 in Luke 11:20 where Jesus claims the Moses-like power to drive out demons by the finger of God, and Jannes and Jambres are mentioned directly by name in 2 Timothy 3:8: "Just as Jannes and Jambres opposed Moses, so also these teachers opposed the truth," a verse where Paul uses the story to discredit rival teachers who were spreading misinformation and challenging his authority. We do not know if it was a Jew or a Christian who first composed the Apocryphon of Jannes and Jambres, but the mention of Jannes and Jambres in the New Testament certainly encouraged Christian interest in the story, and it was Christianity that subsequently disseminated it throughout the Middle East, Europe, and North Africa in various versions and translations into languages like Latin, Coptic, and Ethiopic.

There is evidence from rabbinic sources and manuscript fragments in Coptic that there were once multiple stories of Jannes and Jambres, but the narrative recorded in the Apocryphon of Jannes and Jambres is an early version of the story that became well known among Christians in late antiquity and the Middle Ages.[6] The surviving fragments of the apocryphon do not preserve the whole narrative, but one can get the gist of the story, which begins when Pharaoh orders Jannes to use his magic against Moses and Aaron. Jannes complies, but he is soon felled by a terrible illness that compels him to declare, "This is the power of God. I am not able to accomplish anything." The Apocryphon of Jannes and Jambres did not make explicit the verses on which it was basing itself, but the words of the sickened Jannes seem to conflate "This is the finger of God" from Exodus 8:15 with the magicians' response to the plague of boils in Exodus 9:11, where they are no longer able even to stand before Moses, much less perform any more magic.[7] But whereas in Exodus the magicians' illness marks their last appearance in the narrative, in the apocryphon Jannes's sickness sets the stage for the main action of the story.

Jannes goes on to accompany Pharaoh's army to the Red Sea and perishes during the expedition, but his younger brother Jambres remains behind, and he uses knowledge gleaned from a magical book to conjure Jannes's spirit from hell. In the final part of the story before the manuscripts break off, the brother returns to describe his torment in hell and to warn his brother to repent of his magic lest he suffer the same fate. In the earliest manuscripts, Jannes's speech is only partially preserved, but a version is also known from an eleventh-century Latin work known as "The Penitence of Jannes and Jambres," and it is possible that it approximates what Jannes says to his brother in a now-lost section of the Apocryphon of Jannes and Jambres:[8] "I your brother did not die unjustly but indeed justly, and the judgment will go against me since I was wiser than all wise magicians, and I withstood the two brothers Moses and Aaron, who performed great signs and wonders. On this account did I die, and I was removed from among men to the netherworld where there is great burning and the lake of perdition, whence no one ascends. And now my brother Mambres [an alternative spelling of Jambres], take heed in your life to do good to your sons and friends."[9] The codex includes an illustration of Jannes emerging from hell to warn his brother, showing us some of the demons tormenting him there (figure 10).

The inclusion of a "confession" in the story—a first person admission of one's sins—reflects the influence of confession as a literary genre in late ancient Christianity. The most famous example is the *Confessions* of Saint Augustine, and the genre developed into an important vehicle of religious instruction in late antiquity and the Middle Ages. The story of Jannes and Jambres developed in the light of this genre into a warning against sorcery. Whether this warning had any effect on Jannes's brother is unclear—there is no testimony that Jambres gave up on sorcery at that point, and according to one report, he was buried with Jannes in a tomb that became known as a place inhabited by demons, suggesting that he too failed to renounce demonic magic in time. We will see evidence, however, that others did pay heed to Jannes's warning against demonic magic, and that the brothers' fate had a deterrent effect.

The Jannes and Jambres story reached a far bigger audience than the Talmudic version of the magicians' story, circulating widely in the

FIGURE 10. An eleventh-century rendering of Pharaoh's magician Jambres in hell. From the archive of the British Library, Cotton MS Tiberius B V/1, fol. 87v. British Library / Granger Historical Archive.

Christian world from the Middle East to Africa to northern Europe.[10] One sign of its influence are references to the story in another work about a legendary sorcerer that was widely circulated in its own right, the Confession of Cyprian, a story told in the first person by a sorcerer from Antioch in Syria that ends with his repentance, conversion to Christianity, and martyrdom.[11] In one scene, Cyprian recalls meeting the devil face-to-face, and the latter addresses him as a "new Jambres."

In another he recalls the moment when the brothers recognize "the finger of God" and compares his own situation to theirs: "I outdid the famous magicians Jannes and Jambres. They [at least] acknowledged the finger of God while performing their magic, but I was wholly convinced that God did not exist. If God did not pardon them, even though they recognized him in part, how could he pardon me, who did not recognize him at all" (Confession of Cyprian of Antioch 17.3–4). In the version of the magicians' story known to Cyprian, Jannes and Jambres fail to secure God's forgiveness, but he knows from Exodus 8:15 that they made an attempt to acknowledge God, and he has that example in mind as he considers whether he should attempt his own confession of sin.

The Apocryphon of Jannes and Jambres, together with the Confession of Cyprian, connected the story of Pharaoh's magicians to the act of repentance and confession, and that association seems to have persisted for a long time. An example of its influence in a much later period comes from the writing of a scholar considered one of the Renaissance's greatest experts in magic, Henry Cornelius Agrippa (1486–1535), author of a three-volume study entitled *The Occult Philosophy*, first published in 1510, which offers an encyclopedic overview of different kinds of magic, including demonic magic.[12] Because of his fascination with demonic magic, Agrippa's critics condemned him as a Faust-like figure, a sorcerer who allied himself with the devil. Agrippa was not prosecuted for his study of magic as others accused of sorcery were, but he faced such accusations during his lifetime; opponents tried to block the publication of *The Occult Philosophy*; and the pressure was enough that he felt impelled to publish a recantation where he expressed regret for the youthful curiosity that led him to study demonic magic and offered to retract *The Occult Philosophy*. The retraction initially appeared in a work known as *The Vanity of Arts and Sciences*, and Agrippa later appended it to a revised edition of *The Occult Philosophy*, which he had decided to republish but with the recantation added as a disclaimer that he was not thereby endorsing the use of demonic knowledge but sharing its secrets only in order to help protect people against it.[13]

The recantation has garnered a lot of attention from scholars both for what it suggests about Agrippa himself and for what it reveals about the origins of a literary figure known from the plays of Christopher

Marlowe and William Shakespeare—the remorseful sorcerer who renounces his magic.[14] What is relevant for us is the passage's mention of Jannes and Jambres as a warning to those tempted to enlist demonic magic:

> But of magic I wrote about while I was very young three large books which I called *On Occult Philosophy*, in which what was then through the curiosity of my youth erroneous, I now being more advised, am willing to have retracted by this recantation. I formerly spent much time and cost in these activities. At last I grew so wise as to be able to dissuade others from this destruction.
>
> For whosoever do not in truth, nor in the power of God, but in the deceits of devils, according to the operations of wicked spirits, presume to divine and prophesy, and practicing through magical vanities, exorcisms, incantations, and other demoniacal works and deceits of idolatry, boasting of delusions and phantasms presently ceasing, brag that they can do miracles, I say all these shall with Jannes and Jambres and Simon Magus, be destined to the torments of eternal fire.

As appended to Agrippa's revised version of *The Occult Philosophy*, these paragraphs form the conclusion to the entire work, ending it with a reference to Jannes and Jambres as a warning of the terrible punishment to befall those who engage in "the deceits of devils" to conjure false miracles—they will join Pharaoh's magicians in suffering the eternal torments of hell.

Agrippa was not alone in using the reference to Jannes and Jambres in 2 Timothy 3:8 to condemn heresy, and in fact, over the next century, a period of intense religious strife in Europe, the verse would often be invoked in this way against Christians suspected of heresy or treason. One such example involves the Quakers, a Protestant group that broke away from the Church of England following the English Civil War. The founder of the Quakers, George Fox (1624–1691), was accused by critics of "bewitching" people as if he were a sorcerer allied with the devil, and his followers were often likened to Jannes and Jambres, false teachers opposed to Moses.[15] It is not known whether Agrippa was ever likened by critics to Jannes and Jambres, but his references to the story can be understood as an attempt to preempt that kind of accusation by positioning him as a different kind of magician, knowledgeable in demonic magic but aware of its dangers, committed to God himself, and mindful of what awaits those who enlist it for the wrong reasons.

What adds a twist to Agrippa's use of the story is the recantation's similarity to another aspects of Jannes's story, the speech where Jannes returns from hell and warns his brother against magic. Jannes's recantation of magic, in a section that has now been lost, might even have once included a retraction of magic books similar to Agrippa's: the apocryphon makes several references to a book from which Jannes and Jambres draws their spells, and it has been suggested that in the now-lost ending of the story, a regretful Jannes orders his brother to destroy or hide the book, similar to how Cyprian burns his magic books after he repents.[16] It is possible that even as he was distancing himself from Jannes and Jambres, he was also to some extent emulating them through his own version of a confession. Agrippa had an ambivalent relationship to demonic magic, and scholars argue that his recantation may be less straightforward than our reading of it has acknowledged, but even if we only take it at face value, it still tells us that the story of Jannes and Jambres continued into the early modern period as a cautionary tale against the use of demonic magic. It also suggests the continued importance of repentance and confession to this story. What began in Exodus 8:15 with the magicians' recognition of God's power had by the age of Agrippa and the fictional characters Faust and Prospero evolved into the trope of the repentant sorcerer who renounces magic and orders his magical books to be destroyed or hidden.

From Sorcerers to Charlatans

While Agrippa's reference to Jannes and Jambres shows that their story remained well known to Christians into the early modern period, magic itself in this period was undergoing profound changes. The belief in demonic magic was alive and well—in fact, it was a cause of widespread panic in Agrippa's day, fueling a wave of witch trials that began in Europe in the 1420s.[17] But magic as understood in this period was conceptualized very differently from how it had been in the days of the book of Jubilees, the Talmud, and the Apocryphon of Jannes and Jambres. Agrippa's conception of magic, for example, was influenced by Neoplatonic philosophy, a Christianized version of Kabbalah, an early form of natural science, and Protestantism.[18]

Three ideas about magic were especially important for understanding how the story of Jannes and Jambres was reinterpreted during the period of the Renaissance and the Reformation: (1) the subdivision of magic into different categories that included demonic knowledge but also encompassed forms of magic that were considered divine and beneficial to humankind; (2) a deepened interest in magic as optical illusion and trickery; and (3) the displacement of supernatural magic by the concept of artificial magic, magic that could also be used for nefarious purposes but was the result not of demonic power but of human ingenuity and skill.

The Occult Philosophy reflects the partitioning of magic into different categories, including forms of magic rooted in divine power rather than demonic power and considered beneficial to humankind. It so happens that one of the most important branches of good magic was also associated with ancient Egypt: Hermetic magic, so named because it was traced to an ancient Egyptian sage named Hermes Trismegistus who was thought to have left behind a body of esoteric knowledge known as the Corpus Hermeticum. Although Hermes and his magic were known to Christian scholars in the Middle Ages, they garnered a whole new level of attention during the Renaissance when a monk brought the texts from the Byzantine Empire to Italy and handed them over to Cosimo de' Medici, a patron of art and scholarship. Cosimo happened to be a patron of Marsilio Ficino, a Catholic priest and philosopher, and with his support Ficino published a translation from Greek into Latin in 1471, followed by additional translations and commentary produced by other scholars. The publication of such works put this corpus at the center of Renaissance scholarship, newly recovering a form of ancient Egyptian magic considered so beneficial to humankind that its study drew the support of Pope Alexander IV.[19]

FIGURE 11. Moses and the sage Hermes Trismegistus, as pictured in a mosaic from the Church of Siena created by Giovanni di Stefano (1488). Pixaby.

Consisting of secret knowledge about various philosophical, astrological, alchemical, and medical topics, Hermetic magic was a very different kind of magic from that wielded against the Israelites in Exodus, corresponding to what we would call natural science and philosophy, and it was thought to be consistent with what Moses taught through the Torah, revealing more about divine wisdom. In fact, some Renaissance scholars thought that Moses may have learned his wisdom directly from Hermes, as illustrated by a mosaic laid down in 1488 near the entrance of the Church of Siena that shows Hermes handing his writing to a deferential Moses (figure 11).

In reality, the Hermetic corpus probably consists of writings from the Hellenistic or Roman period, but its historical origins were unknown in this period, and connecting Hermes to Moses served an important function. At a time when the Inquisition was on the lookout for the devil's minions and people were being executed on the charge of sorcery, it was potentially lethal to be associated with magic, but the belief in Hermes made it possible for scholars to justify the study of nondemonic magic, and it also made it possible for church officials to lend their support to this kind of scholarship.[20] Agrippa was one of many Renaissance scholars of magic to engage in the study of Hermetic magic, often quoting from the Hermetic corpus; indeed, he came to be identified with it so closely that he was even referred to as a new Hermes Trismegistus.

I have not found an example where Hermes is placed side by side with Jannes and Jambres, but the rise of Hermetic magic had an indirect impact on how the latter were understood. In the Confession of Cyprian, Jannes and Jambres represent the evil of pagan magic in a general sense, whereas by the time of the Renaissance, they represented an illicit form of demonic magic placed in opposition to other forms of religiously permitted magic like Hermeticism. This is how they were understood by Agrippa; he mentions them in the context of a chapter about a certain kind of magic, the specific branch of magic that drew on demonic power to deceive people, and by reminding the reader of what happened to them, he was not meaning to renounce magic altogether. Moses himself, as Agrippa described him, practiced another kind of magic referred to as Mercaba, which involved the use of sacred names and seals to summon divine and angelic power, and this is what the prophet was drawing on to perform the plagues and other wonders depicted in Exodus.[21] In the light of Agrippa's partitioning of magic, Moses's contest with the magicians became a contest not between magic and divine power in a general sense but between two kinds of magic, the demonic magic associated with Jannes and Jambres versus the divinely powered magic associated with Kabbalah, Jewish mysticism.

In addition to being sidelined by Hermes Trismegistus, Jannes and Jambres also saw their magic emptied of much of its power by coming to be more deeply associated with optical illusion. We saw such an idea reflected in the Talmud's version of the story, but the association of demonic power with illusionism and sleight of hand was much more pronounced in early modern Europe because of that culture's pronounced distrust of vision as a source of reliable information.[22] The panic that fueled witchcraft trials was driven in part by a fear of demonic optical trickery: the devil did not have the power to directly harm people in a physical sense, but he and his minions could lure them to their destruction by taking on the appearance of someone as a disguise or by leading them astray through hallucinations. The threat posed by the devil's manipulation of vision was of such concern that it drew intensive investigations like Johann Christian Frommann's *Tractatus de fascinatione* (1675), a thousand-page tome that explained how the devil and his minions manipulated the operations of the eye and the mind.

An example of how this focus on optical illusion influenced the story of Jannes and Jambres comes from a work called *Dialogicall Discourses of Spirits and Divels* (1601). The authors of the work, the Protestant divines John Deacon and John Walker, speaking through characters named Lycanthropus and Physiologus, discuss how Pharaoh's magicians were able, with the devil's help, to *counterfeit* the miracle of transforming the staffs into serpents by manipulating what onlookers saw, or believed they were seeing.[23] As Physiologus explains, the devil took advantage of the fact that the onlookers in Pharaoh's court had just had their imaginations primed by seeing Aaron turn his staff into a serpent, exploiting the lingering afterimage to shape their interpretation of what happened next, and then he used his extraordinary speed to remove the staffs and put serpents in their place before anyone noticed.[24] This kind of effort to expose the trickery of Satan reflects an impulse to uncover fake wonders and imposture that was widespread among Protestant scholars of the day and was also reflected in efforts to disprove the miracle stories cited by the Catholic Church to justify its doctrines and religious practices.[25]

A related idea that also put a new spin on the story of Jannes and Jambres was the concept of artificial magic, magic not derived from demonic power or natural sources but created through human intelligence and skill. A few decades after Agrippa, the Italian theologian Tommaso Campenella (1568–1639) defined artificial magic as the use of "things made by art or the use of things made by nature in an artful way to produce usual effects."[26] This kind of magic was godlike in its ability to produce wonders like automata, ingenious machines that replicated the movements of human beings, but like demonic power, it too could be used to do harm to people. The deceptive mode of artificial magic was similar to Satan's trickery in the *Dialogicall Discourses*, but it was the product not of demonic enmity but of human deviousness.

A portrait of Jannes and Jambres as practitioners of deceptive artificial magic appears in another important work about magic composed in this period, the 1584 treatise known as *The Discoverie of Witchcraft* by Reginald Scot.[27] In Scot's version of the story, Jannes and Jambres operated as what people at the time called jugglers, not performers who know how to keep tossing balls in the air continuously but charlatans who use artificial magic to fool people. Scot has occasion to mention jugglers active in his own day like Thomas Brandon, hired as an entertainer in the court of Henry VIII, and some have speculated that Scot's use of "Jannes" and "Jambres" were references to other contemporary jugglers. On the surface, however, he was referring to Pharaoh's magicians as stand-ins for the whole profession, magicians who use sleight of hand, secret accomplices, and psychological manipulation to deceive people.

In Scot's version of the Jannes and Jambres story, the brothers never enlist the help of demons. This is not because they are virtuous but because, in Scot's view, demons have no real power to influence the world or to form compacts with human beings. Instead, Jannes and Jambres are practitioners of artificial magic who use their own cunning, skill at misdirection, and understanding of human psychology to pull off tricks. The exception are the magicians' feats in Exodus 7–8, their ability to replicate the turning of their staffs into serpents and to copy the first two plagues. These were truly extraordinary acts that involved the creation and transformation of matter, but according to Scot, they were not performed with demonic help since demons did not have the power to change material reality. He knew the Talmudic tradition that demons couldn't create anything smaller than a barley grain, which he used to argue that demons did not have the power to create anything at all, and since demons could therefore not have created serpents, blood, or frogs, it followed for Scot that the power that made it possible for the magicians to reproduce the first few plagues came from another source—from God himself. Why would God have given the magicians the power to reproduce his own miracles? Scot suggests that he was seeking to lure Pharaoh into thinking that his magicians had more power than they really did.

During the third plague, however, God decided it was time to expose the magicians as the charlatans they really were and thus withdrew from them the power to reproduce the plague. Moses as Scot depicted him was opposite of a juggler, a truth-seeker, and he recognized in the magicians' inability to reproduce the plague of lice a chance not just to expose the magicians' impotence but to get them to confess to the world that their magic was a sham: Moses "confounded all magick, and made the world see, *and the cunningest magicians of the earth confesse,* that their own doings were but illusions, and that his miracles were wrought by the finger of God" (*Discoverie of Witchcraft,* chapter 31; italics mine). In other words, the effect of the third plague in Scot's telling is not just to compel the magicians to recognize God but to compel them to "confesse . . . that their own doings were but illusions." This version of the episode as an effort to extract the truth out of suspect magicians brings to mind the witchcraft trials that occurred with particular frequency in England in Scot's day, but in this case the purpose of extracting a confession was to expose the accused not as witches but as frauds.

The difference between this early modern version of the Jannes and Jambres story and the ancient-medieval version is brought into sharp relief by comparing how the phrase "This is the finger of God" was used in each telling. In the Apocryphon of Jannes and Jambres and the Confession of Cyprian, the phrase is understood as a declaration of faith, an acknowledgment of God's power. In Scot's version of the episode, it takes on a related but distinct meaning: "confesse" is not to declare one's faith but to reluctantly admit guilt. Scot's goal in composing the *Discoverie of Witchcraft* was to expose magicians as charlatans, and he seems to have read Exodus 8:15 as a precedent for this very campaign, portraying

Moses as a debunker like himself and even applying the expression "the finger of God" to his own impulse to expose "all counterfeit devises of mans braine . . . deceitful arts, and circumventing inventions" (chapter 34).

Scot's depiction of Jannes and Jambres reflects the distinguishing qualities of early modern magic identified above—the distinction between good and bad magic, the focus on illusionism, and the concept of artificial magic—and it also reflects its age in another way as well. In an effort to bring witchcraft trials to an end, scholars in Scot's day made the case that demonic magic could not harm people because it was not real or powerful enough to influence material reality. The *Discoverie of Witchcraft* was a part of this effort, responding to juggling as a threat to the public but also seeking to refute the claims of Jean Bodin, remembered today as a philosopher but also the author of an influential book on demonology that depicted witchcraft as worse than treason and urged judges to use torture to expose it. Scot's depiction of Jannes and Jambres appears in this light not just as a caricature of the juggler but as a counter to Bodin's claim that their magic was demonic in origin.[28] By demoting them from sorcerers to charlatans, the *Discoverie of Witchcraft* helped to lay the ground for a change in the status of magic in European imaginations, making it appear far less real and therefore far less threatening than people believed it to be, and in turn that shift helped to end the witch-hunting and prosecutions that had killed tens of thousands of people in Europe between the fifteenth and eighteenth centuries.

Scot's use of the biblical story to de-supernaturalize and defang demonic magic brings us to modernity and another period in the history of magic, one distinguished by the rise of stage magic, the simulation of supernatural magic as a form of entertainment. Magic had been used to entertain people long before, but the nineteenth century saw a merger of that practice with what we referred to earlier as artificial magic generated through human skill and technology. The last magician we will be focused on, Jean-Eugène Robert-Houdin (1805–1871), brought these two traditions together, combining his ability as an inventor able to contrive automata and other mechanical wonders with his skill as a performer and producer to create what is now known as stage magic, the performance of magic illusions as mass entertainment. Robert-Houdin only referred fleetingly to Jannes and Jambres, but the reference is a telling reflection of how the story of Pharaoh's magicians was transformed by modernity into a contest between magic and science.

Modern Disenchantments

The use of magic to entertain people goes back to antiquity, but modern entertainment magic began to achieve success only after the end of the witchcraft trials in Europe in the seventeenth century when showmen like Isaac Fawkes (1675–1732) made a fortune by performing before audiences that included the king of England. This kind of magic would reach its pinnacle nearly two centuries later during the so-called Golden Age of Magic, between the late nineteenth and early twentieth centuries, when stage magic became a highly popular form of entertainment.[29] Ironically, this was also a golden age of *exposing* magic—proving to audiences that mediums and others claiming supernatural or psychic powers were what Scot would have called jugglers.[30]

Robert-Houdin was not the first modern stage magician to play the role of debunker, but he was at the center of the most sensational magical exposure of the nineteenth century, a kind of magical contest that came about in 1856 when he was commissioned by the French government to help quell restive tribes in Algeria. Napoleon III thought he needed the help of a magician because the source of the problem, it seemed to the French, was a group known as the marabouts, Muslim military chaplains and guides believed to have magical powers, and it was suspected that they were using their powers to encourage resistance. Napoleon III wanted Robert-Houdin to prove to the Algerians that French magic was stronger than their magic, and the magician accepted the mission, traveling to Algeria to offer a series of performances for tribal leaders.

The tricks he performed included the Light and Heavy Chest, where a light chest suddenly becomes too heavy to lift; the Gun Trick, where someone from the audience shoots a gun at the magician's heart that leaves him completely unharmed; and yet another trick where a young

Arab man disappeared, a trick that was so terrifying to the tribesmen, according to Robert-Houdin's memoirs, that they bolted from their seats and rushed to the exits. However, the point of the performances was not only to amaze and terrify the Algerians but to expose the magic of the marabouts as fake by revealing that it could be reproduced though the art of prestidigitation: this Robert-Houdin did by enlisting translators to follow his performance with an explanation to the audience that his feats were performed not through sorcery but through skill. It is not clear that the performances had much of an impact on the Algerian tribesmen: Robert-Houdin only offers two anecdotes to show that he had unsettled their confidence in the power of the marabouts' magical abilities. Back in Europe, however, the episode did enhance Robert-Houdin's stature as a magician; to some, it even called to mind how Moses had defeated Pharaoh's magicians.[31]

It so happens that in one of the books where he recounts this episode, an 1868 book entitled *Secrets of Conjuring and Magic, or How to Become a Wizard*, Robert-Houdin himself mentions Jannes and Jambres as experts of "pretended magic . . . who ventured to compete with the miracles of Moses."[32] The brothers appear at the head of a list of legendary magicians known for their knowledge and power, including Hermes Trismegistus, but whose abilities paled in comparison to those of the modern stage magician. The achievements of these venerable wonder-workers were doubtless impressive for the era in which they lived, Robert-Houdin acknowledges, but if they were performing before modern-day "enlightened" spectators, their feats would make very little impression because of all the scientific wonders of the modern age. He then asks the reader to picture these ancient magicians transported to the present to attend a lecture by a professor of science. As he imagines the scene, the professor gives a lecture about the marvels made possible by pyrotechnics, steam power, electricity, and photography, and the sorcerers in attendance are so amazed that they react to the professor as if he were a divine being.

If this scenario seems familiar, it is because, I would argue, it is a secularized retelling of the magicians' capitulation in Exodus 8:15. Like that episode, it imagines a kind of contest between two types of wonder-working—the false magic of legendary sorcerers who include Jannes and Jambres pitted against the superior wonder-working of the professor, here playing a role akin to Moses as the agent and representative of the Truth. Robert-Houdin turns the magician subplot into a contest between two kinds of magic, not demonic magic versus Hermetic or Kabbalistic magic but the pretend miracles of premodern magic versus the real marvels of science.

The exhibition-contest envisioned here likely reflects Robert-Houdin's experience in Algeria, which he writes about in the same book, and it anticipates a genre of stage magic performance that would become very popular at the end of the nineteenth century and in the early twentieth century—a public contest between a stage magician and a rival claiming real magical powers. Some of these duels involved a contest with an exotic magician from the Orient (or someone claiming to be such a magician)—an Indian, Arab, or Chinese wonder-worker who claimed mysterious supernatural powers. Others involved contests between the stage magician and spiritualists who claimed to be able to contact the dead, figures like Daniel Dunglas Home (1833–1886), a Scottish medium, and the Davenport brothers, Ira and William, who were sometimes compared by Christian critics to Jannes and Jambres.[33] Some of the most successful professional magicians of the era made a name for themselves by challenging rival magicians or spiritualists either directly in a joint or coordinated appearance with their opponent or by using their performances and publications to expose the trickery of their rivals. Among those who followed Robert-Houdin in this regard were John Maskelyne, John Henry Anderson, and none other than Harry Houdini, whose stage name was meant as a tribute to Robert-Houdin.

The historian Erika White Dyson has suggested that such duels were meant to resonate with Christian audiences familiar with the story of Jannes and Jambres from sermons and Sunday school lessons.[34] Whether a parallel to the biblical story was intended or not, they certainly brought it to mind, as illustrated by a column in a 1926 issue of the magazine *Life* commenting on Houdini's contests with spiritual mediums. After noting that this kind of conflict went back to the time of Moses's contest with the magicians, the author cheekily remarks that those who believe in reincarnation might suppose Houdini's former self to have been one such magician.[35]

These contests were staged in various forms. One involving a medium named Charles Colchester, a spiritual adviser to Mary Todd Lincoln, took place in the context of an actual trial in 1865 after Colchester was indicted for having performed sleight of hand without a license. What drew the press's attention above all was the participation of two stage magicians called on as expert witnesses, John Henry Anderson and John Macallister, "the Great Wizard of the World," who sought to prove that Colchester's spiritual manifestations were fakes by reproducing them before a jury (which reached a verdict of guilty in about ten minutes). Other contests were framed as scientific experiments, as in the much-publicized confrontation between Houdini and a séance medium named Mina Crandon; the rules that she agreed to required her to do her conjuring under scientific test conditions. Faculty at my home institution, the University of Pennsylvania, launched a similar investigation in 1884 known as the Seybert Commission that, after a careful investigation which included attending a mock séance arranged by the stage magician Harry Kellar, concluded that spiritualism was unverified and probably fraudulent.[36]

While the conflict between stage magic and spiritualism sometimes played out in judicial and academic settings, for the most part it was performed before audiences as a stage act in its own right. Both stage magicians and spiritualists quickly figured out that it drew press attention and ticket-buyers to court controversy, and they set about generating it by staging contests with their opponents.[37] There was nothing new about simulating magical duels on the stage; indeed the tradition goes back to medieval mystery plays that used trickery and crude special effects to reproduce the duel between Moses and the magicians.[38] What was new about the theatrical magical duels of the nineteenth century was the hype—new uses of advertising and publicity stunts to call attention to them, including the manufacturing of controversy. Debunkers like Houdini may have been completely sincere in wanting to expose fraud and cure the public of its credulity, but the use of publicly staged contests and challenges was also a part of their act.

The sensationalizing of the magical duel, its transformation into an entertainment performed before an audience, was another shift in magical culture that affected the retelling of Moses's contest with the magicians, and we can see this reflected already in Robert-Houdin's brief reference to Jannes and Jambres. In his version of the story, the duo, summoned to the present, do not act as jugglers as they do in Scot's *Discoverie of Witchcraft*; they do not make any attempt to reproduce the miracles performed by the professor or perform magic of their own. Instead, their role is that of an audience who watches the spectacles on the stage. The impressive list of illustrious magicians assembled for the professor's lecture mirrors Robert-Houdin's efforts to draw real-life high-class people to his shows, which were offered in an elegant auditorium in the Palais-Royal, while his belittling description of the sorcerers' credulous response registers his contempt for naïve spectators who mistook his illusions for real supernatural magic.[39]

Secrets of Conjuring and Magic begins by distinguishing stage magic from earlier kinds of magic, but what it is also doing in the vignette is distinguishing two kinds of audience—the unenlightened audience represented by Jannes, Jambres, and the other legendary magicians of yore, and the enlightened audience with whom the reader is to identify, an audience that understands science well enough to appreciate the true impressiveness of stage magic. By incorporating Jannes and Jambres into a story about how not to respond to stage magic, Robert-Houdin was conveying a message like the one he sent to the Algerians when he tried to teach them how to respond to stage magic as an enlightened spectator from France would have.[40]

In some respects, Robert-Houdin's version of the Jannes and Jambres story is similar to that of Reginald Scot: the brothers represent false magic of the human rather than the demonic kind, and the scene in Exodus 8:15 has been transformed into a scene of humiliating exposure by a truth-seeking opponent. But at the same time, he was telling a very different story: the contest with Moses has been transformed into a stage performance; the jugglers Jannes and Jambres are now passive and naïve spectators; and they have been joined by representatives of other kinds of magic once considered great but now recognized as ineffectual and self-deluded. In this version of Exodus 8:15, it has become a story about the triumph of modernity—represented by the professor's use of technology—over premodern and non-Western forms of magic like that of the marabouts, magic now exposed as pathetic compared with the astounding marvels of science.

Robert-Houdin's take on Exodus 8:15 reflects a distinctively modern story about magic that was told in many different ways during the nineteenth and early twentieth centuries—a story about the triumph of modern scientific rationality over magic. A particularly influential version of this story is reflected in the sociologist Max Weber's concept of "the disenchantment of the world," the idea that the Enlightenment and science have driven magic from the modern world by refusing to submit any longer to mysterious supernatural forces and displacing them with rational explanation. Recently, it has been argued that this account of modernity is a myth in its own right that exaggerated the displacement of magic by science, a claim supported by the fact that even leading scientists in the nineteenth and twentieth centuries entertained spiritualism as a credible possibility.[41] Whether it is right to call the decline of magic in the West a "myth" is debatable, but it is correct to see this idea as a story that modernity has told itself again and again, and stage magic helped to disseminate it by repeatedly dramatizing the conflict between magic and rationality in the form of a duel where the stage magician as representative of the Enlightenment defeats the medium as representative of a fake supernatural magic. This is the story Robert-Houdin projected onto Jannes and Jambres, producing a version of Exodus 8:15 as a moment when premodern magic is forced to acknowledge the superiority of modern science.

Belief in demons persists; magic is still used to con people; there are still plenty of psychic mediums out there who claim the ability to contact the dead and to read minds; and there are still debunkers who see it as a moral duty to expose fake magic, but thanks in part to the efforts of people like Scot and Robert-Houdin, magic is not nearly as threatening to Western publics as it used to be—there hasn't been a witchcraft trial in the United States since 1878, a case that was dismissed—and the diminished sense of menace has drained the story of Jannes and Jambres of much of its relevance. The brothers did get a brief mention in a 2006 televised performance by the magician duo Barry and Stuart, but that is only because the theme of that particular show was tricks inspired by the Bible. Apart from a reference here and there, the once great and terrible Jannes and Jambres, even when remembered by modern-day magicians, only merit a moment of acknowledgment for introducing the trick of turning a staff into a snake.

But their present-day obscurity does not take away from the influence that the story of Jannes and Jambres has had on how people think about magic, and it still exerts this influence in indirect ways. Among its progeny, as noted earlier, is the legend of the scholar Faust, who rues selling his soul to the devil in exchange for knowledge. The persistence of Faust's story, continuously retold in its own right, is proof that the tradition of retelling the third plague as a story of sorcerers renouncing their secret arts survives in how people imagine science as a form of magic that is both powerful in its ability to match the miracles of God and deeply regrettable.

4

The Fourth Plague

A SHELTER IN THE SWARM

EXODUS MAKES clear in its description of the first three plagues that their reach extended throughout the entire land of Egypt, and for some of the story's interpreters, that raised a question: Did the Israelites suffer from the plagues as well, or were they somehow spared from their impact? In later midrashic retellings, the Israelites are miraculously spared from the plagues—the water turned to blood only when the Egyptians tried to drink it, for example, remaining unchanged for the Israelites—but that was a later elaboration of the story, and it is only when the biblical account arrives at the fourth plague that Exodus itself offers an explanation for how the Israelites were able to survive the plagues: they had been living in a region of Egypt known as Goshen, which God had set apart to insulate them from the plague: "I will set apart in that day the land of Goshen where my people are stationed, so that no swarm of flies will be there, so that you will know that I am the Lord in the midst of the earth, and I will put a division between my people and your people" (Exodus 8:18–19).

Some interpreters have inferred from this passage that this was how the Israelites had survived the earlier plagues as well, taking shelter in a Goshen shielded from what befell the rest of the land. In some midrashic retellings, for example, the Israelites were able to keep drinking during the seven days of the first plague because they had access to miraculous water from Goshen that hadn't been turned into blood.[1]

Exodus itself, however, makes no mention of Goshen before the fourth plague, and it refers to it directly only once more, during the seventh plague, when it notes that no hail fell in Goshen (Exodus 9:26). This dearth of description led later Jews and Christians to fill out what Goshen was like through retellings and illustrations—interpretations that often reflect the reteller's conception of a "safe space" in the most concrete sense of safety, a space where one could feel protected from physical harm but that also imagine Goshen as a model for other kinds of refuge as well, psychological, social, and cultural. In this chapter, we will explore these different ways of imagining Goshen as a shielded and semi-utopian space, situated in a dangerous environment and yet offering a safe harbor.

These various interpretations, it is worth noting, were aided by yet another lacuna in the biblical account—a dearth of information about the physical setting in which the plagues took place. The Bible's description of Egypt's environs was a largely blank canvas that people filled in differently in light of their own surroundings. Exodus only mentions a few specific places within Egypt—the Nile and the streams that branch off from it, the houses of Pharaoh and the Egyptians, and the slave cities Pithom and Ramses mentioned in Exodus 1:11—and its description of these places offers so few details that readers have to conjure what these places were like from their own imagination or from their knowledge of Egypt in their own day.

This was true of the land of Goshen as well. The Bible offers a few clues about its location and characteristics but does not reveal very much. In its account of how the Israelites first came to settle in Goshen, Genesis explains that Joseph, brought to Egypt as a captive but now serving as a minister on Pharaoh's behalf, bestowed its territory on his brothers so that they would be living near him as a high-ranking member of Pharaoh's court (Genesis 45:10). But where was the court of Pharaoh based at this time? The biblical account does not make this clear. We also learn from Genesis that Goshen was the best part of Egypt—bountiful and a good place to graze cattle—and that the Israelites flourished there before the exodus, becoming populous. But we are told nothing else about the place or its subsequent history. What happened to it during the period of Israel's oppression? Were the slave cities Pithom and Ramses built there or somewhere else? Was it near the house of Pharaoh in Exodus or in some other part of the land? None of these questions can be answered from the information provided by the Torah itself, allowing later retellings of the Bible a lot of room to maneuver in their depictions of Goshen.

For thousands of years, people have tried to pinpoint the exact location of Goshen. The name is not mentioned in ancient Egyptian sources, but other clues place it in northeastern Egypt. The Septuagint (the earliest Greek translation of the Hebrew Bible) refers to Goshen as "Gesem of Arabia"—the name "Arabia" in this context referring not to the area of modern Saudi Arabia but to the eastern region of the Nile Delta—and on this basis early Christians came to identify Goshen with Heroonpolis, a city near the mouth of an ancient canal built to connect the Nile to the Red Sea.[2] Some modern scholars agree with this identification, but Benjamin of Tudela, a twelfth-century Spanish Jew who chronicled his travels across Europe, Africa, and Asia, placed Goshen near the city of Memphis, one hundred kilometers from Heroonpolis.[3]

Just as interpreters have placed Goshen in different locations, so too they have elaborated on what it was like to live there in different ways. In my judgment, the most interesting depictions of Goshen, verbal or visual, are those that find some way to combine two characteristics of Goshen as depicted in Genesis and Exodus that are at odds with each other. On the one hand, Goshen bears a certain resemblance to the land of Canaan itself as a place of safety and prosperity. On the other hand, it was still in Egypt, and though it serves as a safe harbor for the Israelites during the plagues, it is possible to suppose that by that point, it had become a site of slave labor, suffering, and oppression. Some retellings of the story emphasize the first role, others the second, but what makes the history of how people have reimagined Goshen all the more interesting are retellings that acknowledge and fuse the utopian and dystopian into a single place.

I have tried in this book not to get weighted down by too much theorizing, but I have been guided by certain approaches, and one that is important for this chapter is known as third space theory, introduced by the postcolonialist thinker Homi Bhabha.[4] A " third space" is a hybrid space that brings together and combines the qualities of spaces that people normally think of as separate and even opposed—home and work, the familiar and the foreign, the inside and the outside. The third space exists beyond these binaries. As Bhabha puts it, quoting the political philosopher Frantz Fanon, it is a "site for the assimilation of contraries," where people can act and interact outside the social norms that restrict them in ordinary life.[5]

After being introduced by Bhabha in the 1990s, the concept of the third space came to be embraced by a wide range of scholars—political theorists, media scholars, architects, and educators—and is now so widespread that it has also come to be used commercially as the name for cafés, bars, and other places branding themselves as alternatives to both home and work.[6] As the concept has become popularized, it has lost a lot of its novelty and theoretical punch, but I have found it a useful guide for thinking about the role that Goshen came to play in people's imaginations as a space outside the binary of home and exile, or freedom and slavery.

To shelter the Israelites from the fourth plague, God introduced a divider between Goshen and the rest of Egypt, what Exodus 8:19 refers to in Hebrew as a *pedut*. The biblical account never clarifies whether the term is referring to a physical barrier or something else, but this divider is described as a "sign" in its own right that somehow marks the distance or separation between the Israelites and the Egyptians. The quality of Goshen as a separated, secluded space would prove important to how people in later ages described or visualized it, as it gave them license to imagine the inside of Goshen as a realm of semi-freedom not obtainable for the Israelites in the land of bondage outside. Egypt would become a symbol for environments and circumstances that were hostile, brutal, repressive. Canaan symbolized freedom and independence. Goshen represented something in between, a realm situated within the heart of an oppressive landscape that nonetheless offered room to act with a measure of autonomy. This chapter is a history of people reimagining the land of Goshen and drawing on its example to envision a space for themselves somewhere between the land of bondage and the Promised Land.

Goshen as Rebel Base

Many modern scholars today identify the biblical Goshen with a city known as Avaris, the seat of power for the Hyksos dynasty that ruled the northern part of Egypt from the 1630s BCE until around 1550 BCE. The Hyksos have made a mark on biblical scholarship because their history—their migration into Egypt from the region of Canaan and Syria, their century-long reign in northern Egypt, and their eventual expulsion from Egypt by a ruler named Ahmose—strongly parallels the story of Joseph and the exodus. Already in the first century CE, the Jewish historian Josephus identified the Hyksos as the ancestors of the Israelites, and his description of Avaris, though not mentioning Goshen explicitly, includes elements that seem inspired by the biblical account and thus offers an opportunity to explore an early attempt to fill out what it was like.

Josephus's account of the Hyksos, narrated in a work known as *Against Apion*, is based on a history of Egypt produced by Manetho, a scholar thought to have been an Egyptian priest who lived in the third century BCE.[7] Manetho's history is an important source of information about ancient Egypt that has been partially corroborated by other sources. This is true of what it says about the Hyksos capital Avaris, a city now identified with the archaeological site of Tell ed-Dabʿa.[8] Yet Manetho's work as we know it from Josephus is also polemical. Resentful of the presence of Jews in the Egypt of his own day, he created an account of their history that vilifies them as a diseased and violent group of renegades who threaten the social and religious order of Egypt. The historian Amos Funkenstein once argued that Manetho's account of the Hyksos was a "counternarrative" to the Exodus story, an attempt to disparage the Jews by subverting or parodying the Jews' own account of their origin.[9] If we view Manetho's description of Avaris with this in mind, it becomes possible to read it as a deliberately distorted image of Goshen, a physical-spatial manifestation of all the negative traits he ascribed to the Jews: a contemptible ancestry, a misanthropic rejection of other people's gods and traditions, an association with impurity and disease, insularity, and a long history of insurrection, killing, and destruction.[10]

Josephus cites two lengthy excerpts from Manetho's history that, when read in tandem, describe the origin of the Jews in two stages. The first suggests that the earliest ancestors of the Jews known from Genesis were Hyksos, which it depicts as marauding shepherds who invaded Egypt from the east and wreaked havoc there, burning its cities, razing its temples, and massacring and enslaving its population. The regime the Hyksos established was able to rule a portion of Egypt until kings in other parts of the land rose up against them, forcing them to take refuge in the garrison of Avaris, where a stalemate emerged. Unable to overcome the walls of the city, the Egyptian king, a figure named Thoumosis, negotiated a settlement with the Hyksos whereby they agreed to evacuate Egypt, and from there, according to the excerpt, the Hyksos traveled to Judea, where they built the city of Jerusalem (Josephus, *Against Apion* 1.75–92).

In the second excerpt, Manetho tells of how, at a later point, an Egyptian king named Amenophis decided to segregate lepers and other polluted peoples from the rest of the Egyptians by forcing them to work in stone quarries on the eastern side of the Nile. This group is distinct from the Hyksos of the earlier excerpt, but the two peoples later intersect: after having toiled in the quarries for many years, the lepers petitioned the king to settle in Avaris, the city once inhabited by the Hyksos but since abandoned. The king agreed, though he later came to regret the concession because, shielded by the walls and fortifications of Avaris, the lepers were able to plot a rebellion. Their leader was a priest named Osarseph, and his first move was to issue a new set of laws: the lepers would be forbidden from socializing with the Egyptians and from worshiping their gods. Osarseph then dispatched a message to the Hyksos in Jerusalem, calling on them to return to Egypt and join him in a war against Amenophis.

Uniting at Avaris, the two groups commenced a campaign that forced the Egyptian king to flee to Ethiopia, leaving the country to be despoiled by the invading force. As they had done in their earlier occupation of Egypt, the Hyksos behaved cruelly, destroying cities, pillaging temples, mutilating the images of the gods, and forcing the priests to slaughter their sacred animals. The excerpt makes the connection to the exodus explicit when it notes that the priest who led the leper rebellion, Osarseph, changed his name to Moses (Josephus, *Against Apion* 1.232–250).

As for the link between Manetho's Avaris and the biblical Goshen, the two are located in the same part of Egypt, but there is no connection between the two names, and the descriptions of the two places differ in several important ways: according to Genesis, Goshen is a pastoral setting where Jacob and his family tend their flocks, whereas the Avaris of Manetho's account is a huge city fortress, a region of 10,000 *arourae* (an *aroura* is equivalent to about 2,500 square feet) that the Hyksos enclosed within a massive wall in order to secure their possessions and spoils. Goshen is granted to the Israelites by the Egyptian king, and they tend the pharaoh's cattle there on his behalf, whereas Avaris is beyond the control of the Egyptian king, protected by its walls. Goshen is where the Israelites were sheltered from the plagues according to the book of Exodus, whereas Avaris was ground zero for disease and disaster, thanks to its occupation by the lepers.

Since Manetho never quotes or refers to the Bible in any discernible way, it is impossible to know for certain whether his description of Avaris was modeled on the biblical Goshen, but it is by no means a stretch to suggest that the exodus story was familiar to a non-Jewish scholar in Hellenistic Egypt unable to read the Hebrew of the Bible. In addition to the Septuagint, the Greek translation of the Torah that was available to scholars in the Library of Alexandria, there survive from this period brief excerpts of works that recount the exodus in Greek, including a history written by a scholar named Artpanus and a play by a writer named Ezekiel, which recounts the exodus in the form of a Greek tragedy (though there is no mention of Goshen in the surviving excerpts). Unfortunately, while Manetho clearly knew some version of the exodus story, recounting events that parallel it in several ways and even mentioning Moses by name, we cannot sort out what he knew about the Bible or prove that he had read its description of Goshen.

If we read Manetho's account carefully, however, there is reason to think that his history of Avaris was indeed modeled on or influenced by the biblical account of Goshen, or some paraphrase of the exodus story. Manetho, as Josephus cited him, offers two accounts of the origin of the Jews, one narrating the foundation of Avaris and its settlement by the

Hyksos, the other telling the story of how Moses and his leper followers settled the city in a later period and used it to launch a rebellion. Why tell two stories about Avaris, one associated with the Hyksos, the other focused on the lepers? Perhaps Manetho drew each account from a separate source, as some scholars suggest, but another possibility is that each stage of Avaris's history was meant to correspond to one stage of the Torah's two-stage description of Goshen's history in Genesis and Exodus.

In this reading, Manetho's first story about the city corresponds to the first mention of Goshen in Genesis 45–46. The Hyksos in this first account are depicted as shepherds (Josephus claims that the word "Hyksos" means "shepherd kings"), which corresponds to how Jacob's family is described in Genesis 46:32 ("The men are shepherds, keepers of flocks"). Josephus himself saw the similarities between this story and the events of Genesis and drew a specific connection to the story of Joseph's captivity. In the second excerpt, Avaris becomes the refuge for Moses and his leper followers, and that corresponds to the role of Goshen in the book of Exodus. The two excerpts, though cited in Josephus's narrative as if they were unrelated episodes, snap together into a single coherent story when read in light of the Torah's depiction of Goshen.

If we read Manetho's account in this way, what does it tell us about its author's understanding of Goshen? Avaris/Goshen, as Manetho represented it, corresponds to what philosopher Michel Foucault called a heterotopia—a secluded space to which people considered deviant, undesirable, and difficult to manage are consigned.[11] The two groups associated with Avaris, the Hyksos and the lepers, exemplify this kind of person. The former are foreign invaders of ignoble origin and savage impulses who seek to destroy the temples and sacred animals of the Egyptians; the latter are native Egyptians, but their disease, which the Egyptians regarded as a source of impurity, is so threatening to Egypt that its king feels he must remove them from the land. Once the two groups find protection within the walls of Avaris, they prove to be even more dangerous, using the city as a base to launch a full-fledged attack against Egypt and its temples. If this description reflects Manetho's understanding of Goshen, he saw it not merely as a refuge but as a rebel stronghold beyond Egypt's control and threatening its political and religious order.

This is Goshen as imagined by a Hellenized Egyptian who was deeply resentful of the Jews. There is no sign that it was based directly on the biblical account, and if Josephus was citing Manetho accurately and not adding anything of his own, it does not tell us anything about how Goshen was understood by Jews (though Josephus's citation of Manetho's history as semi-reliable corroborating testimony for the events of Genesis and Exodus raises the possibility that he accepted the identification of Avaris with Goshen). We do not know very much about Jewish life in Hellenistic Egypt, but evidence from the later Roman period suggests that Jews in Alexandria were concentrated into a certain part of the city that was socially segregated to some degree from the Egyptians and Greeks there, not a ghetto but an ethnically concentrated enclave of some sort. Philo refers to two Jewish districts in the city, while Josephus mentions a single area established during the time of Alexander's successors that, as the historian explains, allowed Jews to minimize interaction with non-Jews.[12] Perhaps Manetho's description of Avaris reflects ethno-religious tension in the Alexandria of his day, projecting onto it his suspicion of what Jews were up to in the parts of the city where they could not be completely monitored by outsiders.

Later Jews and Christians did not conflate Goshen with Avaris, drawing on Genesis and Exodus for their understanding of what it was like, but they too recognized it as a semi-autonomous zone within Egypt where their ancestors could act without being closely monitored by the Egyptians and where there was a degree of insulation from the danger and violence of the world outside. The next example that we will look at is a Jewish one, but it developed within the Catholic context of medieval Spain and modeled its version of Goshen on a Christian third space that mixed together the qualities of the urban and the natural, and the earthly and the spiritual.

Goshen as an "Enclosed Garden"

Goshen did not receive all that much attention from rabbinic interpreters of the plague story, but when they did focus on it, they imagined it as a place where their ancestors were able to carry on their traditions within Egypt, and to study the Torah. In the best known of such traditions, Goshen was imagined as the home to an academy established by Joseph's brother Judah at the behest of his father, Jacob (Tanhuma Vayyigash 11; Genesis Rabbah 95.3). Although the Torah would only be revealed much later at Mount Sinai, the rabbis embraced the anachronistic idea that the study of its laws was already underway by the time of Jacob and Joseph within the walls of a study house established in Goshen, and this academy was understood as a precursor to the *bet talmud* or *bet hava ʿad,* where the rabbis themselves would study the Torah and Talmud.

When Jews tried to envision a space where they could be free from the control of outsiders, they often thought, of course, of the biblical Canaan and especially Jerusalem. Here and there, however, Jews did draw on the midrashic Goshen to imagine an alternative space where they could at least be safe from external control and violence in a provisional way. In 1940, as the Holocaust was beginning, Joseph Isaac Schneersohn (1880–1950), the rabbi who brought the Chabad Lubavitch Hasidic movement from Poland to the United States, established an organization called Mahane Yisraʾel that was meant to encourage the study of the Torah, and it is not a coincidence that he compared it to Goshen protecting the Jews from the violence taking place in the world beyond.[13] Nor is it a coincidence that, in 1973, after the Israeli army had crossed the Suez Canal to within one hundred kilometers of Cairo during the Yom Kippur War, a rabbi named Mordechai Halperin established a *yeshivat Goshen* for the religious soldiers stationed there.[14] These institutions were attempts to create spaces where Jews could study their tradition in a hazardous foreign environment, and the midrashic Goshen came to mind as a model because of its role as a place where the biblical Israelites had been able to sustain the study of the Torah even within Egypt.

I want to focus this section, however, on another way of imagining Goshen that also emerged within a Jewish community but conceived Goshen as a different kind of refuge.

This version of Goshen appears in a medieval manuscript of the Haggadah known as the Hispano-Moresque Haggadah, produced in Spain, probably in Toledo, in the late thirteenth century or early fourteenth century. One of the earliest known examples of an illustrated Haggadah, the manuscript devotes a folio page to visualizing life in Goshen in the period when the Israelites were sheltering from the fourth plague. The illustration is crude by comparison with the best Christian art of the day but nonetheless offers much to take in (figure 12).

Most of the illustration is taken up by the facade of a three-story palace, with two figures on the top of the tower blowing rams' horns to celebrate a marriage ceremony taking place amid the plague. In the center is a figure wearing a headdress and looking out from a window. His crossed eyes indicate that he is looking down, and the direction of his gaze calls attention to the scene below, where a veiled woman is flanked by two men, the one to the right holding a ring and a lily. There are two rings in the scene, but the viewer is probably meant to understand that they are one and the same ring—the man on the right is shown offering it to the woman, and she is shown holding it up for inspection in what appears to be a betrothal ceremony. Below, an archway frames a herd of cattle passing by, one of the herds that Israel kept in Goshen (Genesis 46:31–34), and the Hebrew writing at the top of the whole scene makes the connection to Goshen and the fourth plague explicit, citing Exodus 8:18: "I will set apart in that day the land of Goshen."

The only full-fledged study of this illustration is by an art historian named Julie Ann Harris, who has made a number of observations that can help us decode what is happening.[15] The preceding illustration in the Haggadah, as Harris notes, is a visualization of the fourth plague that depicts it as a brutal attack of lions devouring the Egyptians. Why lions? Though the translation offered at the start of this chapter refers to it as a plague of flies, that rendering masks the fact that the underlying Hebrew word, *ʿarov*, is of unknown meaning and has been understood in various ways. Its translation as a plague of flies assumes that the word means "swarm" (the root letters of *ʿarov* can mean "mixture"), an interpretation that goes back to the Septuagint in the third or second century BCE, but midrash records two views: Rabbi Nehemiah taught that the plague consisted of hornets, while for Rabbi Yehuda, the plague was a mixture of wild animals like lions and bears (Exodus Rabbah 11.3). The illustration in the Haggadah draws on this latter interpretation, but, as Harris notes,

FIGURE 12. The land of Goshen as illustrated in the Hispano-Moresque Haggadah. From the archive of the British Library, OR 2737, fol. 73r. British Library / Granger Historical Archive.

the depiction of the plague as a lion attack is also a visual pun that plays on the name of the kingdom based in Toledo, Castile-León, whose coat of arms bore the image of a lion. The symbolism likens the violence committed by the kingdom of Castile-León to a biblical plague, ferocious but targeted not at the Jews but at those trying to harm them.

Turning to the illustration of Goshen itself, Harris detects another visual pun in the lily that the man is holding. The Hebrew for "lily," *shoshanah,* evokes the name of one of Toledo's most prominent Jewish families, the Ibn Shoshan family, and Harris takes that as a clue that the wedding depicted in the scene reflects a real-life wedding connecting the Ibn Shoshan family to a member of another prominent Toledo Jewish clan, the Ibn Hasdai family, who are also alluded to in the Haggadah via images of a stork (*hasidah* in Hebrew) included in some of its illustrations. The Hispano-Moresque Haggadah may itself have been created as a wedding gift for the couple to take into their new home, and the Goshen scene and other illustrations that adorn it, visually emphasizing the theme of fecundity, may have been meant to encourage them to have children, recounting the exodus as a story of how the Israelites survived their plight in Egypt by being fruitful and multiplying even in the midst of hardship and violence.

By using Goshen as a backdrop for this celebration, the Haggadah implies that the Jews of Toledo have found a Goshen-like space within Castile-León, and that kind of security was not to be taken for granted in the period when this Haggadah was composed. Although the Jews of Castile-León were recognized as a protected minority under Alfonso X (1221–1284), they were still subject to theological condemnation by Christians, were never fully integrated into civic life, and were occasionally ensnared in the violence of the realm's politics. Life became especially difficult in 1281, when Alfonso, angry with his Jewish tax collector, Don Çag de la Maleha, condemned Çag to be hanged, ordered the imprisonment of other Jewish tax gatherers, and took the male members of the community as hostages, confining them in their synagogues for a ransom of twelve thousand gold *marividas* per day. It is not known when during this period the Hispano-Moresque Haggadah was created, but the illustration suggests that the Jews of the community at the time lived within or had access to a walled space in the city where they felt secure enough to mount a celebration. It is even possible that the Haggadah attempts to depict an actual place within Toledo: Jews during the rule of Alfonso X were concentrated in a special urban district enclosed by walls and gates known as the *judería*, where they were segregated from the city's Christian population but also to some extent insulated from it.[16]

We can gain a deeper understanding of the Haggadah's depiction of Goshen as a specific kind of refuge by placing it in the broader context of Christian artistic convention, on which this and other Haggadot produced in Spain in this period sometimes drew.[17] The relevant Christian prototype for the Haggadah's illustration of Goshen was the depiction of Mary or some other devout or virtuous woman sitting in an enclosed garden, where she is protected from the outside world. Such scenes, known as *hortus conclusus* (Latin for "enclosed garden"), were inspired by the biblical book of Song of Songs, understood by Catholics at the time as an allegory about Mary, and in fact the phrase *hortus conclusus* itself comes from the Latin translation of Song of Songs 4:12: "My sister is an enclosed garden." The garden in these scenes is separated from the outside world by a wall, fence, or hedge, and Mary—or another woman ascribed Mary-like virtue—is shown seated in the midst of the garden among trees and flowers.[18] The flowers in the garden symbolized the extraordinary fecundity of the woman at the center of the garden, while the garden's seclusion from the outside symbolized her inviolate purity.

Men sometimes appear in the scene, too, but only as attendants or as figures positioned outside the walls of the garden, looking down on the woman with a threatening gaze; the woman is protected from male lust by the walls, which is what allows her to relax, to focus on socializing with other women or reading.[19] Different artists introduced their own innovations into the scene, but they invariably included a barrier separating the garden from the outside and were focused on a female figure at the center of the garden positioned amid flowers and trees.

Artistic renderings of the *hortus conclusus* theme were produced in Castile-León in the period when the Hispano-Moresque Haggadah was produced, as demonstrated by an illustration in a poem cycle called the *Cantigas de Santa Maria*. Produced during the reign of Alfonso X, the

FIGURE 13. Late thirteenth-century Spanish illustration of Mary in an "enclosed garden" of lilies, from the *Cantigas de Santa Maria, Cantiga* 10. *The Index of Medieval Art*, Princeton University, system number pap20191031013.

Cantigas features 420 songs attributed to the king himself, although many if not all were produced by court musicians, and each tells a story about Mary or praises her. The songs are illustrated, and the tenth one, shown in figure 13, features a *hortus conclusus* scene that puts its own spin on the trope's conventional motifs: Mary sits under an arch in an enclosed garden of lilies and other flowers, and she holds a lily in her right hand.[20]

The similarity to the Goshen illustration is by no means obvious, at least not at first, since there is no garden in the Goshen scene. But we can see parallels when we look more closely. The Goshen illustration also puts a woman at the center of an enclosed space with an archway over it, and the presence of a veil and a lily, implying her chasteness and purity, has a counterpart in the veil on Mary's head and the lily in her hand. While the woman does not appear in the midst of a flowering garden in the Goshen scene, she does appear in a protected space, and the scene suggests fecundity through the vines bordering the scene, the herd of animals passing by at the bottom, and the use of the color green throughout the illustration. Another detail that recalls the *hortus conclusus* is the man looking down on the woman from a window, recalling scenes where a man is looking down on the woman in the *hortus conclusus* from a window or ladder above.[21]

The fact that the enclosed garden symbolized the protected space of a virtuous woman's sexuality may help to explain why the Goshen scene drew on its elements—the illustrator was seeking to make a similar statement about the sexuality of Jewish women. In Castile-León at the time, religious authorities were anxious to maintain sexual boundaries among Jews, Christians, and Muslims. Alfonso X himself was concerned enough about this issue that he imposed the death penalty on Jewish and Muslim men found to be sleeping with Christian women, while rabbinic authorities in the kingdom, also alarmed by the blurring of sexual boundaries, used their legal authority and influence to try to dissuade Jews from having sexual relations with Christians or Muslims.[22] As Harris notes in her analysis of the Hispano-Moresque Haggadah, several of the illustrations in the Haggadah can be understood to be referring in symbolically coded ways to the experiences of the Jewish community of Castile-León, using the exodus to highlight the role of heroic women in sustaining the community in circumstances that threatened its safety and demographic future. The Goshen scene fits into this extended visual allegory as an episode capturing a community where women are able to sustain their virtue and flourish, protected from the sexual menace posed by outsiders as symbolized by the man looking down from the window.

By transferring the qualities of the Christian enclosed garden to the land of Goshen, the illustrator of the Hispano-Moresque Haggadah transformed it into a different kind of refuge from the fortress depicted by Manetho or the *yeshivat Goshen* of midrashic tradition. This Goshen was not a rebel base where outcasts and outlaws had the freedom to plot rebellion against their enemies; it was not a study house founded as an intellectual-spiritual refuge for Jewish men seeking to sustain their obligation to study the Torah in a foreign environment; it was a place of life being sustained by women and producing more life in an environment insulated from animalistic violence and sexual predation, constructed in the very midst of Egypt but not unlike the Garden of Eden as a place where one could be fruitful and multiply as commanded by God.

Goshen as a Back Porch

Seven hundred or so years later, in 1939, the writer and anthropologist Zora Neale Hurston offered readers a novelistic version of the exodus story, *Moses, Man of the Mountain,* that depicted the prophet in light of Afro-Caribbean and African American folklore. Hurston's version of the exodus registered the oppression endured by Black people under slavery and the segregationism of Jim Crow, but it was also about gender, using its depiction of Moses to imply a critique of male leadership within the Black community. Most relevant for our purposes is the part of the novel situated in Goshen, and I want to devote the last section of this chapter to making a case for this version of Goshen as yet another kind of third space remolded into a model of how to thrive in the midst of racism.[23]

Hurston's decision to recount the life of Moses situates her as part of a centuries-old religious-literary tradition within African American culture that used the exodus to reflect on contemporary Black experience. In the seventeenth century, White Puritan leaders in New England often described their experience in the colonies as a reenactment of the exodus, casting North America as a New Canaan bequeathed to the colonizers by divine providence. That rhetorical tradition was passed on to Black Africans when they were imported into New England as human chattel and converted to Christianity. By the beginning of the eighteenth century, the preacher Abraham Jones, a former slave turned Methodist lay minister, was calling on his congregants to ponder the similarities between the affliction of the Israelites and the suffering of slaves in the United States. By the middle of the century, the comparison was a commonplace in African American preaching and hymnody. The analogy was also explored in fiction, including in the novel *Blake*, by Martin Delaney (1812–1885), which describes a fictional exodus of slaves to Canada, and the epic poem "Moses: A Story of the Nile," by Frances Ellen Watkins Harper (1825–1911), who retold the story in a way that credited the Israelites' liberation to cross-racial cooperation between Moses's (Black) mother and the (White) daughter of Pharaoh.[24]

There were two biblical spaces that were especially important in this analogy: "Egypt" was applied to the United States or the South as a place of enslavement, while "Canaan" referred to any space that lay beyond slavery and oppression, either a physical place beyond the South—the North, Canada, Africa—or the state of freedom itself. Goshen, a space *within* Egypt where the Israelites could find a measure of security and prosperity, did not easily fit into this binary, and often it was simply ignored. Communities throughout the United States, both White and Black, took on the name of Goshen, but usually as a way of referring to a site as a fertile place good for farming, and I could scarcely find any examples where the name was meant to evoke Goshen's status as a refuge from oppression. One exception was a ward of Richmond, Virginia, where the city's Black population was confined as a result of post–Civil War gerrymandering, which came to be known informally as Goshen, and it did represent a kind of refuge from racism; indeed, it was there, in 1904, that the earliest successful campaign to use a boycott to reverse segregation in the South was waged.[25] For the most part, however, the name Goshen was simply used for places that were considered good sites to farm or raise cattle. This was the relevant aspect of Goshen even for the abolitionist Frederick Douglass when he visited what he took to be the actual Goshen during a trip to Egypt in 1887—he marveled at how its fields were still green and its camels still grazing as in the time of Jacob without mentioning its role as a refuge from slavery.[26]

Given the importance of the exodus story in general in Black American culture, why didn't Goshen's role in the story resonate more? One reason for this may be that many African Americans did not find a corresponding space for themselves within the United States. This, at least, was the conclusion drawn by the abolitionist David Walker (1796–1830) in an 1829 work entitled *Appeal, in Four Articles; Together with a Preamble, to the Coloured Citizens of the World but in Particular, and Very Expressly, to Those in the United States*. Walker invoked the biblical Goshen to argue that American slavery was so pitiless that there was simply no room for such a place in the United States. The Egyptians had also enslaved the Israelites, but at least they had offered them land where they might support themselves. By contrast, a Black man in America could labor night and day to pay for a small piece of land, labor to build a house there, and move his family into it, yet White people would still take it from him even if it was in a mud hole.[27] Walker's representation of America as even worse than biblical Egypt was part of a critique so daring for its day that it might have gotten him killed; he was found dead in his shop in 1830 shortly after publishing the *Appeal*, possibly as a result of poisoning.

While its role in the African American imagination was marginal compared with Egypt and Canaan, however, Goshen still sometimes appears in retellings of the Bible from Black thinkers and writers as a metaphor for a kind of space between slavery and freedom. One such representation appears in an essay published in 1900, by the mathematician and sociologist Kelly Miller (1863–1939), entitled "The Modern Land of Goshen."[28] Although now overshadowed by his contemporary W.E.B. Du Bois, Miller was a highly influential leader of the era, and the essay spelled out a plan that looked back to Goshen as a model for how Blacks could build a better life for themselves within a White America by absorbing wisdom from the Egyptians (that is, White people) and then using it to develop a zone of economic and social autonomy in the South: "We are indebted to the banks of the Nile for most of our norms of knowledge, and it may be that we have to go back to Egypt for sociologic wisdom. . . . The Land of Goshen was set apart for [the Hebrews'] especial use, where they remained until they acquired a goodly measure of the discipline and culture of the Egyptians. . . . Under the recurrence of similar circumstances history must repeat itself."[29] Foreseeing that White people would never grant them equality, Miller called for Blacks to focus their energies and resources on creating a new Goshen in the American South, a self-supporting economic enclave comprising Black-owned agricultural industries, businesses, and manufacturing. If Black people used this zone to import Yankee industriousness into the South while disentangling themselves from the White economy, he argued, they could achieve the independence and equality that neither migration nor attempted integration with Southern Whites had been able to achieve. This was the wisdom to be learned from Goshen.

Hurston was thus not the first African American writer to use Goshen to think about the experience of Black people in America, but her version of Goshen is different from that of Miller. Goshen, as she imagined it, is no business zone but something akin to a plantation or prison where the Israelites are subject to harsh restrictions and punishments, ongoing surveillance, and terrible violence. As her novel opens, the Hebrews, who had begun to build houses beyond Goshen, have been shoved back into it by a new pharaoh who imposes a series of merciless decrees; these recall the plantation rules that masters demanded their slaves follow, and there are elements in Hurston's description—Goshen is ringed in by steel and patrolled by secret police—that also recall a state-run prison farm or even a concentration camp.[30] As terrible as Hurston's Goshen is, however, Pharaoh and his soldiers cannot control everything happening in it, and this small measure of unsurveilled seclusion is enough to allow for a certain level of independent expression and action. The Hebrews talk among themselves, they venture some sarcasm about their masters every now and then, they gossip, and once Moses arrives, they plan an escape.

To understand Hurston's version of Goshen, it is instructive to note its resemblance to a kind of space that shows up again and again in her writing. The Jim Crow South, as oppressive as it was, contained areas where Black people enjoyed a zone of limited autonomy, where they could speak their minds and act on their creative impulses. These spaces were created by segregation and rendered invisible by their marginality, but their position on the edges of White Society allowed for a certain measure of seclusion and freedom within their borders, enough to allow Black people to express themselves openly and to develop a life and culture of their own.

One such space was the all-Black town of Eatonville, Florida, where Hurston was raised—a "pure Negro town," as she described it in her memoir *Dust Tracks on a Road*. Eatonville was one of some sixty all-Black towns that emerged in the South following the Civil War, towns that developed their own banks, stores, schools, churches, and law enforcement. In fact, as Hurston describes it, Eatonville was the first town in the country to be self-organized and led by Black people (her father had served as its mayor), and she recalls it with nostalgia as a "safe cocoon" insulated from the cruelty of White racism.[31] While many Blacks at the time were opposed to segregation, Hurston saw something protective and even liberating in the spaces for Black self-determination it had created—spaces like Eatonville. To the consternation of integrationists, it was this view that led her to publicly oppose school desegregation: she had seen segregated spaces where Blacks did not have to integrate with Whites and were able to thrive independently of them.[32]

Hurston's best-known novel, *Their Eyes Were Watching God*, is set in Eatonville, and its fictional depiction of the town includes other kinds of segregated space that provide refuge from surveillance and external control.[33] The front porch of the house is depicted as an enclave of relative leisure, freedom, and un-self-censoring expression for the novel's Black male characters, a place where, because "the sun and the bossman were gone," the men could enjoy a modicum of power and respect as "lords of sounds and lesser things."[34] Women were excluded, forced to congregate on the house's back porch, but there they found a corresponding space of their own where they could gossip, complain about the men, and share secrets. The novel itself is framed as a story recounted during a back-porch conversation between the narrator and her friends.

FIGURE 1. Angels pouring out the apocalyptic plagues described in Revelation 16, from an illustrated version of the New Testament completed in 1531. The Ottheinrich Bible, p. 298. Alamy.

FIGURE 2. The ten plagues as a cell phone display, from Eli Kaplan-Wildmann's *The Recreated Haggadah*. Image reproduced with permission from Eli Kaplan-Wildmann.

FIGURE 7. John Jensen's concept for the frog plague in Cecil B. DeMille's *The Ten Commandments* (1956), an episode filmed but eventually cut from the movie. Image courtesy of Heritage Auctions / HA.com.

FIGURE 8. Medieval illustration of "and a frog came up" (Exodus 8:2) from the Golden Haggadah. From the archive of the British Library, MS 27210, folio 12v. British Library / Granger Historical Archive.

FIGURE 9. The plague of frogs as glimpsed through a rotating wheel included in Abraham Silbermann, *The Children's Haggadah*, 3rd ed. (London: Shapiro, Vallentine, 1942), 13. Courtesy of the Library at the Herbert D. Katz Center for Advanced Judaic Studies, University of Pennsylvania.

FIGURE 10. An eleventh-century rendering of Pharaoh's magician Jambres in hell. From the archive of the British Library, Cotton MS Tiberius B V/1, fol. 87v. British Library / Granger Historical Archive.

FIGURE 11. Moses and the sage Hermes Trismegistus, as pictured in a mosaic from the Church of Siena created by Giovanni di Stefano (1488). Pixaby.

FIGURE 12. The land of Goshen as illustrated in the Hispano-Moresque Haggadah. From the archive of the British Library, OR 2737, fol. 73r. British Library / Granger Historical Archive.

FIGURE 13. Late thirteenth-century Spanish illustration of Mary in an "enclosed garden" of lilies, from the *Cantigas de Santa Maria, Cantiga* 10. *The Index of Medieval Art*, Princeton University, system number pap20191031013.

FIGURE 15. Angel summoning hail and fire from the heavens in the *Cloisters Apocalypse* (France, ca. 1330). Metropolitan Museum of Art, New York.

FIGURE 16. The plague of darkness as depicted in the Vatican Octateuch. Reproduced with permission of the Vatican Apostolic Library, vat. Gr 747, fol. 83v.

FIGURE 17. Christ breaking into the blackness of hell, as depicted in an eleventh-century Byzantine mosaic from the Monastery of Hosios Loukas in Greece. Wikimedia.

FIGURE 20. Marc Chagall, *Moses Spreads the Darkness over Egypt* (1931).

FIGURE 21. Miriam Beerman, *Plague of Darkness* (1986). Image courtesy of James Yarosh Associates Gallery, with permission from William Jaffe.

FIGURE 22. The Lamb of God as depicted in the van Eyck brothers' *Adoration of the Mystic Lamb* (Ghent, 1432). Alamy.

FIGURE 23. Erastus Field's depiction of the slaying of the firstborn (1865–1880). Metropolitan Museum of Art, New York.

Hurston's version of Goshen similarly turns out to be an enclave of sorts, despite what it shares with the plantation, the prison, and the concentration camp. Pharaoh has spies there, and people are often afraid to speak, but they can crack jokes, mutter complaints, and spread rumors and gossip. What connects Goshen to the back porch, in particular, is that it is only in Goshen that the women of Israel can assert themselves to some degree. When Moses returns to Goshen after many years away in the land of Midian, he is surprised to discover that the person in charge is a woman, his sister, Miriam. She was hardly free in Goshen, yet she had more power and status there than she does after Moses takes charge and leads the Israelites into the wilderness. Hurston's depiction of Goshen is similar to Miller's in the sense that it too is conceived as a realm of autonomy formed in the heart of the land where Black people are oppressed, but Miller's version of Goshen is a zone of Black economic independence, whereas Hurston's Goshen is a place of relative psychological and linguistic seclusion, where the oppressed find ways to evade the notice of their taskmasters and express themselves freely.

Hurston's Goshen is certainly no land of Canaan, but in her telling it does have some advantages over that land. Moses wants his people to be free, but all the people want from him is to be a strong, authoritative ruler—a king—and when it comes time to pass leadership on to Joshua, the prophet himself has second thoughts about freedom, advising Joshua against giving the people too much of it. Hurston's Canaan is a morally murky place, a locus of hope but also an environment where authoritarianism can take root. The prison camp of Goshen offered something in between Egypt and Canaan, a terribly punishing and constricted space but one that, precisely because it was so disempowering for the men of Israel, left room for women to assert agency over their lives. Even as she chronicled the oppressiveness of Egypt, Hurston discovered in Goshen a temporary refuge within Egypt similar to Eatonville and other segregated Black towns, the juke joint (informal clubs set up on the outskirts of Southern towns where plantation workers and sharecroppers could spend time relaxing, dancing, and gambling), and the back porch where women were free from the gaze of men and could speak their minds freely.

As we will see, Exodus's account of other plagues has played a bigger role in the history of freedom—the sixth plague featured prominently in debates about the freedom of the self, and the tenth plague has played a significant role in struggles for the emancipation of slaves—but the fourth plague made its own modest contribution. It introduced into our collective imagination a way to envision a temporary shelter from enslavement, with Goshen serving as a scriptural model for imagined third spaces where it was possible to exercise a partial freedom within a violent and oppressive environment. The biblical account in Exodus did not offer later readers a lot of raw material to work with, only mentioning Goshen twice and revealing almost nothing about what it was like, but it proved possible for Hurston and other retellers to fill in its gaps by fusing into the biblical story experiences of protected spaces found in their own environs like the yeshiva, the enclosed garden, and the back porch. People can be incredibly resourceful when it comes to finding refuge, locating it in very cramped, out-of-the-way, barely habitable spaces beyond where most people would think to look. Something like that kind of creativity is reflected in the history of people reimagining the land of Goshen, a record not just of biblical interpretation but of people envisioning safety and freedom in circumstances where they are extremely constricted and vulnerable and have almost no control of the space around them.

5

The Fifth Plague

THE GREAT CATTLE MASSACRE

IN 2006, a team of scientists, policy experts, and public health officials came together to imagine what it would be like if the fifth plague, the plague in which all the cattle of Egypt died, occurred in the United States. The simulation exercise, held at Case Western Reserve University, was meant to give the group a chance to rehearse how they would respond to a bioterrorism attack that involved hoof-and-mouth disease, an animal disease that causes illness in cows, pigs, and sheep. Someone came up with the name "the Fifth Plague," and a recording of the exercise posted online offers a glimpse of what might happen if the country ever faced an attack like the one the Egyptians did when God struck down all the cattle of Egypt.[1]

The organizers of this exercise were not biblical interpreters, but by choosing to name the simulation "the Fifth Plague," they were continuing a long tradition of interpreting Exodus 9:1–7 as the paradigmatic cattle plague, a plague that threatens all society by striking down the domesticated farm animals on which it depends for food and other essentials. The agricultural and economic consequences of such an outbreak can send entire nations into crisis. A cattle plague that struck England in 1865—a since-eradicated disease called rinderpest—killed so many cattle, for example, that it affected the country's livestock trade for the next twenty-five years. More recently, in the 1980s, an outbreak of mad cow disease, a fatal brain disease known as bovine spongiform encephalopathy, caused widespread panic in Britain and elsewhere, requiring the slaughter of four million cattle to contain the disease and costing the British economy billions of dollars.

In earlier such crises, religious authorities would often recall the fifth plague to help explain the outbreak as a divine punishment, and to call on people to repent of their sins. In response to the cattle plague of 1865, many preachers spoke of how "the hand of the Lord" had fallen upon the nation, adopting the phrase from Exodus 9:3 to drive home the idea that the pestilence was God punishing the nation for its sins.[2] No fewer than fifty-four sermons using the phrase are known to have been published as pamphlets during this crisis, and these often made explicit reference to the fifth plague.[3] The biblical episode did not play an overt role in the public responses to the outbreak of mad cow disease in the 1980s and 1990s, but even in that case, it exerted an influence reflected in interpretations that explained the outbreak as a consequence for modern-day farming practices such as turning cows into cannibals by using the parts of other cows as animal feed. There was a scientific basis for this claim, but the core idea that the disease was a punishment for abominable human behavior drew moral and emotional power from the centuries-old tradition of interpreting cattle plagues on the model of the biblical cattle plague.[4]

In this chapter I want to trace the history of how people have retold the plague of cattle, and what I want to focus on is a relatively recent shift in those retellings. For most of the Bible's history, interpreters have assumed that what made the plague so terrible was its impact on the Egyptians, not on the cattle themselves. An example is a 1747 sermon from the Anglican minister Morgan Powell in response to an outbreak of distemper, a sermon entitled "The Hand of the Lord upon the Cattle."[5] Powell shows some sympathy for the cattle, acknowledging that they did nothing to bring the pestilence upon themselves, but the question of why the animals had to suffer on the behalf of humans was not something that Powell thought even to ask, much less to address. The cattle, he writes, were "only the Instruments from which [God]punishes their offending Masters," and their groaning was to be heeded only in relation to its utility for humans, intended by God as a message to awaken in people a sense of guilt, motivate them to reflect on their sins, and thereby move them to repent and save themselves. In line with earlier Christian interpretation of cattle plagues, Powell did not acknowledge anything inherently wrong about the cattle's suffering in part because it would have been heresy to question the justness of divine punishment but also because, in his view, a cow, a horse, or a sheep did not have a moral claim of its own to justice, a right not to suffer for the behavior of its owner.

In more recent retellings of the story, however, there has been a shift in perspective: cows are no longer mere instruments of God but victims. Their deaths are treated as a tragedy, a noble sacrifice, or even a miscarriage of justice that needs to be rectified. As we move in this chapter from ancient to medieval to modern retellings of the fifth plague, my goal will be to shed light on when and why the cattle of Egypt ceased to be seen as mere property of the Egyptians, instruments in the hand of God, or collateral damage in his effort to chastise humans and instead came to be seen as sentient beings with a claim to life transcending their role in God's plan.

On *Not* Counting Sheep

If we were to survey the earliest Jewish and Christian interpretations of the fifth plague, we would scarcely find any empathy at all for the cattle of Egypt, and no recognition of anything unfair about their fate during the fifth plague. Josephus did not even think to mention the cattle plague in his retelling of the plagues, while rabbinic interpretation of the episode includes a midrash that expresses regret that God did not go far enough; the author of the midrash inferred from mention of cattle later on in the ten plagues that God had not killed all the domestic animals of the Egyptians during the fifth plague, and had he not spared some of them, the midrash concludes, the Egyptians would not have had horses to help them chase after the Israelites when they left Egypt (Mekhilta de-Rabbi Ishmael on Exodus 14:27, beshallah 2.28).[6] Early Christian interpreters were no more compassionate toward the cattle. In his sermon on the ten plagues, the third-century Christian scholar

Origen justified the death of the cattle as God's way to make clear to the Egyptians their foolishness in worshiping such animals as gods.[7]

The first-century-CE Jewish philosopher and biblical commentator Philo of Alexandria, one of the earliest known interpreters of the ten plagues, is an instructive example of this kind of response because he is one of the few early biblical interpreters to spell out his view of animals in general, and we can situate his interpretation of the cattle plague in that context. Philo thought a lot about animals, composing a treatise that addressed their subjective experiences, and he acknowledged their capacity for suffering. But he denied that animals possessed the rationality and moral capacity that he thought elevated humans over all other created things—a view that helps to explain what he says about God's use of animals to punish the Egyptians.

Philo lays out his interpretation of the ten plagues in the first volume of his *Life of Moses* (96–146), a kind of biography of the prophet written in Greek and informed by Philo's knowledge of philosophy and other intellectual fields.[8] One of the most intriguing aspects of Philo's interpretation of the plagues is that it does not follow their order as narrated in Exodus but instead reorganizes them in a sequence based on Philo's understanding of physics and metaphysics. The material world, in his view, was created out of four core elements that moved from the denser elements (water and earth) to the lighter ones (fire and air). Everything in the material world—objects, animals, humans—was composed of a different combination of these elements, and that included the plagues, rearranged by Philo according to a scheme that moved upward from the material to the non-material. First God sent plagues made of the denser elements, water and earth—the plagues of blood, frogs, and gnats. Then came three plagues that involved the lighter elements of air and fire: the fiery hail, the locusts, and the darkness. The plague of boils combined earth and air, so it came next, and the last three plagues originated from beyond the material world altogether: the flies, the cattle disease, and the slaying of the firstborn.

It is not clear at first why Philo moved the cattle plague from the fifth position to the ninth, but a closer look at his interpretation reveals an explanation. What united the first three plagues in his sequence was not just that they were made out of water or earth but that the one who brought them about was Aaron, the lowest-ranking member of the three agents involved in executing the plagues—Aaron, Moses, and God. The second set of plagues, involving the lighter elements of fire or air—the hail, locusts, and darkness—were said by the Torah to have been carried out by Moses, who in each case stretched out his hands to the heavens to summon them down to earth. The plague of boils was anomalous for Philo for two reasons: it alone transgressed the boundary between lower and higher elements, combining the lower element of earth with the higher element of air, and it alone was performed by both Moses and Aaron according to Exodus. For these reasons, Philo moved it from the sixth to seventh position, in keeping with his view that the number seven was the most anomalous of the numbers one through ten.

This left the three plagues that Philo could not identify with any kind of matter—the flies, the cattle plague, and the slaying of the firstborn. What united them as a group in Philo's understanding of the story is that they were all brought about by God directly, without any intervening action by Aaron or Moses. This is a point that Philo makes explicitly about the plague of cattle, noting that it came about without any human cooperation: "There followed again a chastisement brought about without human cooperation, the death of the livestock; for great herds of oxen and sheep and goats; and every kind of beast of burden and other cattle, perished as by a single agreed signal in a single day, whole droves at a time, thus announcing the destruction of men which was about to follow, just as we find in epidemics. For pestilential disorders are said to be preluded by a sudden murrain among the lower animals" (*Life of Moses* 1.133). What motivated Philo to relocate the cattle plague was the logic of his overall understanding of the plagues: because it did not involve water, earth, fire, or air and because it was not brought about by Aaron or Moses, it belonged in his view to the highest category of the plagues that came directly from God along with the flies and the slaying of the firstborn. Why make it second to last within this group? Philo compares the last two plagues to the unfolding of an epidemic where the cattle are affected just before humans are, a sequence that our own era can explain as a consequence of interspecies disease transmission but that people in Philo's day recognized as a god's way of giving humans a final warning before their own demise.[9]

Despite the elevated status that Philo assigned the cattle plague in his philosophically driven reorganization of the plagues, he did not hold the cattle of Egypt in especially high regard. To the contrary, as he makes clear throughout his writing, he had particular contempt for the animals of Egypt—the crocodiles, the asps, and especially the cattle—because of their role in Egyptian animal veneration, an egregious form of idolatry that Philo considered the worst of the Egyptians' sins.[10] Cattle were especially offensive from this perspective because of the prominent role of cattle gods in the Egyptian animal cult, such as the bull god Apis and the ram god Amun. In a commentary known as *Questions and Answers on Exodus,* Philo posed the question of why it was that on the last night of the plagues, God chose to command the Israelites to sacrifice lambs, and his answer is that God, as a way of showing the vanquishment of Egypt's gods, wanted the Israelites to slay the very animals that the Egyptians revered as divine (1.8).[11]

But even apart from his particular animus for the animals of Egypt, Philo did not have very high regard for animals in general, treating them as mere assets or tools for humans to use for their own benefit, without any claim to justice of their own. In a commentary known as *Questions and Answers on Genesis* (2.9), Philo briefly addressed the question of why God allowed animals to die in the flood even though they had not committed any sin themselves. His answer was pitilessly anthropocentric: since, in his view, animals were created by God not for their own sake but only for human benefit, it follows that if the humans who own them die, there is no longer any reason for the animals to live. Philo does not offer such an explanation for the death of Egypt's cattle, but his utilitarian approach to animals suggests why their death left him unmoved: in contrast to humans, who were meant by God to be elevated above the rest of material creation, the "lower animals" did not have any inherent claim to life. Their value was purely instrumental. If God had a reason to dispose of them, there was no reason not to do so.

This view was heartless, but it was not thoughtless. As mentioned earlier, Philo devoted a whole treatise to animals, known as *On Animals,* which survives in an Armenian translation that has been judged by scholarship to be authentic. Framed as a debate between himself and his nephew Tiberius Julius Alexander about whether animals can be held morally accountable for their actions, the treatise focuses on the question of whether animals are rational, with Tiberius arguing that they are and Philo countering that they are not. Philo used the treatise to make a case that, lacking rationality, animals simply aren't eligible to be treated as moral beings: they cannot understand the difference between good and evil or make a choice to do one or the other, and it makes no sense to think of them as beings that can be treated justly or unjustly.[12]

Philo's treatise on animals emerged out of a larger philosophical debate in the Hellenistic and Roman world that we know of from three treatises on animals written by the second-century-CE scholar Plutarch, as well as from later sources.[13] Philo's view was aligned with Stoicism, which insisted on a sharp difference between humans and animals. Animals had souls, according to Stoics, but they lacked the highest part of the soul that made reasoning possible. Because they lacked reason, they could not participate in the system of morality and justice that governed how humans interacted. Philo's biggest criticism of the Egyptians, as mentioned earlier, was that they blurred this difference. To be an animal, according to Philo, was to be led by one's body, to follow appetite and instinct unrestrained by reason, and the core problem with the Egyptians' veneration of animals was that by elevating animality to a divine status, it encouraged people to allow the animal side of their souls to ride roughshod over the higher reasoning power that God had bestowed on them when creating them in his image. Ascribing rationality to animals blurred the human-animal distinction in the opposite direction: whereas animal worship turned humans into animals, believing that animals had rationality falsely granted them equal status to humans.

Like the Stoics, Philo also believed it was morally permissible to use animals to benefit oneself. This is why God had created them in the first place, and in Philo's retelling of the plagues that involve animals, he consistently stresses their instrumental value in serving a divine purpose. The fish die during the blood plague in order to make the experience more unbearable for the Egyptians by adding a stench (*Life of*

Moses 1.100); the gnats' diminutive stature sends a message to the Egyptians that God is so powerful that he can use even the tiniest creature to defeat his opponents (1.109–112); while God turned to the vicious dog fly (the plague of flies as Philo imagined it involved a creature that combined the qualities of the dog and the fly) as another weapon, a javelin that fixes itself firmly to its victim (1.131–132).[14] Philo's interpretation of the death of the cattle is consistent with how he understands the role of animals throughout the plagues. Their demise did not register as unjust because, from his perspective, cows, sheep, and horses, as nonmoral beings, have no claim to being treated justly in their own right; their death was simply another blow that God used to assert power over the Egyptians and punish their sin.

Philo's interpretation of the cattle plague can serve us as a useful before-and-after foil for the more compassionate interpretations we will consider in the following sections. In focusing on it, however, I do not mean to suggest that premodern peoples couldn't have felt compassion for the suffering of the cattle, couldn't have ascribed to them moral agency, or couldn't have recognized the injustice of their having to die for the Egyptians' sins. Philo's own writing shows that in the first century, a morally untroubled reaction to the death of the cattle was not the only possible response. By this time, another school of thought—represented in Philo's *On Animals* by his nephew Tiberius—afforded animals intelligence, dignity, agency, and moral accountability. We also know of retellings of the ten plagues from this time that anthropomorphize the animals of the plagues, ascribing to them humanlike characteristics. In fact, we have already seen an example of such a retelling, in the midrash about the frog martyrs of the second plague who are depicted as pious devotees of God worthy of human emulation.

To date, however, I have found no similar portraits of the cattle of Egypt in interpretations of the ten plagues that happen to survive from antiquity, and it is only in the early modern period, the seventeenth century, that there emerge retellings that take a strikingly different approach to the cattle, versions of the story where the suffering of the cattle is ascribed significance and where their deaths register as a tragedy or an injustice. I am not suggesting that these ways of retelling the fifth plague were widespread in the early modern period. The view that cattle were mere instruments continued to shape interpretations of the fifth plague. But a more empathetic attitude does emerge in some retellings of the episode, which, as we will see, reflect broader changes in the religious and moral status that early modern Christians ascribed to animals.

Cattle Conversions

Morgan Powell was, perhaps unsurprisingly, not the only preacher to compose a sermon in response to a devastating outbreak of cattle disease that had beset England beginning in 1745. In the town of Northampton, the minister Samuel King delivered a sermon about the same event, entitled "The Hand of the Lord upon the Cattle Considered and Improved." King's sermon asserted that the recent death of cattle was "the finger of God" sent to punish and instruct the people of England, just as God had punished the Egyptians. The country, he warned, was currently on the same path as the sequence of plagues in Exodus and would soon suffer a more lethal phase of God's wrath, which would only end when the nation repented of its sins.

What I want to call attention to in King's sermon is its acknowledgment that the cattle struck down by the plague were sentient beings deserving of pity. King wanted his listeners to know that God has high regard for the lives and feelings of brute creatures: they lack reason but "are not void of sensations both of pleasure and pain," and he takes care to provide for them.[15] He would make such creatures suffer, King insists, only under extreme circumstances, when doing so is necessary to save humans from complete destruction.

Nearly a century earlier, in 1656, the celebrated poet Abraham Cowley had likewise granted the cattle of Egypt a measure of compassion. In marked contrast to the plague as depicted in Philo, Cowley's retelling in a poem called "The Plagues of Egypt" accentuates the innocence of the animals killed during the plague, the agony of their suffering, and the tragedy of their deaths.[16] One way it does this is by giving the reader brief glimpses of the animals' lives before they were felled by the plague. The poem depicts the oxen dropping dead before the plow they pulled throughout their lives. It tells of a horse whose nostrils can no longer delight in the smell of his dappled mistresses. It speaks of sheep too sick to eat anymore, bleating their innocent souls out into the air. Cowley drives home the pathos of the episode by describing how onlookers were affected by the deaths, mentioning the gasping of a dog as it watched the animals that it was protecting die and a lute-playing shepherd halted mid-tune by his grief.

Cowley created this narrative by grafting the biblical account in Exodus onto a poetic description of a cattle plague in the third book of Virgil's *Georgics* that describes what seems to have been a real-life outbreak, possibly caused by anthrax.[17] Virgil's account, which catalogs how different species of cattle were felled by the plague, was drawn on by Christian poets long before Cowley as a model for how to describe the plagues of their own eras.[18] But in Cowley's case, by fusing it with the biblical account in Exodus, he was able to create a moving rendition of the fifth plague that conveys a sense that the animals deserve the reader's sympathy. He did not question the justice of God in killing the cattle, but he did emphasize their innocence and nobility, and he reminded readers that they had had full lives before the plague, feelings, and relationships. They were not just property to be disposed of, and their deaths were a tragedy.

I cannot pin down when this more empathetic approach to the cattle of Egypt first emerged, but there is research to suggest that it is tied to other changes in how animals in general were understood within Christianity. One important development was the emergence during the Middle Ages of the idea that among the consequences of the sin of Adam and Eve in the Garden of Eden was a reorganizing of the animal world. God had intended animals to be beneficial to humankind, and some species continued in that role, but others, following the serpent's lead, turned antagonistic, rebelling against human rule and posing a threat to them. Most of the animals involved in the ten plagues—the frogs, gnats or lice, flies or wild animals, and locusts—would have fallen into this latter category of unruly animal, what medieval and early modern Christians in Europe came to refer to as vermin, creatures thought inimical to human well-being.[19]

This was a view expressed, for example, by the Anglican bishop Godfrey Goodman in a 1616 treatise entitled *The Fall of Man*:

> Behold the dumb creatures who were made only for mans use and service cast off their yoeke, and are now become dangerous and obnoxious to man, from the greatest to the least. We stand not only in feare of fierce Lions, cruell Tigers, ravening wolves, devouring Beares, but Gnats, Flies and the least wormes doe serve to molest us; let not the plagues of Aegypt seem so incredible, when as within our memorie . . . the Mice so swarmed and abounded. . . . It cannot be that the government of man over the creatures should so farre bee impeached, were it not, that there is some connivencie and toleration from above.[20]

Ever since the fall of humankind, Goodman maintains, humans have had to contend with the hostility of all kinds of creatures, great and small—wild creatures like lions and tigers but also smaller noxious creatures like gnats and flies. The former were more frightening, but they lived in locations at a distance from people and were encountered relatively rarely, whereas vermin were nearby and constantly encroaching into the human realm, and they were all part of an animal rebellion against humankind that had been underway since the sin of Adam and Eve. As the literary scholar Lucinda Cole has suggested, this interpretation of the animal world arose in response to environmental changes introduced by the Little Ice Age, a centuries-long period of cold weather and agricultural precarity that increased the threat posed by rats, insects, and other small and noxious animals that could cause a life-threatening famine by destroying a crop or killing livestock.[21] The concept of vermin as animal rebels also likely resonated in light of the politics of an era riven by the Protestant Reformation. Although serving as a bishop in the Church of England, Goodman himself developed second thoughts about England's break from the Roman Church, and given his delicate position as a Catholic sympathizer amid suspicious Protestants, it is tempting to explain his description of a rebellious animal world as a reflection of his own feeling of vulnerability in a society encompassed on every side by religious insurgents.

Goodman's brief reference to "the plagues of Aegypt" suggests that he understood the plagues as a continuation of the war between animals and sinful humans, but he only touches on the story, and a more developed example of how the concept of vermin shaped people's understanding of the ten plagues appears in the aforementioned retelling by Abraham Cowley. One trait that distinguished vermin from other kinds of animals is that they were thought to have formed spontaneously out of dead or corrupted matter, rather than being created directly by God. This is, according to Cowley, exactly how the frogs of the second plague came to be, rising up out of the Nile as if formed from "rotting Fish and unconcocted Gore."[22] Another characteristic of vermin that Cowley emphasizes is their invasiveness—they are always threatening to overrun and despoil the spaces of human habitation. The frogs take over all the towns, houses, temples, and palaces of the Egyptians, even reaching into their silky beds. There is no escape from the flies, either—not for humans seeking shelter in their houses nor for the cattle in the field, who are so tortured by them that they wish upon themselves the disease that would soon kill them with the fifth plague. Then come the locusts, "wretched Pillagers" who leave nothing left to farm at all.[23] Whereas other retellings of the plagues depict the creatures involved as wild animals, Cowley's version shapes them in the image of marauding vermin that threaten the boundary between humans and animals by invading humans' living spaces and pillaging their produce.

Alongside this notion of the vermin came another category of animal that shaped Cowley's depiction of the cattle of Egypt. The opposite of the verminous creature, in this early modern vision of the animal kingdom, was the domestic animal, the animal that retained its original God-created role as a servant to human beings. What distinguishes this conception of the animal from Philo's is that the domestic animal was not merely an instrument in the hands of God or humankind but a sympathetic being, an innocent creature benignly disposed to humans, loyal, kind, admirable. Such animals were clearly subordinate to humans, who were authorized by God to use and kill them for their needs, but they were now recognized as also deserving of protection, gratitude, and pity, qualities that Cowley brought to the fore by using his poetic skills to convey, for lack of a better word, the humanity of each kind of cattle felled by the plague. In this version of the episode, the death of the cattle registers not just as lamentable but as a Christlike sacrifice, necessary to accomplish God's purpose but undeserved and deeply heartrending.

Why did people in this period put more emphasis on the suffering, innocence, and agency of domestic animals? The answer may also relate to the Protestant Reformation. The scholar Robert Watson argues that, in places like England, the Reformation may have triggered greater sympathy for animals by motivating Christians involved in the revolt against the Catholic Church to develop a sense of identification with other innocents suffering under the oppressive rule of cruel authorities. In support of this connection, Watson observes that early opposition to animal cruelty came mostly from Protestant circles, who imputed bullfighting and other forms of animal cruelty to their Catholic opponents. For instance, shortly after establishing the Massachusetts Bay Colony, the Puritans introduced one of the earliest provisions against animal cruelty in 1641: "No Man shall exercise any Tirranny or Crueltie toward any brute Creature which are usually kept for man's use." Even those advocating for the protection of animals accepted their characterization as "dumb beasts" bereft of reasoning and communicative ability, but the absence of intelligence was now taken as a sign not of inferiority and thingness, the absence of agency, but of innocence and freedom from sin. Domestic animals were ascribed other virtues esteemed by Protestants too, including meekness, gentleness, and dutifulness.[24]

It may not be a coincidence that in this same period, there emerged in Europe other signs of a greater empathy for animals, such as a revived debate about whether animals have the capacity to reason.[25] Whether it was the Reformation or some other social or cultural change that was driving this new, more sympathetic attitude toward animals I cannot pin down, but the shift does account for a change in how some retold the fifth plague. Reading the biblical account in light of the animal categories that prevailed in their own age, early modern minds saw a distinction among the animals involved in the ten plagues that wasn't known or relevant to how Philo understood the story. He lumped together all animals, wild and domestic—serpents and crocodiles but also cattle—as incarnations of appetites and instincts of the soul that were disgusting and dangerous. In early modern Christianity, by contrast, people made a distinction between vermin and domestic animals, vilifying the former as an unruly menace and idealizing the latter as innocent, noble, and deserving of care and compassion. This recategorization of the animal world made the cattle of Egypt more relatable, not just instruments in God's plan for humanity but innocents whose suffering resembled that of Christians persecuted for their faith.

This view anticipates an even more empathetic approach to the animals of the ten plagues that has emerged in the last century, but it should be distinguished from it. The early modern sermons and poetry I have mentioned treated the cattle of Egypt as worthy of compassion but were nonetheless operating from a perspective that judged animals as good or bad based on whether they benefited humankind. Later animal rights advocates rejected not only the theology that underpinned this view but its human exceptionalism as well—the idea that humans have a moral status and intellectual capacity that elevate them over animals even though the latter also deserve sympathy and respect—and such advocates argue that animals not only are entitled to protection from abuse but ought to be liberated from their subjugation by humans.

Nevertheless, the emergence of the cattle of Egypt as beings capable of feeling, innocence, and virtue does represent an important point of transition to the modern approach to the fifth plague episode that I want to explore in the next section. Part of what distinguishes contemporary understandings of cows and other animals is their identification by at least some people as fellow *persons*—not just fellow suffering creatures but, in a sense, fellow citizens of the world with rich inner lives, social relationships as dear to them as ours are to us, and a claim to justice in no way subordinate to that of human beings. This is not a universally shared view of animals by any means, as witnessed by the fifth plague simulation where the death of the cattle is treated as an economic loss for humans rather than as a victimization of the animals themselves, but it is an increasingly common one, as the philosopher Peter Singer has demonstrated by showing how the *New York Times* has shifted from using "that" in reference to cows to "who," the pronoun used of persons.[26] Early modern sermons and poetry that mourn the death of the cattle of Egypt, still justifying it as a divine punishment or chastisement for sin but acknowledging the animals' innocence, expressing compassion for their suffering, and marking their death as a tragic, Christlike sacrifice, reflect an early stage in this transition from understanding the cow as a thing to perceiving the cow as a person.

Liberating the Lamb

Moving into the nineteenth century, this kind of compassionate response to the death of the cattle was further encouraged in England by the cattle pestilence of 1865 mentioned at the beginning of the chapter—an outbreak so severe that it affected the country's livestock trade for the next twenty-five years. In response to the death of so many cattle in a short amount of time, the Scottish poet Janet Hamilton wrote a poem that addressed the dead cattle directly:

> For your suff'rings, sinless things
> Weeps the Muse even while she sings:
> Guilt not yours brought down the rod
> Of a just and righteous God.[27]

The poem's mention of "the rod of a just and righteous God" connects it to the ten plagues, recalling the staff used to bring about some of the plagues, but Hamilton combined this motif with deep feeling for the cattle she saw dying, addressing them in the second person as victims completely undeserving of the suffering inflicted on them.

While the poem shows the persistence of the kind of sympathetic interpretation developed centuries earlier by Cowley, the cattle plague about which it was written proved another turning point in how people perceived and interacted with cattle. So argues Joseph Hardwick, a scholar focused on the role of animals in British religious history, who has recently argued that the 1865 outbreak, which killed an estimated four hundred thousand cows, had a lasting impact on how people in England related to nonhuman animals; it moved clergy to urge their congregants to treat their animals more compassionately, to stress the close communal bond between humans and cattle, and to encourage people to interpret the pestilence as retribution for the abuse of animals.[28] In some ways, these changes were continuous with trends that began in the seventeenth century, but they went further: people were emboldened to question the prayers offered in response to the outbreak because they failed to take note of animal suffering, and some went so far as to call on God to suspend the punishment of humans on the animals' behalf, as did a hymn composed by John Mason Neale in 1866. The hymn provoked opposition at the time from clergy who felt it went too far in blurring the distinction between men and brutes and distracted from the distress that the pestilence caused to humans, but as Hardwick shows, Neale's impulse to intervene with God on behalf of the cattle was representative of a broader trend.

Why did this particular cattle plague provoke a different kind of religious response from earlier outbreaks? Apart from the scale of the animal suffering involved, another factor at work was the success by that point of an organized effort in England to prevent the abuse of animals. Earlier centuries had seen the introduction of anti–animal cruelty legislation, but the campaign to protect animals through legal reforms had taken off by the time of the cattle plague of 1865. In 1751, the painter William Hogarth published a series of prints under the title *The Four Stages of Cruelty*, meant to expose the barbaric treatment of animals in the streets of London; and in the following years, the cause was embraced by religious leaders such as Humphrey Primatt, author of a *Dissertation on the Duty of Divine Mercy and the Sin of Cruelty to Brute Animals* (1776), a foundational document in the movement to prevent cruelty to animals. Such efforts soon led to legal changes.[29] The nineteenth century brought major legislative victories in this regard, like Martin's Act, a law passed by the British Parliament in 1822 that made it illegal to inflict unnecessary suffering on cattle, and then thirty years later, the Grammont Act of 1850, the first French law against animal cruelty, which prohibited the abuse of domestic animals in public.

The shift is also reflected in literature and art from the period—cruelty to animals became a prominent theme in nineteenth-century fiction by the likes of the Brontë sisters, Charles Dickens, and Thomas

Hardy, as well as in painting and photography.[30] The same change was at work within the Church of England, and the cattle plague of 1865 can be seen as another watershed moment in this regard, reviving theological discussion of the question of whether animals have souls and, as in Neale's case, provoking the composition of prayers and hymns that were not just sympathetic to cattle but called for divine intervention to rescue them from their suffering.[31] Even animal advocates did not put animals on the same level as humans, but in the wake of the political and cultural changes underway, heightened sensitivity to animal suffering penetrated ever more deeply into mainstream popular culture in the second half of the nineteenth century. Yet another critical catalyst in this regard was the publication of Charles Darwin's *On the Origin of Species* in 1859, and then *The Expression of Emotions in Man and Animals* in 1871, works that championed the idea that animals suffer and feel emotions in ways that are not just similar to what humans experience but biologically and genealogically related.

The changing status of animals in this period had an impact on people's understanding of the Bible, and in turn, biblical interpretation played an important role in disseminating these ideas to a Christian public. Like other social reform movements of the era, early animal welfare organizations like the Society for the Prevention of Cruelty to Animals were grounded in Christianity, and their reliance on the Bible as a source of inspiration and guidance posed something of a dilemma because of its endorsement of violence against animals. But precisely for this reason, some animal activists thought it important to show that the Bible also counseled or even required compassion toward animals. An example is an 1880 work for Sunday school teachers called *The Biblical Museum*, which explains "the righteous man" in Proverbs 12:10, who "knows the life of his animal," as a person who "tries to know the feelings and life even of the brute beast . . . especially the animal that in any way renders him service."[32]

By this period, compassion and pity for animals had evolved in some corners into a recognition that animals have a *right* not to be tortured or killed unnecessarily. One of the earliest expressions of this idea comes from a philosophical book about horses by the writer John

Lawrence (1753–1839); the concept was soon embraced by prominent figures like the philosopher Arthur Schopenhauer (1788–1860) and the diplomat Henry Bergh (1813–1888), founder of the American Society for the Prevention of Cruelty to Animals; and by the end of the nineteenth century, it too had made its way into biblical interpretation.[33] In an explanation of Deuteronomy 25:4 ("Do not muzzle the ox while it is treading out the grain"), the theologian Theodore Munger, author of *The Rights of Dumb Animals* (1898), explained that the law reflected not only compassion for the laboring oxen but a recognition of a hard-won right: the oxen have earned a claim to the grain because they worked to produce it. The very purpose of this law, he continued, was "to teach Jews that animals have rights which men are bound to respect."[34]

Although most early animal welfare activists were Christian, it is important for understanding the reinterpretation of the fifth plague in our own era that some were Jewish, such as Lewis Gompertz (1783–1861), a founding member of the Society for the Prevention of Cruelty to Animals and author of an early important book on the subject, *Moral Inquiries on the Situation of Man and of Brutes*. Such was the influence of the animal rights movement among European Jews in this period that the Yiddish and Hebrew writer Sholem Yankev Abramovitsh (also known as Mendele Mocher Sforim), in an 1873 novella called "The Mare," identified the movement with the Haskalah itself, a campaign to persuade Jews to embrace modern secular culture. The story tells of a young Westernized Jew named Isrolik who tries to intervene when he sees a group of Russian bullies tormenting a mare, feeling the animal has a "right" to his assistance. Isrolik appeals to the Russian Society for the Protection of Animals to intervene but soon learns that it refuses to help until the mare learns to behave in a way that is worthy of their commiseration, and that response eventually drives him mad. The tale depicts the Russian animal welfare movement as hypocritical, imperious, and callous, but it also registers what drew Jews to the cause: a feeling of solidarity with animals suffering abuse from a cruel society. For Abramovitsh himself, the sense of identification with abused animals was so strong, and so personal, that he went on to write an autobiographical piece called *The Book of Cattle* in which he recalls protecting an orphaned heifer from mistreatment only to make himself a target.[35]

Where this history eventually intersects with the interpretive history of the ten plagues is the twentieth-century Passover Haggadah. God's killing of animals during the exodus began to be experienced as a moral embarrassment by Jewish animal rights activists, vegetarians, and vegans who wanted to celebrate Passover but had to figure out what to do about the part of the story that involved the killing and sacrifice of animals. It was one thing to remove meat from the Seder—people came up with various vegetarian or vegan substitutes for the lamb shank bone and egg traditionally displayed on the Seder plate[36]—but it was another challenge altogether to remove the killing of animals from the Passover narrative, as the Haggadah is thoroughly implicated in the killing of cattle. In addition to the references to the cattle plague, there is also the service's commemoration of the Passover sacrifice of lambs in the Temple, not to mention the singing of "Chad Gadya" near the end of the Seder, an Aramaic song that begins by recalling a goat being eaten by a cat, followed a few rounds later by an ox being slaughtered by a butcher.

One of the most influential responses to these ethical challenges is *Haggadah for the Liberated Lamb*, published in 1988 by the Jewish animal rights activist and poet Roberta Kalechofsky.[37] Kalechofsky's Haggadah draws on midrash to transform the exodus into a story of animal liberation. In one midrashically inspired passage, her version of the Haggadah makes compassion for animal suffering a defining trait of Moses's role as savior. The passage explains that when the prophet was a shepherd, he once had to chase a lamb that had run away. When he found it drinking at a pool of water, he realized that it had been driven by thirst and must now be tired from its flight, so he put it on his shoulders and carried it back. In a move that aligned the animal liberation movement with the exodus itself, Kalechofsky's Haggadah explains that Moses's effort to save a lamb is what inspired God to choose him to lead Israel out of slavery.

Kalechofsky also included a rabbinic story about an encounter between Judah the Patriarch, the sage credited with producing the Mishnah, and a calf on its way to being sacrificed. Turning to the rabbi for help, the calf could not have been more pitiable, hanging his head on the edges of the rabbi's garment and weeping, but the rabbi was unmoved and dismissed the calf with the words, "Go! For this purpose you were created." The rabbi's response was so heartless that God sent a series of afflictions against him until the rabbi had learned his lesson: seeing his maidservant sweeping baby weasels out of his house, Judah feels moved to protect the animals, and his merciful intervention on their behalf moves God to have mercy on him in turn (b. Bava Metzi'a 85a). *The Liberated Lamb* does not, like the earlier interpretations we have considered in previous sections, merely render animals in a sympathetic light but advocates for intervention to stop the killing of animals as a fulfillment of how God wants animals to be treated.

Given these efforts to inscribe compassion and activism for animals into the experience of the Seder, how does the Haggadah approach the part of the exodus story in which God himself kills animals to liberate Israel? Kalechofsky was not willing to remove the recitation of the ten plagues altogether, including the plague of cattle, but she did insert additions that reframe the story. The title of the Haggadah itself transforms the sacrificial lamb of Exodus 12 into an animal that is being rescued from death, and Kalechofsky also appended to the plagues section a story about another biblical plague that, in her reading, dramatizes God's disapproval of meat eating. The episode in question comes from the book of Numbers (11:31–34), the story of how God sends a plague to punish the Israelites after they eat quail that has been blown into their camp by the wind. Kalechofsky treats the episode as a warning against eating meat in general.

The Liberated Lamb did not expand on the fifth plague, but it laid the groundwork for a later version of the Haggadah that does. The Haggadah in question was produced by Jewish Veg, a nonprofit with the mission of persuading Jews to embrace a plant-based diet as an expression of their Jewish values. Adorned with a cover that shows a young girl gently kissing a lamb, the *Vegan Haggadah* goes a step beyond *The Liberated Lamb* by equating the plagues with the suffering that society causes animals. The plague of blood is associated with the pollution of the waters with blood and animal waste generated by the animal agricultural industry, while the tenth plague conveys how "calves are taken immediately from their mothers in the dairy industry [and as a result], cows, who love and care for their young, must suffer the intense pain of loss for them." The Haggadah reimagines the death of Egypt's cattle in a similar way: "The animals that the Egyptians relied on for their labor, travel, food, and many aspects of everyday life grew sick and suffered under the hardheartedness of the Pharaoh."[38]

We have seen interpretations from earlier centuries that show compassion for the cattle of Egypt and lament their death, but they do not call out their deaths as unjust, still subordinating the interest of the animals to that of God and the Israelites. What distinguishes the retelling of the *Vegan Haggadah* from earlier empathetic accounts is its refusal to recognize anything redemptive about the death of the cattle: the only lesson to learn from the episode is to feel obligated to fight the abuse of farm animals today by boycotting the poultry and egg industries.

What I have not found an example of is a retelling of the fifth plague where the cattle are imagined speaking for themselves. This has always been a curse for cattle; as noted by the philosopher Vinciane Despret, this inability to communicate their views in a form that humans can understand has condemned sheep and other animals to a fate of being mistaken as passive beings without opinions of their own.[39] So far, no one has figured out how to bridge the communication divide, but some have used observation, empathy, and imagination to reconstruct what is going on inside the minds of cows and other domestic animals, ascribing to them intelligence, emotional sensitivity, a complex social life, and self-awareness.[40] I have yet to find a version of the fifth plague where someone has conferred that high degree of personhood on the cattle of Egypt, but some activists have come close by recognizing the cattle as a "who" rather than a "that," and by associating their deaths with modern-day violations of animal rights.

6

The Sixth Plague

HABITS OF A HARDENED HEART

AS THE COVID-19 pandemic spread around the globe, researchers struggled to understand why so many people were reluctant to accept social distancing and other health measures. One of the factors they identified, beyond the impact of conspiracy theories and distrust of government, was a widespread feeling of fatalism, a sense of powerlessness. People came to believe that there was nothing they could do to protect themselves from the disease, and that belief, valid or not, had dire real-world consequences. Researchers estimated that this "fatalism effect," people giving up on health measures out of a sense of inevitability, cost the U.S. economy billions of dollars.[1]

While the pandemic was spreading feelings of futility, however, it also revealed that people have a deep need to feel in control of their lives. Another study showed that within days of the global shutdown, people were finding ways to reassert their autonomy—creating new routines, seeking out learning opportunities, and adopting Zoom in order to connect with others, all in the effort to restore the sense of self-control they were accustomed to feeling and exercising.[2] Feeling trapped and perceiving a loss of control could induce depression, and many sought to counteract such feelings by asserting even more agency over their lives than had been the case before the pandemic, resolving to become more deliberate, mindful, and self-determining in their behavior.

The experience of powerlessness in the face of an overwhelming force comes to the fore in Exodus's description of the sixth plague. Already by the time of the second plague, Pharaoh is beginning to bend to God's power and declares himself ready to let the Israelites go in exchange for God removing the frogs. It is clear, however, that he is not completely defeated. He hardens his heart again as soon as the plague is removed, as he does after the third, fourth, and fifth plagues as well. The Bible does not have much to say about the sixth plague, a plague of boils that spreads out across the entire land of Egypt, but what it does suggest is that it was even more debilitating than the other plagues. Pharaoh's magicians, in their very last appearance in the biblical account, not only make no attempt to reproduce the plague: they can no longer even stand up before Moses (Exodus 9:11). Pharaoh too seems completely overwhelmed by the plague—this time, for the first time, Exodus makes no mention of him hardening his heart after it comes to an end.

The fact that Pharaoh does not simply let the Israelites go at this point brings us to a major twist in the biblical account: at the very moment when the king loses the will to resist, God intervenes to take control of his reaction, again hardening his heart and compelling him to renew his resistance to Moses. This is a puzzling moment. If the whole point of the plagues was to force the Egyptians to comply, why would God want Pharaoh to keep refusing? Why prolong the suffering of the Israelites more than was necessary? And why make Pharaoh more obstinate than he needed to be? In an earlier moment in Exodus 7, before any of the plagues, God had revealed to Moses that he was going to harden Pharaoh's heart so that he would refuse to free the Israelites, creating an opening for God to multiply his signs and wonders and thereby demonstrate the extent of his power. The sixth plague is the moment in the story when God intervenes in this way, and if God had this kind of control over Pharaoh's response, why not assert it earlier, and why do so now in a way that only thwarted the goal of freeing the Israelites?

The verse is also perplexing because of what it suggests about the relationship between human will and God's power. It was one thing for Pharaoh not to be able to stand up to the overwhelming power of the plagues and all the pain and destruction they imposed, but Exodus 9:12

reveals a whole new level of powerlessness. Pharaoh cannot defy God because he isn't even in control of his own response and decision-making, acting under the compulsion not of external violence but of something intervening internally in what the Bible refers to as Pharaoh's "heart," the part of the self that reacts to input from the external world, forms intentions, and makes decisions. This remains the case for the rest of the plagues. From the sixth plague forward, after each remaining plague, the biblical account reports that the Lord hardened Pharaoh's heart—this is true even after the tenth plague when it seems to be God who impels Pharaoh to send his army chasing after the Israelites to the Red Sea—and there is no clear indication in Exodus that the king was ever again acting of his own volition, according to what he himself would have decided to do if God had not intervened to redirect his response.

This twist in the ten plagues story caught the attention of both Jewish and Christian readers of the story because it raised questions about the extent of human agency in a world controlled by an all-powerful God. If, as Exodus 9:12 suggests, God controls people's thoughts, or at least does so whenever he has reason to steer them in a particular direction, does that mean that the human mind is not truly free, that our feeling of authoring our own actions is an illusion? If that is the case, why then does God address humans as if they were independent agents? Why does he demand that they choose to obey him, and why does he hold them accountable when they make wrong choices? To some, it seemed profoundly unfair that God held Pharaoh to account for his actions when God was the one who made Pharaoh hard-hearted, and no less unfair that God might hold us to account if we are simply thinking, acting, and responding as God, pursuing his own plans for the world, wants us to think, act, and respond. Others maintained that Pharaoh did have some measure of genuine self-determining autonomy during the first five plagues—why else would the biblical text report that he hardened his own heart?—but wondered how to square that freedom with the control that God asserts over Pharaoh during the remaining plagues.

Jewish and Christian interpreters wanted to understand what motivated the switch from "Pharaoh hardened his heart," which appears after each of the first five plagues, to "the Lord hardened his heart," which appears in the remainder of the narrative, as a way of better understanding the biblical story itself, but they had another goal as well—to make sense of their own contradictory position in the world as autonomous beings with the power to make decisions and shape what happens next yet whose thoughts and actions, like everything else in the universe, must also be determined by an all-powerful God. The hardened-heart subplot in Exodus was thought not only to register this contradiction but to hold a key to making sense of it, and that has led to many interpretations and retellings of the story that use the figure of Pharaoh—and whatever change was signified by the switch to "the Lord hardened his heart"—to work out the relationship between the "fatalism effect" and the human need to feel in control.

Pharaoh's Heart Philosophized

Philosophers today use the expression "the free will / determinism debate" to refer to an intellectual debate about whether humans are genuinely autonomous or merely think they are. If all events in the universe are determined by preceding events, how is it possible for humans to be exempt from this determinism? How can their intentions and decisions be truly voluntary and self-directing if the body and mind are subject to the same cause and effect that govern the rest of reality? For people who believe in God, the idea that people are free to make their own decisions and determine their own fate, to act independently of external compulsion, led to theological puzzles as well. If humans are truly independent, deciding on their own what they are going to do, how does that not compromise and limit God's power? How can free will and divine omnipotence coexist if human autonomy means that God has less control over the world? And finally, there is a moral dimension to the debate as well; if people act as they do out of necessity or under the control of God, how can they be judged as good or evil, praiseworthy or damnable? How can it be fair to punish people who are only acting as they are compelled to act?

The contradictions that drive the free will / determinism debate do not surface as major concerns in the Hebrew Bible. Its authors recognized a tension between human desire and divine control, and between the unpredictable contingency introduced by human decision-making and God's plans for Israel and humanity, but they did not frame those tensions as philosophical problems to be investigated and debated. Ancient Greek philosophers, by contrast, explicitly took up these puzzles and contradictions, and the various conclusions they reached partly distinguished philosophical schools like Stoicism and Epicureanism from one another. During the Hellenistic period that followed the conquests of Alexander the Great, ancient Jews were exposed to these different schools of thought, and that encouraged a new kind of attention to the Bible—Jews reading it in ways that either increased the space for human free will or shrank it.

Indeed, if we accept the testimony of Josephus, the first-century CE, Greek-writing Jewish historian, the question of how much control individuals had over their fate was one of the major points of contention among the most prominent religious parties in Jerusalem during the Hellenistic and Roman periods: the Essenes, the Sadducees, and the Pharisees. According to Josephus, the Essenes, a relatively small group that had settlements of its own throughout Judea, had a deterministic perspective on the world, believing that fate governed all human affairs. The Sadducees, a faction of high priests and aristocratic families, were theological "libertarians" in modern parlance, emphasizing humans' power to choose between good and evil. The Pharisees, the most popular of these groups, subscribed to a compromise position, what modern philosophers call compatibilism, acknowledging that humans are subject to fate but have some measure of control as well (Josephus, *Antiquities* 13.171–173).[3] Josephus presented his people in terms that Hellenized readers would find relatable, and it is possible that he was exaggerating the similarity between the sects of Judaism and Greek philosophical schools, but scholars have learned from the Dead Sea Scrolls, Philo, and Josephus himself that Jews from this period did develop views similar to and in some cases demonstrably influenced by Greek thought.

At this early point, however, there is little evidence that this debate had an impact on how Jews interpreted Pharaoh's hardened heart. The versions of the ten plagues story found in Jubilees, Philo, and the Dead

Sea Scrolls simply omit phrases and verses in the Exodus account that were at odds with their respective views. In the version of the story in Jubilees, God is in control of everything that happens. It is the demon Mastema, not God, who instigates the Egyptians to persecute the Israelites, but Mastema is unaware that he was only doing what God and his angels permitted him to do: even demonic resistance to God is divinely controlled in this version of the story. This version of the story simply does not wrestle with the phrases that seem to imply that Pharaoh was making decisions on his own during the first five plagues, nor does it make any effort to account for the switch to "The Lord hardened his heart" after the sixth. A retelling of the exodus story found among the Dead Sea Scrolls moved the story in a similar direction by telling of how God hardened the heart of Pharaoh from the start of the plagues (as opposed to only after the fifth plague), a change that saps Pharaoh of the self-determining power he seems to assert in the first plagues while accentuating God's control throughout the plagues.[4]

Falling at the libertarian end of the free will / determinism debate was Philo of Alexandria, who believed that humans have free will notwithstanding God's control over the universe. In his account of the exodus in *The Life of Moses,* Philo removed the parts of the story where God intervenes to harden Pharaoh's heart, leaving the king in charge of his own responses throughout. The authors of such sources were pulling the biblical story in the direction of their own determinist or libertarian positions, but they did not draw conclusions from Pharaoh's example about the larger theological and moral issues at stake, and none wrestled with or even acknowledged the shift that Exodus registers from a Pharaoh who hardens his own heart to a Pharaoh whose heart is hardened by God. Each used the retelling of the story not to explain but to mask the switch from one to the other and thereby evaded the puzzlement that it provokes.

There is, however, one text that focuses attention on the hardened-heart language of Exodus, and it became quite important in later Christian debates about free will. The passage in question comes from chapter 9 of the New Testament's Letter to the Romans, where Paul, the earliest known author to interpret Jesus's life, death, and role in the human-divine relationship, is responding to a story in Genesis in which God chooses Jacob over his twin brother, Esau, while they are still in the womb. Since neither brother had even been born yet, much less done anything good or bad, it might seem unfair that God favored one over the other, but one should not doubt God's justice, Paul insists. God shows mercy to whom he shows mercy for reasons of his own, and it is not for people to understand his reasoning or to think that they can do something themselves to win God's favor.

By the same token, Paul continues, God chooses to make some people hard-hearted at his own discretion too. As Paul reads the exodus story, Pharaoh was created by God for the very purpose of being hard-hearted; he did not choose this disposition on his own but was made that way by God in order to help accomplish God's purposes.[5] Paul's reference to the story is very brief, but as part of the Christian Bible, Romans had much more influence than Jubilees or Philo, and this passage would become central in later Christian debate over free will. On the surface, it would seem to place Paul on the fatalistic end of the free will / determinism debate, suggesting that God predetermined Pharaoh's hard-heartedness for his own mysterious reasons, but that did not stop later Christians from wanting to carve out some room for human self-determination within God's plan nonetheless, and Paul's language was vague enough in its own right to allow proponents of both deterministic and compatibilist arguments to align it with their perspectives.

These are the sources we have from before 100 CE, and they suggest that Jews and Christians at that point did not take much interest in the story for what it might teach about the free will / determinism debate, though the debate itself was familiar to some of them. This situation changed in the third century, however—in following centuries the story became a major scriptural touchstone in the debate—and the catalyst was the early Christian philosopher Origen of Alexandria (ca. 185–253 CE), the most brilliant Christian scholar before Augustine.

Origen's distinctions include being the first thinker to develop a Christian theory of free will, and in developing this theory, he found a way to reinterpret Paul's seemingly deterministic perspective to allow Pharaoh—and by extension all humans—a role in shaping their fate.

According to Origin, God does not decide to make some people good and others evil. A good and loving God would never want to make someone evil—to the contrary, he always wants to be merciful to people across the board. But by endowing humans with rationality, the ability to reason and to make a decision, God endowed them with freedom, and it was therefore for human beings to choose for themselves whether they are going to be open to that mercy or resist it. God's intervention with Pharaoh was as merciful as it was with every person, but humans have it within their power to decide how to respond to that intervention, and Pharaoh made the wrong choice by refusing to obey Moses, turning divine mercy into hard-heartedness. Why the king responded in that way is not something Origen explains, but the choice to accept or resist God was Pharaoh's to make, and he can therefore be held accountable for the consequences even though it was also true that his hard-heartedness was the result of an act of divine intervention.

Though Origen was posthumously declared a heretic, his effort to reconcile Paul's views with free will had a major impact on the thinking of later Christians.[6] In the following centuries, Christians would turn again and again to the story of Pharaoh's hardened heart to try to work out whether humans have self-determining power in a world controlled by an all-powerful and all-knowing God. In fact, at certain points in Christian history, the story became a flashpoint in intra-Christian debates over free will, and the positions staked out in such debates often referenced Origen's reading of Paul's reading of Pharaoh's hard-heartedness.

One such flashpoint was a theological controversy that pitted Augustine, positioned close to the deterministic end of the spectrum, against a monk named Pelagius, who was a theological libertarian. Augustine believed that the sin of Adam and Eve in the Garden of Eden was freely undertaken but had had a highly damaging effect on the human soul and mind, especially the will, and when Adam and Eve had children, they passed this damaged will to them as a biological-spiritual inheritance, making it impossible for them to form the desires and intentions needed to reason properly or make good choices. The resulting corruption of human nature, perverting people's free will into defiance and transgression, would have condemned all of humankind to destruction were it not for God's graciousness in giving humanity a chance to rid itself of the sin inherited from Adam and Eve through the sacrifice of his son, but humans must overcome their corrupted wills and submit themselves fully to God to secure such forgiveness.

This is the famous doctrine of original sin that became so important to later Christian theology, but Pelagius, a British or Celtic theologian who lived between 354 and 410, rejected the idea. In his view, people's natures were not determined by what they had inherited from Adam and Eve but rather remained open-ended. It is in their power to choose to do good and evil, which means in turn that their ultimate salvation is in their own hands and does not depend on God rescuing them from sinful urges they cannot control through their own decision-making.

Thanks to a sermon discovered in 1903—which, if not written by Pelagius himself, was composed by a follower of his—we know that Pharaoh's hardened heart played an important role in the effort to justify Pelagianism.[7] Known as *On the Hardening of Pharaoh's Heart*, the sermon represents another attempt to carve out a space for self-determination within the parameters established by Paul and Origen. Yes, God hardened Pharaoh's heart, but this act did not mean that God intervened to harden a heart that wasn't already hard. Pharaoh's heart had already been hardened through his own evil actions, and God merely completed that process, not by intervening to take control of Pharaoh's heart but by the opposite, fully relinquishing control so that Pharaoh's heart would be left fully exposed to the devil. In this reading, the phrase "The Lord hardened Pharaoh's heart" did not mark the end of Pharaoh's autonomy; in fact, it made him even more free than before by completely liberating Pharaoh from divine influence. Of course, as we know from how things turned out according to Exodus, Pharaoh doubled down on his bad choices, but even so, it always remained within his power to change course, to *un*harden his heart, and that, in fact, is what happens in the sermon's version of the story: the king eventually recognizes God as his maker and repents, a development inferred from what Pharaoh says to Moses in Exodus 9:27: "I have sinned this time: the Lord is the one in the right."

Pelagianism did not persist beyond the sixth century—in part because it was declared a heresy in 418 by a council that Augustine convened in Carthage—but that did not mean that the story of Pharaoh's hardened heart lost its importance as part of intra-Christian debates about the autonomy of the will in a world controlled by God. Another highly consequential conflict over the meaning of "The Lord hardened Pharaoh's heart" broke out in the early sixteenth century, and it happened to involve two of the most important thinkers in the emergence of modernity and modern Christianity: Erasmus (1469–1536), a scholar who personifies the Northern Renaissance and humanism, and Martin Luther (1483–1546), whose religious dissent fomented the rise of Protestant Christianity. Erasmus expressed his views, which amount to a version of theological libertarianism, in a work called *On the Freedom of the Will* in 1524, while Luther responded a year later with *The Bondage of the Will*, in which he argued that the soul was entirely enslaved to God. Such was the impact of this debate that it has been described as the very moment when Renaissance humanism and the Reformation went their separate ways.[8]

The debate between Erasmus and Luther made explicit a struggle between two different concepts of the will developing among intellectuals at the time. Some emphasized the will as a powerful agent and driver of human behavior, while others became distrustful of the will, emphasizing its weakness.[9] The Catholic Church settled on an in-between position known as synergism, which envisioned a path to salvation through a combination of free will and divine grace, but many contested that compromise position. In the debate between Erasmus and Luther, the former aligned himself with the Catholic perspective, while the latter broke with the Catholic view by treating the will as a captive of a dark force beyond its control.

Because Erasmus decided to confine himself to using Scripture as his evidence, a good portion of *On the Freedom of the Will* was devoted to compiling biblical verses that seemed to endorse the idea of free will. But he also had to address biblical passages that seemed to contradict the idea, and that included, first and foremost, the story of Pharaoh's hardened heart as interpreted by Paul. While Paul's reading of the story, on its face, seems to negate any role for the human will in a person's salvation, Erasmus countered that understanding of Paul by invoking Origen's interpretation of the story: "The Lord hardened Pharaoh's heart" means not that God hardened his heart in a way that overruled Pharaoh's freedom of choice but merely that he created an occasion for Pharaoh to exercise a choice about how to behave. An all-knowing God foresaw what Pharaoh was going to do, but Pharaoh was created with a will that could turn either way. He made his choice and bears responsibility for the resulting punishment.

Luther rejected these arguments and added many insults too. Free will, as he saw it, is like the empty titles that kings claim for themselves: it is supposed to elicit deference but confers no actual power. One can tolerate such titles in a king because no one is really deceived by them, but "free will" is a different matter because it gives rise to the dangerous illusion that God is less than omnipotent. The concept of free will imposes a limit on God's power even as it exaggerates the power of the human will, which is so feeble that it is unable to control what it wills or to stop itself from willing. Luther compares the will to a beast of burden caught between two masters: If God rides it, it goes where God wills. If Satan, it goes where Satan wills. It cannot choose to go to one rider or the other; it can only go in the direction its rider sets for it.

Luther went on to explain that by hardening Pharaoh's heart, God was merely revealing the nature of a person already destined to be evil. Pharaoh's will was driving him along, but it was acting out of necessity, not freely, set on its course by the evil character instilled in Pharaoh and by the reaction that kicks in whenever the will finds itself thwarted in the pursuit of its goals. Why God did not intervene to redirect Pharaoh's will toward the good is a mystery beyond human comprehension, Luther acknowledged, but be that as it may, the Bible's claim that it was the Lord who hardened Pharaoh's heart plainly teaches that his sinfulness was not in any way the result of the Pharaoh's own will, notwithstanding Erasmus's learned efforts to prove otherwise. Pharaoh was never actually free, even when he was acting in defiance of God.

The conflict between Erasmus and Luther did not yield a clear winner, and different theologians responded differently to it. Erasmus's arguments granted so much autonomy to the human will that some of his fellow Catholics wanted to ban his writing. Meanwhile, it didn't take long before some of Luther's fellow Protestant theologians began adjusting his arguments to make more room for free will. The French reformer John Calvin (1509–1564), famous for his association with the idea of predestination, took the biblical story in a deterministic perspective. He rejected the idea that God granted permission to Pharaoh to act on his own will in favor of the idea that God handed Pharaoh over to Satan to further harden his heart, a version of the story in which Pharaoh is never actually in control of his own will but simply passes from the control of God to that of Satan, in line with what Luther had suggested (Calvin, *Institutes of the Christian Religion* 2.4.3–4).[10] But other Protestant theologians tried to bend Luther's position toward a more compatibilist view. Luther's associate Philipp Melanchthon (1497–1560) was one such figure, positing a will too weak to achieve its salvation through its own efforts but free enough at least to make a choice to accept God's words.[11] Calvinism would come to be associated with predestination, the idea that God determines who will be saved and damned, while Melanchthon's effort to allow for some free will went on to play an important role in evangelical theology, and the difference between these different forms of Protestantism was anticipated by how Calvin and Melanchthon understood the hardening-heart motif.[12]

To this day, Christian theologians can still make use of the story of Pharaoh's hardened heart to express different positions on the freedom of the will, and the debate was never resolved for two main reasons. The first has to do with the Bible's ambiguity: the Torah's account is unclear and inconsistent in ways that cannot be definitively pinned down, and Paul's reading of the story in Romans 9, though suggesting that Pharaoh's hard-heartedness was planned by God in advance, did nothing in the long run to conclusively solve the puzzles generated by the Exodus narrative. The second has to do with the inherent irresolvability of the free will / determinism debate itself: neither religious or secular philosophy has been able to resolve the debate, and arguments in one direction or the other inevitably provoke strong counterargument.[13] Thanks to this convergence of biblical opacity and philosophical inconcludability, the figure of Pharaoh has been reshaped in the image of practically every position along the spectrum between determinism and libertarianism, sometimes aligned with one end of the spectrum and sometimes the other but often ending up in the muddled middle between fatalism and complete freedom.

The Unrepentant Heart

Christians were not the only ones who read the story of the ten plagues for insight into the range and limits of human autonomy within a world controlled by God. So too did Jews. Christian and Jewish retellings of the story of Pharaoh's hardened heart differ, in part, due to theological differences between the two communities. But they were also building on different versions of the story inherited from antiquity: whereas Christians read the story in the light of Romans 9 as interpreted in turn by Origen and other church fathers, Jews viewed it through the prism of rabbinic tradition, such as the following midrash that appears in Exodus Rabbah 13.3:

> "For I have hardened his heart" (Exodus 10:1). Rabbi Yochanan said: Doesn't this provide an opening for heretics to say that he was not able to undertake repentance as it says, "For I have hardened his heart." Rabbi Shimon ben Lakish said to him: Let the mouths of the heretics be sealed. . . . When the Holy One Blessed be He warns a man once, twice, three times, and if he does not turn back to him, God will lock up his heart from repentance in order to exact punishment on him for his sins. But with the wicked Pharaoh, God sent five warnings to him and he took heed of the matter. God then said: "You have stiffened your neck and hardened your heart; so I will add defilement to your defilement." And thus [it is possible to understand], "For I have hardened his heart." What does "I have hardened (*hikhbadti*)" mean? The Holy One blessed be He made his heart like a liver (*kaved*) where liquid cannot penetrate it even if you boil it twice. Thus the heart of Pharaoh became like the liver, unable to receive the words of the Lord.

When the Torah reports that the Lord "hardened" Pharaoh's heart, what it means according to this midrash is that he turned his heart into a liver, an organ thought to be extremely impermeable—the joke turns on the fact that the verb "harden" has the same root letters as the Hebrew word for "liver." Beyond humiliating Pharaoh with a clever pun, however, the midrash has the more serious goal of addressing a deeply disturbing question raised by the biblical account. By hardening Pharaoh's heart, God had stripped him of the ability to repent of his sins. Why would a deity who wants people to be good and is known for being merciful and forgiving have stopped an evil human being from having a change of heart and doing the right thing?

The world as the rabbis conceived it required both justice and mercy—a sin-prone humankind would have been destroyed long ago if it had been governed by justice alone—and repentance was meant to keep the world going by making it possible for humans to appeal to divine mercy and allay God's punishment. But repentance required free will, the ability to decide to stop sinning and choose a better course, and what is disturbing about the ten plagues story from this perspective is the idea that God took away Pharaoh's power to repent, condemning him to punishment even though Pharaoh was ready to relent and might have been forgiven. The heretics mentioned in the midrash may be Gnostics or members of some other sect using this problem in the biblical story to claim that the God of the Jews was not a good or loving God.

In addressing this challenge, what the midrash comes up with is yet another kind of compatibilism, not just a compromise between free will and divine control but also a compromise between divine mercy and divine justice. The Yochanan cited in the midrash worries that heretics will seize on God's claim to have hardened Pharaoh's heart as proof that God does not want people, or rather non-Jews, to repent. Shimon ben Lakish aims to allay Yochanan's concern by showing that, in fact, God gave Pharaoh not one chance or even three chances (as is God's wont) but *five* chances to repent by warning him during the first five plagues. He did finally intervene to harden Pharaoh's heart, foreclosing the possibility of forgiveness by depriving him of any further opportunity to repent but only after going well beyond what he normally does to give people a chance to change course. Pharaoh had it in his power to relent, God warned him multiple times to do so, and only after the king repeatedly disregarded such opportunities did God finally withdraw the possibility of forgiveness.

Just as Paul's reference to hardened hearts shaped subsequent Christian interpretation, this midrash influenced later medieval Jewish interpretation. It helped make repentance important to how later Jews would understand the story, and it also called attention to the sixth plague as a fatal turning point in Pharaoh's narrative when he becomes unredeemable.

The single most influential elaboration of this way of retelling the story within Jewish tradition was developed by the medieval physician, philosopher, and Torah scholar Moses Maimonides, who was born in Spain in 1138, died in Egypt in 1204, and came to be regarded as the greatest medieval Jewish philosopher. To better understand what Maimonidies did with this tradition, however, it will first help to note another factor distinguishing Jewish from Christian interpretations of this theme—the impact of Islam on how medieval Jews understood the Torah.

During the Middle Ages, the majority of the world's Jewish population lived in Islamic contexts where the free will / determinism debate was such a major point of theological contention that Muslim theologians, influenced by Aristotle and other Greek philosophers, split into different schools of thought over the topic.[14] Early on, there developed two main schools of thought—the libertarian school of Qadariyya and the deterministic Jabariyya school—with other schools emerging thereafter. Jewish scholars living in Islamic lands, including Saadia ben Josef, Bayya ibn Pequda, and Maimonides, developed their views under the influence of this debate. While they used the Bible rather than the Qur'an to express their views, they nevertheless drew on what Muslim scholars had to say about the Qur'anic Pharaoh and his ability to repent.[15]

The portrait of Pharaoh in the Qur'an is different from the Pharaoh of Exodus, but it presents its own share of ambiguities and puzzles. In the Qur'an, for example, there comes a moment when Pharaoh seems to repent and declare his belief in God—not during the plagues but as he is drowning in the Red Sea (10:90). If Pharaoh repented before his death, commentators wondered, why does the Qur'an go on to report that he drowned in the sea. Many commentators concluded that Pharaoh's repentance must have been too late to save him, or insincere, motivated by self-preservation rather than by true faith, but the wording of the Qur'an was vague enough to allow for the possibility that he had indeed repented, and some believed that he was spared from death—this was the view of the great Andalusian mystic and poet Al-Arabi (1165–1240).[16]

This latter position influenced how some Jews understood the biblical account. As the scholar Arnon Atzmon has demonstrated, earlier midrash originating from the Christian Byzantine Empire rejected the idea that Pharaoh repented in the end—the midrash in Exodus Rabbah cited earlier falls into this camp—but later midrash composed within the Islamic orbit can assert that Pharaoh repented and survived.[17] Islamic influence is also reflected in how Jews understood the hardened-heart theme. Maimonides, for instance, developed his views of Pharaoh's closed heart under the influence not just of the midrash cited earlier but also of Qur'anic commentators like the tenth-century jurist Abu al-Layth al-Samarqandi.[18]

Maimonides was a theological compatibilist, finding a way to reconcile God's control over the world with human self-determination. A follower of Aristotle, he believed in the determining effect of causality, but he also regarded freedom of the will as "the pillar of the Torah," arguing that it was an essential prerequisite for the entire system of mitzvot, or divine commands, at the core of Jews' relationship with God. If the Israelites lacked the ability to choose between right and wrong, what would have been the point of giving them commandments in the first place? And why would God have spent so much time warning the Israelites not to sin and calling on them to repent if they didn't have the ability to choose to take a different course? Repentance, he believed, is an especially important way that the mind asserts its freedom, giving humans the ability to shape their fate through the recognition of sin and the decision to change.[19]

In line with this compatibilist perspective, Maimonides developed a version of Pharaoh's story that, like the midrash in Exodus Rabbah, begins with Pharaoh able to exercise free will and ends with the king forfeiting that power. When the Torah refers to the Lord hardening Pharaoh's heart, Maimonides claims, it is referring to the moment when Pharaoh loses the capacity to repent that he had during the first five plagues (*Mishneh Torah*, Laws of Repentance 6.3). The philosopher describes Pharaoh's loss as divine retribution, but God's involvement does not mean that he suspended the laws of nature to change Pharaoh's character miraculously. Rather, as the scholar Shira Weiss has explained, Maimonides understood Pharaoh's loss of his free will as a naturally occurring process that took effect after he hardened his own heart too many times.[20]

One of the lessons that Maimonides took from Aristotle was an understanding of how a person can lose free will over time. According to Aristotle, people's choices about how to act can, over time, instill in them a second nature, a newly formed disposition to act in a certain way that shapes their subsequent proclivities (*Nicomachean Ethics* 3.5). We call this habit—a disposition that initially emerges from decisions we make voluntarily, like the decision to smoke or the decision to exercise, but that can come to feel compulsory after a time. One can improve one's character by forming good habits, but the process can also go wrong, ruining a person's character in a way that can become difficult to undo. In fact, individuals can reach a point where, because of how their nature has been reshaped through repeated bad decisions and bad habits, it is no longer possible for them to decide to become better people simply by wanting to do so.[21]

Maimonides drew on the Aristotelian concept of habit to develop an explanation of how God hardened Pharaoh's heart that did not involve the suspension of causality or the laws of nature. There was no miracle involved; the hardening resulted from a simple process of habituation and character formation. Despite warnings from Moses, Pharaoh chose of his own free will to commit sin several times, and by the sixth plague, those decisions had hardened into an evil nature that made it impossible for Pharaoh to change even when he wanted to do so. The shift to "The Lord hardened his heart" marks the point of no return in a process of habituation, a will sapped of its freedom by having repeatedly exercised its freedom in the wrong way.

Like Christian theology, Jewish theology never settled on a single view of how to reconcile free will with divine control of the universe. However, almost all Jewish thinkers who addressed the topic fell somewhere in the compatibilist middle ground between theological determinism and libertarianism, acknowledging God's control while also leaving room for human accountability and repentance. Between the extremes, however, there existed many possible ways of reconciling free will and divine control along the spectrum between determinism and free will, with some commentators minimizing Pharaoh's autonomy while others maximized it.

The French-born Levi ben Gershom, or Gersonides (1288–1344), is representative of those interpreters who fell closer to the determinist pole. Gersonides's understanding of the Torah was grounded in what he learned through writing a commentary on the Muslim philosopher Averroës (or Ibn Rushd, 1126–1198), who emphasized God's omnipotence at the expense of human freedom,[22] and he came to embrace a version of determinism known as astral determinism. According to this theory, the cosmos is governed by the "active intellect," an Aristotelian term for the divine mind that exerts its influence through astral bodies whose motions have an effect on the material world, including the human body and mind. A person's temperament is determined by the position of the stars at the moment of birth, and astral influences continue to direct a person's thoughts throughout their life.[23] Yet despite this belief in the controlling influence of the stars, Gersonides also saw ways to overcome the influence of the stars through the exercise of reason. Non-Jews, he believed, could cultivate their reasoning power—and hence their power to overcome astral influence—through the study of philosophy and astrology, while Jews could achieve it by studying and following the laws of the Torah.

In Gersonides's version of Pharaoh's story, when Pharaoh appears to be hardening his own heart during the first five plagues—that is, acting on his own free will—it is really the influence of the stars at work, as they have determined his character, predisposing him to behave in a wicked way. In contrast to Maimonides's reading of the first five plagues, in other words, Gersonides's reading is deterministic, ascribing

Pharaoh's hard-hearted response to the plagues to astral influence. Despite being compelled to be hard-hearted, however, Pharaoh still had a choice about how to behave. His astral-based temperament inclined him to respond in a certain way, but the stars were not completely deterministic: he still could have exercised his reason to counter their effects. This is the situation until the sixth plague, at which point, according to Gersonides's version of the story, the active intellect stopped Pharaoh from repenting in order to ensure that events went in the direction that would advance Israel's spiritual development.

Representing a more libertarian perspective is the reading advanced by Joseph Albo, a Jewish philosopher from Christian Spain who lived at the end of the Middle Ages (1380–1444). Albo's most important work is *The Book of Principles*, or *Sefer ha ʿikkarum*, which was completed in 1425 but not published until 1485, when it appeared as one of the first works of Jewish philosophy to be disseminated through the printing press.[24]

Albo flipped the midrashic version of the story on its head. During the first five plagues in Albo's version of the story, Pharaoh isn't making his own decisions: he is operating under the extreme duress created by the plagues, like a disobedient slave being beaten by his master. When it seems like he is on the verge of relenting, that is only because he is motivated by pain and fear; as soon as the beating is over, as soon as the plague subsides, he reverts back to his wickedness. This is what Pharaoh does after each of the first five plagues. What happens when God hardens Pharaoh's heart, according to Albo, is not that God takes away Pharaoh's free will but that he gives him the courage to act on what he really wants to do, an idea that Albo supported by pointing to the Hebrew word used in Exodus 9:12—often translated as "harden" but reflecting a distinct root more literally rendered as "strengthen" (*yehazzeq*). Albo understood the word in this latter sense to mean that God gave Pharaoh a courage he lacked during the first five plagues.

Only after God instills courage in Pharaoh is the king able to act without the fear of being punished, and it is from this point forward, according to Albo, that his responses to Moses reflect a genuinely free will. Of course, Pharaoh ends up making bad decisions, refusing to repent and dooming himself, but the fact that he now has such a choice at all is possible only because God intervenes to end the compulsion Pharaoh experienced during the first five plagues.

Albo's reading of the story points to something that distinguished medieval Jewish readings of Pharaoh's story from those of Christians and Muslims, a difference that reflects their relative social and political positions. Theologians from all three communities were similar in reading the story philosophically in the context of the free will / determinism debate, even influencing each other directly in some cases, but for Jews living under Christian or Muslim rule, the debate was also inflected by their experience as a religious minority. In such circumstances, Jews were subject to the control of other people and vulnerable to physical coercion.

Shira Weiss has suggested that Albo's version of Pharaoh's story was partly a response to the persecution of Jews in Christian Spain during the fifteenth century, an era when Jews and Muslims were coerced into becoming Christians.[25] Albo himself had been forced to participate in a debate with a Jewish convert to Christianity named Geronimo de Santa Fe that was staged as a way to pressure Jews to convert. Indeed, during the debate, hundreds of Jews were forced into the hall and made to declare their conversion to Christianity. In this context, Albo's retelling of Pharaoh's hardened heart can be seen as exposing the problem with coercing people to undergo a change of heart: even pressure from a divine power was not enough to effect a genuine change in Pharaoh, whose heart was hardened as soon as each plague was over and his fear was gone.

But Albo was not exactly a wholehearted libertarian either. In his version of events, once God liberates Pharaoh from fear, Pharaoh does not repent. Instead, he becomes a heretic, refusing to recognize God's role in the plagues and seeking out "causes and pretexts" to explain how the plagues came about as the result of chance. Fear of punishment does not allow for true repentance, but Pharaoh's behavior after he gains true freedom shows that the complete elimination of fear poses its own threat because it can lead to apostasy. The ideal mindset, according to Albo, is a combination of freedom and fear—not a fear of physical punishment, which eliminates the freedom of thought needed for genuine piety, but what Albo calls the "fear of God," an uncoerced respect for God's power, governance, and justice.

While the earlier compatibilist readings of Maimonides and Gersonides sought to balance human freedom and God's control of the universe, Albo's compatibilism added a new dimension, making room for the freedom of the will but also for the freedom of conscience, the ability to think one's own thoughts without coercion or fear of punishment. Albo recognized that such freedom posed its own danger—being liberated from fear allowed Pharaoh to pursue heretical thoughts—but without it, he was not doing the right thing either because, as someone acting under duress, he was not making decisions that reflected his true convictions or that he would stick to once his fear faded. Whereas midrash and Maimonides had imagined Pharaoh losing his freedom by the sixth plague, Albo believed that was the moment when he gained it, but that did not avail the king, for in Albo's version of the plagues, such freedom, released from external compulsion but also without the internal constraint imposed by faith, ends up self-destructing.

The Self-Hardening Heart

Since the Bible does not play the role in contemporary philosophical culture that it did in premodern Europe, the story of Pharaoh's hardened heart is no longer at the center of the free will / determinism debate. Yet as we will see in one last retelling of Pharaoh's hardened heart—formulated by the philosopher Eleonore Stump in response to a seminal essay on free will by the philosopher Harry Frankfurt—its influence has not entirely disappeared.[26]

Frankfurt's earlier argument, in a nutshell, was that people can be considered to have free will only if they are free to have the will that they want. What many of us mean by a free will is a will that is free to act on its desires and intentions, that is not constrained by some external force or obstacle. But that understanding leaves open a question: How does the will choose which desires to have? Is there not something behind the will that causes it to want what it wants? And is that meta-will, what

Frankfurt calls "second-order" volition, free in its own right? Not all wills want what they want. An alcoholic who wants a drink may not *want* to want a drink. To be free, Frankfurt argued, a will has to be able to choose what it wills, to want to desire what it desires.

Frankfurt's analysis of the will inspired a new approach to Pharaoh's hardened heart developed by Stump, an American philosopher known for enlisting medieval religious thinkers and concepts to address modern philosophical questions. In 1988, she published an essay entitled "Sanctification, Hardening of the Heart, and Frankfurt's Concept of Free Will" that aimed to refine Frankfurt's division of the will into first-order and second-order volitions.[27] She formulated the following question: If Frankfurt is right that the mind needs a second-order will to decide what the first-order will ought to want, doesn't there need to be a third order of volition to tell the second order of volition what it is good to want? And what about the preferences of this third order of volition? How does this kind of analysis of the will avoid falling into an infinite regress, positing a third-order volition to tell the second-order volition want to want, then a fourth-order volition to guide the third-order volition, and on and on? Conceptualizing the will as a limitless layering of volitions, each regulated by a higher level of volition, seemed like an absurd way of thinking about how the will works, so Stump developed an alternative to Frankfurt's analysis, arguing that what regulates a person's will is not a higher level of volition but the intervention of another mental faculty with the ability to make judgments about what is good or bad to want—reason.

I must leave it to philosophers to weigh the pros and cons of Frankfurt's and Stump's conceptions of the will and how each one accounts for the freedom of the will.[28] What I want to focus on is how she brings the story of Pharaoh's hardened heart into the picture. It first comes up tangentially—not through a direct engagement with the biblical text but by means of an anecdote about a Nazi that evokes the language of the hardened heart, an episode that Adolf Hitler's propagandist Joseph Goebbels recorded in his diaries. The incident involved Goebbels's reaction when watching a newsreel of the German invasion of Poland. As a committed Nazi, he entirely approved of the brutal things that the

Germans were doing in Poland, but as he viewed the images of the invasion, his resolve faltered. He found himself feeling pity for the Poles, a desire to help them. Goebbels was experiencing an involuntary first-order volition, a desire to help the Poles; and in response, he instructed his own heart, "Be hard, my heart, be hard."

Following Frankfurt's account of a hierarchically arranged will, Stump divides Goebbels's will into a first-order desire to have mercy and send help to the Poles and a second-order desire that aimed to control the first-order desire—in this case, to repress it. The first-order desire was instinctive, something that Goebbels felt despite himself, while the second-order desire was under the control of his reasoning powers, the part of cognition able to make judgments about what is good to want and what is bad, and to steer his will accordingly. As he watched the newsreel, Goebbels briefly lost control over his first-order volition but then reasserted control over it by making a conscious effort to suppress the desire he was feeling to be compassionate.

According to Stump's account, Goebbels's success in controlling and ultimately repressing his first-order desire to be compassionate means that his will was acting freely, that it was controlling its own desires. Of course, there is nothing to celebrate about Goebbels's free will, which led him to tremendous evil, but Stump's analysis reveals the depth of his culpability. If Goebbels committed his crimes from an instinctive impulse to be evil, or out of a fear of being punished if he acted otherwise, one could argue that he was not really culpable for them because his will wasn't truly making its own decisions. But Goebbels's admitted ability to control his first-order volition, his hardening of his own heart, proves that his actions as a Nazi were not merely voluntary (in the sense of being uncoerced) but were born of a reasoned choice *to want* to do terrible things. According to Stump's analysis of what makes a will free and in charge of itself, that choice is what makes Goebbels truly accountable for the evil that he brought about; his will was instinctively impelled to be merciful, and by exercising his second-order will for it to be otherwise, he proved that it was free and therefore responsible for its hard-heartedness.

After discussing Goebbels's hardened heart, Stump then turns her attention to the biblical story itself, and that part of her argument, interestingly, converges with Albo's reading. The biblical account makes clear that Pharaoh intends to oppress the Israelites from the very beginning. God does not need to implant that desire in his head because it is already something he wants to do. But it is not clear at this point that Pharaoh's will is free, that he is in control of his first-order volition. What the words "The Lord hardened Pharaoh's heart" signify, Stump proposes, is a divine intervention akin to that of reasoning in her account of Goebbels's hardened heart—God gives Pharaoh the power to control his first-order volition to oppress the Israelites, just as Goebbels exercised control over his first-order volition by reasoning about what it was good to want. After that moment, Pharaoh was not only doing what he wanted but *wanting* what he wanted—his will was free—and that is why, from the sixth plague onward, he can be judged accountable for his cruelty in a deeper way than was true of his decisions in the first five plagues.

Stump's use of the hard-hearted Pharaoh to illustrate her conception of the will was an intentionally old-fashioned move. Philosophers today often argue that the will itself is an illusion or a misunderstanding of what is happening inside the mind, and volition is now often treated as a subject not of philosophical inquiry but of scientific investigation to be pursued through the methods of psychology or neuroscience. By contrast, Stump's style of reasoning, and especially her use of the story of Pharaoh as a case study, ties her argument to an earlier era of philosophical and theological tradition that includes Origen, Augustine, and Martin Luther.

Like all the other examples we have considered, however, her version of Pharaoh reflects a contemporary concept of the will. In all the previous examples we have looked at, the question of the will's freedom was tied to questions about God's control over creation. If Pharaoh, or humans in general, were truly free to decide their own actions, that would mean that God wasn't fully in control of the world and theologians had to struggle to reconcile the unpredictability and uncontrollability this introduced with God's omniscience and omnipotence. For Stump, the hardening of the heart is not the result of divine intervention but an internal mental process, something the mind does to itself, and thus it does not raise questions about divine control and justice that she feels the need to address. The essay reflects its age in other ways as well, responding, for example, to the moral challenge of the Holocaust, including the efforts by Nazi subordinates and collaborators to evade culpability for their role in its atrocities.

What nonetheless ties it to the earlier retellings we have surveyed in this chapter is the way it uses the story of Pharaoh's hardened heart to wrestle with a tension at the core of human experience between people's awareness of themselves as impelled by forces beyond their control and their sense of being in charge of their own decision-making. From the time of Origen onward, theologians and philosophers have seized on the inconsistencies in the ten plagues story, including the switch to "The Lord hardened his heart" after the sixth plague, as a reflection of this paradox of experience, and Stump's dissection of Pharaoh's heart is true to that tradition.

7

The Seventh Plague

SIGNS JUST BEFORE THE END

ONE OF the most important reasons that people have taken an interest in the ten plagues story is that it was thought to give a glimpse of how the world was going to an end. The idea first surfaces in the Hebrew Bible itself in prophetic texts that imagine ten plagues–like catastrophes befalling the enemies of Israel, and later Jewish and Christian interpreters built from this idea a kind of script for the eschatological age, what Jews call the End of Days and Christians call the Apocalypse. God would bring this world to an end and create a new heaven and earth in its place, and the transition from one to the other would come about through a series of plagues resembling the plagues in Exodus, though even more devastating and enveloping all humankind.

While the Torah itself never claims that the plagues were anything other than one-time events, it does imply that they were part of a recurrent pattern in God's relationship to Israel, a pattern in which God allows Israel to be taken captive by foreigners and then rescues them by afflicting the enemy with calamity. The first time this occurs is in Genesis 12, when Abraham and Sarah are forced by a famine in Canaan to migrate to the land of Egypt: Sarah is taken prisoner by the pharaoh at the time, and while Abraham can do nothing to help her on his own, she is rescued after God sends "great plagues" against the king that force him to let her go (Genesis 12:10–20). In this and similar episodes involving Abraham's descendants, Genesis sets up the exodus from Egypt as a manifestation of a pattern of divine intervention that occurred whenever the ancestors of the Israelites were taken captive by foreigners, an intervention on a much bigger scale than ever before but that was essentially repeating what God had done for the patriarchs and matriarchs of Genesis when they found themselves subjugated in Egypt.[1]

Other biblical authors, the ones who created the prophetic books of Isaiah, Jeremiah, and Ezekiel, projected this pattern onto the future. Long after the exodus, after the Israelites had settled in Canaan, they faced threats similar to what their ancestors had suffered in Egypt, suffering subjugation by foreigners like the Assyrians, the Babylonians, and the Egyptians themselves. Throughout this period, there were prophets who sought to reassure the Israelites that God would deliver them as he had done for their ancestors, and some evoked the exodus as a precedent and paradigm of this future deliverance, as in the following oracle from Isaiah 19:

> On that day there will be an altar to the Lord in the center of the land of Egypt, and a pillar to the Lord at the border. It will also be a sign and a witness to the Lord of hosts in the land of Egypt when they cry to the Lord because of oppressors; he will send them a savior, a defender, and he will deliver them. The Lord will make himself known to the Egyptians, and the Egyptians will know the Lord on that day and will worship with sacrifice and burnt offering, and they will make vows to the Lord and perform them. The Lord will strike Egypt, striking and healing, and they will return to the Lord. (Isaiah 19:19–22)

The passage, referring to Egypt of the eighth century BCE, envisions a day when the Egyptians would come to know God themselves and even begin to worship him—and does so by casting these future events as a reiteration of what God did to the Egyptians in the time of Moses. While we cannot tell for certain that the author was referring to the exodus story as we know it from the Torah, several phrases signal that he had in mind some version of the story. The phrase "a sign and a witness" echoes Exodus's description of the plagues as "signs and wonders" (Exodus 7:3); the passage's mention of a savior (*moshia* ʿ) evokes Moses's role and even his name (Moshe); the line, "The Lord will make himself known to the

Egyptians," echoes what God tells Moses in Exodus 7:5 ("The Egyptians shall know that I am the Lord"); and the description of God "striking" Egypt calls to mind the plagues themselves. Already in the period of the First Temple, the passage shows, prophets were repurposing the story of the plagues as a prediction, using it to reassure their distressed listeners that God would save them from their present-day enemies.

There was something else in the Exodus account that encouraged later Jews and Christians to read the plagues as an anticipation of future events—its description of the plagues as "signs and wonders." The underlying Hebrew words, *ʾot* and *mophet,* are brought together for the first time in Exodus 7:3 and then appear some thirty more times in the Hebrew Bible and New Testament, and the combination of the two terms has come to be understood as a reference to the miracles that God performs to manifest his power or to confirm the truth of a prophecy. As I have noted, however, the translation of *mophet* as "wonder," bringing the concept of miracles to mind, reflects a particular understanding of the term, and the Septuagint's alternative rendering of the term as "portent" encouraged readers to think of the plagues as signs of the future.

Although projecting the ten plagues story onto the future has its roots in the Hebrew Bible, it appears to have had particular appeal for early Christian readers of the Bible who were likely influenced by the importance of divine portents in ancient Greek and Roman culture of their day. Pre-Christian pagan literature includes many examples of the gods sending warnings to humans in the form of strange and terrifying events that occurred in clusters or as a sequence, just as the plagues do in Exodus. The Greek historian Polybius, born around 200 BCE, even referred to such events with the phrase "signs and wonders" (*Histories* 3.112.8),[2] and he probably did so without knowing that this same phrase was used in the Septuagint of the ten plagues. The similarity between the Greco-Roman portent and the Bible's description of the plagues encouraged early Jews and Christians to conflate the two, generating visions of the future where a series of ten plagues–like calamities function as warnings of a more terrible catastrophe to come—the final punishment of the sinful in the time of the messiah's appearance. The retelling of the plagues as a way of depicting an apocalyptic end of the world is what we will focus on in this chapter, starting by showing that the most influential description of the end times, the New Testament book of Revelation, is really an elaboration of the ten plagues and then tracing how its version of the story led to other retellings of the plagues in modern secular forms.

But why attach this discussion to the seventh plague, the plague of hail? Most of the other plagues also came to be associated with the apocalyptic age, and the plague of hail wasn't even the last or most terrible one: it was followed by the locusts, darkness, and the slaying of the firstborn. For reasons I will explain later, however, the hail of the seventh plague served as a distinctive signifier of the Apocalypse, and it would come to play an especially important role as a point of continuity between premodern religious accounts of the Apocalypse and modern-day apocalyptic narratives that reframe the end of the world in a scientific and space-age context.

From Plague to Portent

At first blush, hailstorms would seem too commonplace to qualify as miracles, much less as signs of the Apocalypse. According to the National Weather Service, in 2023 in the United States, there were 4,811 severe hail events. That same year, according to the European Severe Weather Database, Europe witnessed 9,267 large hail events.[3] Storms are not common in Egypt, but they do occasionally happen, as in one recorded by an ancient text known as the Tempest Stela from around 1550 BCE that did extensive damage to temples and tombs. But the hailstorm of the seventh plague was no ordinary weather event. At two points in Exodus 9, the text stresses that this hailstorm was unprecedented—in verse 18, we are told that "there had been nothing like it in Egypt since the day it was established," and again, in verse 23, "there had been nothing like it in Egypt since it became a nation." What marked this hailstorm as an act of divine intervention was that it was unlike any previous hail strike that Egypt had ever suffered.

But what precisely was so unprecedented about this storm? One might reasonably assume that the distinction was its destructiveness, and indeed, later retellings of the episode expand on its singularly devastating impact. In an early retelling of the exodus from the third century BCE, for example, a historian named Artapanus added an earthquake to the plague, reporting that it killed those who were not killed by the hail.[4] But while the biblical account in Exodus 9 certainly accentuates the catastrophic impact of the hail, reporting that it killed every human and animal that did not take cover, struck down every plant, and broke every tree, interpreters also noticed that its hail was different from that of an ordinary hailstorm in other respects as well.

For many interpreters, part of what revealed the hailstorm as a divine intervention was the size of the hailstones it produced. The Bible nowhere specifies the dimensions of the hail, but it does note that the hail was "very heavy," which has been interpreted as a reference not just to the intensity of the downpour but also to the weight and size of the stones. This was the view of the historian Josephus, who remarked that the stones were larger than what fell in the northernmost regions during winter (*Antiquities* 2.304). Others believe that what distinguished this hail is that it was on fire, a detail inferred from Exodus 9:24: "There was hail with fire flashing in the midst of it." While the biblical author was likely referring to flashes of lightning in the midst of a hailstorm, the Hebrew for "in the midst of it" can also be understood as "inside of it"—that is, the text can be understood to be reporting that fire flashed inside each hailstone. For some early Jewish interpreters, it was this impossible combination of fire burning inside ice without melting it that distinguished the hail of the seventh plague from ordinary hail, producing what one rabbinic sage referred to as a "miracle inside a miracle" (Exodus Rabbah 12.4).

There was one other detail in the biblical account that distinguished the seventh plague from an ordinary hailstorm in early Jewish and Christian interpretation of the episode. When Moses announces that the tenth plague, the death of the firstborn, is about to happen, he declares that a great cry will go out throughout Egypt "such as never happened before *and will never happen again*" (Exodus 11:6). The Torah also describes the hailstorm as an event that has never happened before in the history of Egypt, but early interpreters noticed that, in contrast to

Exodus 11:6, it does not rule out such an event happening again. Some took that omission to be intentional, a warning that a similar plague of hail would happen again in the future. When would it occur? According to one midrash, at the time of Gog and Magog, the enemies mentioned in biblical prophecies of the messiah's final apocalyptic battle with God's enemies (Exodus Rabbah 12.2). From this perspective, the seventh plague was not just a disaster in its own right: it foreshadowed another terrible hailstorm to happen at the End of Days.

The reading of the ten plagues as a template for the Apocalypse is what led the author of the book of Revelation, the New Testament's most fully developed vision of the apocalyptic age, to the idea that the end of the world would include devastating hailstorms. The catastrophes envisioned in Revelation fall into three distinct lists of seven plagues. The first set of plagues, which are released when the messiah, depicted as a lamb, opens up seven seals of a mysterious scroll, does not mention hail specifically, but its description of what follows the opening of the sixth seal resembles it: there is a great earthquake as in Artapanus's account; the sky darkens; and stars fall from the sky like unripe figs falling from a tree (Revelation 6:12–13). The second set of plagues, each of which is released when an angel blows a trumpet (8:6–11:19), include hail and fire mixed with blood after the first trumpet (8:7) and more hail after the seventh trumpet (11:19). The third set of seven plagues, recounted in Revelation 16, culminates with a plague of hail that is more precisely similar to the seventh plague of Exodus, including flashes of lightning, crashing thunder, an earthquake "such as never been since man was on the earth" (again as in Artapanus), and gigantic hailstones weighing a talent each, about a hundred pounds.

The hail mentioned in the book of Revelation was modeled on the book of Ezekiel and its description of a battle where God uses hail to punish Israel's enemies: "I shall exact justice against him with pestilence and with blood, and I will cause to rain on him, and on his forces and on the many peoples with him a torrential rain and great hailstones,[5] fire and brimstone" (Ezekiel 38:18–22). But the author of Revelation put his own spin on this motif, and there is a lot about its account that remains mysterious. Why three sets of plagues and not a single sequence as in Exodus? Why seven plagues in each set instead of ten? And why make hail the last of the plagues in the final set? There is no consensus among scholars about how to answer these questions, and for that matter we cannot tell whether its description of plagues was a prediction of future calamities, referred to disasters that had already happened, or was even intended to be taken literally. It would take an entire book to recount the many ways people have understood the apocalyptic plagues in Revelation, and despite that long history of interpretation, what they are referring to; why there is a tripling of such plagues; and why they play such a central role in Revelation's larger vision of the end remain puzzles that scholars are still trying to solve.[6]

I would venture one observation, however: the importance of meteorological events in its narrative—stars and hail falling out of the sky—likely reflects the importance of heaven-sent portents in the Roman Empire at the time. As noted earlier, ancient Roman historians record many such events. One episode reported by Livy, for instance, occurred during the reign of Tullus, the third king of Rome, and involved a rain of large hail stones accompanied by the sound of a mighty voice emanating from a nearby grove (*History of Rome* 1.31.8). As with comets and other omens from the sky, the hail in this episode portended dramatic change—in this case, the defeat of an early rival to Rome—and the apocalyptic hail of Revelation likewise signified a violent transition to a new epoch, only on a cosmic scale that involved the end of one world and the beginning of another. While the events portended in Revelation—God's vanquishment of his enemies, the enthronement of the messiah, the judgment of the wicked, and even the use of hail to punish the enemy—were drawn from Jewish prophetic and apocalyptic tradition, the idea of a terrible hailstorm as a portent of world-shaking change was also one that the author of Revelation shared with non-Christian Romans and Greeks who saw hailstorms and meteors as harbingers of war, political upheaval, and the rise of new rulers.

Revelation is the earliest Christian text to project ten plagues–like calamities onto the apocalyptic future, but the idea was soon picked up and developed by other early Christian visionaries who elaborated on it, such as the author of a brief text known as the Apocalypse of Thomas, often dated to the fifth century CE. In this work's vision of the world's end, the arrival of the apocalyptic age is depicted as a series of escalating calamitous signs that unfold over seven days and culminate with the deliverance of the elect on the eighth day. By around 1000 CE, this version of the end times had expanded into a catalog of disasters, known as the Fifteen Signs before the Day of Judgment, which were expected to occur over fifteen days leading into the Apocalypse. There developed different versions of the list, but most included the seas rising above the mountains, blood-sweating trees, collapsing buildings, and falling stars from the heavens that spew fire, and some versions added hailstorms.[7] The signs were recounted in sermons and poetry, and they were also visualized in book illustrations, sculptured reliefs, and stained glass windows, such as one in the parish church of All Saints in York that presents all fifteen signs.[8] This tradition became very widespread in the Christian world over the course of the Middle Ages, and such was its influence that it inspired a very similar Islamic tradition of cataloging the signs expected to occur before the Day of Judgment.[9]

The fifteen signs tradition was influenced more by Revelation than by Exodus, but the ten plagues story continued to exert its own influence on how Christians imagined the end of the world in other ways. One example emerged from the followers of an abbot named Joachim of Fiore (1135–1202), one of the Middle Ages' most influential apocalyptic thinkers, who believed that the present was following a pattern laid out in the Old Testament. Joachim himself did not leave behind an apocalyptic reading of the ten plagues, but one of his followers did, producing a short apocalyptic work that developed the correspondence between the ten plagues and the seven phials of plague described in Revelation 16 to argue that humanity was in the sixth of seven stages of history leading to the messianic age envisioned in Revelation.[10] The association of the ten plagues with the signs of the end also inspired another of Joachim's followers, Toribio of Benavente (1482–1565), to produce a work that described the history of New Spain—today's Mexico—as a series of apocalyptic signs leading to the return of Christ. Toribio, also known as Motolinía, was one of "twelve apostles" sent to Mexico to convert its inhabitants, and in his description of its history before their arrival, he depicts events as a new ten plagues leading to the establishment of a new Jerusalem, chronicling the disease, war with the Aztecs, famine, and a seventh plague during the construction of Mexico City that involved death from above—people felled by falling beams from newly constructed buildings or crushed during the demolition of buildings.[11] These were all warnings to the native people, the Nahua, to repent of their sins, as some of the Egyptians had done in response to Moses's warnings, and the arrival of Toribio and his fellow missionaries was part of this divine scheme, the next stage in the Nahua's salvation.

In these and other elaborations of the ten plagues, the sequentiality of the plagues—the expectation that they will occur in a preordained sequence over a week or fifteen days—became very important to the story, sending advance warning of the Apocalypse and giving people a chance to prepare. This too is arguably an element adapted from the ten plagues story—and more specifically, the plague of hail. In some of the earlier plagues, God had used Moses to announce what he was going to do before he did it, but there is no mention of the Egyptians doing anything to protect themselves from what happened. Before the plague of hail, by contrast, Moses instructs the Egyptians that there is something they can do to save themselves—move themselves and their animals under shelter. The seventh plague thus introduces an idea that would be important to the story as a literary template for the Apocalypse. There was nothing people could do to stop the catastrophes from occurring in the sequence foreordained by God, but they could hope to be delivered if they recognized the disasters of their day as the prophesied warnings of the coming Apocalypse and made sure that they repented of their sins before it was too late.

Cosmic Impacts

In the eighteenth and nineteenth centuries, in both Europe and the United States, hailstorms came to be understood as naturally occurring events—not acts of divine punishment or signs of the end but haphazard events that had no inherent religious significance. In the same period, the fireballs that fall from the sky also underwent a similar process of de-theologization: what were once seen as portents of coming cataclysm were now recognized as stones falling from space.[12]

The emergence of a scientific approach to such events did not, however, put an end to the practice of interpreting them as signs of the Apocalypse. In fact, it spawned a modern offshoot, an old-yet-new apocalyptic narrative in which the fiery hail of Revelation was transmuted into other world-ending threats from the skies. By this point, science had reconceived the "heavens" as a vast expanse of outer space that included planets, stars, and comets, but as vast and mysterious as this realm was, it was still possible to interpret it in light of Revelation by transferring the apocalyptic significance of hail and falling stars in its vision of the end to naturally occurring celestial events, especially comet strikes and celestial collisions. A new form of cosmic apocalypticism emerged that fused Christian belief with what astronomers were observing through their telescopes, and the result was a celestialized version of the apocalyptic plague of hail as a world-ending event that fulfills the prediction of Revelation while also adhering to what astronomers were learning about outer space and the history of the cosmos. In this section, we will be exploring this transformation—how the story of the apocalyptic plague of hail came to be retold in modern times as a scientifically informed story about how the earth is going to end.

It should be noted that the connection between the Apocalypse and comets in particular long predates the rise of modern astronomy, originating from ancient divination and then undergoing a process of Christianization in late antiquity. According to Thomas Aquinas, it was the fourth-century Christian scholar Jerome, translator of the Vulgate, who first associated the comet with the events predicted in Revelation, by including it among the fifteen signs of the end (*Summa Theologica*, supplement to part 3, question 73, article 1), and Christians interpreted comets as signs of the end throughout the Middle Ages well into the modern era.[13] By the eighteenth century, comets had come to be much better understood thanks to the work of astronomers like Edmond Halley (1656–1742), who discovered that the comet later named for him passed by Earth on a regular basis. Nevertheless, people continued to interpret the arrival of these celestial bodies apocalyptically. Thus, an

1811 comet that was visible from across Europe, occurring at a time of dramatic upheaval in the wake of Napoleon's conquest in Europe and invasion of Russia, was regarded as a biblically prophesied portent of the end times, and a century later, in 1910, the return of Halley's Comet was similarly understood as the sign of an impending apocalypse.[14]

In a certain sense, the rise of scientific astronomy even breathed new life into apocalyptic interpretations by revealing how the world-ending events foreseen in Revelation could actually come about. In the fifteenth and sixteenth centuries, the astronomers Jean Pena and Tycho Brahe calculated that comets were much farther from Earth than people had understood, and that they came and returned as part of their orbit around the sun. For some, such discoveries undercut the apocalyptic interpretation of comets—writing in the eighteenth century, the philosopher Denis Diderot observed that "it has been a hundred years since comets signified anything."[15] But scientists in earlier centuries believed that what they were observing about comets did signify something, falling in line with the events of the end times as envisioned in Revelation.[16]

A case in point is Tycho Brahe (1546–1601). A Danish astronomer, Brahe is recognized as an important forebear of the scientific study of comets, establishing an observatory called the Uraniborg (named for the Muse of Astronomy), constructing astronomical instruments, and carefully recording his observations of a comet that passed by Earth in 1577. But he was also a Protestant reader of the book of Revelation, and he interpreted the comet in light of its description of the apocalyptic age. Although he rejected the idea advanced by others that the comet seen over northern Europe in 1577 was a portent of an impending judgment day itself, he offered his own prediction that its arrival would initiate a new era that would include a battle with Gog and Magog (the latter identified by Brahe with Moscow), followed by the millennium of peace foreseen in Revelation 20.[17] Another example of such intermingling between science and Christian apocalypticism comes from the theologian and mathematician William Whiston (1667–1752), a disciple of Isaac Newton and successor to his professorship at Cambridge. Whiston is remembered for proposing the earliest prediction of a comet destroying

Earth in a work published in 1696 called *A New Theory of the Earth*. Although Whiston was proposing a new role for comets in the history and development of Earth, he believed himself to also be explaining how the end as foreseen in the book of Revelation would come about.[18]

Responsible scientistic forecasters today do not try to reconcile their predictions of a future cosmic collision with the prophecies of Revelation, but the two scenarios for the world's end, scientific and apocalyptic, were not always so separate in public consciousness, and they continue to intermingle. The first comet collision–related mass panic of which I am aware occurred in 1773, triggered by a rumor that the astronomer Jerome de Lalande had predicted two approaching comets would incinerate France. Although Lalande had only said such a scenario was possible, not that it was going to happen, people panicked when they heard the news, and some responded as if they had heard the fifteen signs of doomsday were underway, rushing to repent of their sins.[19] Subsequent comet flybys triggered similar responses well into the twentieth century. In 1950, for example, the psychoanalyst Immanuel Velikovsky published *Worlds in Collision*, a book that proposed the idea that the ten plagues were the catastrophic effects of a near collision with a comet ejected from Jupiter and predicted that the world was going to come to an end through a similar collision.[20] A more recent—and tragic—example involves an apocalyptic interpretation of the Hale-Bopp Comet, which passed near Earth in 1997. Marshall Applewhite and Bonnie Nettles, founders of a sect known as Heaven's Gate, convinced their followers that there was a UFO in the tail of the comet that was coming to rescue them from the impending end predicted in Revelation.[21] In order to beam up to this ship, the thirty-nine members of the group believed they had to shed their physical bodies, which they did by committing suicide.

As these examples show, the apocalyptic interpretation of comets as signs of the Apocalypse persisted into the twentieth century mostly in the context of UFO-centered religious sects like Heaven's Gate and countercultural movements opposed to establishment science, but the fusion of astronomy with apocalypticism did find its way into the mainstream through another medium: science fiction, which has popularized the idea of an Earth-ending comet. Science fiction bases its descriptions of the future on scientific discoveries and theories, and that is also true of doomsday science fiction that imagines a world-ending comet strike or planetary collision, a scenario based on theories like that proposed by the Nobel Prize–winning scientist Luis Alvarez, together with his son and other colleagues, which claims that an asteroid collision triggered the extinction of 75 percent of the world's animal species some sixty-six million years ago.[22] However, historians of science fiction have also recognized that the genre borrowed—and continues to borrow—from Revelation, and that includes the role of falling stars and hail as apocalyptic events. Following this motif from Revelation into science fiction will help us to understand how the plague of hail has proved so resilient as a sign of a coming doomsday that it plays this role even in modern visions of the end that otherwise reject Christian apocalypticism.

Signs of the Anti-Apocalypse

This genre of science fiction emerged not long after the earliest comet-inspired mass panic, and its earliest exemplar is a doomsday novel that imagines the end of the world, a prose poem from 1805 called *Le dernier homme* (*The Last Man*) by Jean-Baptiste Cousin de Grainville. This work was soon emulated by other writers, including Mary Wollstonecraft Shelley of *Frankenstein* fame, who in 1826 published *The Last Man*, a novel that describes a pandemic that sweeps across the world in the twenty-first century.[23] These works are true intermediaries between science and apocalypticism: they draw on the science of their day to envision the world's end, but they also draw on Revelation, modeling their plots and characters on it.

Jean-Baptiste Cousin de Grainville (1746–1805) was an ordained priest who lived through the events of the French Revolution and the beginning of the Napoleonic era. During the Reign of Terror (1793–1794), when some priests were imprisoned and even executed for refusing to take an oath that acknowledged the nation's authority over religious matters, he was forced to take such an oath and then marry a cousin in violation of his vows; when France later returned to a more traditional Catholicism, his status as a married priest made him a pariah. Eventually, he succumbed to despair, committing suicide before *Le dernier homme* was published. The novel nevertheless made such an impression that it inspired others to publish similar stories—Shelley's book along with the astronomer Camille Flammarion's 1894 *Omega: The Last Days of the World*—which have inspired many subsequent retellings and imitations in the last two centuries.

Le dernier homme is a kind of fictionalized retelling of Revelation, although it also draws from John Milton's *Paradise Lost*. Its main characters, Omegarus and Syderia, are modeled on Milton's Adam and Eve, but Omegarus's name, an allusion to Revelation 1:8, where Jesus declares, "I am the Alpha and the Omega," signals that he is also modeled on Jesus in his role as an agent of the end time. The story begins when the narrator enters a cave in Syria where he finds an enchanted mirror that reveals the earth in its final days. There is but one couple left, Omegarus and his wife, Syderia, but God, rather than instructing them to repopulate the earth, wants to stop them from doing so, so that he can create a new heaven and earth, sending none other than Adam himself to foil their plan. Before Adam reveals his identity, Omegarus explains that he had been born into an age when a very advanced human race was on the verge of extinction after exhausting all its resources, and as a result, the future of humanity now depended on the children he produces with Syderia. Adam then reveals his identity to Omegarus and convinces him to leave Syderia and seal the world's fate. The rest of the novel depicts the end as a bleak realization of the prophecies of Revelation, setting the stage for the creation of a new heaven and earth but with no humans left to inhabit it. Though the end does not come about through a comet collision, comets do appear in a reddened sky as a sign of the world's impending death.[24]

Shelley's novel tells a very similar story. It too begins with an experience that the narrator—here Shelley herself—has in a mysterious cave that once belonged to a sybil, an ancient prophetess who left behind a collection of texts that foretell the end of the human race. From these texts, the character Shelley learns of the last man, a twenty-first-century Englishman named Lionel Verney, and the bulk of the novel is a first-person account of his experiences as the sole survivor of humanity's demise, relating how he and other survivors of the pandemic move from one country to another, perishing one after another until only Lionel is left to wander the world alone. Readers of Shelley's more celebrated novel *Frankenstein,* published eight years prior, may recognize how this story mirrors the increasing isolation of Dr. Frankenstein as the monster he had created picks off his family and friends one at a time, leaving him all alone.

Like de Grainville's novel, *The Last Man* alludes to Revelation and borrows elements from it, but Shelley meant to subvert its vision of the end. In a number of scenes, she evokes Revelation but only to highlight a contrast between its vision of a catastrophic apocalypse with the consistently anticlimactic end that she imagines for humanity. In one scene, for example, Shelley conjures an image of the dramatic and noisy events of Revelation only to deny that such events were taking place in this version of the end:

> Do you not behold the clouds open, and destruction lurid and dire pour down on the blasted earth? See you not the thunderbolt fall, and are deafened by the shout of heaven that follows its descent? Feel you not the earthquake and open with agonizing groans while the air is pregnant with shrieks and wailings—all announcing the last days of man?
>
> No! None of these things accompanied our fall![25]

In Revelation, the whole of creation reacts to what is happening to humans: the heavens shout and wail while the earth convulses with pain. In Shelley's vision, humans are going extinct, and the rest of creation does not pause to take notice. The air is balmy, flowers are blooming, and the birds are chirping, as if Nature were completely oblivious to the downfall of humankind.

The novel takes a similar turn in another episode that recalls the falling stars of Revelation. Near the end of the novel, the survivors witness a sight that makes them fear for their lives: "Suddenly, a wonder! Three other suns, alike burning and brilliant, rushed from various quarters of the heavens toward the great orb. They whirled around it. . . . Suddenly the three orbs united in one, and plunged into the sea. A few seconds afterward, a deafening watery sound came up with an awful peal from the spot where they had disappeared." Yet again, the narrative draws on Revelation, especially its description of a large star that falls into the waters of the earth (Revelation 8:10–11). The biblical parallel is not lost on the people within the narrative, to whom it appears as if the Day of Judgment were at hand: "It appeared as if suddenly the motion of earth was revealed to us—as if no longer we were ruled by ancient laws but were cast adrift in an unknown region of space. Many cried aloud, that these were no meteors, but globes of burning matter, which had set fire to the earth, and caused the vast cauldron at our feet to bubble up with its measureless waves; the day of judgement was come they averred, and a few moments would transport us before the awful countenance of the omnipotent judge."[26] Here, too, Shelley summons the book of Revelation to mind, only to immediately annul the comparison: the meteor shower does not lead to any day of judgment. It creates a wall of water so immense that it appears poised to drown the world in a flood only to peter out before it reaches the precipice on which the onlookers are standing.[27] Even as the novel subverts its readers' apocalyptic expectations, however, it nevertheless ties itself to Revelation, incorporating elements of its visions—including the falling stars of the sixth seal—into its depiction of the world's demise.

The apocalyptic cosmic strike—an object descending from space to annihilate humankind—would only grow in importance as a doomsday scenario in apocalyptic science fiction, thanks in part to growing public fascination with space in general and comets in particular. The spectacular comet visitations of the nineteenth century, enhanced by the sensational news reporting and public panic and speculation they inspired, captured the imaginations of authors like Edgar Allan Poe in "The Conversation of Eiros and Charmion" (1839) and Jules Verne in *Off on a Comet* (1877). The return of Halley's Comet in 1910, which incited mass panic (people were scared that its tail would asphyxiate humankind), only magnified the appeal of this kind of story, as did the introduction in the same period of the medium of cinema.[28] Six years later, in 1916, the first-ever feature-length disaster movie came out, the Danish science fiction film *Verdens Undergang* (known in English by the title *The End of the World*), and it is not a coincidence that its disaster involves a comet. The film's plot and imagery reflect other recent disasters as well—the sinking of the *Titanic* and World War I—but the main inspiration was Halley's Comet and the apocalyptic terror that it triggered.[29]

Verdens Undergang is itself evidence of how the book of Revelation continued to shape the genre of doomsday science fiction into the twentieth century, as the title used for the German release of the film all but made explicit: *Das jungste Gericht* (The last judgment). God does not make a direct appearance in the film, but it does feature a prophet who in the opening scene declares that the comet is God's punishment; it includes a scene where the wealthy villains of the story seek refuge in underground mines, recalling Revelation 6:15, where the powerful of the earth seek to hide from the falling stars by hiding in caves; and, more importantly, it concludes with a comet bringing judgment to Earth, killing the sinful while sparing the virtuous.

By the standards of early twentieth-century special effects, the comet strike is spectacular, and there are moments in its visualization that suggest a connection to the apocalyptic plague of hail. The still in figure 14, taken from a scene where fireballs are raining down on Earth, captures the escalating destruction that precedes the arrival of the comet itself. The imagery evokes the then-ongoing bombing raids of World War I, but it was inspired by the apocalyptic imagery of biblical illustrations, such as a rendering of fiery, blood-mixed hail used to illustrate Revelation 8:7 in a fourteenth-century French manuscript known as the *Cloisters Apocalypse* (figure 15).

While the film clearly draws on the imagery associated with the apocalyptic hail of Revelation, however, it also deploys at least one plot element that goes back to the earlier plague of hail recounted in Exodus 9. In the Exodus narrative, as noted earlier, many of the Egyptians refuse to heed Moses's warning and are destroyed, but some of Pharaoh's officials "fear the word of the Lord" and are able to save themselves. *Verdens Undergang* makes a similar distinction by dividing the characters in its story into reprobates who refuse to believe the prophet's warning and perish, and a small group of innocents whose faith saves them from

FIGURE 14. Destructive fireballs raining down on a city from a comet in the 1916 film *Verdens Undergang*.

FIGURE 15. Angel summoning hail and fire from the heavens in the *Cloisters Apocalypse* (France, ca. 1330). Metropolitan Museum of Art, New York.

destruction. At the center of the film is a pair of sisters: Dina, a social climber who abandons her fiancé to marry a greedy mine owner named Frank Stoll, and Edith, who remains faithful to her childhood friend Reymers, with whom she falls in love. Stoll is an opportunist who exploits news of the coming comet to get rich, and he and the self-centered Dina get their just deserts when they are asphyxiated in the mines in which they have taken shelter by poison gas released from the comet. Meanwhile, Edith and Reymers's survival recalls that of Noah—both escape from rising seas—and at the end, they are reunited as a new Adam and Eve who will go on to repopulate the earth.

The genealogical connection between the killer-comet film and the seventh plague is by no means direct, as it runs through many intervening generations of retelling that include the book of Revelation, the history of its interpretation, and early science fiction writing—each of which expanded on and reframed what it inherited from the original story in Exodus in profound ways. And yet my point is that certain elements from the seventh plague account in Exodus 9 were passed on as well, including, most essentially, the destruction of a population by fiery rocks from the sky that spare only a small group of the faithful who heed the warnings in time to save themselves. The transmission of this narrative core is what marks all the examples we have surveyed in this chapter as retellings of the seventh plague, despite the changes of setting, content, genre, medium, emotional tonality, and meaning they have introduced along the way.

And this tradition continues into the storytelling of our day. The Earth-killing-comet story has been retold many times since *Verdens Undergung*, but I want to look at just one more example, the 2011 film *Melancholia*, directed by another Danish director, Lars von Trier. Here, the killer cosmic object heading toward Earth is not a comet but an immense rogue planet, Melancholia, as the characters refer to it, and it is not barreling toward Earth in a straight line but has gotten caught up in a spiraling "dance of death" that slingshots it toward Earth, then away, and then back toward Earth for a final collision. Those are not the only details that distinguish it from the scores of killer-comet and asteroid films produced over the twentieth century: the film also stands out for a mysterious opening montage; for a deeply melancholic tone; for visual and musical allusions that enmesh its story within religious, mythological, and cinematic tradition; and for an ending bereft of hope. *Melancholia* has been interpreted in many ways: as a meditation on art in an age of cynicism and catastrophe, as an anticapitalist rejection of Hollywood escapism, and as an attempt to convey the absolute finality of death, among other themes identified in the film.[30] However one interprets it, like *Verdens Undergang,* it signals a connection to the Bible, and some of its narrative elements go back to the ten plagues story.

In fact, the film hints at a connection to the story of Exodus in particular early on in an opening montage that offers a synopsis of the whole story scored with music from the prologue of Richard Wagner's *Tristan and Isolde*. In one of the scenes, very fleetingly, one can see a glimpse of a burning bush through the window of an alcove, recalling the scene in Exodus where God appears out of a burning bush to announce to Moses that he is going to send plagues against the Egyptians. The image has been explained as an homage to the Soviet filmmaker Andrei Tarkovsky, director of an apocalyptic film of his own entitled *The Sacrifice* and an artistic hero for von Trier who used fire as a visual leitmotif in several of his films, but it is also a foreshadowing of the film's fiery end and an invitation to look for other allusions to the Bible.

The film goes on to evoke the book of Revelation as well, ending, for example, with several characters taking refuge in a tent constructed out of sticks that one of the sisters, Justine, describes as a "magic cave"—an allusion to Revelation 6:15 and its description of the rich and powerful seeking shelter in caves as stars fall on them from the sky. But like Shelley's novel, von Trier's film evokes the Christian apocalypse only in order to subvert it. In *Verdens Undergang,* like Revelation itself, the Apocalypse spares a small group of the righteous who are able to start over. In *Melancholia,* the characters are too three-dimensional to sort into neatly divided categories of the saved and the damned—Justine is a prophetic figure but reckless, insensitive to others, and deeply depressed; Claire is brittle, unable to assimilate the truth of what is happening to her but also loving and attentive—and everyone in the film, good or bad, is headed for the same fate, doomed to die in an atmospheric conflagration unleashed by the planetary collision. There is no new heaven and earth; here, the end is the rumbling sound of a burning world and then silence as the screen grows dark for several unnerving minutes.

Despite this bleak ending, however, the film does connect itself to apocalyptic tradition, and one of the ways it does so is by including a hailstorm just before the end of the world. For most of the film, Claire has been in denial about what is coming, and by this point, she has grown so desperate that she simply tries to run away with her son, but she is unable to do so—neither sister is able to get over the bridge that connects the estate to the rest of the world. The planet is now so close that it fills most of the sky; electrical lines are glowing menacingly; and it is at this moment that a hail shower begins, catching Claire on the estate's golf course. The scene is a major turning point in her story. Until now, she has been unable to accept what is happening, yet when the hail shower appears, she gives up and falls to her knees with her son in her arms.

Why include a hailstorm near the end of the movie? The opening montage offers one small clue by briefly showing Claire clutching her son as she walks off the golf course past a flag marking the nineteenth hole. As many fans of the movie have noted, golf courses only have eighteen holes, and there has been much speculation about what the nineteenth hole is meant to symbolize. Since "the nineteenth hole" is a name often used for lounges that golfers go to after finishing a round, some believe that it refers to the afterlife, symbolically signaling an ending beyond death. Von Trier himself has reportedly explained it as a symbol for limbo, a realm where those who are neither saved nor damned languish for eternity. Since, as the movie makes clear at several points, there are only eighteen holes on a golf course, however, it is also possible that it symbolizes the unreality of the afterlife, making it one of a number of elements in the film that evoke God and religious faith, only to then thwart the promise of divine rescue as an escape route from death, such as Justine's horse, named Abraham, who refuses to carry her over a bridge leading off the estate. *Melancholia* uses the hail in a similar way to evoke the eschatological hope at the heart of

Christian faith, but only in order to snuff it out; what the end brings in *Melancholia* is true extinction: Justine, Claire, and Leo in their magic cave all perish.

What the hail signifies in this context is something like the falling stars of Shelley's *Last Man*. It announces the imminent end of humankind as in Revelation, but as in Shelley's anti-Apocalypse, there is no judgment or redemption that comes after, and here too the end is marked by anti-climax—a downpour of hail, a raging fire, but then darkness and silence. Even as it upends apocalyptic expectation, however, *Melancholia* also attests to the continued vitality of Revelation as a narrative of the end; in fact, von Trier counted on the familiarity of that narrative in assuming his audience would recognize the hail as a signifier of the coming Apocalypse and form their expectations and interpretation accordingly.

By tracing a line of continuity from the seventh plague to *Melancholia*, I do not mean to deny the profound transformations of the story over the millennia. Revelation reframed the hail as part of its vision of an apocalyptic future. Shelley incorporated elements and images drawn from Revelation's version of the Apocalypse to form a deflationary anti-Apocalypse that negates the end of the world as an act of judgment and redemption by a God who cares about humanity; *Verdens Undergang* turned Revelation into an allegory about the connection between the disasters of the *Titanic* and World War I and capitalist greed; and von Trier transmuted the stories of Revelation and *Verdens Undergang* into a story about depression, death, and the flimsy shelter provided by art and cinema. Each story stands on its own, responding in some new way to the circumstances of the author and the story's immediate audience. And yet none was creating from scratch—they each built on the storytelling of earlier generations, and at the very beginning of this tradition, I have tried to show, was the plague of fire and ice recounted in Exodus 9.

People have long turned to the Bible to help them imagine what the end of everything will be like, and the ten plagues story has emerged in this context as one narrative model, used for thousands of years to give structure to the future as a sequence of mounting disasters that humans have brought upon themselves through their sins. The sequence leads to a final catastrophe, but not without giving people time to save themselves—those who heed the signs. Because of the influence of Revelation, the hail stands out from the other plagues of its visions as the *penultimate* sign of the coming apocalypse, the catastrophe that occurs as a warning just before the final day of judgment, and such is its impact on imagination that it shapes apocalyptic storytelling even among those who don't believe humanity will be saved in the end.

8

The Eighth Plague

JAWS

IN MAY 2020, large stretches of western India were beset by an infestation of desert locusts that endangered hundreds of millions of people. The outbreak, which comprised massive swarms that stretched over hundreds of miles, had been triggered by a cyclone in the Arabian Peninsula in 2018 and then spread into Africa and across central Asia. By April 2020, the locusts had reached twenty-three countries, including India, where they posed a major threat to the country's food supply. It is estimated that 150 million locusts consume as much food in a day as thirty-five thousand people; the swarms that spread across Africa and Asia in 2019–2020 involved billions of such insects.

In the midst of this crisis, a young Bollywood actress named Zaira Wasim, a Muslim born to a family from Kashmir, created a firestorm when she posted the following tweet: "So we sent upon them the flood and locusts and lice and frogs and blood: signs openly self-explained; but they were steeped in arrogance—a people given to sin."[1] The tweet, posted without explanation, is a quotation from the Qur'an, Sura 7:133, a one-verse account of the plagues of Egypt. The locust plague takes up all of one word in the verse, but in the face of the threat posed by a present-day locust plague, it jumped off the page, stirring up a hornet's nest of outrage and mockery from those who understood her to be referring to poor farmers or non-Muslims as the arrogant sinners who had provoked God's punishment of India through their lack of faith. The backlash was so strong that Wasim temporarily deactivated her social media accounts and, shortly thereafter, announced she was no longer an actress.

As this episode illustrates, the plagues story resonates powerfully not just for Jews and Christians but for Muslims as well, a religious community comprising some two billion people worldwide. But the version of the story that Wasim posted, the version known from the seventh sura (or chapter) of the Qur'an, known as Al-'Araf (The Heights), departs from the biblical account in several respects. It only mentions five plagues, lists them in a different order from what appears in Exodus, and adds a flood to the story nowhere mentioned in the Torah's account. Elsewhere in the Qur'an, in Sura 17:10, the narrative speaks of nine signs, reflecting a different way of counting up the miracles of the exodus, but why then mention only five such signs in 7:133? Did the author not know of the other plagues mentioned in Exodus, or might there be a reason the story was retold in this way? These are the questions we will explore in this chapter.

Although Sura 7 squeezes the plagues into a single sentence, that sentence contains more than its fair share of interpretive puzzles. Why does the verse refer to a flood not mentioned in Exodus? Why does its reference to the locusts, lice, and frogs go in the opposite order from the sequence in Exodus? Is "the blood" a reference to the turning of water into blood or some other plague not mentioned in the Bible, as some Qur'anic commentators believe?[2] The main question I want to focus on, however, has to do with the locust plague: Why was it included when other plagues—the boils, the hail, the darkness—were left out? The Qur'an does not answer this question directly, and it is possible that its author's choice of which plagues to mention was arbitrary and not carefully thought through. Yet, as we will see, all the plagues mentioned in the verse share something in common that distinguishes them from the plagues that were left out, and I think that commonality can lead us to a deeper understanding of why the author of the Qur'an told the story in this particular way.

The plague verse in the Qur'an, as understood in Islamic tradition, is not considered a *retelling* of the biblical story originally recounted in the book of Exodus: for Muslims, it records a divine revelation to the prophet Muhammad of what really happened, and it is the biblical account in the Torah, a corrupted record of divine revelation, that represents a distorted recounting of events. For our purposes, however, and following modern critical scholarship on the Qur'an, we will treat its version of the plagues story as a retelling of the biblical account informed by earlier Jewish and Christian interpretive tradition. There now exists an impressive body of scholarship demonstrating what the Qur'an shares in common with midrash and Christian biblical interpretation and perhaps learned from earlier Jewish and Christian sources known in Arabia, and that includes its treatment of the exodus story.[3] Reading Sura 7:133 from this perspective, it can be understood in the way we have approached other retellings of the ten plagues that rearrange and expand on the story to make a point and engage a particular audience.

After we explore how the Qur'an retells the plagues, we will also reflect on the legacy of what it says about the locusts in particular. It so happens that locust outbreaks are particularly common and consequential in precisely those parts of the world where large Muslim populations reside: North and East Africa, the Arabian Peninsula, the Levant, and central Asia. Muslims would come to refer to locusts as "God's army" because they experienced them as a powerful invasion force that left immense destruction and hardship in their wake, but in part because of their role in Moses's confrontation with Pharaoh, locusts were also recognized as a manifestation of divine love and as allies for the faithful. The Qur'an's version of the plagues story, as brief as it is, gave religious meaning to a terrible environmental catastrophe by helping to transform the locust into a mysterious revelation of God's power experienced as both a trial and a blessing.

A Warning with Wings

The traditional conception of the Qur'an understands its authorship based on clues from the Qur'an itself and authoritative testimony about the words and actions of Muhammad included in hadith, a collection of reports about the prophet from his companions that have been passed on and collected. According to that tradition, the Qur'an records a series of revelations disclosed to Muhammad by the angel Gabriel over twenty-three years. The suras are believed to come from different periods of Muhammad's life, and Sura 7 has been situated in a period when the prophet was still in Mecca, his hometown, before departing for Medina, and was facing skepticism, mockery, and threats from opponents who rejected his claim to be a messenger of God.

Like other suras near the beginning of the Qur'an, Sura 7 is long and covers a lot of ground, so I am not going to try to summarize all its content. But it is important to note that it situates the conflict between Moses and Pharaoh within a long, cyclical history of the divine sign. The divine sign was of much interest to the author of the Qur'an; it uses the Arabic word for "sign," *ayah*, more than 350 times, and follows a consistent view of why God communicates through signs, what can serve as a divine sign, and why humans so often discount them.[4] Sura 7 reflects this view as well, framing the Egyptians' resistance to the signs of Moses as a continuation of an age-old pattern in humanity's response to God that always ends in disaster.

Again and again, according to the sura, God sent messengers to warn people to repent of their arrogance and idolatry—Noah, Hud (an Arabian prophet who may be equivalent to the biblical Eber), Salih, Lot, Shuaib (identified with Moses's father-in-law Jethro), and then Moses and Aaron—and some even offered miraculous signs to prove that they were speaking on God's behalf, but the people they were trying to save failed to heed the warnings, dooming themselves by arrogantly rejecting God's messengers. Situated as a part of this story, the signs that Moses delivers to the Egyptians, including the plagues, are another example of humans rejecting the signs that prophets deliver to humans to prove they have been sent by God. Pharaoh and his advisers are so egregiously arrogant that they refuse to believe Moses even when he presents to them multiple miraculous signs attesting to the truth of his message. He turns his staff into a serpent and makes his hand appear white to onlookers, but Pharaoh remains unconvinced; indeed, he refuses to believe the prophet even when his own magicians become believers in God, and this obstinacy is what leads to the plagues cataloged in verse 133.

Initially, the Egyptians plead to Moses to intercede with God on their behalf, but once each plague is lifted, they backtrack in keeping with humans' propensity to forget God and reject his messengers and signs.

Zeroing in on the plagues themselves, one can see that the Qur'an's version of the story is similar to some extent to the biblical account, but it omits several of the plagues, presents them in a different order, and begins with a plague that is not mentioned at all in Exodus—a flood. The Arabic word for "flood," *tufan*, possibly related to the English word "typhoon," is used of the flood of Noah, and Qur'anic commentators assumed it referred to a terrible rainstorm that drowned many Egyptians, in some cases associating it with the plague of hail. No such flood is mentioned in Exodus, but we do know of an ancient retelling of the story from the Jewish Hellenistic historian Artapanus (the same ancient historian who added an earthquake to the plague of hail) where the first calamity that Moses unleashes against the Egyptians is not the turning of the waters of Egypt into blood but the flooding of the Nile.[5] Before the Aswan Dam was built in the 1960s, rainstorms in the highlands of Ethiopia would send floodwaters down into the Nile, and the overflow of its banks would cause the fields of Egypt to be covered in heavily silted reddish-brown water each year. The renewing of the land's fertility in this way was celebrated with an annual festival by the ancient Egyptians themselves, but for Artapanus, the flood was not a blessing but a divine punishment initiated by Moses. A possible explanation for the mention of a flood in Sura 7:133 is that the Qur'anic author was not working from the biblical account as we know it from Exodus but was drawing on an alternative formulation of the story similar to or even based on the version known to Artapanus many centuries earlier.

Why mention only five of the plagues—the flood, locusts, lice, frogs, and blood—and not the death of the cattle, the boils, and the other missing plagues? One possibility, a partial answer, is that the author focused on those plagues that involved animals. Animals play an important role in the Qur'an as divine signs; indeed, earlier in Sura 7 itself, in verses 73–79, there is a story about a miraculous she-camel in the time of Salih, a prophet not known from the Bible, that is described as such a sign. Addressing himself to the people of Thamud, an Arabian tribe,

Salih offers the she-camel to prove the truth of his message, instructing the tribespeople to allow it to graze on their land and warning that if they harm it, they will be punished, but just as earlier generations had rejected the messengers of their day, so too the tribe members of Thamud refuse to believe Salih, hamstringing the camel and then taunting the prophet to bring on the punishment he has threatened. In response, God kills them with an earthquake. It is possible that the Qur'anic author highlighted the animal signs in the Moses story to accentuate the pattern that shapes the sura as a whole, sharpening the similarity to the she-camel episode in particular.

The most obvious problem with this explanation, however, is that it does not account for the other two plagues mentioned in the verse, the flood and the blood. Animals play an important role as divine signs in the Qur'an, but God can deploy any aspect of creation as a sign—the stars in the sky, mountains, even the body of Pharaoh becomes a sign after he is swallowed by the sea. Throughout the heavens and the earth, there are signs visible to those who have faith, the Qur'an declares on more than one occasion (10:6; 45:3–4), and its version of Moses's story illustrates the variety: God does indeed send animals as signs, but he also uses the weather as a sign (the flood in 7:133) and the human body (Moses's turning his hand white is counted as a divine sign).

In searching for an alternative explanation for the verse list, I have noticed one other attribute shared by all five signs—an association with the staff that Moses uses to perform his miracles. Most of the plagues omitted from the verse—the flies, the cattle plague, the boils, and the slaying of the firstborn—are those where the staff plays no role in bringing them about according to the biblical account: in these cases, Aaron and Moses initiate the plague with only their hands, or God intervenes to inflict the plague without human mediation.[6] But in the case of the plagues listed in Sura 7:133, there is testimony either from the Bible itself or from postbiblical tradition that the staff was considered instrumental to how each one came about.

To be sure, in Exodus's account of Moses's confrontation with Pharaoh, it is not the prophet himself who wields the staff during the serpent episode and the first three plagues but his brother Aaron. In some early Jewish retellings of these episodes, however, the staff is transferred to Moses. The best example is the retelling of the plagues by Artapanus, where Moses uses the staff to bring about the flooding of the Nile and all the other plagues in that account—the summoning of winged creatures against the Egyptians (which cause the boils), the frogs, the lice, the locusts, and the flies. The staff's power is so impressive according to Artapanus that the Egyptians themselves paid homage to it by installing staffs of their own in their temples, albeit dedicated to the goddess Isis. While Artapanus's account is from centuries before the Qur'an, it was transmitted by Christians in late antiquity, and it is conceivable that a similar version of the story, or even Artapanus's own account, lies behind the version of the story in Sura 7.

Even if the Qur'an's selection of signs to enumerate was simply following the source it happened to be relying on, however, there is also reason to think that its author had his own reasons for highlighting the plagues associated with the staff. It so happens that the staff plays a prominent role in Sura 7, surfacing in its narrative at three other points. The first mention appears in verse 106, where, in response to Pharaoh's demand that he show him a sign to prove the truth of his words, Moses throws the staff down before the king, and it turns into a snake. The staff is mentioned a second time in verse 117, when Moses throws it down again and it swallows the fake staffs-turned-serpents of the magicians, causing them to become devout believers in God. The third mention is in verse 160, when Moses uses it to strike water from a rock. All these episodes are based on scenes in Exodus, but the Qur'an expands on the role that the staff plays in the Torah. Beyond proving the truth of Moses's words, it also wins over converts to God, so impressing the magicians with God's power that they not only prostrate themselves before God but refuse to disavow him even when Pharaoh threatens to crucify them (7:119–126).[7]

Why does the Qur'an elaborate on the role of the staff in this way? My answer to that question is that the author recognized the staff as a precursor to the Qur'an itself. As Sura 7 makes clear, Muhammad stands in a long line of prophets sent to human beings to warn them against sin and urge their submission to God. The earliest of these messengers do not wield any divine signs at all, and they are simply disbelieved, but when the prophet Salih is able to produce a miraculous sign, the miraculous camel, he has more success: it too is rejected by the elite of the Thamud tribe, but it does convince the common people who declare their belief in Salih as God's messenger (7:75). Muhammad refuses to produce a sign when called on to do so, but the Qur'an itself can be considered such a sign, a miracle sent by God as a warning to disbelievers (Sura 29:47–51). The Qur'anic author enlarged the role of the staff because he viewed it as a precursor to the Qur'an's own role as an instrument of divine communication and chastisement.

Although there is no way to prove any particular explanation for the list of plagues in Sura 7:133, the evidence cited here suggests that it may not be a coincidence that it mentions only those plagues associated with the staff while omitting most of the others. In one other place in the Qur'an, it should be noted, its account of the exodus has been notably reworked to give the staff a bigger role than it has in the Bible. In the biblical account of the parting of the Red Sea, God instructs Moses to lift up his staff, but the narrative then goes on to report that Moses used his hand to part the sea, not the staff (Exodus 14:21). By contrast, in Sura 26:63, Moses uses his staff, not his hand, to split the sea. The Qur'an's selective listing of the plagues can be seen as another modification of the biblical account to give the staff a more prominent role in the story.

Reading the plagues verse in the larger context of Sura 7 puts us in a position to tease out a little about its one-word reference to the locust plague. At first glance, it seems to be playing the same role that the locust plague does in Exodus, but its meaning has been changed by being relocated within the sura's account of prophetic history. Like the earlier signs recounted in the sura, the true audience for the signs delivered to Moses was not the Egyptians themselves but later generations meant to learn from what happened to them on account of their arrogance. The narrative implies that God had already planned for Pharaoh and his nobles to reject the signs, sealing their hearts so they would not believe them no matter how many there were or how clear their meaning. The intent, rather, was to warn later gener ations in a position to see the terrible consequences of the Egyptians' disbelief, just as they were meant to learn from the drowning of the people who rejected Noah's warning (Sura 7:64), the earthquake that destroyed the tribe of Thamud for killing Salih's miraculous camel (7:78), and the earthquake that destroyed the townspeople of Shuaib, Moses' father-in-law, after they pressured him to abandon his faith (7:96). The locust plague as it is narrated in Sura 7 is framed as one of a long series of prophetic warning signs that fail to convince disbelievers at the time but leave a trail of sudden catastrophe and misery that later people were meant to learn from, lest they disbelieve as well and perish in the same ways.

The Qur'an's reframing of the locust plague helps to explain its significance for later Muslims like Zaira Wasim. Following the backlash to her tweet, Wasim posted a follow-up message in which she explained what she had been trying to say. The Qur'an's purpose was to inspire people to engage in reflection about their own lives, and it was in that spirit that she was citing Sura 7:133, she explained—not to condemn others as sinners responsible for the calamity swooping down on them but to encourage them to reflect on the Qur'anic story, to avoid the mistakes of the Egyptians, and to return to God.[8] What made it possible for her to apply such a view to a present-day locust invasion was not just the one-word reference to locusts in Sura 7:133 but also the conception of the sign developed in Sura 7 and throughout the Qur'an—the idea that God uses all of creation, including the tiniest of animals, to send reminders of who he is to people prone to forget him, that he repeatedly warns them to repent despite knowing that many will reject his messengers, and that he sends calamities as signs not just to punish the wicked but to try to save the generations who come later before they doom themselves as well.

Oracles with an Appetite

As depicted in Sura 7, the locust is not ascribed any special characteristics that might distinguish it from the other animals involved in Moses's confrontation with Pharaoh. It appears among several animals identified as signs—the camel revealed to the tribe of Thamud, the snake and serpent appearing from Moses's staff, and the frogs and lice of the other plagues—and nothing stands out about it among these other creatures. As developed by later storytellers, however, the locust's status as a divine sign deepened, and this change, I will argue, had a big impact on how Muslims interacted with the locusts they encountered in their own lives.

In Sura 7:133, the flood, locusts, lice, frogs, and blood are described as signs that are "openly self-explained" or, as some have translated the term, "obvious." In other words, they were signs that were simply too patently clear to miss. Though Pharaoh and his accomplices do not believe them, there is no suggestion in the Qur'an that they had any difficulty understanding the signs; it does not depict them puzzling over how to understand them or being mystified by them. They even accept them initially, acceding to Moses while each plague is ongoing and only reverting to their former foolishness after it has subsided.

But that is not how the locust is depicted in later hadith, anecdotes and sayings from the prophet Muhammad and his companions collected by later Muslim scholars and that serve as a source of guidance second only to the Qur'an itself in authority. As it happens, hadith contain all kinds of stories that involve Muhammad and locusts.[9]

In some hadith, the prophet is remembered opining about various legal questions raised by the locust—whether it is permitted to kill locusts and in what circumstances, and whether Muslims are allowed to dine on them (locusts were considered a nutritious and even tasty food in parts of the Islamic world, but there was also legal debate about whether they were halal, meat that Muslims were legally permitted to eat).

Some traditions fill in the background of the locust, like one that explains that they were created from the clay left over after the creation of Adam out of the ground. Others associate them with the coming day of judgment, *Yawm al-Qiyamah* in Arabic—such as a tradition where Muhammad teaches that they are destined to become the first creature to perish when the world comes to an end. According to one story, when Muhammad's companion and father-in-law, 'Umar (582–644 CE), began to receive reports that there were no locusts to be found anywhere in Muslim territory, he recalled Muhammad's teaching and feared that the Day of Judgment was at hand, sending messengers to Syria and Yemen to confirm whether the reports were true. When one returned with a handful of locusts, 'Umar seemed greatly relieved, declaring "Allahu akbar" (God is great) three times.

Most relevant for our purposes are hadith where Muhammad is depicted interpreting the wings of the locust, whose markings are taken as cryptic writing. The Muhammad of hadith resembles Moses in many ways, even carrying a staff, but here he is an interpreter of the locust rather than their commander, and his understanding of the locust as a divine sign goes beyond anything the Qur'an claims for Moses as a medium of divine signs. According to one hadith, cited in an entry on the locust in the fourteenth-century work *Hayat al-Hayawan al-Kubra* (*The Life of the Great Animal*), a zoological encyclopedia compiled by an Egyptian scholar named ad-Damiri (1341–1405), after being asked to explain the strange markings that appear on the locust's wing, the prophet, recognizing that the markings were Hebrew letters, explained that they recorded a threatening proclamation from the locusts: "We are the army of the great God, and we lay ninety-nine eggs. If the number of them is completed to a hundred, we shall eat the world and what there is in it."[10] The association of the locust with the end of the world brings to mind one of the apocalyptic calamities envisioned in the book of Revelation, an attack by monstrous locusts who use their scorpion-like tails to sting and torment people for five months (Revelation 9:1–11). In this hadith, it is the locust's mouth the endangers the world: locusts are so ravenous that if each were to lay just one more egg, there would be enough of them to devour everything.

Another hadith recorded in the same entry from *The Life of the Great Animal* involves an episode witnessed by Muhammad's companion Abd-Allah: "Once when a locust fell on a table, Abd-Allah took it and asked, 'What is there written on it?' . . . [Muhammad] replied, 'There is written on it, "I am God, there is no deity but me. I am the Lord of locusts and their sustainer. To some people, I send them as a food if I wish, to others I send them as a trial."' At this, Abd-Allah said, 'This is a part of the secret knowledge'"[11] Here, too, Muhammad is depicted as able to decipher the coded message inscribed into the locust's wing, but this time the message comes from God himself, who declares the locust as both a blessing and a trial—to some people a source of nourishment but to others an ordeal that ruins their livelihoods. By revealing a divine answer to a theological question—it was God that gave the locust its strange power to both nourish and ravage—the locust's wing functions like ancient divination, especially the practice of reading the markings on the body parts of animals as portents of good fortune or calamity.

The locust as depicted in this hadith isn't just an enigmatic sign; it is a puzzlingly paradoxical one, revealing the insect as a contradictory combination of blessing and trial. The hadith does not explain why God uses the same creature in two ways, nor does it shed light on why God sends the locusts as a blessing to some and an ordeal for others. It simply asserts that the locust combines both roles, leaving the companion to whom Muhammad revealed this secret, Abd-Allah, impressed but also mystified. "This is a part of the secret knowledge," he responds.

This aspect of the hadith also reflects a conception of the oracle known from the Greek world. An oracle is a divine message sent through an intermediary, and in the ancient Greek world at least, such messages were a combination of revelation and secrecy, disclosing divine secrets to humans but expressed in ambiguous and paradoxical language that was hard to make sense of. The best-known examples come from the Oracle of Delphi, messages from the god Apollo delivered through a priestess in response to questions people would pose to it. As the philosopher Heraclitus explained, the Oracle neither spoke nor concealed but only communicated through signs, evidently understanding the latter to involve something in between speaking and concealing, and we know from other Greek sources that the oracles of Delphi often took the form of slyly vague, riddle-like pronouncements and prophesies that were difficult to make sense of and easy to misinterpret—sometimes tragically so, as when the king Croesus mistakes an ambiguous Delphic oracle as a prediction of a victory when it was really a prediction of his own kingdom's defeat.[12]

The messages that Muhammad finds inscribed into the wings of the locust are not ambiguous in the same way, but they involve a similar combination of disclosure and concealment, divulging something of why God sends locusts to humans but not everything. The last example, where the writing on the locust's wing reveals the creature to be both a blessing and a trial, can be considered a kind of riddle or paradox similar to the Delphic oracle in the way it leaves Muhammad's companions puzzling over a divine secret they do not fully understand.[13]

Operating under a similar understanding of the divine sign as paradoxical, medieval Qur'anic commentators sometimes took note of and highlighted the paradoxical quality of the animals mentioned in the Qur'an as a manifestation of divine intelligence.[14] Why was it, for example, that when God sent a sign to the people of Thamud in the time of the prophet Salih, he enlisted a camel as the sign? According to the fourteenth-century Qur'anic commentator and historian Ibn Kathir, it is because the camel embodies a paradoxical combination of strength and yielding: although it is stronger than humans, the camel is willing to submit to them. Al-Qurtabi, a thirteenth-century scholar from Spain, understood this subordination of a great creature to a small one to be "a sign of creation"—Qur'anic language that refers to elements of the natural world that reveal the divine intelligence and benevolence that created it—and the camel was not the only such sign to have a paradoxical quality; so too did other creatures, such as the bee, the bird, and the human, though the last did not always achieve the marvelous balance between the beneficial and the noxious, and between power and submissiveness, in the way the camel did.[15]

The locust, as depicted in the entry from ad-Damari cited earlier, signifies in a similarly paradoxical way. One of the stories recounted in the entry, for instance, involves a Bedouin farmer who, after witnessing his field mowed down by locusts, marvels at God's creation of a creature that is strong and weak at the same time: "Praised be to him who kills the strong—the eater—at the hands of the weak—the eaten one." Why respond in this way? The story does not explain why exactly God sent the locusts, but suggests that he did so as a lesson to the Bedouin who evidently realizes as he looks over his devastated crops that he was the eater who has now been eaten. In this story, the locust in its role as an enigmatic and paradoxical divine sign reveals that people are not as strong as they think they are, owing their ability to control nature to a god with the power to undo their dominance in an instant by turning something they eat into an agent of famine and starvation. The Bedouin seems to understand this, which is why, rather than cursing his fate, he resigns himself to it, praising God for revealing his power to him through the locust.

The understanding of the locust as a Delphic-like oracle is very different from its role in Sura 7. Elsewhere, the Qur'an distinguishes between those of its verses that are clear, and therefore reliable as a source of knowledge, and those that are ambiguous, cause uncertainty, and require expert interpretation to explain (see Sura 3:7).[16] The locusts as they are described in Sura 7, like all the other signs mentioned in its account of prophetic history, correspond to the former kind of verse. Their meaning is clear and self-evident; the Egyptians reject them not because they are hard to understand or deceptively presented but because Pharaoh and his nobles in their arrogance had decided in advance to reject any sign that Moses delivered to them. As reconceived in hadith and Qur'anic commentary, the locust was transformed into the other kind of sign. Their meaning, encoded in cryptic language and paradox, was no longer obvious, and it required guidance from someone with divine understanding like Muhammad to understand them.

Muslim representations of the locust thus mirrored a larger change in the concept of the divine sign, but there was also something else motivating the insect's evolving religious significance—Muslims' interactions with locusts in their own experience. The locust played contradictory roles in people's lives as a source of nourishment but also as a ravenous pillager that caused so much havoc and hardship that it seemed like a marauding army. The Qur'an does not register this contradiction in its brief reference to the locust as a warning sign to Pharaoh, but later Muslims developed their image of the locust in light of it, and the reinterpretation of the locust as a cryptic divine sign, a Delphic-like oracle, opened a way to understand the double role of the locust in people's lives as a religious paradox. The result was a deepening of the locust's significance as a lesson to humankind not to underestimate God's power or overestimate its own.

Fighting God's Army

The locust is not the only insect ascribed this paradoxical quality. The bee was recognized as a similar combination of blessing and pain, offering honey from one side of its body and a sting from the other. What distinguished the locust, however, was the scale of the pain and death it could inflict. Locust outbreaks happened fairly frequently in the parts of the world inhabited by large Muslim populations, and the famines they triggered could cause a loss of life comparable to that caused by a war. Locust attacks were a part of people's experience in the Middle East throughout antiquity and the Middle Ages, and modernity has seen some devastating outbreaks too: a locust invasion in Algeria between 1864 and 1875 caused a famine that, together with the spread of disease, killed an estimated eight hundred thousand people, while a locust outbreak in Syria and Palestine in 1915 is thought to have precipitated the deaths of up to two hundred thousand people.[17] Hadith and Qur'anic commentary might help to account for such events as part of God's creation, but they did not stop the starving and suffering they caused.

Given the threat posed by locusts, it is no surprise that Muslim farmers, like others affected by locust swarms, developed various ways to protect against them. And given their religious beliefs, it is also unsurprising that these techniques often involved seeking God's help through prayer and other supplicatory rituals. Muslims were by no means the first to enlist divine help in response to locust outbreaks. The various peoples of the ancient Near East all used prayer to enlist the help of the gods against locusts; so too did the ancient Greeks—indeed, we know of an example or two where people consulted the Oracle of Delphi for Apollo's guidance about how to end a locust infestation; and the Israelites appealed to their god for help in a not dissimilar way, as we know from the book of Joel, where a prophet calls on his people to fast, weep, and pray to God for mercy.[18] Muslims also turned to God to defend against locust attacks, using some of the same basic religious techniques—prayer, repentance, and other supplicatory practices—but they developed these into their own distinctive ways of soliciting God's help.

Muslims also, of course, deployed nonreligious techniques to fend off locusts—that is, techniques that depended on human effort rather than divine intervention, such as searching out and destroying locust eggs to prevent the insects from reproducing. But alongside such measures, they also turned to God precisely because of his role as "Lord of the locusts," the deity who created them and directed their movements. I could fill this whole chapter with examples of the prayers, amulets, and other measures developed over the centuries to combat the locust—a variety that reflects the environmental and cultural diversity of the Muslim world that stretches from Africa and Europe to East Asia. From the Middle Ages into the nineteenth century, Muslims in Syria employed an elaborate procedure to attract a flock of mysterious birds known as the *samarmar*, drawing them by various ritual practices—Sufi prayers, communal ceremonies, and the use of sacred water carefully imported from Iran—to swoop in and consume all the locusts.[19] In sub-Saharan Africa, Muslim farmers would guard their crops against locust incursions by tying leaves of paper inscribed with a prayer of Muhammad to sticks that they placed in their fields.[20] My favorite example comes from Yemen, where some communities would enlist a local rabbi-mystic to intercede with God on their behalf and send the locusts in another direction.[21]

Such practices resembled and sometimes borrowed from non-Muslim anti-locust measures. In the case of the Syrian ritual, we know from the Roman scholar Pliny that long before the rise of Islam, people living in the region would pray to Jupiter to send birds to eat the locusts that were plaguing them (*Natural History* 10.17), while the amulets used by sub-Saharan Muslim farmers to ward off locusts were an adaptation of earlier Hausa practice. What could complicate Muslim efforts to defend against the locust, however, was the role of the locust in Islamic interpretive tradition, lore, and legal tradition. While there were hadith that permitted Muslims to kill locusts in self-defense, as one was permitted even to kill a fellow Muslim, the locust was thought to be under God's control, an army that he deployed to punish the wicked and warn people to repent, and even when he sent them against the faithful, it was thought that he had his reasons for doing so. To try to fight against the locust, therefore, was to fight against God, to resist him in the way that Pharaoh did—an act as futile as it was impious.

The religious dilemma this situation could create came to the fore in the first half of the twentieth century when Westerners sought to intervene in various Muslim societies in Africa and Asia to help local farmers overcome the locust threat. European Christians had also relied on prayer and other religious measures to combat the locust, but by this point, Britain and other European powers had embraced a scientific approach to locust control pioneered by a Russian-born scientist named Boris Uvarov (1888–1970), the founder of the field of acridology, the scientific study of grasshoppers and locusts. Uvarov had come to understand the environmental factors that trigger the formation of locust swarms, and he used that knowledge to develop forecasting and population-control methods that Britain and other colonizing powers soon exported to the various territories that came under their sway.[22] While such methods were supposed to give local farmers a better way to combat locusts, they could clash with traditional religious beliefs, including those regarding the role of the locust in Islamic theology and lore, and the result in some cases was resistance, passive and active—a refusal to accept the help of Western powers.

Consider what happened in Palestine, then under the control of the Ottoman Empire, when locusts caused a devastating famine in the region in 1915–1916. According to Western reports from the time, rather than accept the help of outsiders or take any steps of their own to combat the locusts, locals simply resigned themselves to the destruction. The locusts, they believed, had been sent by God, and so they were helpless to fight them.[23] The early Zionist Alexander Aaronsohn (1888–1948), writing of his brother's effort to organize a campaign against the locusts at the behest of an Ottoman military ruler, described the locals in similar terms, also suggesting a religious motivation: "The Arabs are lazy—and fatalistic besides, they cannot understand why men should attempt to fight *Djesh Allah* [God's army] as they call the locusts."[24] One can imagine many other reasons that would explain why locals gave up in this way—perhaps this particular locust attack was simply too overwhelming; perhaps people resented the menial, poorly compensated work of egg collection; perhaps they were not inclined to cooperate with foreigners or Zionists like Aaronsohn—but according to these reports, they couched their resignation in religious terms, as an act of submission to God's army.

The pious capitulation registered in these sources was not limited to Palestine. The earliest example I have come across is from the eighteenth century: an Italian official based in Cyprus, then under Ottoman rule, reported that the Turks did not allow peasants to search out locusts' eggs to destroy them "because they deem it a capital sin to rebel against a Divine judgement."[25] This attitude persisted into the twentieth century, into and beyond World War I. In a report submitted to the League of Nations in 1926, for instance, a British official complained of the "habitual apathy and fatalism toward the locust scourge" among the population in Iraq.[26]

In two places, the Russian-dominated emirate of Bukhara and British-controlled Somaliland, the introduction of Western pest-control methods ignited violent uprisings. The first revolt, in Bukhara in 1920, was a reaction against a Russian and then Soviet anti-locust campaign between 1905 and 1920 wherein the Russians exerted a lot of pressure on the population to introduce a new and very labor-intensive method to combat the locusts that involved finding young locusts before they could fly and burying them in ditches.[27] The Somaliland revolt in 1945, led by a preacher named Sheikh Bashir, was a reaction against the British-introduced use of toxins in locust baits.[28] Both rebellions were driven by economic, political, and ecological grievances. Farmers in Bukhara resented being forced to leave their farms to join a backbreaking effort they didn't think would work and was upsetting the region's ecological balance. In Somaliland, people suspected that the baits were a plot to poison the cattle and drive people from their land. However, both uprisings, fanned by clerics and preachers, were also fueled by the belief that the anti-locust campaigns were a rebellion against God and needed to be resisted as a matter of faith.

In trying to understand Muslim resistance to the methods of European locust control, it is important to keep in mind that Western accounts of how Muslims in this period behaved were often influenced by an orientalist stereotype that exaggerates Muslim passivity and fatalism.[29] The historian Samuel Dolbee has recently demonstrated such bias at work in an 1886 report compiled by the French consul in the Iraqi city of Mosul. The report explains the locals' inertia in the face of locust outbreaks by citing some of the hadith I have already mentioned as evidence of an ingrained fatalism.[30] Dolbee shows, however, that the author, a Christian diplomat, edited what he took from ad-Damiri's entry on the locust to make Muhammad look more one-dimensionally fatalistic than hadith, in the aggregate, actually represent him to be. For instance, the author cites the hadith in which Muhammad learns from reading a locust's wing that locusts are just one egg shy of being able to eat the whole world. What the diplomat leaves out is the prophet's response once he learns this: he does not simply resign himself to being destroyed by the locusts but calls on God to destroy them and make their eggs unproductive.

Even factoring in that Muslim fatalism is exaggerated, however, it seems likely that religious belief played some role in fomenting resistance to modern pest control. Of particular importance is the theological concept known as *tawakkul,* or trusting in God, which can shape how some Muslims respond to calamities to this day. The core idea is that people should always trust in God's plans even when those plans require the faithful to suffer and die, and for some Muslims, that ruled out taking self-protective measures, such as wearing armor in battle, carrying provisions on a trip across the desert, or taking medicine when ill. According to some interpretations of the concept of *tawakkul,* Muslims who truly submitted themselves to God would not need such measures to protect themselves; it showed a lack of trust to use them; and it would be futile to try to thwart or evade God's plans anyway since he was all-powerful.[31] Even today within some Muslim countries, there are public health experts who argue that present-day adherence to the concept of *tawakkul* is so strong among many Muslims that it poses a societal risk, endangering people by encouraging them to resist taking precautionary measures.[32]

We saw this kind of attitude reflected in the hadith about the Bedouin who resigns himself to seeing his crops destroyed by locusts. He was left destitute, but there was nothing he could do to stop them, and he could only praise God for creating the locusts. In the light of such stories, we cannot simply dismiss the testimony of Western sources that report Muslims refusing to cooperate in anti-locust campaigns because they deemed it impious to fight God's army. The threat posed by locusts is never to be underrated—based on the number of people endangered by locust-initiated famines, they are arguably the single most dangerous animal that humans have faced in their history, with the possible exception of the mosquito. But it was one thing to turn to God for help against the locust; it was another to try to operate independently of that control by using foreign and secular methods to defeat God's army. The latter could be considered a lack of faith in God comparable to that of Pharaoh when he turned to magic to challenge Moses, and such defiance was even more dangerous than a locust swarm.

Beyond this theological objection, however, another factor may have led Muslims to resist Western locust-control campaigns—the special status of the locust in Islamic tradition. The perception of locusts as God's army, an enforcer used to punish sin and warn people to repent, meant that their removal, whatever immediate relief it brought, also removed one of the instruments that God used to prepare people for the final judgment. Poisoning locusts thus might have triggered the apocalyptic anxiety felt by the prophet's companion ʻUmar when he thought that there were no more locusts to be found within Muslim territory. If pesticides were to eliminate locusts, wouldn't their disappearance portend the end of the world? It is also possible that people felt a need to protect the locust from extermination because of the insect's role as an ally for the faithful. Locusts were supposed to be feared as God's army, agents of the irresistible power that created the world, enforcers of justice, and signs sent to warn people to repent, and seeing unbelievers try to wipe them out may have been harder to abide than even the damage inflicted by locusts themselves: so suggested an angry Bukharan emir Said ʻAbd al-Ahad Khan when he complained that only infidels could conceive of "destroying locusts sent by God."[33]

The locust uprisings in Bukhara and Somaliland were soon repressed, and it did not take long before Western-style anti-locust campaigns resumed in both places: in fact, a team operating under the direction of Uvarov returned to Somaliland just five years after the end of the revolt, though there was still some concern about encountering hostile mobs there. Today, pesticides and other Western-originated scientific methods of locust removal are used in countries with large Muslim majorities throughout the Islamic world, and those governments that fail to keep locusts under control can suffer politically, as the Muslim Brotherhood in Egypt learned when it found itself mocked for having failed to stem a locust outbreak in 2013.[34] The Taliban in Afghanistan, which returned to power in 2021, is known for seeking to create a pure Islamic state based on the Qur'an, but nothing in its understanding of the Qur'an and Islamic law prevented it from accepting forty thousand liters of the pesticide malathion from India in 2024 to curb infestations that threatened up to a quarter of the country's wheat harvest. In a 1943 essay titled "The Locust Plague," Uvarov depicted the biblical locust plague as the beginning of a long and tragic history of locust-caused agricultural ruin and famine that the world now had the power to end through scientific research and international cooperation.[35] Although locust outbreaks continue as a major environmental threat, Uvarov's science-driven vision of preemption and management has prevailed worldwide in both Muslim and non-Muslim countries.

But thanks to the continued sacrality of the Qur'an and hadith, the theological understanding of the locust and the locust plague also remains alive and well for millions of Muslims. Even in an age that uses advanced monitoring systems and drones to suppress locust outbreaks, the insect still poses a threat that humans struggle to manage and contain. For present-day Muslims like Wasim, the Qur'an offers a way to make sense of this vulnerability and even to draw something redemptive from it by presenting its readers with the example of a locust outbreak functioning as a sign, an epiphany, not just the punishment of sin but a lesson that humans are not as strong and independent as they think they are.

9

The Ninth Plague

DARKNESS VISIBLE

EVEN IN a light-saturated world, darkness can still pose a menace. On August 14, 2003, a hot summer day, a power surge triggered a blackout that reached from the northeastern United States into the Midwest and all the way into Canada, cutting off power to some fifty-five million people. It is the most widespread blackout to date in U.S. history, and at the time the second-largest blackout in world history. While it caused no mass panic, the loss of power introduced enough hazards that, according to one study, the mortality rate increased by 28 percent that night. The heat was a major factor in many deaths, but the darkness killed too: poor lighting contributed to a rise in car crashes, while being stuck in the dark in subways and elevators precipitated heart attacks.[1]

A blackout is one of the few moments when a person today—those of us living in an economically developed country—feels the vulnerability to darkness that has characterized the experience of most human beings for the entirety of our species' existence. Modern humans have figured out ways to keep the darkness at bay, but for most of history, the safest bet was to stay shut inside because of how much danger lurked in the night.[2] Not only were there predators lurking in the shadows, animal, supernatural, and human, but sickness was thought more likely to attack at night; and the earth itself became more treacherous: in an unlit, unpaved world, the perils of the night included falls and drownings. Darkness remains a menace today for the large part of humanity afflicted by "light poverty" that increases accidents and other health risks.

As terrifying as darkness can still be today, however, it was even more frightening in a premodern era when light was harder to come by. In a midrash about humanity's first experience of darkness, Adam, at the end of his first day in the garden, is terrified by the impending nightfall. This will be his first experience of night, and he is worried that something is coming to attack him (Genesis Rabbah 11.2). The story, which registers fear of the dark as the most primordial of fears—felt by Adam before he had any reason to be afraid even of mortality itself—captures what seems to be a shared inheritance of humankind. Despite their theological differences, Judaism, Christianity, and Islam all associate darkness with very negative experiences—terror, isolation, complete and absolute vulnerability, and death itself.

The deep-seated nature of this fear can help us appreciate what was so terrifying for early readers of the Bible about the ninth plague, the plague of darkness. As described in the book of Exodus, the darkness of the plague lasted much longer than both the brief yet frightening blackout of an eclipse and the ordinary darkness of nighttime, persisting for three days. One of the earliest retellings of the episode was that of Philo, who added that there was no relief to be found in any kind of artificial light source: lighting a lamp or a torch did not work to illumine the darkness of the plague, he explains, because the flames would be smothered by the winds of a storm. As described in Exodus, the darkness is said to have been so total that the Egyptians could not see each other or move about. Philo understood its effect to have been psychologically immobilizing as well; the darkness trapped the Egyptians in a state of mass catatonia that left them unable to speak or even eat, to the point of starvation (*Life of Moses* 1.124–125).

The biblical text sheds little light on the darkness of the plague. Yet, as we will explore in this chapter, in recounting the story of the ninth plague, artists have been able to draw detail from out of the shadows of the Bible's description as Philo did in his expansion of the episode. The key difference from his example, though, is that they operated visually rather than verbally, producing versions of the episode where, by dint of the painter's brush or an engraver's tool, the darkness acquires a shape, texture, and color, and can reveal landscapes, people, animals, objects, and even sources of light beyond what the Egyptians themselves were able to see. By turning our gaze from retellings to illustrations of the biblical story, in this chapter I will seek to illumine how the opacity of the ninth plague was reimagined as a revelatory visual experience.

Reading in the Dark

Interpretations of the ninth plague can be divided into two categories: those that conceive of the plague as a form of blindness, an impairment of the Egyptians' ability to see or interpret what they are seeing, and those that understand the darkness as atmospheric, a result not of God interfering with the Egyptians' eyesight but of a cessation or blocking of light. My main focus will be on this latter approach, but before turning to it, I first want to consider a retelling from the tradition that presents the darkness of the plague as a spiritual, intellectual, or moral blindness.

My chief example of this way of interpreting the darkness comes from a previously mentioned Hellenistic text from the second or first century BCE, the Wisdom of Solomon. The darkness in this version of the episode is presented as a self-imposed hallucination: the Egyptians have convinced themselves that they are enshrouded in darkness, even though light shines all around them: "For the whole world was illumined with brilliant light, and went about its work unhindered, while over those people alone heavy night was spread, an image of the darkness that was destined to receive them; but still heavier than darkness were they to themselves" (17:20–21). What sent the Egyptians into a panic was not atmospheric darkness, a physical turning out of the lights, but an "image of the darkness that was destined to receive them"—that is, it was a mental visualization of the darkness awaiting them in death. In actuality, the world around them was bathed in light, and had the Egyptians a correct understanding of reality, recognizing God's control of the cosmos, they would have been able to see it and had nothing to fear, because God, according to the author of this text, rewards those who believe in him with eternal life. Without that knowledge, they were trapped in a darkness generated by their own minds, a hallucinatory externalization of the fear of death.

The Wisdom of Solomon was composed in Greek, and its rendering of the plague of darkness bears a striking resemblance to a famous depiction of darkness in another Greek work known at the time, Plato's allegory of the cave in his dialogue *The Republic* (514a–520a). The allegory describes a group of prisoners chained to a wall in a cave in a way that prevents them from seeing the world outside; all they can see are the shadows projected onto the wall of the cave as things pass in front of its entrance. The allegory is meant to illustrate how we are captive inside a material world that conceals from the mind the true nature of reality beyond what eyes can see.

While the Wisdom of Solomon does not explicitly cite the allegory of the cave, scholars have long suspected that it was influenced by Plato, in part because of the ideas they share in common.[3] As I discussed in the chapter on the plague of blood, justice is a major theme in the Wisdom of Solomon—which develops a reading of the ten plagues as psychologized measure-for-measure justice—and that focus is the first point of connection to Plato's *Republic,* the philosophical dialogue that features the allegory of the cave and whose central task is to illuminate the very concept of justice. More specifically, the two texts construct very similar scenarios: an allegorical light shines outside—a light that symbolizes truth or wisdom—but those trapped inside the darkness, depicted as prisoners who mistake specters and shadows for actual beings, cannot apprehend it. In both stories, moreover, the way out of the darkness is a kind of enlightenment. For Plato, the escape is philosophy, understood as a guide that can lead the mind out of the illusory realm of material existence. In the Wisdom of Solomon, the way out is "the imperishable light of the law" (18:4)—that is, the Torah—which this author understood as being similar to philosophy, involving a form of study meant to shed light on wisdom and justice.

Plato introduced a distinction between the kind of light accessible to the senses, the light generated by the sun, and another kind of light that came from somewhere beyond the sun, a source of mental illumination accessible not to the eyes but only through the sort of reasoning cultivated by philosophy.[4] The author of the Wisdom of Solomon drew on this idea to cast the Torah as the equivalent to philosophy, "a reflection of eternal light . . . more beautiful than the sun" (7:26), and he used the plague of darkness to create something like Plato's cave, a realm of darkness where the darkness is understood as a mental failure, an inability to apprehend the true nature of reality as a nonmaterial and imperishable realm of thought beyond sense perception.

Because the Egyptians do not understand what the universe is really like—because they do not grasp the invisible God, the invisible principle of justice that governs the universe, or the invisible soul that will live beyond the death of the physical body—they languish under a misunderstanding of physical death that confines them in a prison of terror and delusion. The Israelites, on the other hand, have no such fear because they see reality in the light of the Torah.

The Wisdom of Solomon, especially well known to those who regard it as a part of the Bible, inspired its own tradition of interpretation and retelling that extends into our own day. In the twentieth century, for example, the Swiss theologian Hans Urs von Balthasar interpreted the plague of darkness as an allegory for the soul struggling with the anxiety of being distant from God.[5] In this tradition, the darkness of the plague is a spiritual, intellectual, or moral blindness that prevents the Egyptians, stand-ins for humanity, from apprehending the truth. I would also venture to include as a possible heir to this tradition the 1995 novel *Blindness* by the Portuguese Nobel Prize–winning writer José Saramago, a story about a city stricken by an epidemic of blindness. (Saramago, incidentally, seems to have been fascinated by the allegorical potential of darkness; his novel *The Cave* was inspired by none other than Plato's allegory of the cave.) It may not be a coincidence that these figures were Catholic or, in Saramago's case, were reacting to Catholicism, because the Wisdom of Solomon is included in the Catholic Bible—and is not a part of the Jewish and Protestant Bibles—and thus had far more of an impact on how readers in Catholic contexts understood the ninth plague than it did on Jewish and Protestant interpretations.

The other way of imagining the darkness, which will be my primary focus in what follows, is as an atmospheric condition, not blindness but a shrouding of Egypt in physical darkness. This kind of darkness was easier for visual artists to represent; and indeed, it gave the ninth plague a special appeal for such artists—darkness has long been a subject of fascination for painters, whose artistry requires a skillful manipulation of light. However, it also posed its own distinctive challenges. What does darkness look like? How does one distinguish the special miraculous darkness of the ninth plague from the ordinary darkness of nighttime? How does one show the viewer what happened during the ninth plague when such events were not visible to those involved in the episode? The history of how artists have addressed these challenges gives us a chance to pay more attention to illustration, the translation of a verbal text into a visual experience, as a mode of retelling the ten plagues. This history also offers an opportunity to further explore how people's understanding of the darkness of the plague has been influenced by their understanding of darkness in general, a condition universally experienced by humans as frightening but taking on various intellectual, emotional, moral, and metaphorical associations in different cultures and circumstances, as it does, for example, in Plato's allegory of the cave.

The earliest attempt to visualize the darkness plague of which I'm aware is a scene in a Byzantine Octateuch from the eleventh century. An Octateuch is a truncated biblical manuscript, comprising only eight books—the five books of Moses plus the historical books of Joshua, Judges, and Ruth in their Greek translation. The practice of publishing the Bible in this form emerged in the Byzantine Empire, the Christianized eastern part of the Roman Empire that split from its western part in the fourth century and survived as a kingdom until the fifteenth century. There is evidence of Octateuchs as early as the fifth and sixth centuries, and since we know that other biblical manuscripts were already being illustrated by this period, it is possible that they were also adorned with images. However, the only surviving examples of illustrated Octateuchs come from a later period between 1050 and 1300, and these manuscripts preserve the oldest known visualizations of the plague of darkness that I have come across.

In the scene pictured in figure 16, which comes from one of the earliest of those manuscripts (known as the Vatican Octateuch),[6] the darkness

FIGURE 16. The plague of darkness as depicted in the Vatican Octateuch. Reproduced with permission of the Vatican Apostolic Library, vat. Gr 747, fol. 83v.

of the plague is clearly visible on the right side of the illustration, rendered in a dark black. Pharaoh is in the center of the illustration, enveloped within the darkness along with two other Egyptians whose crouching posture and elevated arms signal their intimidation and alarm. The two figures on the left side of the illustration, Moses and Aaron, are adorned with golden halos radiating from their heads that contrast with the monochromatic darkness that entraps the Egyptians.

In contrast to a verbal retelling, an illustration like this can employ light and darkness as a part of its representation, and the Octateuch illustrator has done so by dividing the scene into light and dark zones to create a mirroring effect between the two sides of the picture. This contrast is significant. Art historians have shown how Byzantine art deployed a contrast between bright color (especially gold) and blackness to signify the luminosity of the divine presence and its absence, respectively.[7] The illustrator of this scene has incorporated this contrast into his depiction of the plague, opposing the darkness, painted in a deep black, with the shimmering golden halos of Moses and Aaron and the bright variegated coloring of their clothing.

FIGURE 17. Christ breaking into the blackness of hell, as depicted in an eleventh-century Byzantine mosaic from the Monastery of Hosios Loukas in Greece. Wikimedia.

It may not be a coincidence that similar color contrasts are used elsewhere in Byzantine art to draw out the opposition between heaven and hell, as in figure 17, a mosaic from the monastery of Hosios Loukas in Greece that depicts Christ breaking into hell. This illustration pictures a scene that was often represented in Byzantine art, Christ's descent into hell to save Adam and Eve and other sinners imprisoned there before the Resurrection. Its depiction of the darkness of hell is different in many ways from the Octateuch's representation of the darkness of the ninth plague: it takes up much less space in the scene, it is not shown imprisoning anyone—in fact, this is a prison break; the objects shown in the darkness are broken pieces of the gate of hell—and Christ is standing over it victorious. What the two scenes do share, however, is a similar color scheme organized around the contrast between the golden luminosity of divine presence and monochromatic charcoal blackness as a signifier of divine absence and the experience of imprisonment.[8] It is even conceivable that the Octateuch illustration was meant to suggest the darkness of hell itself. The Christian scholar Jerome, translator of the Vulgate, suggested a connection between the two kinds of darkness when he prefaced the word "darkness" in Exodus 10:12 with an adjective he used elsewhere of hell, *horribilis* ("there came *horrible* darkness on the land of Egypt"), while midrash went so far as to claim that the darkness of the plague actually originated in hell (Exodus Rabbah 14.2).[9] The deep enveloping blackness of the Octateuch scene, calling to mind the cave- or prison-like darkness of hell in Byzantine art, may have been an effort to encourage a similar association, as if to visualize the conception of the plague as an expansion of the darkness of hell into Egypt.

The illustrator of the Octateuch was neither the only artist to seize on the contrast between the darkness and light mentioned in the biblical account nor the only artist to invest this contrast with symbolic meaning. In what follows, I single out for closer analysis three illustrations that also deploy the contrast between light and dark to deepen the meaning of the ninth plague: an engraving by the nineteenth-century French biblical illustrator Gustave Doré (1832–1883), a painting by the twentieth-century modernist artist Marc Chagall (1887–1985), and a more recent painting by the abstract expressionist Miriam Beerman (1923–2022), part of a series of ten plagues–inspired paintings. While all three artists were working within the narrative parameters established by the brief account in Exodus 10:21–23, within those confines, they created strikingly different retellings of the story, including different renditions of how the darkness of the episode relates to the light shining over the dwellings of the Israelites. The idea that the darkness of the plague manifested hell on earth was an ancient one, but all three artists transmuted this tradition into renderings of the darkness as distinctively modern versions of hell.

A Dark Cloud over Egypt

Many interpreters of the ninth plague have imagined the darkness as a cloud that was so thick that it was palpable. Two details in Exodus suggest such an interpretation: the use of the word ʾ*afelah* to describe the darkness, a word that elsewhere in the Bible connotes dark clouds or mist, and a puzzling phrase in Exodus 10:21, "a darkness which may be felt." The Hebrew does not make any sense grammatically and might be the result of a copyist's mistake, but the phrase has been taken by many to mean that the darkness had texture and substance. Philo, as noted earlier, associated the darkness with storm clouds, and Josephus described it as a thick dark cloud that smothered to death all those who came into contact with it (*Antiquities* 2.307–310).

Among modern interpreters who associated the darkness with clouds was Gustave Doré. In one of the most circulated illustrations of the ninth plague, intended for a Bible published in France in 1866, Doré took advantage of an improved engraving process to include more variegated coloring, texture, and shading than was previously possible. The engraving was part of a set of biblical illustrations that were such a hit that they were shown in a special gallery in London opened in 1874 just to exhibit them, and they have been in circulation ever since, republished as book illustrations, church decorations, and picture cards, as well as on the internet.[10] Of most interest to us is Doré's depiction of the darkness as a serrated cloud blanketing the land of Egypt (figure 18). In the distant horizon, there is a break in the cloud that hints at the light shining over the Israelites, but the focus in this image is the terrified Egyptians. What frightens them is not just the darkness itself but the lions and crocodiles coming out of the darkness; their menacing presence may be Doré's way of accounting for why the Egyptians could not rise from their places, as stated in Exodus 10:23.

Doré's version of the plague, shaped by his understanding of the Bible as a grand epic, looks to be very pious, but it is also distinctively modern, a product of the nineteenth century, and one reflection of this era is the way the illustration mimics some of the qualities of photography, introduced less than thirty years earlier, in 1839. That very year saw the first photographs of Egypt, including its ancient monuments, and by the 1850s, a book of photographs entitled *Egypte, Nubie, Palestine et Syrie*, produced through a collaboration between the writer Gustave Flaubert and the photographer Maxime du Camp, achieved great commercial success.[11] Pressure to compete with such photographs helps to explain why Doré included Egyptian ruins and exotic wild animals from Africa in the scene, popular subjects of photography at the time.[12]

FIGURE 18. Engraved illustration of the plague of darkness in Doré's Bible. Alamy.

In my reading of the illustration, however, such details were not merely decorative but tie this version of the plague of darkness to Africa. Darkness took on a new kind of resonance in the nineteenth century in the wake of European colonial expansion. As European countries were beginning to colonize Africa, the language of light and darkness emerged as a metaphor for the difference between Europe and Africa, as witnessed by the title of the era's best-selling English-language account of a colonial expedition, *In Darkest Africa* (1878), by Henry Morton Stanley, the explorer who paved the way for Belgium's colonization of the Congo. Doré's illustration plays on this association between darkness and Africa, transforming the ninth plague into a story about how Africa became a "dark continent."

The light/dark metaphor grew out of the self-image of European colonization itself. The British, French, and Germans all justified colonization as an extension of the Enlightenment, a way of bringing the light of education, science, rational governance, and Christianity to non-European peoples.[13] Darkness connoted the spiritual benightedness of non-Christians, as well as scientific ignorance, and by the nineteenth century, of course, it was also racially coded by the association of blackness with Africans and other non-Whites and non-Christians beyond Europe.[14] In an 1890 map of Africa used by missionaries, for instance, non-Christian regions were represented with black or dark shading, while a lighter shade or white was used for regions where Christianity was gaining ground—with missionary stations marked as points of light.[15]

Rudyard Kipling, in his now infamous poetic celebration of colonization, "The White Man's Burden," offers a contemporary example of how this colonial metaphor could be extended to the darkness of the ninth plague. A reference to the plague appears near the end of the poem in the context of a complaint from the natives who resent being brought to the light: "Why brought he us from bondage, our loved Egyptian night?" (line 40).[16] At first glance, the Egypt that Doré depicts in his illustration seems to be different from the Egypt evoked in Kipling's poem. Doré's Egyptians are racialized as White, and the grandeur of the buildings implies a highly developed culture. Yet a closer look reveals ancient Egypt at the point of its collapse, succumbing to the barbarism of its environs in Africa. This is suggested by the encroaching lions and crocodiles coming out of the darkness to attack the Egyptians, as well as the fact that the Egyptian buildings in the scene have already fallen into ruins. Doré's plague of darkness can be read as an origin story for the darkness of Africa, a depiction of ancient Egypt as an enlightened civilization but one that is beginning its descent into the savagery that darkness was used to represent.

Doré's illustration, so interpreted, is a visual counterpart to a story that emerged in the second half of the nineteenth century about how ancient Egyptians were related to Black Africans. While there was disagreement among scholars in Europe and the United States about how to racially classify ancient Egyptians—some argued they were White, while others held that they should be classified as Black or as descending from some other race—there was a general consensus among such scholars that the civilization of the ancient Egyptians had been very advanced, while that of later Black Africans and Arabs was inferior. Some accounted for the difference by depicting the history of Africa as a history of societal and cultural decline and racial degeneration through misrule, miscegenation, or Muslim conquest.[17] For example, in an 1887 book entitled *Light in Darkness*, which offers a history of Protestant missionary efforts in Africa, the American Methodist ministers John Godbey and Allen Godbey claim, "Once Africa was the nursery of science, art and literature, when Egypt was the first of kingdoms. But long since has the prophecy been fulfilled which declared that Egypt should become the basest of nations. . . . The mystery that today shrouds Egypt, and the deadly blight which has so long rested on it, the mental and moral degradation of its inhabitants combine to give it the title of 'the Dark Continent.'"[18] The only hope for the present-day Africans and Arabs trapped in this darkness, the Godbeys proceed to argue, is outside intervention, the light brought by modern European civilization and Christianity. Doré used the story of the plague of darkness to imply a similar narrative of African decline. The light that once bathed the ancient Egyptians is now seen to be at a great distance, the great buildings pictured in the scene are already falling into ruins, and the land is becoming the savage jungle that nineteenth-century Europeans took Africa to be.

This brings us to the darkness itself, the dark cloud bank that dominates the top half of the illustration. Doré was not the first to depict the plague as a dark cloud, but it too can be understood as part of the illustration's allegorical origin story for Africa. In the nineteenth century, as my former colleague Projit Mukharji has shown, clouds came to be associated with the spread of disease—an offshoot of the ancient idea that plagues were caused by noxious air—and this idea was often rendered visually.[19] Take, for instance, George Wither's book about the great plague of London, *Britain's Remembrancer*, whose frontispiece features an image of a "dismall Cloud, exceeding blacke," which contains within it "all plagues and punishments." In the nineteenth century, following the first cholera pandemic in 1817–1821, what Wither used as a metaphor became literalized through the belief that cholera was

FIGURE 19. Joseph Légaré, *Cholera Plague, Quebec*, c. 1832, National Gallery of Canada, Ottawa.

transmitted through colored or darkened clouds. An 1832 painting by the Canadian Joseph Légaré, for instance, visualizes a cholera epidemic in Quebec as a dark cloud looming over the city (figure 19).[20]

How does this connect to Africa? Cholera clouds were often thought to originate in India or Africa, regions where hot weather and the decay of vegetation were thought to promote the disease. Indeed, cholera's categorization as a specifically African disease is demonstrated by none other than Doré himself, who once personified cholera as an old Black man, in contrast to influenza, depicted as a White man.[21] Mukharji cites a newspaper account from the *Chicago Daily Tribune* that tells of a black cholera cloud thought to have traveled from Africa to Italy, where it was first spotted by a crowd gathered at a castle near Rome. Citing eyewitnesses, the article reports that the cloud looked like "the two wings of an enormous bat."[22]

Dark clouds had another connection to Africa as well: they were often used as a symbol for the trouble that beset the continent and held it back. Missionaries seem to have been especially fond of this metaphor. A memoir published by William Crocker (1805–1841), a missionary in West Africa, laments that a "dark cloud hangs over Africa." In 1864, the missionary Hollis Read wrote that "we see light for Africa . . . in the very thick cloud which has so long hung over her," and in 1878, the Reverend J. E. Carlyle similarly decried the "dark cloud of superstition" that brooded over the minds of Black Africans.[23] The metaphor persisted into the twentieth century, applied to maladies that include slavery, war, superstition, and locusts, and it was often accompanied by an aspiration to dissipate the dark clouds through Christianity, emancipation, colonialism, or new public health measures.[24] Doré's illustration of the ninth plague as a dark plague looming over Egypt—which to this day is frequently republished as if it were a faithful rendering of the biblical account—is yet another application of this motif, using the black cloud over Africa as a way to convey the continent's darkening after the ruination of ancient Egypt.

Painting the World Dark

A little over sixty years after the publication of Doré's illustration, another ambitious effort in France to illustrate the Bible yielded a different rendering of the darkness. In 1931, the art dealer Ambroise Vollard proposed to Marc Chagall that he create a series of etchings to illustrate the Bible. Although Chagall had abandoned religion as a teenager, he sustained a lifelong fascination with the Bible, describing it as a source of deep insight into creativity and art itself; as he once put it, "To read the Bible is to perceive a certain light."[25] Accepting the commission, he worked on the project to the point of obsession, traveling to Palestine for inspiration, to Vilna in Lithuania in order to rekindle the spirit of traditional Bible study he knew from his youth, and to Amsterdam to study Rembrandt's biblical paintings. The project was halted in 1939 when World War II forced Chagall into exile, but he revived it in 1952 and carried on producing illustrations for it until 1956. The resulting Bible-inspired portfolios and related etchings, numbering in the hundreds, are regarded as a great achievement of twentieth-century art.

In the series, Chagall embraced numerous artistic traditions. His influences range from Russian Orthodox Christian iconography and Yiddish and Hasidic folklore to futurist, expressionist, and surrealist European art. He also brushed into his images memories and emotions from his own life, which moved from a childhood in the Jewish Pale of Settlement in Russia, to art training in Paris, to officialdom as a commissar for visual arts in the Soviet Union, to France again, to exile in the United States during World War II, and then back to France—a life that involved loss, displacement, and generative collaborations with leading artists along the way.[26] The resulting illustrations are visually powerful, emotionally evocative, and symbolically overloaded, and include among them a depiction of the plague of darkness, originally composed in 1931, entitled *Moses Spreads the Darkness over Egypt* (figure 20).[27]

In the painting, Moses appears as a large figure in the bottom right corner, a position conventionally reserved for figures with which the artist identifies, and a smaller Aaron looks up at him. Dead animals are strewn across the distant landscape; and we can see in the bottom left corner a trench ladder, as if the scene were a battlefield, and a small figure next to it raises his arm in alarm or grief. In the top right corner, an angel appears overhead, dropping the luminescent letters of the divine name toward Moses. The darkness forms a blackened backdrop infused with swirls of smoke that, in the version of the illustration that I have focused on for this chapter, billow out from the inferno on the left side of the picture.

Although this painting evokes earlier works of art in several ways, Chagall put his own spin on that legacy. An example is his depiction of two beams of light emanating from Moses's head, a detail derived from a western European artistic tradition that visualizes Moses as a horned figure. The idea originates from a passage in Exodus 34 that describes how, after returning from Mount Sinai, the prophet's face was shining in a way that terrified the Israelites. The passage uses a word for "ray," *qeren*, that can also be understood as "horn," and this translation, embraced by Jerome, spawned a Catholic artistic tradition of horned Moses images that includes Michelangelo's statue of Moses in the Church of San Pietro in Vincoli in Rome.[28] An interpretation found in Rashi's commentary, which Chagall studied as a child, understood the

FIGURE 20. Marc Chagall, *Moses Spreads the Darkness over Egypt* (1931). © 2025 Artists Rights Society (ARS), New York / ADAGP, Paris.

term to refer to beams of divine glory that project outward from the prophet's head like horns (see Rashi on Exodus 34:29), but medieval Christians came to associate the horns with the devil, and it became part of an anti-Semitic stereotype of the Jews as demonic minions of Satan. Familiar with both the Jewish and Christian traditions, Chagall's painting fused them in a way that evokes divine rays and satanic horns simultaneously. In the distance, a large fire releases flames that form into the shape of a demonic fiend with what look like two horns of fire coming from its head, calling to mind William Blake's rendering of Satan in his illustration of *Paradise Lost*. This infernal figure, towering over the battlefield, appears as a satanic mirror image of Moses, reflecting his upraised arm and the two beams of light coming from out of his head. Drawing on both traditions of a radiant/horned Moses, Chagall created a doubling effect: evoking the prophet as a luminous holy figure but one with a fiendish and destructive alter ego.

Chagall declined to explain the meaning of the symbols he used in his art, insisting that it speak for itself, but it is possible to tease out some of what he was seeking to convey. One clue comes from a preface that he wrote for a book that celebrated the opening of a museum devoted to his biblical art, the Marc Chagall National Museum in the city of Nice. The essay emphasizes the importance of color, which Chagall claimed revealed the artist's character and message.[29] In Chagall's own painting, color was meant to manifest the life force that he identified with light, love, and creativity, the force that the Bible also expressed, albeit through language rather than image.[30]

Like the illustrations from the Vatican Octateuch, Chagall's vision of the darkness plague was also organized around the contrast between bright and dark, though he deployed the contrast differently. Divinity is signified by brightness—the angel and the divine letters are in white—but, unlike in the Octateuch, there are no clearly segregated zones of light and darkness, nor are there any figures positioned outside the darkness, not even the angel who seems to be flying in the darkness. Moses as he appears in the 1931 version of the painting is colored in a way that positions him in between light and darkness. His garb is colored in a greenish yellow and shot through with black streaks and splotches. Even the beams emanating from his head are not colored in white but instead shade into increasingly dark colors as they extend upward.

The darkness itself is also colored in a complex way. Rather than depict it as jet black, Chagall uses a black mixed with lighter paint strokes that make it appear billowy and smokelike. Also suggesting an association of the darkness with smoke, as the art historian Maya Balakirsky Katz pointed out to me, is the position of Moses's left hand: raised to his neck, it can be interpreted as a choking gesture, as if the prophet had inhaled the smoke coming from the inferno. Departing from Philo's interpretation that the darkness was so dense it extinguished the flames of torches, Chagall's image contains a fire, like a funeral pyre raging over the landscape, and its burning in the dark evokes John Milton's depiction of hell as a furnace that emits no light.

In their effort to reconstruct Chagall's artistic motivations, scholars frequently turn to his autobiographical writing for clues. Especially germane to this illustration was his experience during World War I, which he reflected on in an early autobiography completed in 1922.[31] He reports that while living in Petrograd, where he and his wife moved during the war, "[the Germans'] repeated mustard attacks choked me at 46 Litenaya Street [his residence] *and my painting was suffocated*."[32] Chagall found ways to infuse the trauma of the war into his art, and this illustration of the plague of darkness is a complex example. The darkness it shows includes a burning battlefield-like landscape littered with the dead, a sky shrouded by choking smoke, and a Moses who wears greenish clothes that evoke battle fatigues, wields a staff that resembles the batons that soldiers used in the trenches, and seems to be choking on the smoke around him.

Later in life, after World War II, Chagall would use his art to protest war, attending peace congresses and producing the "Peace Window," a fifteen-foot-tall blue stained glass window on display at the United Nations headquarters.[33] The window was inspired by a passage in Isaiah 9:1–7, which begins with the imagery of darkness and light: "The people that walked in darkness have seen a great light." One could interpret his depiction of the plague of darkness as a similar biblical allegory, using the plague of darkness to protest against the horrors of war, but I see something more going on in it, a reflection on painting itself as a way of responding to war.

Chagall's Moses is a fusion of a soldier and a painter. While the staff he holds looks like a trench stick, it also resembles a painter's long brush, and in using it to cover Egypt in darkness, he is in a way acting as a painter, coloring the world dark. This is a painting about painting, about Chagall's own use of light and darkness, and it seems to be implying that Chagall's painting, or painting in general, has been darkened by the death and destruction of World War I. For someone familiar with his other biblical illustrations, the inferno in the background also calls to mind his depiction of the burning bush where Moses encounters God. Even Moses's position in relation to the inferno corresponds to his position in relation to the bush in Chagall's version of the scene.[34] For Chagall, the burning bush symbolizes artistic inspiration, the revelation not just of God but of light, the source of all color, but Chagall here has inverted it, using the plague of darkness to create a kind of negative image of revelation, an image that reverses the light and darkness of the burning bush. What is revealed to Moses from this fire, moreover, is no angel but rather something satanic, and the prophet himself has been transformed from an inspired artist infusing the world with light into a combatant caught in the midst of death and destruction.

Yet Moses is not the only figure in this picture. The angel at the top right of the scene also recalls warfare, resembling an airplane on a raid, but it is painted in the color of light itself, the opposite of the darkness in the rest of the painting. It is modeled, I believe, not on a bombing run but on the use of airplanes to drop flares onto the battlefield. Suspended from small parachutes, these would ignite at a certain height, giving the soldiers below a few minutes of light to see the advancing enemy as the flares slowly descended to earth. While Chagall's Moses is painting the world dark, the angel is coming to the rescue by parachuting light into the world.

That light appears to take the form of four Hebrew letters, the divine name, which Chagall elsewhere deploys as a symbol of revelation. A closer look, however, reveals that they do not actually spell the divine name, Chagall having changed YHWH to YHYH through a small alteration of the third letter from *waw* (ו) to *yod* (י). Since Jewish custom discourages the writing of the divine name, this change might seem to be an act of piety, but once one notices the small alteration, it becomes apparent that Chagall was communicating something else: the letters YHYH evoke the word for "let there be" (YHY) in Genesis 1:3, the word that God speaks in order to create light. The flare-like word that the angel parachutes into the darkness is not a religious revelation. It is a flash of creativity, inspiration, of art infused with light.

What I find encoded in the symbolism of Chagall's plague of darkness is a story about two different kinds of art: an infernal art darkened by war and a redemptive art associated with light. If we understand the Moses as a projection of Chagall's self-image, the painter finds himself entrapped in the darkness, fire, and choking smoke of the hell-like world created by war, and Chagall is implicating himself in that world as an artist transformed by the militarization, destruction, and death in the world around him. His art has taken on the hues of the battlefield; the lights that emanate from his head are unable to penetrate the darkness; and the only color spread by his staff-like painter's brush is black. But the searchlights coming from his head also imply that Chagall's Moses is looking for something, and what arrives is the angel, symbol of a revelatory mode of art meant to bring light to the darkness. Chagall has thus used the plague of darkness to make a statement about art in the time of war, implying that the artist's embrace of creativity and light offers some kind of rescue from the darkness of World War I.

Chagall's painting illustrates something about the visualization of the plague of darkness that has been true of the other examples we have looked at as well: each one plays with the relationship between light and darkness in ways that communicate meaning without the use of words. The Octateuch segregates light and darkness into two clearly demarcated zones that correspond to the light-filled realm of God and the absolute blackness of hell. The light and the dark are balanced against one another, and there is a sharp divide between the two realms, in keeping with a concept of the world as a binary place where God is either present or absent. Doré's version of the plague represents the light as far away, shining on some distant locale. If what I have suggested about this picture is correct, the remoteness of the light suggests allegorically that the light of civilization has gone somewhere far from Egypt.

In Chagall's version of the ninth plague, the whiteness of the angel contrasts sharply with the rest of the scene, but the darkness is mixed together with light, bleeding with other colors into a putrid yellowish green and an infernal orange evocative of the flames of hell. The mixing of colors adds to the ambivalence of Chagall's Moses, allowing the qualities of destructiveness and creativity to bleed into each other. Chagall was by no means the first to interpret the ninth plague allegorically—we have traced such interpretations back two thousand years—but he revealed so much more between the lines of the biblical episode by using color, composition, and contrast to portray war as an artistic plague of darkness and the infusion of light as a mode of artistic rescue.

Wounded Witness

I want to conclude this chapter's tour of different kinds of darkness by looking at one last example of how the ninth plague has been visualized from the twentieth century. In 1986, an American expressionist artist named Miriam Beerman produced a series of large canvases depicting seven of the plagues.[35] Several of the paintings show the ghastly faces of humans or animals suffering torment or death, and this is true of Beerman's plague of darkness as well (figure 21).

There is nothing in this version of the darkness to anchor the viewer's perspective—no Moses looking at the darkness and no landscape. All that can be made out are ghoulish and mangled faces crowded together in the darkness, though each is oblivious of the others. An especially unsettling element of the picture are the unseeing eyes, hollowed out or wounded. Several of the faces are looking up as if crying for help, but there is no indication of a light shining from anywhere in the scene, and each seems trapped within a particular kind of torment.

As is true of all the earlier depictions of the plague that we have examined, Beerman's version reflects the era in which it was produced. Although she was born in Rhode Island and did not suffer through the Holocaust, she was from a Jewish background, grew up during the 1930s, and developed a sympathy for what was happening to the Jews—and artists—in Europe. From that childhood experience there emerged a lifelong preoccupation with representing the evil and suffering that the Holocaust exemplified, a preoccupation that led her to focus on depicting bodies and faces that have been disfigured by distress or torture:

FIGURE 21. Miriam Beerman, *Plague of Darkness* (1986). Image courtesy of James Yarosh Associates Gallery, with permission from William Jaffe.

"There are some who feel they have to bear witness," she once said in an interview, "and I happen to be one of them."[36]

Beerman's depiction of the ten plagues reflects this preoccupation with bearing witness. In an artistic statement posted on her website, she remarks that she was drawn to the plagues as a theme because she recognized in them a presaging of the Holocaust, the bombing of Hiroshima, and the threat of nuclear annihilation, and the impression left by those past or impending horrors is reflected in every one of the plague paintings. Her version of the plague of blood shows the bodies of dead fish floating in a river of blood. With the plague of gnats, the viewer sees faces caught up in a tornado-like storm coming out of a twisted corpse. The plague of cattle, set against an apocalyptic backdrop, centers on a disturbing image of a cow with a human face lying down amid the skeletal remains of other cattle that have died off. The slaying of the firstborn is a scene of corpses hanging from a gallows.[37] In every painting, there are corpses, deformed bodies, and faces twisted by suffering or death, and the series as a whole, registering what Beerman must have seen from photographs of concentration camps, the Vietnam War, and atomic bomb testing, puts the viewer in the role of witness to a nightmarish succession of atrocities.

Beerman's depiction of the plague of darkness, revealing only the faces of the plague's victims, reflects this focus of the larger series: here too, the faces are twisted, wounded, or skull-like. The focus on the eyes of the faces suggests the subject of this painting is in some sense the act of seeing, perhaps even the act of witnessing itself, though it is depicted in a way that suggests eyes that can no longer see. It is impossible to pin the painting down to a specific meaning, but Beerman remarks in her artist's statement that the humans and animals of her paintings are "the angels and demons of an inner perception," a way of giving visual expression to the good and bad of existence as filtered through her own feelings and imagination.[38] The highly personal nature of her art suggests that it is a visualization of Beerman's own feelings as an artist responding to the horrors she was trying to convey through the ten plagues. As I interpret the painting, it manifests her perception of herself as an artist painting in a world imagined as a torture chamber of souls so deadened by suffering that they can no longer see.

While all the earlier illustrations we have looked at played in some way with the contrast between darkness and light, Beerman's version of the plague does not—for her, there was only darkness. There is, however, one important line of continuity. Since antiquity, interpreters of the biblical story have understood and depicted the ninth plague as a hell-like experience. In the Wisdom of Solomon, the plague terrifies the Egyptians by giving them a glimpse of the darkness awaiting them after death. In the artistic renderings of the Vatican Octateuch and the painting of Marc Chagall, the darkness is modeled on hell, the pitch-black cave of a Byzantine hell or the dark flames of Milton's hell. Beerman's plague of darkness strips out the religious elements, but it does preserve this association of the plague with hell as a prison of dark and hopeless torment.

10

The Tenth Plague

THE NIGHT OF REDEMPTION

WE HAVE arrived at the tenth and final plague, where the Israelites are at last redeemed from slavery. As the Torah tells the story, their troubles are far from over—the Egyptians will try to chase them down at the Red Sea; the Israelites will face hunger, thirst, disease, and internal conflict during their journey to Canaan; and life in Canaan itself will occasionally threaten them with plagues of its own. Nevertheless, Jews and Christians have long recognized the tenth plague as a turning point because it is the plague that forces the Egyptians to let the Israelites go and launches them on their journey to Canaan. Few stories have done more to inspire hope than the Exodus story has, and we will see that the tenth plague episode, or rather the act of retelling it, has played a key role in this history by helping people to imagine a future better than the present.

The account offered in Exodus 11–12, as is true of every plague, is rather sparse and thus permits and even requires people to fill in gaps in the narrative with their own interpretive choices. One such gap concerns the mysterious "destroyer" (Hebrew *mashchit*) that God sends to slay the firstborn, mentioned in Exodus 12:23 as someone or something that enters the homes of the Egyptians to slay their firstborn but is stopped from slaying the Israelites by the blood of the Passover sacrifice. Since antiquity, readers have inferred that the destroyer was a winged angel. But as the Exodus account offers no description, the angel has been depicted in many different ways, and there has also always been room to imagine it in non-personified form—in Cecil B. DeMille's *The Ten Commandments*, for example, the "destroyer" is visualized as a mist-like entity that creeps along Egypt's streets as if it were poisonous gas or radioactive fog. The term "Passover" has similarly invited divergent interpretations. Passover, *pesach* in Hebrew, is the name given to the animal that the Israelites sacrifice on the night of the tenth plague to protect themselves. According to Exodus 12:13, the name reflects how God "passed over" the houses of the Israelites, but here too the Bible's ambiguity has allowed people to take the story in different directions. For Philo, the term meant "crossing over," signifying Israel's progression from a life led by bodily impulses, symbolized by Egypt, to the higher spiritual state symbolized by Canaan (*Special Laws* 1.146–147). Greek-reading Christians connected the name to Jesus's suffering on the cross, the Passion, based on the similarity between the Greek Pascha and "suffer" (*pascho*).[1]

Our focus in this chapter will be on the ambiguities of another biblical word from the book of Exodus—the word "redeem," from the root *ga'al* in Hebrew. That word does not actually appear in Exodus 11–12 itself, but it is used earlier in the Exodus account in reference to the plagues, where God instructs Moses to tell the Israelites, "I will redeem you [*ve-ga'alti*] with an outstretched arm, and with great judgements" (Exodus 6:6), a prediction that comes true when the tenth plague compels the Egyptians to let the Israelites go. In the minds of both Jews and Christians, the concept of redemption came to be closely associated with the events of Exodus 11–12. The former made redemption a central theme of the Seder, a commemoration of the nocturnal events depicted in Exodus 11–12, while the latter associated the Passover sacrifice and its blood with Jesus's redemption of humanity through the Crucifixion.

Like the words "destroyer" and "Passover," however, the biblical language of redemption has a vagueness to it that has allowed Jews and Christians to read different notions of redemption into the biblical story. Both groups read Exodus 11–12 as an anticipation of future salvation—the salvation of the righteous in the coming messianic age, or the salvation of the soul from physical death—but they brought to their interpretations and retellings of Exodus 11–12 distinct conceptions of redemption developed out of the word's multiple meanings and associations.

The history of how people have retold the Bible's account of the tenth plague, unfolding over an eventful night that included the first Passover and Israel's departure from Egypt, is simply too vast a subject to squeeze into a chapter. In what follows, however, I want to offer some sense of this history by focusing on three retellings that capture in different ways how the story of the tenth plague intersects with the history of hope. Two of these examples originated in premodern times, but their influence persists today, while the third, arising in more recent centuries, speaks to the role of the tenth plague as part of America's struggle for redemption.

The Price of Redemption

The English word "redemption" signifies the act of saving or being saved, but it also refers to the act of clearing a debt or gaining possession of something in exchange for a payment. The redemption of a slave, for example, refers to the act of freeing the slave by purchasing them out of bondage. This was how some early Christian thinkers explained the redemptive power of the Crucifixion: by offering his own life up as a sacrifice on humanity's behalf, Christ "redeemed" it from sin and death through a kind of payment, just as people were redeemed from captivity through a ransom payment. This compensatory conception of redemption began to take shape in the very earliest period of Christian history, going all the way back to the New Testament. Mark speaks, for example, of how the Son of Man came to give his life as "a ransom for many" (10:45), while the apostle Peter (or whoever wrote the letter known as 1 Peter), suggesting a connection to Passover, wrote of how people were ransomed "with the precious blood of Christ like that of a lamb without defect or blemish" (1:18–19).

This conception of redemption is notably different from the meaning of the biblical term "redeem" in Exodus 6:6, where redemption is depicted as a forceful intervention to free the Israelites, but it also has roots in the Hebrew Bible. According to Exodus 13, God's intervention to slay the firstborn of Egypt imposed a kind of debt on the Israelites: God had given up something on their behalf, and they were obligated to pay God back by offering something of equivalent value—their own firstborn. Yet rather than insisting the Israelites sacrifice their own firstborn, whom he had just intervened to save from the destroyer, God allows the Israelites to redeem their firstborn by sacrificing firstborn animals in place of their own children and, later on in the Torah, by making a monetary payment.[2] The Vulgate rendered this act of offering compensation to God with forms of the Latin verb *redimere*, the ancestor of our word "redeem," but the original Hebrew of the biblical account uses a distinct verb, not *ga'al* but *padah*.

When early Christians conceived the redemption Jesus made possible as an exchange, the offering of something valuable in exchange for human life, they were going back to the model of redemption exemplified by Exodus 13. An even more important influence, however, came from slave-trade practice in the Roman Empire of the day, the manumission of slaves through a payment to their owners.[3] While New Testament authors did not elaborate on the idea of Christ's sacrifice as a redemptive process akin to buying the freedom of a slave or hostage, later Christian theologians like Augustine did, depicting redemption as a process of purchasing the soul from the captivity of Satan or sin.[4] The "ransom theory of atonement," as this way of conceiving redemption has come to be known, was very influential in late antiquity and the Middle Ages.

This way of thinking about redemption influenced how early Christians understood the redemption described in Exodus 12, as did another idea that emerged early on: the identification of Christ with the Passover sacrifice. Christians like the second-century philosopher Justin Martyr developed this connection by drawing out a correspondence between the Crucifixion and the blood placed on the doors of the Israelites' houses to rescue them: "Just as the blood of the Passover offering saved those in Egypt, so also the blood of Christ will deliver from death those who have believed" (*Dialogue with Trypho* 111).[5] The timing of the Crucifixion on the Day of Preparation for Passover, the day before the first day of the weeklong holiday, encouraged the association, tying

Jesus's death to a festival that, in the time of very early Christians like Peter and Paul, was observed in the temple through the sacrifice of lambs in accord with the Torah.

We can observe the impact of these ideas on how Christians understood Exodus 12 thanks to a second-century text known in English as *On the Passover,* attributed to a bishop known as Melito of Sardis. The text reads like a sermon, and some scholars believe that it was composed for the celebration of a Christian version of Passover, a theory based on echoes of the Haggadah in *On the Passover.*[6] Even if the author was familiar with an early form of the Seder, however, he has put a distinctively Christian spin on the festival, retelling the events of Exodus 11–12 in light of the two ideas identified earlier: redemption as a compensatory payment or ransom for the life of another, and the identification of Christ with the Passover sacrifice.

Deploying what would later come to be known as a typological reading of the biblical story, *On the Passover* asserts that the Passover sacrifice of Exodus 12 operated on a double level, saving the Israelites from the lethal angel of the tenth plague but also anticipating the eternal salvation that Christ made possible through his death. What saves the Israelites from death in this version of the story is something that the angel recognizes when he sees the Passover blood: a glimpse of Christ's future sacrifice. After developing the correspondence between the Passover sacrifice and the Crucifixion, the text then uses the analogy to assert a compensatory explanation for the redemptive power of Jesus's sacrifice as a purchase of humanity's release from captivity: "Led as a lamb and slain as a sheep, he *ransomed us* from the world's service as from the land of Egypt, and freed us from the devil's slavery" (lines 459–464, italics mine). Some ancient Jewish sources depict the Passover sacrifice as an apotropaic rite, a ritual meant to turn away a destructive force. In late ancient Jewish translations in Greek Aramaic, for example, the name Passover can be rendered with words that mean "cover" or "protect," as if the translators understood the blood placed on the entrances of the Israelites' houses as a shield from the destroyer akin to an amulet used to ward off an evil spirit.[7] Conflating the Passover sacrifice with the Crucifixion, early Christians suggested a different role for the

Passover sacrifice: its blood functioned like the blood that Christ spilled on the cross, the most costly of payments, to purchase the freedom of the enslaved from the captivity of sin.

The correspondence between Christ and the Passover sacrifice would become even more prominent during the Middle Ages, when Christians in Europe developed an intense spiritual fixation with the redemptive power of Christ's blood. As the historian Caroline Walker Bynum has shown, medieval theologians and artists in Catholic Europe highlighted the role of blood as an agent of redemption: paintings and book illustrations from the time can show Christ's body covered in bloody wounds or gushing blood out in a stream.[8] What to modern viewers appear as gory visions, she argues, were a source of joy for the devout due to a new "blood piety," an intense, worshipful focus on the blood of Christ as manifest during the Eucharistic rite and as represented visually in paintings and other media. During this period, among Catholics, the blood of Christ was considered so powerfully and miraculously redemptive that merely seeing an image of it could be experienced as a transformative event akin to the drinking of the Eucharistic wine, a way of unifying with Christ and participating in his redemptive suffering on the cross.

This new conception of redemption was connected to Exodus 12 by the figure known as Agnus Dei, the Lamb of God, the representation of Christ as an unblemished lamb. The term originated from the Gospel of John, in which John the Baptist refers to Christ as the Lamb of God who takes away the sin of the world (John 1:29). The expression soon gained prominence from its use in liturgical chants and songs as a way of honoring Christ's sacrifice in redeeming humanity from sin, and by the sixth century, it had also inspired a tradition of picturing Christ as a lamb that persists into contemporary Catholicism.[9] Some of these images reflect the kind of piety that Bynum was referring to, depicting the lamb with blood streaming out of its body into a chalice. For instance, in an altarpiece in Ghent, Belgium, known as *The Adoration of the Mystic Lamb*, a famous oil painting completed by Hubert and Jan van Eyck in 1432, the lamb as a stand-in for Christ is shown looking at the viewer from on top of an altar with a crown radiating from its head, a cross nearby, and blood streaming from its body (figure 22).

FIGURE 22. The Lamb of God as depicted in the van Eyck brothers' *Adoration of the Mystic Lamb* (Ghent, 1432). Alamy.

The symbol of the Lamb of God also inspired a custom—dating back to at least the eleventh century and observed until being discontinued by the Second Vatican Council in 1965—that involved stamping an image of the Agnus Dei in wax pendants, which were then blessed by the pope and distributed to the faithful. The medallions were thought to have miraculous protective powers. People tossed them into burning houses to extinguish the flames, dropped them into flooding rivers and stormy oceans to calm the waters down, and laid them on wounds to heal the bodily damage. To infuse the pendants with this lifesaving power, the pope offered a blessing that invoked what God had done in the past to save humankind, and such blessings sometimes explicitly evoked Exodus 12 as a precedent. Here is a version from 1752:

> Humbly we beseech Thee, that Thou mayest deign to bless and sanctify these waxen figures fashioned with the image of the most innocent Lamb that, in their presence, the crash of hailstorms, the storm of whirlwinds, the force of tempests, the rage of winds, the troublesome thunders may dissipate: and, just as the Angel, at the sight of the blood which thy people had sprinkled on the upper door posts and on the side posts did pass over striking without harm upon the houses thus sprinkled, so at the sight of these images may malignant spirits flee and tremble, and may unprovided death not meet devout bearers of these images.[10]

The pope's blessing calls on God to transfer to the wax medallions and their image of the Agnus Dei the protective power that saved the Israelites on that first Passover night. Just as the angel in Exodus 12 was stopped by the sight of the blood on the doorposts of the Israelites' homes, so too the sight of the medallion will protect those wearing it from malignant spirits.

While the Agnus Dei rite was discontinued in the 1960s, the tradition of fusing Exodus 12 and the Crucifixion continues in Christianity today. During the first year of the Covid-19 pandemic, some Catholics sought to protect themselves by attaching a red ribbon on the doorposts of their houses as a way of enlisting the power of the blood of Jesus against the disease. The connection to Exodus 12 was made explicit in online posts about the practice, which often cited verse 13: "The blood will be a sign for you on the houses where you are, and when I see the blood, I will pass over you. No plague will touch you when I strike Egypt." An example is a Facebook account created on April 28, 2020, to call on people to wrap red ribbons around their trees to protect against Covid-19; the page illustrates the practice's fusion of Exodus 12 with the Crucifixion by showing a picture of Christ on a cross flanked by a blood-smeared threshold.[11] Some Christians found the practice objectionable because they believed it was selfish to use Christ's blood to protect oneself and not one's neighbors.[12] For others, it was a way of expressing their faith in God during a difficult period, and of showing support for church members vulnerable to the virus or isolated in their homes. The use of red ribbons to symbolize the blood of the Passover lamb or the blood of Christ was an adaptation of the practice of using colored ribbons to raise awareness of certain issues and express solidarity, but it was also a continuation of the much older Christian retelling of Exodus 12 that interpreted the events of the tenth plague and the Passover sacrifice in light of the redemptive power of Christ's sacrifice.

Reclaiming Redemption

As I have described throughout this book, retellings of the ten plagues story feature prominently within the Passover Seder. There is a case to be made, however, that the entire Seder constitutes, or rather has evolved into, a retelling and reenactment of the events depicted in Exodus 11–12.

The Mishnah, the foundational document of rabbinic Judaism, actually distinguishes two Passovers: the Passover of Egypt, which is celebrated on the night described in Exodus 12, and the Passover of the Generations, which is celebrated by succeeding generations (Mishnah Pesachim 9.5). Among their differences, the Passover of Egypt was observed on only one night, the night of the tenth plague, whereas the Passover of the Generations was a seven-day holiday. The two Passovers were nevertheless clearly interconnected. The Passover of the Generations was meant to recall the first Passover and was, in a sense, an attempt to relive it, as the family comes together for a nocturnal meal that recalls the events of Exodus 12.

Today's Seder is a celebration of the Passover of the Generations as adapted in the wake of the Jerusalem temple's destruction and the end of the Passover sacrifices offered there, but its customs recall the Passover of Egypt: the nocturnal setting recalls the nighttime setting of Exodus 12; the unleavened bread and bitter herbs eaten during the meal are inspired by Exodus 12:8; the shank bone traditionally displayed on the Passover plate evokes the sacrifice that saved the Israelites from the plague; and the structure of the whole experience moves participants along the trajectory of events as described in Exodus 12, advancing from slavery and the plagues to the Passover sacrifice and then to redemption.

What makes it challenging to interpret the Seder as a retelling of Exodus 12, however, is that its elaborations of the Mishnah's skeletal outline developed over such a long time. These elaborations—the practice of reciting the ten plagues, the spilling of the wine, the display of the shank bone—emerged independently of each other in different periods; and we simply lack the evidence to fully understand what motivated their inclusion in the Seder. Rather than trying to analyze the entire Seder as a retelling of the tenth plague, therefore, I want to focus on a specific passage tied to the verse of Exodus 12:12: "I will pass through Egypt on this night, I will strike down the firstborn in the land of Egypt both humans and animals, and against all the gods of Egypt I will render judgments; I am the Lord."

The recounting of the Exodus during the Seder, as I noted earlier in this book, originated from a passage in the Mishnah that called for a father to explain a passage in Deuteronomy 26:5–8 to his son. This passage was understood to refer to the plagues based in part on the reference in verse 8 to signs and wonders: "The Lord brought us out of the Land of Egypt with a mighty hand and an outstretched arm, with terror, and signs and wonders." As it exists today, the Seder offers two midrashic explanations for this verse: a shorter midrash, which I mentioned in the introduction, and a longer explanation, which now appears first in the Seder, even though it was added after the shorter explanation. In what follows, I want to focus on this longer midrash, aiming to clarify what it means and how it works as a retelling of the tenth plague.

Like the Haggadah's shorter midrash on Deuteronomy 26:8, this one also breaks the verse down into smaller phrases, purporting to reveal a hidden meaning for each phrase. It begins with the phrase, "The Lord brought us out of Egypt," which it takes as a reference to what God did on the night of the tenth plague. The first half of the midrash reads as follows:

> *The Lord brought us out of Egypt.* Not by an angel, not by a seraph, not by a messenger but rather [by] the Holy One blessed be he through

> his own glory and his own power, as it says [in Exodus 12:12]: *"I will pass through Egypt on this night, I will strike down the firstborn in the land of Egypt both humans and animals, and against all the gods of Egypt I will render judgments; I am the Lord."*
>
> *"I will pass through Egypt on this night."* [This means] "I and not an angel."
>
> *"I will strike down the firstborn in the land of Egypt."* [This means] "I and not a seraph."
>
> *"Against all the gods of Egypt I will render judgments."* [This means] "I and not a messenger."
>
> *"I am the Lord."* [This means] "I and no one else."

The midrash takes the first few words of Deuteronomy 26:8, "The Lord brought us out of Egypt," as an exclusionary statement—the Lord alone saved the Israelites on that night without any help from an angel or some other assistant, and it backs this claim up by citing Exodus 12:12, breaking it down into smaller, nonredundant units of meaning as well. Each time that God used the pronoun "I" in the verse, according to the midrash, he was not only taking credit for Israel's redemption but denying credit to some other semidivine being—an angel, a seraph, or a messenger. The midrash ignores Exodus's reference to a "destroyer" that most interpreters take to be an angel, and its author was evidently so intent on denying anyone but God a role in Israel's redemption that he also declined to make any mention of Moses's role in the episode.

Why does the midrash insist so adamantly on God as the sole agent of Israel's redemption? Some scholars believe the passage was written in response to a heretical Jewish group that believed God operated with help from a supernatural assistant—an angel, perhaps, or the Logos, a personified form of Wisdom thought to be semi-independent of God. The theory I find more convincing, however, is that the midrash was reacting to Christianity and its claim that God saved humanity through the mediation of Christ.[13] Not only did Christians look to Jesus as a redeemer, but as we have just seen, as early as the second century, some saw that redemptive power at work on the night of the first Passover itself: according to Melito, it was a glimpse of Christ's sacrifice in the blood of the Passover sacrifice that stopped the angel from slaying the Israelites. It is possible that the midrash was countering such efforts to read Jesus into Exodus 12.

The second half of the midrash, proceeding to offer an explanation for the remaining phrases in Deuteronomy 26:8, does not develop the idea of God as the sole redeemer of Israel any further, but here too, I want to propose, there is reason to think that it was reacting to a Christian notion of redemption. It reads as follows:

> *"with a mighty hand."* This is pestilence [which the midrash supports with a quotation from Exodus 9:3, which describes the cattle pestilence as "the hand of the Lord"].
>
> *"and with an outstretched arm."* This is the sword [supported by a quotation from 1 Chronicles 21:16, which refers to a divine sword used to defeat Israel's enemies].
>
> *"and with great terror."* This is the revelation of the Shekhinah [supported by Deuteronomy 4:34].
>
> *"and with signs."* This is the staff [of Moses, supported by Exodus 4:17].
>
> *"and with wonders."* This is the blood [supported by Joel 3:3, which uses the word for "wonders" in association with blood].[14]

After declaring that God did not have a helper during the night of redemption, the midrash goes on to acknowledge that he did use various implements to help defeat the Egyptians and save the Israelites: the pestilence of the fifth plague, a divine sword, the Shekhinah (a manifestation of God's presence on earth that can function like a protective shield for Israel), the wonder-working staff of Moses, and the blood. Some of the items on this list are taken from the ten plagues story—the pestilence, Moses's staff, and the blood, which one might connect to the blood of the first plague—but for some reason, the midrash adds other items nowhere mentioned in the biblical account: the sword and the Shekhinah.

The midrash has exegetical reasons for reading each phrase as it does, using various scriptural verses to fill out the meaning, but the whole makes for a puzzling way to recount the ten plagues story. Why not mention all of the plagues? Why start with the cattle pestilence of the fifth plague? Why add a sword and the Shekhinah? This is not the first time that we have encountered a version of the ten plagues that presents things out of order, or that adds details not mentioned in Exodus, and my approach in those cases was to treat the changes as intentional, to look for some motive or rhetorical goal that would account for the reordering and supplementation of the plagues. Can we apply such an approach to this midrash as well?

We can tell that this midrash was stitched together from earlier midrashic traditions that originated independently of each other. There is textual evidence that the opening part of the midrash where God insists that he alone saved Israel circulated on its own without the rest of the commentary on Deuteronomy 26:8.[15] The midrash's explanation for "a mighty hand" and an "outstretched arm" seems drawn from another source, possibly derived from a midrash known from the commentary Sifrei Numbers (§115) that interprets the same two phrases but as they appear in another biblical passage, Ezekiel 20:33–34, rather than Deuteronomy 26:8. In other words, this midrash was not created from scratch but from a stitching together of two earlier midrashic traditions, neither of which was intended as a commentary on Deuteronomy 26:8, and the composite version in the Haggadah seems to have added some elements of its own as well.

Yet we can also read this passage as something more than a hodgepodge of loosely connected midrashic traditions, by drawing out its resemblance to a Christian tradition known as the Arma Christi, Latin for "the weapons of Christ." By the Middle Ages, it had become commonplace in Christian Europe to enumerate the implements that were used against Jesus during the Crucifixion—the cross itself, the lance used to pierce his body, and every other item that could be associated with the Crucifixion. These were assembled together in illustrations of the Crucifixion, and they were cataloged in lists and poems that describe each item individually, sometimes in scrolls that ran for five or six feet.[16] Since these implements were used to torture and kill Jesus, why were they known as his weapons? Because, paradoxically, they were recognized as the means by which Jesus had defeated sin and the devil. Their display in illustrations, heraldry, and processions that paraded replicas of the implements was akin to the triumphant display of battle trophies, only the victory in this instance was humanity's salvation.

Since the first part of the midrash makes sense as a reaction to Christianity, implicitly contesting Jesus's role as a savior, is it possible that the second half of the midrash is also a response to Christianity, countering the Arma Christi with its own arsenal of redemption? Historically speaking, this is not impossible. The Arma Christi achieved its most fully developed form in European art from the thirteenth century onward, but as the art historian Mary Edsall has shown, an early version of the tradition was already taking hold much earlier.[17] There is evidence that this early form of the tradition was known in the Byzantine Empire, the cultural-religious context in which this midrash, and the Haggadah in general, took shape in the eighth and ninth centuries. A ninth-century sermon, delivered by a patriarch of Constantinople named Photius (820–893), does not depict the implements of the Crucifixion as weapons, but it comes close to the Arma Christi tradition as a catalog of objects associated with the Crucifixion celebrated as instruments of humanity's redemption—the nails, the crown of thorns, and the spear that released blood and water from Jesus's body.[18] It is not at all far-fetched to imagine the midrash developing in response to the role of holy weapons as relics in Byzantine Christianity, the adoration of weapons and implements associated with Christ himself and other sainted figures, including Moses, whose powerful staff was thought to be under the safe keeping of the Byzantine emperor himself and was venerated for its role in protecting and delivering Israel.[19]

This way of understanding the midrash helps explain the specific items that it mentions in its celebration of God's victory. I have noted that the items included in the midrash are baffling—why add a sword and the Shekhinah to the story of Israel's redemption when neither is mentioned anywhere in the Exodus account? If the blood at the end of the midrash is a reference to the first plague, why would that be in the last position? Comparing the midrash to the Arma Christi snaps this puzzle into place, as we can see by considering each of its pieces one at a time.

The Hand of the Lord

The midrash begins by explaining "with a mighty hand" in Deuteronomy 26:8 as a reference to the "pestilence," a word used in Exodus 9 in reference to the cattle plague. Why begin with a reference to the fifth plague? To understand the connection to the Arma Christi tradition, it is important to recognize that what makes this plague relevant in this context is its association with "the hand of the Lord," a phrase used of the cattle plague in Exodus 9:3, and that becomes all the more resonant in the light of the inclusion of hands among the Arma Christi—the hands of the Jews involved in torturing Jesus, hands pulling Jesus's hair or wielding a whip, all counted among the weapons that Christ used to save humankind. In visual depictions of the Arma Christi, the hands often appear disembodied, as if hovering in the air, and shown holding a whip or some other weapon. The midrash can thus be read as pushing back against this motif, citing "the hand of the Lord" in Exodus 9:3 as a way of trumping the role of hands in the Arma Christi tradition.

The Outstretched Arm

The midrash then interprets the phrase "with an outstretched arm" as a reference to a sword that God used to defeat the Egyptians. Exodus never mentions such a sword, but the midrash cites a verse from 1 Chronicles 21:16 ("a sword drawn in his hand, suspended over Jerusalem") to show that God uses a sword against his enemies. This reference, I would propose, could be seen as a response to the spear used to wound Jesus according to John 19:33–34, the "Holy Lance" that produced the five sacred wounds in Jesus's side that were a focus of spiritual contemplation in their own right. The Arma Christi could also include swords, such as the sword that the disciple Peter uses to cut off the ear of one of the officials who had come to arrest Jesus, but the lance was an even more illustrious weapon of Christ, venerated as a relic by the sixth century and included among the Arma Christi early on, as demonstrated by its appearance on the frame of an eleventh-century Byzantine altarpiece in the Basilica of San Marco in Venice alongside the crown of thorns and the sponge used by Roman soldiers to give Christ vinegar.[20] Finding a corresponding weapon for God in the phrase "with an outstretched arm" works as a clever way to counter the salvific power ascribed to the lance in its role as the object that extended the possibility of redemption to humanity by releasing Jesus's blood into the world.

The Great Terror

The third item on the list explains the reference in Deuteronomy 26:8 to "a great terror" as the Shekhinah (dwelling), a rabbinic term for a feminine aspect of God that descends from heaven to reveal itself to Israel and shields it during the exodus.[21] Christians believed that a similar entity, the Holy Spirit, had descended during the Crucifixion to support Jesus, and its presence was signified in visual depictions of the Arma Christia as a dove, such as appears on the eleventh-century altarpiece mentioned earlier.[22] It is not clear why the midrash interpreted the phrase in Deuteronomy 26:8 as the Shekhinah—the only link to "great terror" is a contrived reinterpretation of the Hebrew for "terror" as the similarly spelled "vision," as if the word were being understood to refer to a revelation of the Shekhinah. But reading the midrash as a response to the Arma Christi explains why the author was looking to include the Shekhinah: the role imagined for it during the exodus corresponded to that of the Holy Spirit during the Crucifixion.

The Signs

The midrash connects the word "signs" to the staff that Moses used to perform signs and wonders, and it too has a counterpart in the Arma Christi, in the very cross itself. As noted earlier, the staff was an important relic in the Byzantine Empire, venerated because of its typological correspondence to the cross, and it came to be directly connected to the cross in a widely circulated medieval legend that traced the history of the wood used to make the cross from the tree of life in Eden through Moses's staff to the time of Christ.[23] Perhaps, then, the staff appears in the midrash not only because of its role in Exodus but also because the author, aware of the cross's role in Christianity as an implement of salvation—and particularly how Christians subsumed the staff into the cross—sought to reclaim it as an implement of *Jewish* redemption.

The Wonders

Why is blood the last item mentioned by the midrash? If it refers to the blood of the first plague, shouldn't it have gone first? Here, too, a comparison with the Arma Christi is suggestive, provided that we interpret the blood as a reference not to the first plague but to the blood of the Passover sacrifice. As I noted in the last section, the blood of Christ featured prominently in medieval European depictions of the Crucifixion as the medium of redemption; we saw the example of a painting that highlighted the flowing blood of Christ in the form of a lamb, and other illustrations can show bleeding wounds alongside the Arma Christi as if to count them among the weapons that Christ used to save humanity. These are European Catholic examples from a later period, but there are precedents for the depiction of Christ's blood as the means of salvation in earlier Byzantine art, such as a ninth-century icon from a church in Thebes that shows Christ on the cross with a stream of blood flowing from his side into a chalice.[24] Following the other correspondences to the Arma Christi, the reference to blood falls into place as an effort to counter the redemptive role ascribed to Jesus's blood in the Crucifixion, and perhaps too it was also an effort to reclaim the blood of the Passover sacrifice from Christian biblical interpretation that connected it typologically to the blood of Christ.

There is, these parallels reveal, an underlying logic to the midrash's reading of Deuteronomy 26:8. It was not just throwing together different midrashic traditions about how God redeemed Israel during the exodus in an effort to explain the meaning of Deuteronomy 26:8; it was assembling them on the model of the Arma Christi, finding in the verse an arsenal of divine weapons that correspond point for point to the instruments by which Christ redeemed humanity—the hands of the Jews who tortured Christ, the lance, the Holy Spirit, the cross, and the blood of Christ. The comparison also reveals how the two halves of the midrash work to form a coherent statement about God's redemption: the first part asserts God as the sole agent of salvation over against the role of Christ in Christian theology; the second part asserts the night of the tenth plague and the Passover against the Crucifixion as the key redemptive moment.

We do not know when or in what circumstances the midrash was composed, but it is tempting to suggest that it was triggered by the proximity of Passover to Good Friday, the holiday that commemorates the Passion and Christ's death. By the seventh century, Christians had developed rituals to observe Good Friday that could include venerating relics like the cross and the lance. Read as a reaction to this practice, the incorporation of the midrash into the Seder transformed the commemoration of Israel's night of redemption into a counter–Good Friday.

Perhaps it is not a coincidence that the very next step in the Seder service, a song known as "Dayenu," also seems to be responding to Byzantine worship during Good Friday, mirroring a part of its liturgy known as the Improperia, which goes back to at least the ninth century.[25]

Good Friday, it so happens, was also a time when Christians used the exodus story to denigrate the Jews, and anti-Judaism was a major theme in Byzantine liturgy during the period when the Haggadah was taking shape. The Improperia, for example, uses the exodus to denounce the Jews for having betrayed the God who sought to save them: God had scourged their enemy and its firstborn for Israel's sake, and yet Israel responded by scourging Christ; God had led the Israelites out of Egypt, and yet the Jews responded by leading Christ to the cross.[26] The Arma Christi was likewise used to reproach the Jews: in addition to including the disembodied hands of the Jews who tormented Christ on the cross, some feature a grotesque face of a Jew spitting at him.[27] The midrash never declares that it is responding to such accusations and imagery—openly defying Christian anti-Judaism would have been a risky move for a Jew in a medieval Byzantine or Catholic environment—but it is conceivable that it arose to covertly challenge the anti-Jewish hostility expressed through the Arma Christi, and perhaps, too, the ways that Christians used the exodus itself to disparage the Jews for rejecting Christ as redeemer.

For Christians who saw in Exodus 12 a glimpse of Christ's sacrifice on the cross, the Jews were obstacles to redemption, enemies who had to be vanquished for the rest of humankind to be saved, and the Arma Christi tradition put a paradoxical spin on this tradition by turning Christ's Jewish tormenters into instruments of humanity's redemption in their own right. The midrash countered this view with a retelling of Exodus 12 and the night of Israel's deliverance that not only reasserted God as Israel's sole redeemer but wrested back redemption itself from Christianity by seizing on the Arma Christi to model a counternarrative of Jewish salvation.

God's Terrible Swift Sword

An important turning point in the history of retelling the tenth plague occurred during the English Civil War of 1642–1651, when a new conception of deliverance emerged that transformed the events of the exodus into a road map for political liberation. The English Civil War was a political conflict, but it was also an extension of the broader religious conflict between Protestants and Catholics, and the political and the religious came together in a new way when Protestant dissidents began to use the words "deliver" and "deliverance"—the former used in the King James Bible's translation of Exodus 12:27 to describe God's rescue of the Israelites—in reference to their drive for liberation from the tyranny of the English monarchy, the Church of England, or the pope. Examples from the period include a sermon entitled *Englands Bondage and Hope of Deliverance* by the Puritan Henry Burton, whose ears had been cut off for having criticized the head of the Church of England, and the treatise *England's Deliverance, or, a Great Discovery*, which described England's rescue from an alleged papist conspiracy to reimpose Catholic control over the country.[28] The term "deliverance" resonated biblically as a near synonym for "redemption," but whereas both terms connoted spiritual salvation, "deliverance" also began to be used in this period to signify this-worldly liberation from oppressors.

This political mobilization of the biblical language of deliverance is connected to a new way of retelling the exodus that also first emerged during this period—its use to give expression to the hope for redemption in a political sense. The role of the story as a model of political liberation is the subject of a book by the philosopher Michael Walzer, *Exodus and Revolution*, but the chief example mentioned there—the use of the exodus story as an inspiration and model for political action and activism by Martin Luther King Jr. and the civil rights movement in the 1960s—was following a precedent established in the seventeenth century by Puritans who were reflecting, in turn, the era's retelling of the exodus as a model of political deliverance.[29]

I take note of this conception of redemption as background for a retelling of the tenth plague tied to the effort to end the institution of slavery in Britain and America during the eighteenth and nineteenth centuries. In this version of the exodus story, the exodus served as a precedent or metaphor for the abolitionist movement, the campaign to end the slave trade and then slavery itself, and in this context, the tenth plague developed a new role as a way of describing the climax of this struggle, the moment of maximal violence and heartbreak but also of redemption. The abolitionist reading of the exodus originated in Great Britain in the eighteenth century, but I want to focus this section on its extension to the American Civil War, which occasioned many comparisons to the ten plagues, and to the tenth plague in particular.

The kind of retelling I have in mind surfaces in a number of different sermons and political speeches, but we can begin with an attempt to visualize it, a painting created in the late 1860s by the New England artist Erastus Salisbury Field (1805–1900), now on view in the Metropolitan Museum of Art in New York (figure 23).[30] The painting, which depicts the slaying of the firstborn in Exodus 12, shows a hall full of parents mourning the deaths of their children. Nothing in the painting announces that it is treating the death of the firstborn as an allegory for the American Civil War, but the setting, a large chandeliered room, signals this by evoking the architectural grandeur associated with the South. Field was an abolitionist who often used his paintings of biblical episodes to convey the injustice of slavery, but here his focus was on the devastating consequences for the Egyptians, the grief caused by losing so many firstborn sons.

FIGURE 23. Erastus Field's depiction of the slaying of the firstborn (1865–1880). Metropolitan Museum of Art, New York.

Field's allegorical recasting of the tenth plague to represent the parental grief caused by the Civil War drew on a tradition, present from the onset of the war, in which preachers cast the war as a ten plagues–like punishment for the nation's sins. One of the most fully developed examples of this idea is an article entitled "The Plagues of This Country," which was published in July 1862 by Henry McNeal Turner, a Methodist minister remembered today for having organized one of the first regiments of Black troops in the U.S. Army and for serving as the first African American chaplain.[31] By that point in the war, Abraham Lincoln was still refusing to support emancipation out of fear that doing so might push the border states of Maryland and Missouri to join the Confederacy. Indeed, he even refused to free slaves who had come under the control of Union troops. In the article, Turner argued that the fighting would not end until the country ended slavery, just as the plagues did not end for Egypt until it let the Israelites go.

In Turner's version of the exodus, it is not the Confederacy but Lincoln who is cast as the hard-hearted Pharaoh for refusing to accept the liberation of the slaves, and the plagues are a series of defeats suffered by the Union at the hands of the Confederacy. The first plague is the killing of several soldiers during a riot that broke out between pro- and antislavery militias in Baltimore in 1861, the second is the North's defeat at the Battle of Bull Run, the third is the fall of Lexington, the fourth is the naval battle between the *Monitor* and the *Merrimack*, and the fifth encompasses defeats at the hands of the Confederate general Stonewall Jackson and other recent brutalities. The sixth plague had not happened yet, but Turner believed he knew when it would occur. In 1831, the preacher William Miller had taken the arrival of a great comet as a sign that the Second Coming of Christ was near and predicted it would arrive in 1844. When that year came and went without the Second Coming, it triggered what historians refer to as the "Great Disappointment," widespread religious disillusionment, but Turner believed that Miller had simply gotten the date wrong: an apocalyptic event was still to come in 1866 if the United States did not end slavery by then. This would be the next plague in the sequence, Turner predicted, a world war that would break out among the nations of Europe and America.

Turner was by no means the only Civil War–era abolitionist to assert a correspondence between the war and the ten plagues, and indeed, on one occasion, a whole coalition of abolitionist ministers made such an argument directly to Lincoln himself. A few months after Turner's article appeared, in September 1862, a coalition of Chicago-based clergy came together to formulate a petition known as the Chicago Memorial of Emancipation, which was delivered to the president by a delegation led by Reverends William W. Patton and John Dempster. The memorial declared the war divine punishment of the country for the sin of slavery, and it directly compared the losses inflicted by the war to the ten plagues: "We claim, then, that the war is a Divine retribution upon our land for its manifold sins, and especially for the crime of oppression, against which the denunciations of God's word are so numerous and pointed. The American nation, in this its judgement hour, must acknowledge that the cries of the slave, unheeded by man, have been heard by God and answered in this terrible visitation."[32]

The last line is an echo of the exodus story, an allusion to Exodus 3:7, where God tells Moses, "I have heard their cry." The mass casualties and destruction wrought by the Civil War were God's response to this cry, a terrible plague visited on the nation to punish it for its sins, and the petitioners were now demanding of Lincoln exactly what Moses and Aaron had demanded of Pharaoh: "As Christian patriots we dare not conceal the truth, that these judgements [the deaths of tens of thousands on the battlefield] mean what the divine judgements meant to Egypt. They are God's stern command—LET MY PEOPLE GO!"[33] It is impossible to measure the effect of this kind of argument on Lincoln's thinking, but according to Edwin Stanton, his secretary of war, the memorial carried great weight with him, and perhaps it is not a coincidence that just a week and a half later, Lincoln issued a preliminary form of the Emancipation Proclamation, declaring for the first time that the goal of the war was to free the slaves.

While analogies between the Civil War and the ten plagues were common, references to the tenth plague in particular intensified and sharpened the comparison in a number of ways. In the material I have surveyed, the episode was invoked in several ways. The first is illustrated by Field's painting—the use of the death of the firstborn to symbolize the loss of so many young men to the war, including many who were under eighteen—and he was by no means the first to make the connection. One such reference to the biblical story occurred during the Senate's debate over the passage of the Thirteenth Amendment in 1864, the amendment that would abolish slavery, when one of the senators was moved to exclaim, "Oh! How many of our first-born have been smitten and fallen."[34] Even earlier, in 1863, the pastor John Stevens Cabot Abbott lamented that the wail of the country's firstborn had to drown the roar of battle before the nation would consider ending slavery—a reference to Moses's prediction in Exodus 11:6 that "there will be a great cry throughout all the land of Egypt" once God strikes down the firstborn.[35] Evoking the tenth plague to lament the fallen was not simply a pious platitude; the biblical comparison was born of an effort to make theological sense of the loss of so many young people.

In Field's painting, the comparison with the tenth plague implied that the South had only itself to blame for the loss of its firstborn, suffering the same fate as the Egyptians because it had committed the same sin of refusing to free its slaves. But there may have been another religious concept at work in the comparison as well, the idea that the loss of the firstborn was a Christlike sacrifice required to redeem the country from the sin of slavery. Stories about drummer boys and other children killed during the war often suggested something redemptive about their deaths, casting them as angels staying near the living to protect them or depicting their death as a sacrifice made to remind the living to devote themselves to God, change their sinful ways, and thereby save themselves from damnation.[36] Comparing the war to the slaying of the firstborn justified the death of children as divine retribution, terrible yet just, but may also have been meant to evoke the New Testament's description of Christ as a "first born" (as in Romans 8:29), an innocent whose sacrifice made it possible for others to be redeemed from their sins and live.

A second role for the tenth plague as a description of the Civil War had to do with the "destroyer" of Exodus 12:23, imagined as an avenging angel. Even before the onset of the war, John Brown, the zealous abolitionist hung for leading a raid of a federal armory at Harpers Ferry, was eulogized in a poem that presented him as an avenging angel like the one unleashed in Exodus 12; indeed, the poet went so far as to declare his impending death would be an event worthy of commemoration like Passover.[37] During the war itself, Union soldiers known for being relentlessly punitive—including Ulysses S. Grant when he was a lieutenant—were referred to as "avenging angels."[38] In some cases, such a description was applied sarcastically to soldiers regarded as ruthless and brutal, but it could also be meant more reverentially, applied to Union leaders who pursued their war aims relentlessly and harshly but in service to a sacred cause.

Not every description of an officer or soldier as an avenging angel was a reference to Exodus 12, but it did sometimes evoke the episode, as illustrated by a story told about General William Tecumseh Sherman's burning of Atlanta in 1864. When a Jewish merchant and civic leader named David Mayer, who was living in the city at the time, learned that Sherman was a fellow Shriner, a member of the same Masonic fraternity, he placed a Shriner apron on the doorpost of his home in the hope that it would be spared. According to Ben Mayer, a great-great-great-grandson, Mayer's descendants tell the story every Passover, and there it has a redemptive ending worthy of the holiday—Mayer's house remained intact.[39] There are reasons to doubt the veracity of the story, and the correspondence to Exodus 12 may have grown as the episode was recounted during Passover seders generation after generation.[40] But the anecdote may have had its roots in how Northerners at the time described Sherman's campaign. To slaves liberated by his campaign, according to contemporary reports, the arrival of his army felt like Israel's deliverance from Egypt, and as happened to other Union soldiers, Sherman himself was hailed as a vengeful angel of the Lord inflicting a retribution on the land that was unforgiving but just.[41]

A third reason to invoke the tenth plague was to warn of the intensifying destructiveness of the war. In Turner's version, for instance, each of the enumerated plague-like battles was bigger and more lethal than the one before, and he could foresee that the country was headed toward a far greater disaster if it did not change course. In his scheme, formulated relatively early in the war, it had only reached the fifth plague, but others pushed the analogy all the way to the tenth plague, as in a sermon delivered on September 7, 1862, by the Philadelphia minister Edward Lounsbery that drew on Exodus 12 to envision a sword entering every house in the land: "The land that had long groaned with the oppressions of the slave, must now be bathed in the blood of the master. Her first born must die! The devouring sword is commissioned to enter into every house in the land until, in the graphic language of the sacred text, there was not a house in Egypt 'where there was not one dead.'"[42] Lounsbery envisioned a nation headed toward the ultimate destruction of the tenth plague. The Emancipation Memorial, delivered a few days later, made a similar if subtler reference to the tenth plague near the end of its petition, urging the country to pay heed to a voice calling to free the slaves "above the wail of desolated Egypt."[43] Whereas Turner had placed America's tenth plague in the future, the Memorial's allusion to Exodus 11:6 signaled that it was already underway: the last of the plagues had begun; a great cry of grief was going out over the land, and the nation could delay no further in freeing its slaves.

To a good number of people, the war's culminating act of violence was the assassination of Lincoln on April 14, 1865. The timing of events contributed to its interpretation as a religious event, the president's murder occurring on Good Friday and on the fifth day of Passover, and both Christian and Jewish clergy used their sermons that weekend to draw out the biblical comparisons. Rabbis delivered the first sermons that Saturday, and some eulogized Lincoln as a new Moses who had died before reaching the Promised Land. Then Christian sermons on Sunday compared his death to the Crucifixion, the ultimate sacrifice to save the nation.

Among the biblical verses that came up repeatedly in such sermons was Exodus 12:30: "There was a great cry in Egypt, and there was not a house in which there was not one dead," a line used to describe the grief that had spread throughout the North. Thus, the Presbyterian preacher Morris Sutphen compared the pall that had settled over the country to "that which shrouded Egypt on the memorable night of the universal slaughter of her first-born"; Henry Ward Beecher, the renowned abolitionist, made the same connection, noting how "every virtuous household in the land felt [Lincoln's death] as if its first-born were gone"; and even the *New York Times* cited the verse in its description of the nation's mourning: "It is as when 'there was a great cry in Egypt.'"[44] We have seen this verse applied to the loss of a generation of young men. Here it was used to depict Lincoln's death as a final escalation of divine judgment—the last, most terrible blow in a long succession of blows. Because the death of the firstborn and the Passover sacrifice were so closely associated with the Crucifixion, it also reinforced an image of the president first articulated that very Easter Sunday, the perception of Lincoln as a Christlike figure who had died because of the sins of the nation and whose death would help redeem it.

How did the tenth plague come to be used as a metaphor for the Civil War? The beginning of an answer takes us back to the early abolitionist movement in Great Britain of the eighteenth century, for British abolitionists were the first to use the ten plagues story to warn against slavery. An example is the role of the plagues in the rhetoric of one of the eighteenth century's leading abolitionists, Granville Sharp (1735–1813), a biblical scholar and antislavery campaigner whose efforts helped to end the slave trade in the British Empire in 1807.

Nine decades before the Civil War, Sharp pointed to the plagues as "examples of God's severe Vengeance against Slave-holders" and called on slave traders to learn the lesson before they suffered the same fate, for "God will SURELY avenge the Cause of the Oppressed."[45] Such rhetoric was similar to warning people that they were going to hell for their sins, but they involved a national punishment, disasters that would strike down all of Britain and its colonies in the way that the ten plagues decimated all of Egypt, and abolitionists pointed to evidence that they were already underway in the form of hurricanes, epidemics, shipwrecks, rebellions, and other calamities that seemed natural or manmade but were really divine providence intervening in nature to rectify the injustice of the slave trade, as God had done in the book of Exodus.[46]

American abolitionists in the period before the Civil War inherited this rhetorical trope and used it in their own jeremiads against slavery. In an 1828 issue of the *Genius of Universal Emancipation*, for example, the Quaker abolitionist Benjamin Lundy recalled how Egypt had been stricken with ten plagues for enslaving six hundred thousand Israelites, and wondered what punishment America would suffer for subjecting a greater number to more wretched conditions.[47] Another example comes from a speech given in Boston in 1831 by Maria Stewart (1803–1879), the first Black woman in America to publish a political manifesto: "He will not suffer you to quell the proud, fearless and undaunted spirit of the Africans forever; for in his own time, he is able to plead his case against you, and to pour out upon you the ten plagues of Egypt."[48] Even Lincoln himself evoked the ten plagues in this way in an 1852 eulogy for the senator Henry Clay: "Pharaoh's country was cursed with plagues, and his hosts were drowned in the Red Sea for striving to retain a captive people who had already served them more than four hundred years. May like disasters never befall us!"[49]

Many of these predictions of a future ten plagues were vague about the kind of disaster that was coming, allowing for the possibility that it would involve some natural disaster, but as the struggle against slavery in the United States began to grow violent in the 1830s, 1840s, and 1850s, some abolitionists began to use the ten plagues analogy in a new way. In 1843, for example, a young Henry Highland Garnet (1815–1882), an activist abolitionist minister, used a speech at the National Convention of Colored Citizens to urge slaves to inflict their masters with "plagues more terrible than Pharaoh."[50] By then, there had been several uprisings against slavery, including an attempted insurrection by Denmark Vesey in 1822 and an 1831 revolt led by the preacher Nat Turner that killed more than fifty White people, and Garnet paid tribute to such efforts to break free from slavery. Others at the conference, including Frederick Douglass, rejected Garnet's call for violence, but this modification of the abolitionist trope, using the plagues not to warn of impending divine retribution but to urge active resistance, was a sign of things to come, anticipating the use of the ten plagues to describe and justify the violence of the Civil War.

The use of the tenth plague in connection to the war was an extension of this tradition, but it added an important spiritual nuance by evoking the idea of redemption. In some of the examples we have looked at, the tenth plague signifies divine judgment at its most devastating, but in others—the use of Exodus 12 to describe the death of young people or Lincoln's murder—it was used to evoke something Christlike about those playing the role of the firstborn, ascribing to their death the redemptive power associated with the biblical verb *padah*, redemption as substitution, compensation, the sacrifice of a life to save others. Building on the decades-old use of the exodus story to make a religious argument for abolition, some found in Exodus 12 a way to incorporate the human cost of the war into this narrative as a sacrifice of the nation's firstborn that was devastating but necessary to free the enslaved and redeem the nation from its sins.

I want to conclude by looking at one last speech from the era, an example that does not refer directly to the tenth plague but that, I would argue, draws on the tradition we have been tracing here. The speech in question was not a sermon but an official political speech, and one of the most important of the Civil War era—Lincoln's second inaugural speech, delivered on March 4, 1865. Written in anticipation of the war ending very soon (it ended a month later), the speech begins by adopting a conciliatory tone toward the South, but it briefly switches to a more threatening tone in its final lines, transitioning from the New Testament language of mercy to the Old Testament language of judgment. It is the end of the speech that evokes the tenth plague: "Fondly do we hope, fervently do we pray, that this mighty scourge of war may speedily pass away. Yet, if God wills that it continue until all the wealth piled by the bondsman's two hundred and fifty years of unrequited toil shall be sunk, and until every drop of blood drawn with the lash shall be paid by another drawn with the sword, as was said three thousand years ago, so still it must be said 'the judgments of the Lord are true and righteous altogether.'"[51] The passage does not mention Exodus 12 explicitly, but it does echo it. The mention of 250 years of toil imposed on slaves recalls Exodus 12:40 and its reference to the 430 years of Israel's enslavement, and while the biblical citation at the end comes from Psalm 19, not Exodus 12, its language, "the judgments of the Lord," echoes Exodus 12:12 and its description of the plagues as God's judgments ("Against all the gods of Egypt I will render judgments"). The speech does not evoke the plagues directly, but it comes close by warning of a terrible divine judgment to be visited on the nation if it does not free its slaves.

Earlier in the speech, Lincoln had acknowledged that humans could never fully understand the purposes of the Almighty, but realizing that people do not always act on their better angels, he allowed himself to use the language of divine retribution that abolitionists had been using for a century to argue against slavery when they pointed to various recent disasters as signs that the nation was suffering its own version of the ten plagues or warned that such disasters were coming. He had issued such a warning himself at the end of his eulogy for Henry Clay when he offered a brief prayer for the nation to avoid the punishments that God had visited on the Egyptians, but thirteen years later, after a four-year war that had killed hundreds of thousands of soldiers, it was clear such a prayer had not been answered, and Lincoln found it necessary to intensify the trope, to warn of a punishment escalated beyond anything the nation had suffered so far. This, I submit, is what he was trying to summon in the minds of listeners by alluding to Exodus 12 at the end of the speech, elevating a threat of more war into a biblical prophecy of a final judgment, a new tenth plague, if the nation persisted in its hard-heartedness.

A century after the end of the Civil War, civil rights leaders like Martin Luther King Jr. would promote a version of America's story as an exodus from Egypt to Canaan, a march from slavery to freedom. Lincoln's speech also retold the American story as a biblical story, but it was one that called on the nation to recognize itself as a land of bondage that had suffered catastrophe for the sin of slavery and would face an even more grievous punishment if it did not rectify the injustice. This narrative has persisted alongside the narratives of America as a Promised Land and America as a journey through the wilderness, resurfacing in an updated form, for example, in 2020 when James Forbes, the first African American minister of the Riverside Church in Manhattan, gave a speech depicting Covid and the civil unrest that followed the murder of George Floyd as divine punishment sent to requite America for four hundred years of injustice against Black people and to give it a final chance to repent of its racism.[52] Forbes's talk of a "plague of deliverance" that punishes and redeems with the same blow is a descendant of the role of the tenth plague in Civil War rhetoric, and it shows that, among some Americans, the episode still rings powerfully as a wake-up call to heed the cry of the oppressed before it is too late.

Epilogue

LIBERATION

> Liberation is always in part a storytelling process: breaking stories, breaking silences, making new stories.
>
> —REBECCA SOLNIT

AS I explained in the introduction, the initial idea for this book came to me during Passover of the first year of the Covid-19 pandemic when I noticed people online making connections between the pandemic and the ten plagues. But the time has come for me to share a little more about what drew me into this story, and what it was that I was trying to understand by exploring its history.

That first Passover night of the pandemic, as I do every Passover, I tried to take to heart the Haggadah's injunction that every generation is obligated to see itself as if it had personally gone out of Egypt. The Seder is an immersive experience, engaging the senses and emotions through food, wine, singing, and the drama of reciting the plagues one by one and letting the prophet Elijah through the door, and I had always taken that passage to mean that I should try to imagine myself on the inside of the exodus story, not just retelling it but imagining myself a slave witnessing the miracles and tasting freedom for the first time. But I had never taken any of this literally, and the passage itself acknowledged that the time travel involved was virtual, an act of "as if" imagination. The exodus, if it happened at all, occurred in the biblical then: the Seder was now, and it never occurred to me to think I could really transport myself into biblical times.

But that night was different from other Passover nights. The country and much of the world had just gone into lockdown two weeks before; it was not clear yet how the virus spread or how lethal it was; the whole experience was new, frightening, and deeply disorienting; and in these circumstances, I had an intense and uncanny sensation of Covid-19 as the angel of the tenth plague passing from house to house and now drawing near to my own. I am not a very religious person in the sense of believing in the supernatural: I have never experienced an epiphany or any kind of miracle, and as someone grounded in academic biblical studies, I had been trained to make a distinction between history and myth, between the part of the Exodus account that fit with what scholars knew about history from ancient Egyptian sources and archaeology, and the miraculous "signs and wonders" part of the story that seemed too incredible to be true and in some respects resembled the mythological tales of other ancient cultures. And yet despite what my reasoning powers were telling me, I felt that night as if the boundary between the biblical story and the present had broken down, and that the plagues had spilled out into the world.

It turns out that I was not the only person to have had this kind of feeling. The first testimony I came across was from an online news story published on April 6, 2020, featuring interviews with rabbis and educators about how they were approaching the upcoming Seder, and some of them were feeling the same thing that I did. "That primal Passover experience is going to be very resonant in our mind this year," observed Rabbi David Wolkenfeld, "We will be sitting at the Passover Seder with a plague outside the door. We will be divided in our homes with the blood on the lintel posts, just sitting in fear and not knowing when to go forth." It wasn't just fear that people were feeling; the author Abigail Pogrebin reported a sensation of presence, of the biblical plagues manifesting themselves again, that approximated my own experience: "For me, it has been hard to fathom this idea of plagues. It was so distant, so antiquated. I am not sure I ever believed it. But now I believe the unimaginable thing, the thing you can't stop, the thing you can't control. I just don't think you can read this part of the seder the same way anymore."[1] The experience only lasted that night, but it stuck with me, and as I thought about it, I realized that for all I had learned about the Bible, I did not understand this way of relating to it—not treating it as history or myth but feeling it happening again through one's own life. Many others respond to the Bible in this way, but for me it was a new and bewildering experience.

In a certain sense, this book has been an attempt to explore this sensation of the biblical past intruding into the present. I am not a psychologist, and I could not account for what I had experienced from that perspective, but I thought I could learn something from my own field of expertise, the history of the Bible's reception, delving into it in search of cases where people had retold the ten plagues in ways that blurred the biblical past with the present. This was the initial impetus for the writing of this book, and the phrase "disasters of biblical proportions" appealed to me as a title not only because I was focusing on biblical disasters but because "a disaster of biblical proportions" is an example of the kind of experience I was aiming to better understand, an event that is happening today, in present-day reality, and yet feels biblical at the same time.

In the end, I was only able to explore a small part of this history. The ten plagues have been recounted so many times in so many contexts that it was impossible to do more than offer a mere sampling of how the story has been reimagined. I feel pangs of regret when I recall the many retellings I was not able to squeeze into this book—medieval mystical commentary that uncovers in the story a cosmic drama about the ten sephirot of Kabbalistic tradition; anti-Semitic caricature that twists the plagues into a Jewish conspiracy to poison Egypt; communist versions of the story that turn the plagues into insurrectionist tactics in a revolution; musical renderings such as the ten plagues–inspired tracks recorded in the 2006 album *Plague Songs* that include Stephin Merritt's "The Meaning of Lice" and Laurie Anderson's "The Death of Livestock"; or most recently, spontaneous, one-sentence-long versions of the story that appeared online after U.S. representative Alexandria Ocasio-Cortez called out a Christian nationalist nemesis for not knowing the Bible well enough to name all ten plagues. While I could not cover it all, I do hope to be leaving the reader with a deepened appreciation for the ten plagues as a story continuously re-created by people fusing the biblical account with what they carry into it from their own lives.

The idea that every person can come up with their own version of the exodus story has been given creative expression in a version of the Haggadah that illustrates the passage mentioned at the beginning of the epilogue—the call on every generation to see itself as if it had gone out of Egypt. The illustration appears in the Moss Haggadah, produced in 1983 by the Israeli artist David Moss, which in its original handcrafted form shows portraits of eighteen Jewish men and women from different eras and backgrounds in alternation with inlaid mirrors.[2] The graphic is a playful take on the motif of seeing oneself in the exodus, but for us it also works as a metaphor for the ten plagues as a story that mirrors back something different to each person who reads, recalls, or retells it: some see themselves in Moses as he faces down Pharaoh or in the Israelites sheltering from the plagues, while others recognize themselves in the Egyptian enslavers, Pharaoh's magician accomplices, or the story's animals. What Moss was able to evoke through an image this book has sought to demonstrate as an historical phenomenon, taking its case studies from religion, literature, philosophy, art, war, activism, play, and popular culture.

But there is something else I was trying to convey as well. It is not quite the case that the meaning of the story lies in the eyes of the person beholding it. Another goal of this book has been to show that each version of the ten plagues, however innovative, builds on earlier retellings. The mischievous frog songs and toys of the contemporary Seder emerged from a tradition that goes back to midrashic retellings of the frog plague. The hailstorm just before the end in Lars von Trier's *Melancholia* was modeled on the plague of hail in Revelation's apocalyptic version of the plagues. When the actress Zaira Wasim implied that the locust infestation of 2020 was a replay of the plague of locusts, she was building on how that plague is reframed in Sura 7. Each retelling added something new, adapting the story in ways that reflect the times and the distinctive perspective of the person doing the retelling, but each was also dependent on earlier retellings, which were constructed in turn from still earlier retellings.

Because this process of creating new retellings out of old retellings continues into our own day and age, I want to conclude by looking at one last and very recent example, a short-story rendition of the plagues, or rather about the retelling of the plagues, included in a version of the Haggadah published in 2023. The editors of the Haggadah included the story to make a political point, responding to a controversy raging in Israel at the time; however, I am mentioning it here not to make a political argument but because the narrative in question, a poignant short story entitled "One Plague," written by the Israeli writer Yaniv Iczkovits, captures something about the act of retelling the ten plagues that this book has been aiming to document.[3]

To help us tease out the meaning of this story, it will help to return one last time to the biblical account. Toward the end of Exodus's account of the plagues, in chapter 10, God reveals a new motive for sending the plagues: he wasn't only seeking to free the Israelites or to instill a knowledge of his power in Pharaoh and the Egyptians; he was also seeking to performs signs worth telling one's children about: "I have hardened his heart and the heart of his servants . . . so that you will tell in the ears of your son and your son's son what I have wrought upon Egypt, and the signs that I put there" (Exodus 10:2). A similar moment appears two chapters later in Exodus 12 when Moses instructs the Israelites that after they settle in Canaan, when their children ask why they are making the Passover sacrifice, they will need to explain what happened: "It is the Passover sacrifice: for he passed over the houses of the Israelites in Egypt as he struck down the Egyptians and delivered our houses" (12:26–27). Both passages report that already during the plagues, God was thinking about how the story would be retold in later generations, anticipating the questions that sons would ask when they saw their fathers performing the Passover sacrifice.

Like every other part of the exodus story, this aspect of the biblical account was expanded through midrash, and the most famous example is a midrash incorporated into the Haggadah prescribing how to explain the exodus to four sons who ask different kinds of questions about what happened—a wise son, a simple son, a wicked son, and a son too young to know how to ask. The sons ask different questions about the Passover service according to their moral characters and intellectual capacities, except for the last son, who does not know how to ask, and the midrash instructs the father how to respond to each one in a way he will understand.[4]

Iczkovits developed this tradition into a brief but powerful story about a Seder where a grandmother explains the ten plagues to her grandchild, the story's narrator.

Also important for understanding the story is a ten plagues–related midrash in the Haggadah, a debate among three sages known from the Mishnah, Yose, Eleazar, and Akiba, who draw different inferences from the Bible about how many plagues it took to redeem the Israelites. The midrash appears in the Haggadah after the recitation of the ten plagues as a kind of lighthearted epilogue, shifting the mood of the meal from the gravity of the plagues back to joy, and it has become another very memorable and beloved part of the Seder, but textual evidence suggests that it was not a part of the Haggadah in its earliest Palestinian form, originating as a supplementary reading that was initially considered optional. The midrash is animated by the playfulness we saw reflected in other plagues-related midrash, expanding the ten plagues into hundreds of plagues, and Iczkovits's story can be read as a clever midrash on this midrash.

The midrash presents the views of the three sages one by one, and Yose goes first, inferring from the Torah that in addition to the 10 plagues in Egypt, there were 50 more at the Red Sea; then Eleazar deduces a greater number of plagues, 40 in Egypt and 200 at the sea; and finally, Rabbi Akiba comes up with the largest number of plagues: 50 plagues in Egypt and 250 at the sea. Each sage draws larger and larger numbers of plagues from smaller and smaller portions of the biblical text, and the reader is to understand that Akiba wins the contest by inferring the highest number of miracles. The grandmother in Iczkovits's story inserts herself into this debate with her own view of how many plagues there were, but in contrast to the rabbis, she subtracts rather than multiplies, asserting that there was only one plague that really counted.

As the story begins, the men of the family are sitting at the Seder table, with the narrator's grandfather reciting the ten plagues. One uncle explains that the plagues were meant to gradually punish the Egyptians, another divides the plagues into different categories, and the grandfather offers the observation that while the first nine plagues were all named after the damage they cause, only the tenth plague, the death of the firstborn, was named for its victims. The grandmother and the narrator, a child, are off to the side, speaking of the plagues in a whisper, out of respect for what is happening at the Seder table, but she has her own take on the story, not trying to uncover a hidden pattern in the sequence of the plagues as the uncles do but, like her husband, noticing something about the last plague that distinguishes it from the others.

What distinguishes this plague, she explains to her grandchild, is that it was the only one that had any impact on Pharaoh because he had managed to shield himself from all the others. During the first plague, the palace could draw on the water it had stored for emergencies. The frogs invaded his house, but Pharaoh's guards quickly removed them. Pharaoh had the best doctors to treat the boils, and he ordered lanterns to be lit in his palace when the darkness enveloped the land. His subjects were suffering terribly, but that had no impact on Pharaoh. Only the final plague was able to reach him because it affected him personally by killing his own firstborn child: Pharaoh was so good at insulating himself from the effects of the plagues—his economy was so resilient, his security system so tight, his medical system so advanced—that he had the luxury of ignoring the suffering around him, that of the enslaved but even that of his own people, and it took the death of his own son during the last plague to finally penetrate his defenses.

This then prompts a question from the grandchild-narrator: If Pharaoh finally had to face the consequences of his hard-heartedness, why did he send his army after the Israelites, knowing by that point how things would go and that his soldiers would not return? The answer is that he simply didn't care at that point—the lives of his own soldiers meant nothing to him—and then the grandmother gets to the point, *"and only you will remember that there is another way."* In the four sons midrash, the wise son, in contrast to all the other sons, is the one who hears the story of the Passover and recognizes the obligation that it imposes on him. The grandmother's version of the story is not about redemption in a religious sense, but it also imposes an obligation, calling on the grandchild to learn from the hard-heartedness of the previous generation and to remember that there is another way.

I came across "One Plague" in *The Freedom Haggadah*, an Israeli version of the Haggadah published in the midst of (and for the use of) a protest campaign launched in 2023 against controversial judicial reforms being pushed by the government. The protests, which drew crowds as large as 150,000 people, lasted for months, continuing until the October 7 attacks. Iczkovits's story expresses its own protest against the government. The grandmother represents an older generation of Israelis, angry with the government for its indifference to what people have suffered—the absence of the narrator's parents from the story and the sadness of her eyes hint at what her generation has lost—and the story she tells refers allegorically to a government that has used its power and the resources of Israeli society to insulate itself from the consequences of its actions. The ending of the story, when she urges the grandchild to remember that there is another way, also carries a clear political message, echoing a rallying cry for the Israeli peace movement.

But the message of the story for us isn't only political. In contrast to the uncles, who provide retellings of the plagues that parrot traditional Jewish biblical commentary, the grandmother does not merely repeat what she has heard from others but comes up with her own distinctive version of the story reshaped by heartbreak, outrage, and responsibility to the future. Cleverly mixing biblical past and present, the grandmother's "one plague" captures what this book has been trying to illumine, the role of retelling as a way of fusing the biblical with one's own pain, hope, and creativity.

In the exodus story as recounted in the Bible, the tenth plague is the moment of deliverance for the Israelites, setting them free to begin their journey toward the Promised Land. Thanks to the grandmother in Iczkovits's story, we can end on a liberatory note as well. Retelling a biblical story can be a passive act, simply repeating a story that has been told many times before, but as shown by the grandmother's version of the plagues—and by many other examples we have looked at as well—it can also be used to express agency and creativity. All of these examples are grounded in Exodus and follow it to some degree, but they are not confined by it, moving its story in directions that its author could never have contemplated. The history of retelling the ten plagues begins with Moses's command to the Israelites to tell the story of Passover to their children, but as far back as we can trace, people have not been content to merely repeat the tale as they heard it from others; they have expanded on Exodus to make it say what they wanted or needed it to say, and that process of breaking and remaking its story has proved its own kind of freedom.

NOTES

Introduction

1. See, for example, Sara Brown, "Covid Is Not like the Plagues of Egypt," Tucson.com, April 7, 2020, https://tucson.com/lifestyles/faith-and-values/coronavirus-is-not-like-the-plagues-of-egypt/article_a4888801-a4af-5215-b15a-e2f3c0516bcc.html.

2. Charles Rosenberg, "What Is an Epidemic? Aids in Historical Perspective," *Daedalus* 118, no. 2 (1989): 1–17.

3. For a small sampling of Jewish interpretations in this vein, see the ten plagues–related entries in a feature published by the Jewish newspaper *Forward*: "The 11th Plague: Passover during Coronavirus," April 3, 2020, https://assets.forward.com/pdfs/Shabbat_04.03.20-2.pdf. For a Catholic example, see Gina Christian, "New Video Series Looks at Ancient Plagues, Today's Coronavirus," *Catholic Philly*, April 28, 2020, https://catholicphilly.com/2020/04/news/local-news/new-video-series-looks-at-ten-plagues-coronavirus/.

4. Nolan Lebovitz, "Rafah and the Ten Plagues," *Jerusalem Post*, April 2, 2024, https://www.jpost.com/opinion/article-794847.

5. Anshel Pfeffer, "Israel's Self-Inflicted Ten Plagues since October 7," *Haaretz*, April 22, 2024, https://www.haaretz.com/israel-news/2024-04-22/ty-article/.premium/this-passover-remember-israels-10-self-inflicted-plagues-since-october-7/0000018f-00d0-d6a0-a9ef-c0dce9dd0000.

6. "Kibbutz Be'eri Survivors Hold Seder in Hostages Square; Fiery Protests at PM's Home," *Times of Israel*, April 22, 2024, https://www.timesofisrael.com/israelis-mark-passover-under-shadow-of-war-absence-of-133-hostages-still-in-gaza/.

7. See John Stephens and Robyn McCallum, *Retelling Stories, Framing Culture: Traditional Story and Metanarratives in Children's Literature* (New York: Garland, 1998), esp. 26–60.

8. W. W. Heist, *The Fifteen Signs before Doomsday* (East Lansing: Michigan State College Press, 1952); Shannon Gayk, "Apocalyptic Ecologies: Eschatology, the Ethics of Care, and the Fifteen Signs of Doom in Early England," *Speculum* 96 (2021): 1–37; Robert Lerner, "Sign Theory: Some Scholastic Encounters with 'The Fifteen Signs before the Day of Judgement,'" *Journal of Ecclesiastical History* 73, no. 4 (2022): 720–736.

9. Origen, *Homilies on Genesis and Exodus*, trans. Ronald E. Heine (Washington, DC: Catholic University of America Press, 2002), 260–274.

10. For a translation, see Mary Magdeleine Mueller, O.S.F., trans., *Saint Caesarius of Ares: Sermons*, vol. 2, *81–186* (Washington, DC: Catholic University of America Press, 1964), 85–98 (sermons 100 and 100A).

11. Lucie Doležalová, "Latin Mnemonic Verses Combining the Ten Commandments with the Ten Plagues of Egypt Transmitted in Late Medieval Bohemia," in *The Ten Commandments in Medieval and Early Modern Culture*, ed. Youri Desplenter, Jürgen Pieters, and Walter Melion (Leiden: Brill, 2017), 152–172.

12. Leslie Brubaker, *Vision and Meaning in Ninth-Century Byzantium: Image as Exegesis in the Homilies of Gregory of Nazianus* (Cambridge: Cambridge University Press, 1999), 124–127.

13. For a recent English translation, see Albert Camus, *The Plague*, trans. Laura Marris (New York: Alfred Knopf, 2021).

14. For an English translation of Exodus Rabbah, which has been dated to the twelfth century but records material from an earlier period, see S. M. Lehrman, trans., *Midrash Rabbah: Exodus*, 3rd ed. (London: Soncino Press, 1983). For a critical edition of the Hebrew text, see Avigdor Shinan, *Midrash Shemot Rabbah: Chapters I–XIV* (Tel Aviv: Dvir, 1984).

15. Midrash Leqah Tov on Exodus 8:13; see Solomon Buber, *Midrash Lekah Tov* (Vilna: Ha᾿almanah veha᾿ahim Rom, 1888).

16. See Martin Lockshin, "Rashbam as a 'Literary' Exegete," in *With Reverence for the Word of God: Medieval Scriptural Exegesis in Judaism, Christianity, and Islam*, ed. Jane Dammen McAuliffe, Barry D. Walfish, and Joseph W. Goering (Oxford: Oxford University Press, 2010), 83–91, esp. 86–87.

17. Cited in Menachem Kasher, *Haggadah Shlemah* (Jerusalem: Makhon Torah Shelemah, 1967), 52.

18. For a review of different explanations, see David Golinkin, "What Is the Purpose of the Mnemonic *Dzakh Adash B'ahave* in the Haggadah?," *Responsa in a Moment* 3, no. 7 (April 10, 2009), https://schechter.edu/what-is-the-purpose-of-the-mnemonic-dzakh-adash-bahav-in-the-haggadah-responsa-in-a-moment-volume-3-issue-no-7-april-2009/.

19. Zvi Ron, "Our Own Joy Is Lessened and Incomplete: The History of an Interpretation of Sixteen Drops of Wine at the Seder," *Hakirah* 19 (2015): 237–256. Ron traces this reinterpretation to a Hungarian rabbi named Yirmiyahu Löw (1812–1874).

20. For a translation of this text, see Joshua Kulp and David Gelenkin, *The Schechter Haggadah: Art, History and Commentary* (Jerusalem: Schechter Institute of Jewish Studies, 2009), 233. For the original, see Eleazar of Worms, *Derashah lePesah* [Interpretation of Passover], ed. Simcha Emanuel (Jerusalem: Mekitze Nirdamim, 2006), 101.

21. As, for example, in a teaching attributed to Shalom of Neustadt (1350–1413). See Shlomo Spitzer, *Decisions and Customs of Rabbi Shalom of Neustadt* (Jerusalem: Mekhon Yerushalyim, 1977), 134 (Hebrew).

22. Compare Joanna Bellis, "The Dregs of Trembling, the Draught of Salvation: The Dual Symbolism of the Cup in Medieval Literature," *Journal of Medieval History* 37, no. 1 (2011): 47–61.

23. Central Conference of American Rabbis, *Union Haggadah* (New York: Bloch, 1905), 9. See also Mara W. Cohen Ioannides, *Jewish Reform Movement in the U.S.: The Evolution of the Non-liturgical Parts of the Central Conference of American Rabbis Haggadah* (Berlin: de Gruyter, 2017), 20.

24. Jacques Derrida, *Specters of Marx: The State of the Debt, the Work of Mourning, and the New International*, trans. Peggy Kamuf (Routledge: London, 1994), 100–104.

25. On the origin of the Third Seder, see Ruth Breindel, "The Providence Passover Journal and the Third Seder," *Jewish Rhode Island*, March 14, 2018, https://www.jewishrhody.com/stories/the-providence-passover-journal-and-the-third-seder,8241.

26. This is how the plagues are treated, for example, in a 1955 Third Seder Haggadah produced by the Workmen's Circle chapter in Los Angeles. See "Third Seder Haggadah, 1955," Jewish Histories in Multiethnic Boyle Heights, UCLA Alan D. Leve Center for Jewish Studies, accessed June 11, 2023, https://scalar.usc.edu/hc/jewish-histories-boyle-heights/media/third-seder-haggadah-1955.

27. On the Pan Am protest, see "'10 Plagues' Dumped at a Pan Am Officem," *New York Times*, March 26, 1975, https://www.nytimes.com/1975/03/26/archives/10-plagues-dumped-at-a-pan-am-office.html. On the recitation of the plagues by Extinction Rebellion, note Simon Rocker, "Climate Change Protestors to Hold Demonstration Seder in Westminster," *Jewish Chronicle*, April 16, 2019.

28. Harriete Estel Berman, "10 Modern Plagues," accessed November 17, 2024, https://harrieteestelberman.com/10-modern-plagues; Natalia Romik, "X Plagues," PiraMMMida, August 7, 2020, https://www.pirammmida.life/natalia-romik; Eli Kaplan-Wildmann, "The Re-created Haggadah," Create Unbound, accessed April 29, 2025, https://www.createunbound.com/haggadah.

29. See Sharon Otterman, Eliza Fawcett, and Liset Cruz, "A Night Different from Others as Campus Protests Break for Seder," *New York Times*, April 24, 2024, https://www.nytimes.com/2024/04/22/us/campus-protest-seders.html; *Jerusalem Post* staff, "'Let My People Go!' NYU Students Tell 'Moses' They Don't Support Hamas Releasing the Hostages," *Jerusalem Post*, April 27, 2024, https://www.jpost.com/israel-hamas-war/article-798867; "Police Looking for 6 People Wanted in Connection with Columbia University Admin's House Vandalism," Eyewitness News ABC 7, August 9, 2024, https://abc7ny.com/post/police-looking-6-people-wanted-connection-columbia-university-administrators-home-vandalized-paint-insects/15166695/.

30. John McAuliffe, "Connecting Moses and Muhammad," in *Books and Written Culture of the Islamic World*, ed. Andrew Rippin and Roberto Tottoli (Leiden: Brill, 2015), 326–340; Nicolai Sinai, "Inheriting Egypt: The Israelites and the Exodus in the Meccan Quran," in *Islamic Studies Today: Essays in Honor of Andrew Rippin*, ed. Majid Danrdhgar and Walid Saleh (Leiden: Brill, 2017), 198–214.

31. A survey of the different interpretations of the blood plague in Qur'anic commentary can be found in Ramzi Ghandour, "The Word 'Dam' in Sura 7:133" (PhD diss., University of Exeter, 2014). For the identification of the plague as nosebleeds, see Ghandour, "Word 'Dam,'" 34.

32. Shari Lowin, "Isrāʾīliyyāt," in *Encyclopedia of Islam Online*, ed. K. Fleet et al., 3rd ed. (Leiden: Brill, 2019), https://doi.org/10.1163/1878-9781_ejiw_SIM_0011700.

33. The Ottoman sultan Selim I (1470–1520) claimed to have recovered the staff during his conquest of Egypt, and the Ottoman version of the staff is still on display in a museum in the imperial palace in Istanbul.

34. Ruhollah Khomeini, *Islamic Government: Governance of the Jurist* (repr., Tehran: Institute for Compilation and Publication of Imam Khomeini's Works, 2017), 126. For more on Khomeini's use of the story of Moses's confrontation with Pharaoh, see Houchang E. Chehabi, "Li Kulli Fir'awn Musa: The Myth of Moses and Pharaoh in the Iranian Revolution in Comparative Perspective" (Crown Paper 4, Crown Center for Middle East Studies, Brandeis University, November 2010).

35. As I write this, the group uses a Telegram channel to boast of some of its activities: "Moses Staff," Telegram, accessed April 30, 2024, https://t.me/s/moses_staff_se2.

36. See Alexander Fodor, "The Rod of Moses in Arabic Magic," *Acta Orientalia Academiae Scientiarum Hungaricae Budapest* 32 (1978): 1–17.

37. Jawid Mojaddedi, trans., *Jalal al-Din Rumi: The Masnavi, Book 4* (Oxford: Oxford University Press, 2017), 95, lines 1069–1074.

38. For an English translation of Iqbal's poetic collection, see Syed Ali Shah, trans., *The Rod of Moses: A Declaration of War against the Present Age* (Lahore: Iqbal Academy, 1983). For the staff of Moses as a children's character, see Muhammad Vandestra, *Islam Folklore: The Staff of the Prophet Moses (Musa) and the Wizards of Pharaoh* (Hanover, NH: Scribl, 2019).

1. The First Plague

1. Sky News, "Benjamin Netanyahu and Benny Gantz Deliver Joint Statement on the Israel-Hamas War," YouTube video, 13:52, posted October 11, 2023, https://www.youtube.com/watch?v=dk4RlXt2A4w.

2. Bertha von Suttner, *Lay Down Your Arms* (Cambridge: Modern Humanities Research Association, 2019), 231.

3. On the measure-for-measure principle, see Elaine Phillips, "The Tilted Balance: Early Rabbinic Perceptions of God's Justice," *Bulletin for Biblical Research* 14, no. 2 (2004): 223–240; and Ishay Rosen-vi, "Measure for Measure as a Hermeneutical Tool in Early Rabbinic Literature: The Case of Tosefta Sotah," *Journal of Jewish Studies* 57 (2006): 269–286.

4. See Eric Havelock, *The Greek Concept of Justice: From Its Shadow in Homer to Its Substance in Plato* (Cambridge, MA: Harvard University Press, 1978).

5. Yehoshua Amir, "Measure for Measure in Talmudic Literature and in the Wisdom of Solomon," in *Justice and Righteousness: Biblical Themes and Their Influence*, ed. Henning Reventlow and Yair Hoffman (Sheffield: JSOT Press, 1992), 29–46; see also Ishay Rosen-Zvi, "Punishing Egypt Measure-for-Measure," TheTorah.com, April 12, 2022.

6. Two printed facsimiles of the Venice Haggadah exist: *The Venice Haggadah with Judeo-Italian Translation*, introduction by Tovia Preschel (New York: Orphan Hospital Ward of Israel, 1973); and an edition with an introduction by Bezalel Narkiss (Jerusalem: Mekor, 1974).

7. For a translation of Yagel's work, see David Ruderman, ed., *A Valley of Vision: The Heavenly Journey of Abraham ben Hananiah Yagel* (Philadelphia: University of Pennsylvania Press, 2016) (the passage referred to here appears on 199). For Modena's reference to the principle, see Marc Cohen, trans., *The Autobiography of a Seventeenth-Century Venetian Rabbi* (Princeton, NJ: Princeton University Press, 1988), 110.

8. On the Constantine legend as a source for the midrash, see Ephraim Shoham-Steiner, "Pharaoh's Bloodbath: Medieval Jewish Thoughts about Leprosy, Disease, and Blood Therapy," in *Jewish Blood: Reality and Metaphor in History, Religion and Culture*, ed. Mitchel Hart (London: Routledge, 2009), 99–115.

9. The most influential version of the story appears in the Donation of Constantine, an alleged imperial decree from Constantine granting spiritual, political, and territorial authority to the bishop of Rome. From the eleventh century onward, it was cited in support of the pope's supremacy in the Christian world until it was exposed as a forgery in the fifteenth century.

10. Jeremy Glatstein, "The Watching Night: Print, Power and Jewish Vision in Early Modern Italy" (PhD diss., University of Southern California, 2014), 132–147.

11. David Malkiel, "Infanticide in Passover Iconography," *Journal of the Warburg and Courtauld Institutes* 46 (1993): 85–99, esp. 92–96.

12. Shoham-Steiner, "Pharaoh's Bloodbath."

13. As quoted in Stephen Bowd and Donald Cullington, eds., *"On Everyone's Lips": Humanists, Jews, and the Tale of Simon of Trent* (Tempe: Arizona Center for Medieval and Renaissance Studies, 2012), 158–159.

14. On the history of this accusation, see Ronnie Po-Chia, *The Myth of Ritual Murder: Jews and Magic in Reformation Germany* (New Haven, CT: Yale University Press, 1988); Hannah Johnson, *The Ritual Murder Accusation at the Limits of History* (Ann Arbor: University of Michigan Press, 2012); and Magda Teter, *Blood Libel: On the Trail of an Antisemitic Myth* (Cambridge, MA: Harvard University Press, 2020).

15. Gerrit Lindeboom, "The Story of a Blood Transfusion to a Pope," *Journal of the History of Medicine and Allied Sciences* 9 (1954): 455–459; A. Matthew Gottlieb, "History of the First Blood Transfusion but a Fable Agreed Upon: The Transfusion of Blood to a Pope," *Transfusion Medicine Reviews* 5 (1991): 228–235.

16. See Malkiel, "Infanticide in Passover Iconography," plate 10b.

17. For the early use of "Operation Ten Plagues" as a name for the campaign, note John Kimche, "'Operation Ten Plagues' Broke Egyptian Forces," *Palestine Post*, October 28, 1948.

18. For more on the Israeli battle missive, see Netta Galnoor, "From Jewish Sentiments to Rational Exhortations," *Israel Studies Review* 35 (2020): 130–153.

19. Michal Arbell, "Abba Kovner: The Ritual Function of His Battle Missives," *Jewish Social Studies* 18 (2012): 99–119. For a biography of Kovner, see Dina Porat, *The Fall of a Sparrow: The*

Life and Times of Abba Kovner (Stanford, CA: Stanford University Press, 2010) (Ya'ari's rebuke of Kovner's battle pages is cited on 248). Note also Dina Porat, *Nakam: The Holocaust Survivors Who Sought Full-Scale Revenge* (Stanford, CA: Stanford University Press, 2022).

20. Reuven Shoham, "Intertextual Relations and Their Rhetorical Significance in Abba Kovner's 'Daf Kravi,'" *Hebrew Studies* 37 (1996): 99–118.

21. Quoted in Shoham, "Intertextual Relations," 111–112.

22. Quoted in Alemzhan Arinov, "To Seek Vengeance or Not? How the Evolution of Revenge Propaganda Occurred in the Soviet Military Periodical Press," *Journal of Slavic Military Studies* 34 (2021): 384–402, esp. 387.

23. The story was first recorded in Meir Yellin and Dima Gelpern, *Partisans in Kovno Ghetto* (Moscow: Der Emes State Press, 1948), 12 (in Yiddish). For an attempt to establish the veracity of the story and the related photograph, see Aleks Faitelson, *The Truth and Nothing but the Truth: Jewish Resistance in Lithuania* (Jerusalem: Geffen, 2006), 452–457.

24. For more on the retributionist rhetoric of Markish's 1943 "To the Jewish Warrior" ("Dem yidishn shlaktman") and its use of blood imagery, see David Schneer, "Rivers of Blood: Peretz Markish, the Holocaust, and Jewish Vengeance," in *A Captive of Dawn: The Life and Work of Peretz Markish*, ed. Joseph Sherman et al. (Oxford: Legenda, 2011), 139–156.

25. See Shay Hazkani, "Political Indoctrination of Soldiers in the IDF, 1948–1949," *Israel Studies Review* 30 (2015): 20–41.

26. Cf. Arbell, "Abba Kovner," 107.

27. Compare the analysis of Kovner's religious views in Eli Pfefferkorn, "The Rent Canopy and the Cleft Covenant," *Modern Language Studies* 23 (1994): 11–24.

28. From an unnamed survivor quoted in Stephen Fritz, *Endkampf: Soldiers, Civilians, and the Death of the Third Reich* (Lexington: University Press of Kentucky, 2004), 256.

29. Compare Porat, *Fall of a Sparrow*, 236, citing a reminiscence from Kovner where he says that if he could have dropped the atomic bomb on Germany, he would have.

30. Hanan Hever, "From Revenge to Empathy: Abba Kovner from Jewish Destruction to Palestinian Destruction," in *The Holocaust and the Nakba: A New Grammar of Trauma and History*, ed. Bashir Bashir and Amos Goldberg (New York: Columbia University Press, 2019), 275–292.

31. I thank Penn Libraries, especially staff members Bruce Nielsen and Sara Heim, for sharing its uncataloged collection of IDF Haggadot extending from the 1948 war into the 1970s.

32. Neil Gilman, *Sacred Fragments: Recovering Theology for the Modern Jew* (Philadelphia: Jewish Publication Society, 1990), 202. For other examples of a Jewish theological turn against retributive justice following the Holocaust, see David Seltzer, "An Eye for an Eye: Beauvoir and Levinas on Retributive Justice," *International Studies in Philosophy* 39 (2007): 59–77.

33. Gerald Kirwin, "Waiting for Retaliation: A Study in Nazi Propaganda Behavior and German Civilian Morale," *Journal of Contemporary History* 16 (1981): 565–583.

34. As quoted in Jeffrey Herf, *The Jewish Enemy: Nazi Propaganda during World War II and the Holocaust* (Cambridge, MA: Harvard University Press, 2006), 120–121. For a translation of Hitler's speech, see "Text of Speech by Chancellor Adolf Hitler at Berlin Sports Palace," January 30, 1942, http://www.ibiblio.org/pha/policy/1942/1942-01-30a.html.

35. For divergent interpretations of the *Songs of the Plagues of Egypt*, see Uzi Shavit, *Poetry against Totalitarianism: Alterman and the Songs of the Egyptian Plagues* (Tel Aviv: Zemorah-Bitan, 2003) (Hebrew); and Hanan Hever, *Suddenly, the Sight of War: Violence and Nationalism in Hebrew Poetry in the 1940s*, trans. Lisa Katz (2000; Stanford, CA: Stanford University Press, 2006), esp. 97–139. I have drawn on both for my understanding of the songs. The version of the work itself that I have consulted is *Shire Makkot Mitzrayim* (Tel Aviv: Mahbarot le-sifurt, 1956/1957). The translations here are my own, but an alternative translation of the two songs I focus on, the plague of blood and the plague of lice, appears in Robert Friend, *Selected Poems: Bilingual Edition/Natan Alterman* (Tel Aviv: Kibbuts Hameuhad, 1978), 55–61.

36. On the interweaving of vengeance, messianism, and the ten plagues in late ancient and medieval *piyyut*, see Israel Yuval, *Two Nations in Your Womb: Perceptions of Jews and Christians in Late Antiquity and the Middle Ages* (Berkeley: University of California Press, 2006), 92–109.

37. For the German text alongside an English translation, see Richard Green, *Anthology of Goethe Songs* (Madison, WI: A-R Editions, 1994), xxx–xxxi. The idea to pursue this intertextual connection came from a post by Ilana Kurshan on Alterman's poem; see Ilana Kurshan, "Songs of the Plagues of Egypt," ilanakurshan.com, January 8, 2010, https://ilanakurshan.com/2010/01/08/songs-of-the-plagues-of-egypt/.

38. Shavit, *Poetry against Totalitarianism*, 54–55.

39. Cornelia Essner, "Nazi Antisemitism and the Question of 'Jewish Blood,'" in *Blood and Kinship: Matter for Metaphor from Ancient Rome to the Present*, ed. Christopher Johnson et al. (New York: Berghahn, 2013), 227–243.

40. Nicholas Stargardt, *Witnesses of War: Children's Lives under the Nazis* (New York: Vintage, 2007), 289–314.

41. See Klaus Koch, "Gibt es ein Vergeltungsdogma im Alten Testament?," *Zeitschrift fur Theologie und Kirche* 52 (1955): 1–52.

42. "Israeli Soldier Rabbi Zerbiv Invokes Biblical Ten Plagues in Context of Gaza," *Memo: Middle East Monitor*, January 22, 2024, https://www.middleeastmonitor.com/20240122-israeli-soldier-rabbi-zerbiv-invokes-biblical-ten-plagues-in-context-of-gaza/.

43. Middle East Eye, "Israeli Military Official: Palestinians in Gaza Need to Be Struck with Biblical 'Ten Plagues,'" YouTube Video, April 24, 2024, https://www.youtube.com/shorts/8-ra2jXz3Cg.

44. Sam Sokol, "In Passover Message Netanyahu Vows Imminent 'Painful Blows' on Hamas to Increase Pressure to Release Hostages," *Times of Israel*, April 21, 2024, https://www.timesofisrael.com/liveblog_entry/ahead-of-passover-netanyahu-vows-to-increase-pressure-on-hamas-to-free-hostages/. The word "blows" in this headline translates *makkot* from the Hebrew expression for the ten plagues, and the speech's Passover context and Hamas-Pharaoh comparison clearly show that Netanyahu was not referring to military blows in a general sense but evoking the ten plagues.

2. The Second Plague

1. For the recollections of Lasky and others involved in making *The Ten Commandments*, along with the relevant part of the script cited here, see Katherine Orrison, *Written in Stone: Making Cecil B. DeMille's Epic "The Ten Commandments"* (Lanham, MD: Vestal, 1999), 39–40, 75. For an attempt to reconstruct what the scene was like, see CBDeMilleFan, "Deleted Scene from the Ten Commandments: The Frog Plague (Reconstruction)," YouTube video, 1:06, posted July 15, 2019, https://www.youtube.com/watch?v=eQMbnqNwV_4.

2. David Malkiel, "The Rabbi and the Crocodile: Interrogating Nature in the Late Quattrocento," *Speculum* 91 (2016): 115–148.

3. Charlotte Sleigh, *Frog* (London: Reaktion, 2012), 161–162, referring to Michael Tyler, Richard Wassersug, and Benjamin Smith, "How Frogs and Humans Interact: Influences beyond Habitat Destruction, Epidemics and Global Warming," *Applied Herpetology* 4 (2007): 1–18.

4. For a bibliographic guide to the field of humor studies, see Jennifer Hofmann and Willibald Ruch, "Humor," Oxford Bibliographies, November 25, 2014, https://www.oxfordbibliographies.com/view/document/obo-9780199828340/obo-9780199828340-0127.xml.

5. For an early formulation of this approach, see John Morreall, "Funny Ha-Ha, Funny Strange, and Other Reactions to Incongruity," in *The Philosophy of Laughter and Humor*, ed. John Morreall (Albany: State University of New York Press, 1987), 188–207.

6. A. Peter McGraw and Caleb Warren, "Benign Violations: Making Immoral Behavior Funny," *Psychological Science* 21 (2010): 1141–1149.

7. For a very accessible survey of humor research, see Noël Carroll, *Humor: A Very Short Introduction* (Oxford: Oxford University Press, 2014).

8. Jan Willem van Henten, "Daniel 3 and 6 in Early Christian Literature," in *The Book of Daniel: Composition and Reception*, 2 vols., ed. John J. Collins and Peter W. Flint (Leiden: Brill, 2001), 1:149–169.

9. See Baruch Bokser, "Todos and Rabbinic Authority in Rome," in *Religion, Literature, and Society in Ancient Israel, Formative Christianity and Judaism: Ancient Israel and Christianity*, ed. Jacob Neusner et al. (Lanham, MD: University Press of America, 1987), 117–130.

10. Louise Shier, "The Frog on Lamps from Karanis," in *Medieval and Middle Eastern Studies in Honor of Aziz Suryal Atiya*, ed. Sami Hanna (Leiden: Brill, 1972), 349–358.

11. The complicated compositional history of the Akiba martyrdom story is discussed in Paul Mandel, "Was Rabbi Aqiva a Martyr? Palestinian and Babylonian Influences in the Development of a Legend," in *Rabbinic Traditions between Palestine and Babylonia*, ed. Ronit Nikolsky and Tal Ilan (Leiden: Brill, 2014), 306–354.

12. On this version of the midrash, see Joanna Weinberg, "The Comic and the Serious in Midrash: The Case of the Pious Frogs (Midrash Psalms 28:2)," in *Welcome to the Cavalcade: A Festschrift in Honour of Professor Jonathan Magonet*, ed. Colin Eimer, Elli Tikvah Sarah, and Howard Cooper (Victoria, BC: Kulmus, 2013), 119–126.

13. For the text, translation, and commentary, see Matthew Hosty, *Batrachomyomachia (Battle of Frogs and Mice): Introduction, Translation, and Commentary* (Oxford: Oxford University Press, 2020).

14. For more on the King David midrash, see Alan Cooper, "The Life and Times of King David according to the Psalms," in *The Poet and the Historian: Essays in Literary and Historical Biblical Criticism*, ed. Richard Elliot Friedman (Chico, CA: Scholars Press, 1983), 117–131, esp. 118. As for midrash in Exodus Rabbah 10.6, note also that a similar comic moment occurs in the *War between the Frogs and the Mice*, where the goddess Athena refuses to help the frogs because their noise had kept her up all night (lines 189–91).

15. Daniel Boyarin, *Socrates and the Fat Rabbis* (Chicago: University of Chicago Press, 2009).

16. For more on the rabbis' sense of humor, see, among many studies, Arkadi Kovelman, "The Talmud as Farce," *Review of Rabbinic Judaism* 5 (2002): 86–92; and Eliezer Diamond, "But Is It Funny? Identifying Humor, Satire, and Parody in Rabbinic Literature," in *Jews and Humor*, ed. Leonard Greenspoon (West Lafayette, IN: Purdue University Press, 2011), 33–54.

17. For the scholarly publication of the Golden Haggadah (British Library, MS Add. 27210), see Bezalel Narkiss, *The Golden Haggadah* (Rohnert Park, CA: Pomegranate, 1997).

18. The person who recognized that the smaller frogs are coming specifically out of the butt of the larger frog was the eight-year-old daughter of the art historian Marc Epstein. See his "Frogs, Griffins and Jews without Hats: How My Children Illuminated the Haggadah," *Jewish Review of Books* 3 (2012): 36–38.

19. The classic formulation of the carnivalesque comes from Mikhail Bakhtin, *Rabelais and His World*, trans. Helene Iswolsky (Bloomington: Indiana University Press, 1984).

20. The foregoing description follows the description of the theater historian Shari Troy based on a videotape of the performance. Shari Troy, "On Smiting Borders and Staging Bedlam: The Live Frog as Prop in the Purim Play of the Bobover Hasidim," *Assaph—Studies in the Theater* 11 (1995): 66–74.

21. Troy, "On Smiting Borders," 71–72.

22. Originally entitled "One Morning," the song was first recorded in 1951 by Cohen Steinberg for her personal use in the classroom and remained popular enough some sixty years later

that it was expanded into a children's book illustrated by Ann D. Koffsky, *Frogs in the Bed: My Passover Seder Activity Book* (Millburn, NJ: Behrman, 2014).

23. Osher Werner, *Pharaoh and the Fabulous Frog Invasion* (New York: Judaica Press, 2007), 25.

24. To view this Passover frog riot, see the end of the video "Shalom Sesame: Passover," YouTube video, 6:08, posted December 29, 2015, https://www.youtube.com/watch?v=038ARUy-R5Q.

25. See James Martin, *A History of Childhood: A Very Short Introduction* (Oxford: Oxford University Press, 2018).

26. The film is widely available on streaming platforms, and for the script, see Paul Thomas Anderson, *Magnolia: The Shooting Script* (New York: Newmarker, 1999). The film has both fascinated and confounded scholars, yielding varying analyses and interpretations. An example helpful for understanding its use of the frog plague is Jason Silverman, "'We May Be Through with the Past . . .': *Magnolia*, the Exodus Plague Narrative, and Tradition History," *Religion and the Arts* 20, no. 4 (2016): 459–490.

27. Steven Gados, "'Magnolia' Helmer Ribeted by Novelist's Frogs," *Variety*, February 7, 2000, https://variety.com/2000/film/news/magnolia-helmer-ribeted-by-novelist-s-frogs-1117776227/. Anderson has repeated this claim in many contexts and acknowledges Fort both in the shooting script and in the credits. The book in question is Charles Fort, *The Book of the Damned* (1919; New York: Ace, 1941).

28. Ambrose Heron, "8 and 2 in Magnolia," FILMDetail, December 1, 2008, http://www.filmdetail.com/2008/01/12/8-and-2-in-magnolia/.

3. The Third Plague

1. For more on ancient Egyptian magical lore, see Rana Serida, "Cultural Memory and Motifs of Magician Heroes from Ancient to Islamic Egypt," in *Lotus and Laurel: Studies on Egyptian Language and Religion in Honour of John Paul Frandsen*, ed. Rune Nyord and Kim Ryholt (Copenhagen: Museum Tusculanum, 2015), 351–372.

2. The feat of conjuring darkness appears in a collection of stories known as the Khamwase Cycle, which tells of a duel between an Egyptian magician named Sisose son of Khamwase and an enemy magician from the Nubian kingdom on Egypt's southern border. For a translation, see William Kelly Simpson, ed., *The Literature of Ancient Egypt: An Anthology of Stories, Instructions, Stelae, Autobiographies, and Poetry* (New Haven, CT: Yale University Press, 2003), 470–489.

3. For the meaning of "it is the finger of God" for Philo and other early Jewish and Christian interpreters, see Pieter Van der Horst, "'The Finger of God': Miscellaneous Notes on Luke 11:20 and Its *Umwelt*," in *Sayings of Jesus: Canonical and Non-canonical*, ed. William Petersen et al. (Leiden: Brill, 1997), 89–103.

4. The research on the origin and history of Jewish and Christian belief in demons is voluminous; see Matthew Goff, Blake Jurgens, and Emily Olsen, "Demons," Oxford Bibliographies, February 24, 2021, https://www.oxfordbibliographies.com/display/document/obo-9780195393361/obo-9780195393361-0013.xml.

5. For more on the circulation of the story in antiquity, see Albert Pietersma, The *Apocryphon of Jannes and Jambres the Magicians* (Leiden: Brill, 1994), 12–35; Johannes Tromp, "Jannes and Jambres (2 Timothy 3, 8–9)," in *Moses in Biblical and Extra-biblical Traditions*, ed. Alex Graupner et al. (Berlin: de Gruyter, 2007), 211–226. Pliny refers to Jannes in his *Natural History* 30.2.11, completed by around the year 77 CE.

6. On Jannes and Jambres in rabbinic literature, see Lester Grabbe, "The Jannes/Jambres Tradition in Targum Pseudo-Jonathan and Its Date," *Journal of Biblical Literature* 98 (1979):

393–401. For evidence of an alternative Coptic version of the story, see Frederic Krueger, "Pharaoh's Sorcerers Revisited: A Sahidic Exodus Apocryphon (P. Lips. Inv. 2299) and the Legend of Jannes and Jambres the Magicians between Judaism, Christianity and Native Egyptian Tradition," *Archiv für Papyrusforschung und verwandte Gebiete* 64 (2018): 148–198.

7. On the contrast between midrashic versions of the story, usually tied to specific biblical verses or passages, and the approach of the apocryphon, which rarely connects itself to specific verses, see Jed Wyrick, "The Vanishing Scriptural Scaffolding of the Book of the Words of Jannes and Jambres and Its Kindred Legends," in *Old Testament Pseudepigrapha and the Scriptures*, ed. Eibert Tigchelaar (Leuven: Peeters, 2014), 231–260.

8. So suggested M. R. James, "A Fragment of the 'Penitence of Jannes and Jambres,'" *Journal of Theological Studies* 2 (1901): 572–577.

9. The manuscript in question, cataloged as British Library Cotton MS Tiberius B (fol. 87r, v), is discussed in Pietersma, *Apocryphon*, 277–281.

10. For proof of the story's wide circulation, note evidence for it from Ethiopia (Ted Erho and W. B. Henry, "The Ethiopic Jannes and Jambres and the Greek Original," *Archiv für Papyrusforschung und verwandte Gebiete* 65 [2019]: 176–223); England (Frederick Biggs and Thomas Hall, "Traditions Concerning Jamnes and Mambres in Anglo-Saxon England," *Anglo Saxon England* 25 [1996]: 69–89); and the Near East (Stephen Gero, "Parerga to the Book of Jannes and Jambres," *Journal for the Study of Pseudepigrapha* 9 [1991]: 67–85, addressing Syriac and Arabic material).

11. For the text, translation, and commentary of the texts that describe Cyprian's magic, repentance, and martyrdom, see Ryan Bailey, "The *Acts of Saint Cyprian of Antioch*: Critical Editions, Translations, and Commentaries" (PhD diss., McGill University, 2017).

12. For more on Agrippa, and other learned magicians from the Renaissance, see Anthony Grafton, *Magus: The Art of Magic from Faustus to Agrippa* (Cambridge, MA: Harvard University Press, 2023).

13. The retraction was published in English for the first time in Henry Cornelius Agrippa, *The Vanity of Arts and Sciences* (London: R. Bentley and Dan Brown, 1694), 128. For an English translation of *The Occult Philosophy*, see Donald Tyson, trans., *Three Books of the Occult Philosophy* (Saint Paul, MN: Llewellyn, 2004), esp. 705–706.

14. For a close reading of the recantation, see Chris Miles, "Occult Retraction: Cornelius Agrippa and the Paradox of Magical Language," *Rhetoric Society Quarterly* 38 (2008): 433–456. For the renunciation of magic as a theme in later sixteenth- and seventeenth-century literature, see Andrew Ettin, "Magic into Art: The Magician's Renunciation of Magic in English Renaissance Drama," *Texas Studies in Literature and Language* 19 (1977): 268–293.

15. Pawel Rutkowski, "Papists, Frogs and Witches: Representing Quakers in Seventeenth-Century England," in *Protestant Majorities and Minorities in Early Modern Europe: Confessional Boundaries and Contested Identities*, ed. Simon Burton, Michał Choptiany, and Piotr Wilczek (Göttingen: Vandenhoeck and Ruprecht, 2019), 285–302, esp. 295–296.

16. So suggested James ("Fragment of the 'Penitence,'" 576).

17. On witchcraft and its persecution in Europe, see Brian P. Levack, ed., *The Oxford Handbook of Witchcraft in Early Modern Europe and Colonial America* (Oxford: Oxford University Press, 2013).

18. For a recent overview of differences between medieval and Renaissance magic, see Thomas Willard, "How Magical Was Renaissance Magic?," in *Magic and Magicians in the Middle Ages and the Early Modern Times: The Occult in Pre-modern Sciences*, ed. Albrecht Classen (Berlin: de Gruyter, 2017), 637–655; and for the history of how one evolved into the other, see Mark Waddell, *Magic, Science and Religion in Early Modern Europe* (Cambridge: Cambridge University Press, 2021).

19. For an introduction to the figure of Hermes Trismegistus and the Hermetic corpus, see Florian Ebeling, *The Secret History of Hermes Trismegistus: Hermeticism from Ancient to Modern Times,* trans. David Lorton (Ithaca, NY: Cornell University Press, 2007); and Christian Bull, *The Tradition of Hermes Trismegistus: The Egyptian Priestly Figure as a Teacher of Hellenized Wisdom* (Leiden: Brill, 2018).

20. See Claudio Moreschani, *Hermes Christianus: The Intermingling of Hermetic Piety and Christian Thought* (Turnhout: Brepolis, 2011).

21. See Tyson's translation of *The Occult Philosophy, Three Books,* 700–701. Agrippa's term Merkaba, garbled by a printer's editor as Mercana or Mercara, was based on the Hebrew *merkavah,* used of a school of Jewish mysticism focused on the first chapter of Ezekiel.

22. See Stuart Clark, *Vanities of the Eye: Vision in Early Modern European Culture* (Oxford: Oxford University Press, 2007).

23. John Deacon and John Walker, *Dialogicall Discourses of Spirits and Divels* (London, 1601). This text can be found online at https://quod.lib.umich.edu/e/eebo/A20000.0001.001/1:7.

24. On the belief in this period that Satan was able to manipulate people psychologically, see Darren Oldridge, "Demons of the Mind: Satanic Thoughts in Seventeenth-Century England," *Seventeenth Century* 35 (2020): 277–292.

25. See Rob Iliffe, "Lying Wonders and Juggling Tricks: Religion, Nature, and Imposture in Early Modern England," in *Everything Connects: In Conference with Richard H. Popkin,* ed. James Force and David Katz (Leiden: Brill, 1999), 185–209.

26. Quoted in Grafton, *Magus,* 218–219.

27. Reginald Scot, *The Discoverie of Witchcraft* (London: E. Stock, 1886). This text can also be accessed online at https://www.gutenberg.org/files/60766/60766-h/60766-h.htm.

28. See Jean Bodin, *On the Demon Mania of Witches,* trans. Randy Scott (Toronto: Centre for Renaissance and Reformation Studies, 1995), 63.

29. For more on this history, see Simon During, *Modern Enchantments: The Cultural Power of Secular Magic* (Cambridge, MA: Harvard University Press, 2004); and Sofie Lachapelle, *Conjuring Science: A History of Scientific Entertainment and Stage Magic in Modern France* (New York: Palgrave Macmillan, 2015).

30. John Buescher, "Cornering the Market on Fraud: Stage Magicians versus Spirit Mediums," *Magic, Ritual and Witchcraft* 9 (2014): 210–223. For similar acts of exposure targeted at Indian or Chinese magicians (or White magicians pretending to be Asian), see Christopher Goto-Jones, *Conjuring Asia: Magic, Orientalism and the Making of the Modern World* (Cambridge: Cambridge University Press, 2016).

31. For example, Gustave Vapereau, *L'année littéraire et dramatique* (1858; Paris: L. Hachette et Cie, 1859), 335. For more on this episode as an example of how modern stage magicians sought to distinguish themselves from and elevate themselves over earlier magic, see Graham Jones, "Modern Magic and the War on Miracles in French Colonial Society," *Comparative Studies in Society and History* 52 (2010): 66–99.

32. For an English translation of the 1868 French original, see Jean-Eugène Robert-Houdin, *Secrets of Conjuring and Magic, or How to Become a Wizard,* trans. Louis Hoffman (1877; Cambridge: Cambridge University Press, 2011), 21–22.

33. Note, for example, John Norton, *The King's Ferry Boat: Sermons Preached to Children* (London: Richard D. Dickenson, 1879), 234.

34. Erika White Dyson, "'Gentleman Mountebanks' and Spiritualists: Legal, Stage and Media Contest between Magicians and Spirit Mediums in the United States and England," in *The Ashgate Research Companion to Nineteenth-Century Spiritualism and the Occult,* ed. Tatiana Kontou and Sarah Willburn (London: Routledge, 2012), 231–266.

35. E. S. Martin, untitled column, *Life,* August 12, 1926, 18.

36. Henry Seybert, *Preliminary Report of the Commission Appointed by the University of Pennsylvania to Investigate Modern Spiritualism* (Philadelphia: J. P. Lippincott, 1887).

37. See Simone Natale, *Supernatural Entertainments: Victorian Spiritualism and the Rise of Modern Media Culture* (University Park: Pennsylvania State University Press, 2016), 65–80.

38. See Phillip Butterworth, *Staging, Playing, Pyrotechnics and Magic: Conventions of Performance in Early English Theater* (London: Routledge, 2022), 262.

39. Compare Graham Jones, "The Family Romance of Modern Magic: Contesting Robert-Houdin's Cultural Legacy in Contemporary France," in *Performing Magic on the Western Stage: From the Eighteenth Century to the Present*, ed. Francesca Coppa, Lawrence Hass, and James Peck (New York: Palgrave Macmillan, 2008), 33–60, esp. 48–51.

40. For more on Robert-Houdin's effort to train his Algerian audiences how to be more sophisticated spectators of modern stage magic, see Murray Leeder, "M. Robert-Houdin Goes to Algeria: Spectatorship and Panic in Illusion and Early Cinema," *Early Popular Visual Culture* 8 (2010): 209–225.

41. Jason Josephson-Storm, *The Myth of Disenchantment: Magic, Modernity, and the Birth of the Human Sciences* (Chicago: University of Chicago Press, 2017).

4. The Fourth Plague

1. Other ancient and medieval explanations for how the Israelites were able to find water during the first plague while the Egyptians struggled to find something to drink are collected in a Hebrew-language study by Boaz Shpigel, "What Did the Egyptians Drink during the Plague of Blood? A Study of Midrashim and Rishonim Literature," *Oreshet* 8 (2018): 199–216.

2. For a review of the scholarly debate about the location of Goshen, see William Ward, "Goshen," in *Anchor Bible Dictionary*, 6 vols., ed. David Noel Friedman (New York: Doubleday, 1992), 2:1076–1077.

3. For an English translation of the relevant passage, see Marcus Nathan Adler, ed., *The Itinerary of Benjamin of Tudela: Critical Text, Translation and Commentary* (London: Henry Froude, 1907), 74.

4. Homi Bhabha, *The Location of Culture* (London: Routledge, 1994), 36–39.

5. Bhabha, *Location of Culture*, 56.

6. For the application of the third space concept to the field of urban design (sometimes spelled as Thirdspace), see Edward W. Soja, *Thirdspace: Journeys to Los Angeles and Other Real-and-Imagined Places* (Cambridge, MA: Blackwell, 1996); in political theorizing, see Kevin Bruyneel, *The Third Space of Sovereignty: The Postcolonial Politics of U.S.-Indigenous Relations* (Minneapolis: University of Minnesota Press, 2007); and for media studies, see Karin Ikas and Gerhard Wagner, eds., *Communicating in the Third Space* (New York: Routledge, 2009).

7. For the Greek text and English translation of Manetho as cited by Josephus, see Menachem Stern, *Greek and Latin Authors on Jews and Judaism*, 3 vols. (Jerusalem: Israel Academy of Sciences and Humanities, 1974), 1:62–86; and W. G. Waddel, trans., *Manetho* (Cambridge, MA: Harvard University Press, 1980).

8. Manfred Bietak, *Avaris, the Capital of the Hyksos: Recent Excavations at Tell el-Dab'a* (London: British Museum Press, 1996).

9. Amos Funkenstein, *Perceptions of Jewish History* (Berkeley: University of California Press, 1993), 36–40.

10. For an overview of the different attempts to assess Manetho's testimony, including his possible use of the Bible or Greek paraphrases of the Bible, see Lucia Raspe, "Manetho on the Exodus: A Reappraisal," *Jewish Studies Quarterly* 5 (1998): 124–155.

11. Michel Foucault, "Of Other Spaces," *Diacritics* 16 (1986): 22–27.

12. See Aryeh Kasher, *The Jews in Hellenistic and Roman Egypt: The Struggle for Equal Rights* (Tübingen: J.C.B. Mohr, 1985), a dated but still informative overview.

13. Gershon Greenberg, "Mahane Israel Lubavitch 1940–1945: Active Responding to Hurban," in *Bearing Witness to the Holocaust, 1939–1989*, ed. Alan Berger (Lewiston, NY: Edwin Mellen, 1991), 141–163, esp. 141–142.

14. Moshe Nissenbaum, "The Forgotten Story of Yeshivat Goshen," *Israel Hayom*, April 17, 2018, https://www.israelhayom.co.il/article/545071 (Hebrew). The yeshiva operated for six months until an agreement with Egypt required its disbandment.

15. Julie Ann Harris, "Love in the Land of Goshen: Haggadah, History and the Making of British Library, MS Oriental 2737," *Gesta* 52 (2013): 161–180.

16. There is much Spanish-language research on the medieval *judería* of Toledo. Note the studies collected in Jean Passini and Ricardo Benito, eds., *La judería de Toledo: Un tiempo y un espacio por rehabilitar* (Toledo: University of Castille–La Mancha, 2013).

17. See Marc Epstein, "Another Flight into Egypt: Confluence, Coincidence and Cross-Cultural Dialectics of Messianism and Iconographic Appropriation in Medieval Jewish and Christian Culture," in *Imagining the Self, Imagining the Other: Visual Representation and Jewish-Christian Dynamics in the Middle Ages and Early Modern Period*, ed. Eva Frodmojic (Leiden: Brill, 2002), 33–52.

18. Nancy Miwa, "The *Hortus Conclusus*: Marian Iconography in the Middle Ages" (PhD diss., Drew University, 2011); Liz McAvoy, "The Medieval *Hortus Conclusus*: Revisiting the Pleasure Garden," *Medieval Feminist Forum* 50 (2014): 5–10 (introduction to a special issue devoted to the topic); Liz McAvoy, *The Enclosed Garden and the Medieval Religious Imaginary* (Cambridge: Boydell and Brewer, 2021).

19. Liz McAvoy, "Gendered Spaces of Flourishing and the Medieval *Hortus Conclusus*," in *The Medieval and Early Modern Garden in Britain*, ed. Patricia Skinner and Theresa Tyers (New York: Routledge, 2018), 16–38.

20. For the migration of this theme into medieval Spanish culture, see Lucia Hoess, "The Concept of the Garden in Selected Spanish Works of the Medieval and Golden Age" (PhD diss., University of British Columbia, 1994). A facsimile of the Cantigas de Santa Maria has been published as *Cantigas de Santa María: Edición facsímil del códice B.R.20 de la Biblioteca Nazionale Centrale de Florencia, siglo XIII* (Madrid: Edilan, 1989–1991).

21. For an example from a fifteenth-century manuscript, see the illustration of the soldiers Arcita and Palemone looking down on the woman Emilia in her enclosed garden: *Emelye's Garden*, Luminarium.org, accessed July 30, 2023, https://www.luminarium.org/medlit/garden.htm.

22. For more on the historical context in which Alfonso X and other communal leaders sought to impose sharper social boundaries, including sexual boundaries, among Jews, Christians, and Muslims, see Jonathan Ray, *The Sephardic Frontier: The "Reconquista" and the Jewish Community in Medieval Iberia* (Ithaca, NY: Cornell University Press, 2011), 145–175; and Simon Barton, *Conquerors, Brides, and Concubines: Interfaith Relations and Social Power in Medieval Iberia* (Philadelphia: University of Pennsylvania Press, 2015), 45–73.

23. The novel was published for the first time in 1939 as Zora Neale Hurston, *Moses, Man of the Mountain* (Philadelphia: Lippincott, 1939).

24. For more on this tradition, see Eddie Glaude, *Exodus! Religion, Race and Nation in Early Nineteenth-Century Black America* (Chicago: University of Chicago Press, 2000); Allen Callahan, *The Talking Book: African Americans and the Bible* (New Haven, CT: Yale University Press, 2006), 83–137; and Herbert Marbury, *Pillars of Cloud and Fire: The Politics of Exodus in African American Biblical Interpretation* (New York: New York University Press, 2015).

25. James Brewer, "The War against Jim Crow in the Land of Goshen," *Negro History Bulletin* 24 (1960): 53–57.

26. For Frederick Douglass's description of Goshen, see Henry Louis Gates Jr., ed., *Autobiographies: Narrative of the Life of Frederick Douglass, an American Slave / My Bondage and My Freedom / Life and Times of Frederick Douglass* (New York: Library of America, 1994), 1010–1011.

27. David Walker, *Appeal, in Four Articles; Together with a Preamble, to the Coloured Citizens of the World but in Particular, and Very Expressly, to Those in the United States*, 3rd ed. (Boston: David Walker, 1830), 11–12.

28. Kelly Miller, "The Modern Land of Goshen," *Southern Workman* 29 (1900): 601–607. I thank Jacob Morrow-Spitzer for calling attention to Miller's essay.

29. Miller, "Modern Land," 603.

30. Hurston was familiar with both American prison camps and Nazi concentration camps as they existed in the late 1930s. She interviewed prisoners at convict camps in Florida, recording their experiences in an essay entitled "Turpentine Camp and Cross City," Zora Neale Hurston and the WPA in Florida, Florida Memory: State Library and Archives of Florida, accessed July 30, 2023, https://www.floridamemory.com/learn/classroom/learning-units/zora-neale-hurston/documents/essay/. She also mentions the situation in Germany in a letter to a friend: Zora Neale Hurston to Annie Nathan Meyer, April 25, 1933, in *Zora Neale Hurston: A Life in Letters*, ed. Carla Kaplan (New York: Anchor, 2002), 349.

31. On Eatonville's history and its role in Hurston's life as a "safe cocoon," see Tiffany Patterson, *Zora Neale Hurston and a History of Southern Life* (Philadelphia: Temple University Press, 2005), 50–81.

32. Olivia Marcucci, "Zora Neale Hurston and the Brown Debate: Race, Class and the Progressive Era," *Journal of Negro Education* 86 (2017): 13–24.

33. Compare Dale Pattison, "Sites of Resistance: The Subversive Spaces of *Their Eyes Were Watching God*," *MELUS* 38, no. 4 (2013): 9–31.

34. Citing from the HarperCollins edition of the 1937 novel: Zora Neale Hurston, *Their Eyes Were Watching God* (New York: HarperCollins, 2010), 2.

5. The Fifth Plague

1. Amos Guiora, "Lessons Learned from the Fifth Plague," *Case Western Reserve Journal of International Law* 38 (2007): 605–607. For a video of part of the proceedings, see Case Western Reserve University School of Law, "The Fifth Plague: Keynote Address," YouTube video, 57:33, recorded March 31, 2006, posted September 18, 2009, https://www.youtube.com/watch?v=634xpxoVGXQ.

2. Much has been written about the 1865–1866 cattle plague, particularly in Great Britain. On religious responses, see Matthew Cragoe, "'The Hand of the Lord Is upon the Cattle': Religious Reactions to the Cattle Plague, 1865–1867," in *An Age of Equipoise? Reassessing Mid-Victorian Britain*, ed. Martin Hewitt (Aldershot: Ashgate, 2000), 190–206; Stephen Matthews, "Explanations for the Outbreak of Cattle Plague in Cheshire in 1865–1866: 'Fear the Wrath of the Lord,'" *Northern History* 43 (2006): 117–135; and Marie Robinson, "Plague and Humiliation: The Ecclesiastical Response to Cattle Plague in Mid-Victorian Britain," *Journal of Scottish Historical Studies* 29 (2009): 52–71.

3. Joseph Hardwick, "Cows, Communities and Religious Responses to the 1865–1866 British Rinderpest Outbreak," *Journal of Religious History* 48 (2024): 153–171.

4. On the interpretation of mad cow disease as a form of retribution, see John Fisher, "Cattle Plagues Past and Present: The Mystery of Mad Cow Disease," *Journal of Contemporary History* 33 (1998): 215–228.

5. Morgan Powell, *The Hand of the Lord upon the Cattle: A Sermon Occasioned by the Distemper among the Cattle* (London: S. Austen, 1747), 21.

6. Although Exodus reports that the plague of cattle killed all the cattle of Egypt, the rabbis inferred that some of the cattle must have survived because, a few verses later, the biblical account mentions that there were cattle in the time of the plague of hail (Exodus 9:19). Exodus goes on to note that some of Pharaoh's servants, heeding Moses's warning to take cover, took their cattle into their houses in order to save them, and according to the midrash in Mekhilta de-Rabbi Ishmael, these included the horses that the Egyptians would eventually use to hunt down the Israelites at the sea. My thanks to my colleague Natalie Dohrmann for calling my attention to this midrash.

7. Origen, *Homilies on Genesis and Exodus*, trans. Ronald Heine (Washington, DC: Catholic University of America Press, 1982), 269.

8. I cite the translation of F. H. Colson, trans., *Philo in Ten Volumes*, Loeb Classical Library (Cambridge, MA: Harvard University Press, 1934), vol. 6, with tiny stylistic modifications.

9. For Greek and Roman sources where the death of cattle precedes or accompanies the death of humans during a plague, see Effie Coughanowr, "The Plague in Livy and Thucydides," *L'antiquité Classique* 54 (1985): 152–158.

10. For an overview of how Egyptian animal veneration was seen by Philo and other Jewish, Greek, Roman, and Christian writers, see K.A.D. Smelik and E. A. Hemelrijk, "'Who Knows Not What Monsters Demented Egypt Worships?': Opinions on Egyptian Animal Worship in Antiquity as Part of the Ancient Conception of Egypt," in *Aufstieg und Niedergang der römischen Welt*, vol. 2.17.4, ed. Wolfgang Haase (Berlin: Walter de Gruyter, 1984), 1852–2000; Sarah Pearce, *The Land of the Body: Studies in Philo's Representation of Egypt* (Tübingen: Mohr Siebek, 2007), 241–278.

11. A similar explanation for the Passover sacrifice is suggested by the Roman historian Tacitus: "[The Jews] dedicated, in a shrine, a statue of that creature whose guidance enabled them to put an end to their wandering and thirst, sacrificing a ram, apparently in derision of Ammon. They likewise offer the ox, because the Egyptians worship Apis" (*Histories* 5.1.4). For more on Philo's view of the animals of Egypt, see Pearce, *Land of the Body*, 279–308.

12. For text, translation, and commentary, see Abraham Terian, *Philonis Alexandrini "De Animabilis": The Armenian Text with an Introduction, Translation and Commentary* (Chico, CA: Scholars Press, 1981). For more on Philo's view of animals, see Pearce, *Land of the Body*, 279–308.

13. For translation of these treatises, see Stephen Newmeyer, *Plutarch's Three Treatises on Animals: A Translation with Introductions and Commentary* (London: Routledge, 2021). For further discussion of Plutarch's views, see Damien Miszczynski, "Justice for Animals according to Plutarch," *Mare Nostrum* 10 (2019): 54–76.

14. For more on the ancient debate on whether animals are rational, see Richard Sorabji, *Animal Minds and Human Morals: The Origins of The Western Debate* (Ithaca, NY: Cornell University Press, 1993); and Stephen Newmeyer, *The Animal and the Human in Ancient and Modern Thought: The "Man Alone of Animals" Concept* (London: Routledge, 2017), 44–76.

15. Samuel King, *The Hand of the Lord upon the Cattle Considered and Improved, in a Sermon preached at Northampton, December, 7, 1849. On Occasion of the Present Mortality Amongst the Cattle* (London: J. Bucklund, 1750), 12.

16. "The Plagues of Egypt," one of Cowley's "Pindarique odes," can be found in *The Complete Works in Verse and Prose of Abraham Cowley*, vol. 2, ed. Alexander Grosart (Edinburgh: University of Edinburgh Press, 1882), 32–40.

17. Virgil, *Georgics* 3.478–566. For an English translation, see Kimberly Johnson, "The Plague," *Arion* 13 (2005): 73–76. For an attempt to diagnose the plague as anthrax, see Everard Flintoff, "The Noric Cattle Plague," *Quaderni Urbinati di Cultura Classica* 13 (1983): 85–111.

18. An example of a much earlier Christian poem that draws on Virgil's depiction of cattle pestilence is the fourth- or fifth-century Latin poem "On the Deaths of Cattle" (De mortibus boum) by Endelechius.

19. Mary Fissel, "Imagining Vermin in Early Modern England," *History Workshop Journal* 47 (1999): 1–29; Timothy Desaillan-Olsen, "Vilifying Vermin: Creation of a Noxious 'Kinde,' 1300–1625" (PhD diss., University of Colorado, 2019).

20. Godfrey Goodman, *The Fall of Man: Proud by Reason* (London: Robert Wilson and Richard Boulton, 1618), 219–220.

21. Lucinda Cole, *Imperfect Creatures: Vermin, Literature, and the Sciences of Life, 1600–1740* (Ann Arbor: University of Michigan Press, 2016), 49–80.

22. Cowley, "Plagues of Egypt," stanza 6 line 91 (p. 33 in *Collected Works*).

23. Cowley, "Plagues of Egypt," stanza 12, line 230 (p. 34 in *Collected Works*).

24. Robert Watson, "Protestant Animals: Puritan Sects and English Animal-Protection Sentiment, 1550–1650," *English Literary History* 8 (2014): 1111–1148.

25. See Erica Fudge, *Brutal Reasoning: Animals, Rationality, and Humanity in Early Modern England* (Ithaca, NY: Cornell University Press, 2006).

26. Peter Singer, "The Cow Who . . . ," *Project Syndicate*, February 5, 2016, https://www.project-syndicate.org/commentary/pronouns-greater-recognition-for-animals-by-peter-singer-2016-02.

27. Janet Hamilton, "Lines on the Long and Beautiful Summer of 1865: In Connection with the Cattle Plague Then Raging," in *Poems, Essay, Sketches: Comprising the Principle Pieces from Her Complete Works*, ed. James Hamilton (Glasgow: James McLehose, 1880), 247–248.

28. Hardwick, "Cows, Communities." See also Don LePan, "'Your Suff'rings, Sinless Things': Changing Attitudes towards Non-human Animals and the Cattle Plague of 1865" (paper presented at the 2012 conference of the Society for Literature, Science, and the Arts, Milwaukee, September 29, 2012), https://papers.ssrn.com/sol3/papers.cfm?abstract_id=2491244.

29. William Hogarth, "Progress of Cruelty," in *The Bible of Nature and Substance of Virtue* (repr.; Albany, NY: C. Van Benthuysen, 1842), 177–183; Humphrey Primatt, *Dissertation on the Duty of Divine Mercy and the Sin of Cruelty to Brute Animals* (London: R. Hett, 1776).

30. Ivan Kreilkamp, *Minor Creatures: Persons, Animals and the Victorian Novel* (Chicago: University of Chicago Press, 2018); J. Keri Cronin, *Art for Animals: Visual Culture and Animal Advocacy, 1870–1914* (University Park: Pennsylvania State University Press, 2018), 70–99. On the history of the concept of animal rights as expressed artistically, see Stephen Eisenman, *The Cry of Nature: Art and the Making of Animal Rights* (London: Reaktion Books, 2013).

31. A.W.H. Bates, "Have Animals Souls? The Late-Nineteenth Century Spiritual Revival and Animal Welfare," in *Anti-vivisection and the Profession of Medicine in Britain: A Social History* (London: Palgrave Macmillan, 2017), https://www.ncbi.nlm.nih.gov/books/NBK513717/.

32. James Comper Gray, *The Biblical Museum: A Collection of Notes, Explanatory, Homiletic, and Illustrative* (London: Elliot Stock, 1880), 107. For more on the role of biblical interpretation in the early animal welfare movement, see Michael Gilmour, "Biblical Studies Meets the Humane Society: The Emergence of Animal Activist Exegesis," in *Ask the Animal: Developing a Biblical Animal Hermeneutic*, ed. Arthur Walker Jones and Suzanna Miller (Atlanta: SBL Press, 2024), 101–114.

33. Lawrence's chapter "The Rights of Beasts" appears in *A Philosophical Treatise on Horses and on the Moral Duties of Man towards the Brute Creation* (London: Longman, 1796). On Schopenhauer's view of animal rights, see Stephen Puryear, "Schopenhauer on the Rights of Animals," *European Journal of Philosophy* 25 (2017): 250–269. On Bergh's rather different concept of animal rights, see Darcy Ingram, "The Strange Case of Henry Bergh's 'Declaration of the Rights of Animals,'" *Society and Animals* 30 (2020): 479–491.

34. Theodore Munger, *The Rights of Dumb Animals* (Hartford: Connecticut Humane Society, 1898), 4–6, as quoted in Susan Pearson, *The Rights of the Defenseless: Protecting Animals and Children in Gilded Age America* (Chicago: University of Chicago Press, 2011), 128–129.

35. See Noam Pines, "A Radical Advocacy: Suffering Jews and Animals in S.Y. Abramovitsh's *Die Kliateshe*," *Jewish Social Studies* 23 (2018): 24–47.

36. For some examples of how Jewish vegans and vegetarians have adapted the Seder and other aspects of Jewish tradition in light of their beliefs and moral commitment, see Jacob Labendz and Shmuly Yanklowitz, eds., *Jewish Veganism and Vegetarianism: Studies and New Directions* (Albany: State University of New York Press, 2019).

37. Roberta Kalechofsky, *Haggadah for the Liberated Lamb* (Marblehead, MA: Micah, 1988).

38. Jewish Veg, *The Vegan Haggadah*, accessed June 2, 2024, 17, 16, https://jewishveg.org/wp-content/uploads/JewishVeg_HaggadahBooklet-10MB-1.pdf.

39. Vinciane Despret, "Sheep Do Have Opinions," in *Making Things Public*, ed. Bruno Latour and Peter Weibel (Cambridge, MA: MIT Press, 2005), 360–368.

40. See, for example, Rosamund Young, *The Secret Life of Cows* (Preston, UK: Farming Books and Videos, 2018).

6. The Sixth Plague

1. Jesper Akesson et al., "Fatalism, Beliefs, and Behaviors during the COVID-19 Pandemic," *Journal of Risk and Uncertainty* 64 (2022): 147–190.

2. Eric Anicich et al., "Getting Back to the 'New Normal': Autonomy Restoration during a Global Pandemic," *Journal of Applied Psychology* 105, no. 9 (2020): 931–943.

3. See Jonathan Klawans, *Josephus and the Theologies of Ancient Judaism* (New York: Oxford University Press, 2012), from whom I take the classification of the Essenes, Sadducees, and Pharisees as determinists, libertarians, and compatibilists, respectively.

4. Ariel Feldman, "The Reworking of the Exodus Story in 4Q422," *Megillot* 8–9 (2010): 373–391, esp. 378–379 (Hebrew). My thanks to Nittay Paz for calling my attention to this study.

5. For more on Paul's position in the context of the era's debates about the extent of human agency, see the essays in John Barclay and Simon Gathercole, eds., *Divine and Human Agency in Paul and His Cultural Environment* (London: T. and T. Clark, 2008).

6. For an example of Origen's influence, see Ilaria Ramelli, "The Legacy of Origen in Gregory of Nyssa's Theology of Freedom," *Modern Theology* 38 (2022): 363–388, esp. 380–381.

7. For a translation and analysis, see Bryn Rees, "On the Hardening of Pharaoh's Heart," *Journal of Late Antique Religion and Culture* 6 (2012): 1–54.

8. For English translations of the two works in question, see Ernst Winter, trans., *Discourse on Free Will: Erasmus and Luther* (New York: Ungar, 1961). For analysis, see T.H.M. Akerboom, "Erasmus and Luther on the Freedom of Will in Their Correspondence," *Perichoresis* 8 (2010): 233–277; Clarence Miller, ed., *Desiderius Erasmus and Martin Luther: The Battle over Free Will*, trans. Clarence Miller and Peter Macardle (Indianapolis: Hackett, 2012); and Aku Visala and Olli-Pekka Vainio, "Erasmus versus Luther: A Contemporary Analysis of the Debate on Free Will," *Neue Zeitschrift fur Systematische Theologie und Religionsphilosophie* 62 (2020): 311–335. For an effort to explain the debate's enduring historical significance, see Ricardo Quinones, *Dualisms: Agons of the Modern World* (Toronto: University of Toronto Press, 2007), 23–97.

9. For the elevation of the will's status and power during the Renaissance, see Andrew Escobedo, *Volition's Face: Personification and the Will in Renaissance Literature* (Notre Dame, IN: University of Notre Dame Press, 2017), 57–96. For a countervailing focus on the will's impotence, see Risto Saarinen, *Weakness of Will in Renaissance and Reformation Thought* (Oxford: Oxford University Press, 2011).

10. For more on Calvin's view of the heart and how it hardens and unhardens, see Marjorie O'Rourke Boyle, *Cultural Anatomies of the Heart in Aristotle, Augustine, Aquinas, Calvin, and Harvey* (Cham, Switzerland: Palgrave Macmillan, 2018), 101–133.

11. Timothy Wengert, *Human Freedom, Christian Righteousness: Philip Melanchthon's Exegetical Dispute with Erasmus of Rotterdam* (Oxford: Oxford University Press, 1998).

12. Gregory Graybill's study *Evangelical Free Will: Phillipp Melanchthon's Doctrinal Journey on the Origins of Faith* (Oxford: Oxford University Press, 2010) traces the development of Melanchthon's thought from Luther's position to a distinctively evangelical notion of free will.

13. For a treatment of the free will debate in recent Christian theology, see Leigh Vicens, *Christianity and the Problem of Free Will* (Cambridge: Cambridge University Press, 2023).

14. For an overview of this issue as it was debated in classical Islamic philosophy, see Abdur Rashid Bhat, "Free Will and Determinism: An Overview of Muslim Scholars' Perspectives," *Journal of Islamic Philosophy* 2 (2006): 7–24; and Maria De Cillis, *Free Will and Predestination in Islamic Thought: Theoretical Compromises in the Works of Avicenna, al-Ghazālī and Ibn ʿArabī* (London: Routledge, 2014).

15. Alexander Altmann, "The Religion of the Thinkers: Free Will and Predestination in Saadia, Bahya and Maimonides," in *Religion in a Religious Age*, ed. Shlomo Goitein (Cambridge, MA: Association of Jewish Studies, 1974), 25–51; Arthur Hyman, "Aspects of the Medieval Jewish and Islamic Discussion of 'Free Choice,'" in *Freedom and Moral Responsibility: General and Jewish Perspectives*, ed. Charles Manekin and Marc Kellner (Bethesda: University Press of Maryland, 1997), 133–152.

16. For more on the Qur'an's description of Pharaoh's attempted repentance and death, see Nicolai Sinai, "Pharaoh's Submission to God in the Qur'an and in Rabbinic Literature: A Case Study," in *The Qur'an's Reformation of Judaism and Christianity: Return to the Origins*, ed. Holger Zellentin (London: Routledge, 2019), 303–335. For the debate among later Muslim scholars about whether Pharaoh's repentance was accepted by God, see Eric Ormsby, "The Faith of Pharaoh: A Disputed Question in Islamic Theology," *Studia Islamica* 98 (2004): 5–28.

17. Arnon Atzmon, "Did Pharaoh Repent? On the Development and Transformation of a Rabbinic Motif," *European Journal of Jewish Studies* 13 (2019): 3–27.

18. Adi Shiran, "Not All Minds Are Meant to Be Free: The Textual History of Maimonides' Interpretation of the Hardening of Pharaoh's Heart" (delivered at the Fifty-Second Annual Conference of the Association for Jewish Studies, held virtually, December 16, 2020). I thank Shiran for sharing a draft of the study with me.

19. For further discussion of Maimonides's notion of free will, see Jerome Gellerman, "Freedom and Determinism in Maimonides' Philosophy," in *Moses Maimonides and His Time*, ed. Eric Ornsby (Washington, DC: Catholic University Press of America, 1989), 139–150; and Moshe Sokol, "Maimonides on Freedom of the Will and Moral Responsibility," *Harvard Theological Review* 91 (1998): 25–39.

20. Shira Weiss, *Ethical Ambiguity in the Hebrew Bible: Philosophical Analysis of the Hebrew Bible* (Cambridge: Cambridge University Press, 2018), 51–66. See also Erez Naaman, "Maimonides and the Habitus Concept," *Journal of the American Oriental Society* 137 (2017): 537–542.

21. For more on the Aristotelian notion of habituation and character formation that Maimonides was drawing on, see Thornton Lockwood, "Habituation, Habit and Character in Aristotle's Nicomachean Ethics," in *A History of Habit: From Aristotle to Bourdieu*, ed. Tom Sparrow and Adam Hutchinson (Lanham, MD: Lexington, 2013), 19–36.

22. On the role of causal determinism in Averroës's philosophy, see Catarina Belo, *Chance and Determinism in Avicenna and Averroes* (Leiden: Brill, 2007).

23. I take my understanding of his interpretation of Pharaoh's hardened heart from Charles Manekin, "Levi Gersonides on Hardening Pharaoh's Heart," in *Built by Wisdom, Established by Understanding: Essays on Biblical and Near Eastern Literature in Honor of Adele Berlin*, ed. Maxine Grossman (Lanham: University Press of Maryland, 2013), 305–322.

24. I rely in what follows on David Shatz, "Freedom, Repentance and Hardening of the Hearts: Albo vs. Maimonides," *Faith and Philosophy: Journal of the Society of Christian*

Philosophers 14 (1997): 478–509; and Shira Weiss, *Joseph Albo on Free Choice: Exegetical Innovation in Medieval Jewish Philosophy* (New York: Oxford University Press, 2017). For a critical edition and English translation of *The Book of Principles*, see Isaac Husik, ed., *Sefer Haikkarim* (Philadelphia: Jewish Publication Society of America, 1929–1930).

25. Weiss, *Joseph Albo on Free Choice*, 85–113.

26. Harry Frankfurt, "Freedom of the Will and the Concept of the Person," *Journal of Philosophy* 68, no. 1 (1971): 5–20.

27. Eleonore Stump, "Sanctification, Hardening of the Heart, and Frankfurt's Concept of Free Will," *Journal of Philosophy* 85, no. 8 (1988): 395–420.

28. For another approach to the infinite regress problem in Frankfurt's notion of the will, see Ryan Cummings and Adina Roskies, "Frankfurt and the Problem of Self-Control," in *Surrounding Self-Control*, ed. Alan Mele (New York: Oxford Academic, 2020), 421–433, https://doi.org/10.1093/oso/9780197500941.003.0022. For critiques of Stump's argument, see Sandra Menssen and Thomas Sullivan, "God Does Not Harden Hearts," *Proceedings of the American Catholic Philosophical Association* 67 (1993): 119–134; and David Shatz, "Hierarchical Theories of Freedom and the Hardening of Hearts," *Midwest Studies in Philosophy* 21 (1997): 202–224, which juxtaposes Stump's views with those of Albo.

7. The Seventh Plague

1. For more on the plot structure of Exodus as an often-repeated literary pattern in the Hebrew Bible, see Yair Zakovitch, *"You Shall Tell Your Son . . .": The Concept of the Exodus in the Bible* (Jerusalem: Magnes, 1991), esp. 46–98.

2. For more on the meaning of "signs and wonders" in biblical and nonbiblical sources, see S. Vernon McCasland, "Signs and Wonders," *Journal of Biblical Literature* 76, no. 2 (1957): 149–152; and H.G.M. Williamson, "A Sign and a Portent in Isaiah 8.18," in *Studies on the Text and Versions of the Hebrew Bible in Honour of Robert Gordon*, ed. Geoffrey Khan and Diana Lipton (Leiden: Brill, 2012), 77–86.

3. The statistics for the United States are taken from the website of the National Weather Service Storm Prediction Center, accessed May 5, 2025, https://www.spc.noaa.gov/climo/summary/. For Europe, the numbers and other facts come from Tomas Pucik, "Hailstorms of 2023," European Severe Storms Laboratory, January 23, 2024, https://www.essl.org/cms/hailstorms-of-2023/.

4. Artapanus's history only survives via citations in later Christian authors, and the passage referred to here is cited in Eusebius's *Preparation for the Gospel*, 9.27.33.

5. The meaning of the rare biblical Hebrew word *ʿelgavish*, translated here as "hailstones," is a puzzle, and it has an unusual form for a Hebrew word. A recent effort to explain its origin by connecting it to an Egyptian word for black granite is not convincing, but the author reviews the relevant evidence; see Jonathan Thambyrajah, "A New Etymology for Hebrew אֶלְגָּבִישׁ and Related Lexemes," *Zeitschrift für die Alttestamentliche Wissenschaft* 133 (2012): 346–360.

6. Those interested in such a topic might consult Ian Boxall and Richard Tresley, *The Book of Revelation and Its Interpreters: Short Studies and an Annotated Bibliography* (London: Rowman and Littlefield, 2016); and Timothy Beal, *The Book of Revelation: A Biography* (Princeton, NJ: Princeton University Press, 2018). For a recent attempt to make sense of the numerical symbolism in Revelation's depiction of apocalyptic plagues, see Benjamin Wold, "Revelation's Plague Septets: New Exodus and Exile," in *Echoes from the Caves: Qumran and the New Testament*, ed. Florentino Garcia Martinez (Leiden: Brill, 2009), 279–298.

7. For a version of the fifteen signs that includes hail, see William Heist, *The Fifteen Signs before Doomsday* (East Lansing: Michigan State College Press, 1952), 27–29.

8. Roger Rosewell, "The Pricke of Conscience or the Fifteen Signs of Doom Window in the Church of All Saints, North Street, York," *Vidimus* 45 (2010), https://www.vidimus.org/issues/issue-45/feature/.

9. See Jean-Pierre Filiu, *Apocalypse in Islam* (Berkeley: University of California Press, 2011).

10. See Marjorie Reeves, *The Influence of Prophecy in the Later Middle Ages: A Study in Joachimism* (Oxford: Oxford University Press, 1969), 528.

11. After his arrival to Mexico, Toribio changed his name to Motolinía, "the afflicted one"—the first word he learned in the local language. His description of a new ten plagues in Mexico can be found in Toribio de Motolinía, *Memoriales de fray Toribio de Motolinía: Manuscrito de la colección del señor Don Joaquín García* (Paris: Donnamette, 1903), 17–28. Unfortunately, the English translation of this work in Francis Steck, *Motolinía's History of the Indians of New Spain* (Washington, DC: Academy of American Franciscan History, 1951), omits the whole section on the ten plagues.

12. See Roberta Olson and Jay Pasachoff, *Fire in the Sky: Comets and Meteors, the Decisive Centuries, in British Art and Science* (Cambridge: Cambridge University Press, 1998).

13. For an early modern example of this kind of interpretation of the comet, see Jennifer Spinks, "Signs That Speak: Reporting the 1556 Comet across French and German Borders," in *Religion, the Supernatural and Visual Culture in Early Modern Europe: An Album Amicorum for Charles Zika*, ed. Jennifer Spinks and Dagmar Eichberger (Leiden: Brill, 2015), 212–239.

14. Benjamin Thurston, "The Little Horn: Apocalyptic Literature of the Consulate and the Empire," *French Studies* 58 (2004): 163–176.

15. Denis Diderot, *Lettres à Sophie Volland* (Paris: Gallimard, 1930), 3:216, quoted in Philip Stewart, "Science and Superstition: Comets and the French Public in the 18th Century," *American Journal of Physics* 54 (1986): 16.

16. For more on the intersections between the science of comets and their role in religious imagination, see Sarah Schechner, *Comets, Popular Culture, and the Birth of Modern Cosmology* (Princeton, NJ: Princeton University Press, 2021).

17. Hakan Hakansson, "Tycho the Apocalyptic: History, Prophecy and the Meaning of Natural Phenomena," in *Science in Contact at the Beginning of the Scientific Revolution*, ed. Jitka Zamrzlová (Prague: National Technical Museum, 2004), 211–236.

18. See William Whiston, *A New Theory of the Earth* (London: R. Roberts for Benjamin Tooke, 1696), https://quod.lib.umich.edu/cgi/t/text/text-idx?c=eebo;idno=A65672.0001.001. For more on the porous boundary between the science and religion of comets in the early modern period, see Laura Bland, "Unfriendly Skies: Science, Superstition, and the Great Comet of 1680" (PhD diss., University of Notre Dame, 2016).

19. Stewart, "Science and Superstition," 20–23.

20. Immanuel Velikovsky, *Worlds in Collision* (New York: Doubleday, 1950), which discusses the ten plagues on 138–176 and the end of the world on 286–289.

21. Ted Daniels, "Comet Hale-Bopp, Planet Nibiru, the Mass Landing and Heaven's Gate," in *A Doomsday Reader: Prophets, Predictors, and Hucksters of Salvation* (New York: New York University Press, 1999), 199–223; Benjamin Zeller, "Extraterrestrial Biblical Hermeneutics and the Making of Heaven's Gate," *Nova Religio* 14 (2010): 34–60.

22. Luis Alvarez et al., "Extraterrestrial Cause for the Cretaceous-Tertiary Extinction," *Science* 208, no. 4448 (1980): 1095–1108.

23. For my understanding of the emergence of science fiction and its connection to Revelation, I am indebted to Paul Alkon, "The Secularization of Apocalypse," in *Origins of Futuristic Fiction* (Athens: University of Georgia Press, 1987), 158–191; and Amy Ransom, "The First Last Man: Cousin de Grainville's *Le dernier homme*," *Science Fiction Studies* 41 (2014): 314–340.

24. For a translation of the novel, see Jean-Baptiste Francois Xavier Cousin de Grainville, *The Last Man*, trans. I. F. Clarke and M. Clarke (Middletown, CT: Wesleyan University Press, 2002).

25. Mary Shelley, *The Last Man* (Oxford: Oxford University Press, 1998), 315.

26. Shelley, *Last Man*, 370–371.

27. I take this observation from Melissa Bailes, "The Psychologization of Geological Catastrophe in Mary Shelley's *The Last Man*," *English Literary History* 82 (2015): 671–699.

28. Richard Goodrich, *Comet Madness: How the 1910 Return of Halley's Comet (Almost) Destroyed Civilization* (Lanham, MD: Prometheus, 2023).

29. For more on the cultural and historical context from which this film emerged, see Delia Enyedi, "The Comet Tail: Celestial Apocalypse in Silent Cinema," *Ekphrasis: Images, Cinema, Theory, Media* 2 (2012): 47–53; and Wynn Hamonic, "*Verdens Undergang* (1916) and the Birth of Apocalyptic Film: Antecedents and Causative Forces," *Journal of Religion and Film* 20, no. 3 (2016): article 30, https://doi.org/10.32873/uno.dc.jrf.20.03.30.

30. I draw for my understanding of the film on Christopher Peterson, "The Magic Cave of Allegory: Lars van Triers's *Melancholia*," *Discourse* 35 (2013): 400–422; Robert Sinnerbrink, "Anatomy of *Melancholia*," *Angelaki* 19 (2014): 111–126; and Mark Sandberg, "Apocalypse Then and Now: *Verdens Undergang* (1916) and *Melancholia* (2011)," *European Journal of Scandinavian Studies* 46 (2016): 102–119.

8. The Eighth Plague

1. Wasim's post, shared on X when it was known as Twitter, is from May 27, 2020.

2. For a survey of how Qur'anic commentators have understood the reference to blood in Sura 7:133, see Ramzi Ghandour, "The Word 'Dam' in Sūra 7:133: Muslim Readings of the First Biblical Plague" (diss., University of Exeter, 2014).

3. See, as just one example, Nicolai Sinai, "Pharaoh's Submission to God in the Qur'an and in Rabbinic Literature," in *The Qur'an's Reformation of Judaism and Christianity*, ed. Holger Zellentin (London: Routledge, 2019), 235–260.

4. For more on the Qur'an's view of the sign, see Nicolai Sinai, *Key Terms of the Qur'an: A Critical Dictionary* (Princeton, NJ: Princeton University Press, 2023), 118–129.

5. For an English translation of Artapanus's version of the plagues, see James Charlesworth, ed., *Old Testament Pseudepigrapha*, vol. 2 (Garden City, NY: Doubleday, 1983), 902.

6. The one exception to this generalization is the plague of hail, which is not mentioned in Sura 7:133 but does involve the staff according to Exodus 9:23 ("Moses stretched forth his staff to the skies, and the Lord sent thunder and hail").

7. Moses's confrontation with the magicians was of particular interest to the Qur'anic author, who mentions it more often than any other single episode in the Moses story. In addition to the account in Sura 7, the episode is also narrated in 10:75–92, 20:41–76, and 26:10–51. For further analysis of the Qur'an's treatment of these narratives and their differences from one another, see Andrew Smith, "Moses and Pharaoh's Magicians: A Discursive Analysis of the Qur'anic Narratives in Light of Late Antique Texts," *Journal of Qur'anic Studies* 20 (2018): 67–104.

8. Zaira Wasim (@ZairaWasimmm), posted on X, June 1, 2020, https://x.com/ZairaWasimmm/status/1267403717118005248.

9. Meir Kister, "The Locust's Wing: Some Notes on Locusts in the Hadith," *Le Muséon* 106 (1993): 347–359.

10. Quoted from the 1906 translation of ad-Damiri, *Hayat al-hayawan: A Zoological Lexicon*, vol. 1, part 2, trans. A.S.G. Jayakar, reprinted in *Natural Sciences in Islam* (Frankfurt: Institute for the History of Arabic-Islamic Science at Goethe University, 2011), 10:410.

11. Ad-Damiri, *Hayat al-hayawan*, 410.

12. A story recounted by the historian Herodotus in *The Persian Wars*, 1.53.1–3.

13. It is not impossible that the ancient Greek conception of the oracle as ambiguous and paradoxical had a direct impact on later hadith that depict divine communication in a similar

way. Compare the example of Delphic influence discussed in Alexander Altmann, "The Delphic Maxim in Medieval Islam and Judaism," in *Biblical and Other Studies*, ed. Alexander Altmann (Cambridge, MA: Harvard University Press, 1963), 196–232.

14. Sarra Tlili, *Animals in the Qur'an* (Cambridge: Cambridge University Press, 2012), 153–167.

15. Tlili, *Animals in the Qur'an*, 153–165.

16. For more on the Qur'an's distinction between the clear and the ambiguous, see Gabriel Said Reynolds, "Paradox in the Qur'an," *Journal of the International Qur'anic Studies Association* 9 (2024): 142–163.

17. Brock Cutler, "Evoking the State: Environmental Disaster and Colonial Policy in Algeria, 1840–1870" (PhD diss., University of California, Irvine, 2011); Zachary Foster, "The 1915 Locust Attack in Syria and Palestine and Its Role in the Famine during the First World War," *Middle Eastern Studies* 51 (2015): 370–394. For the frequency of locust outbreaks in Near Eastern history, see Dario Camuffo and Silvia Enzi, "Locust Invasions and Climactic Factors from the Middle Ages to 1800," *Theoretical and Applied Climatology* 43 (1991): 49–73; and Batal Ciplak, "Locust and Grasshopper Outbreaks in the Near East: Review under Global Warming Context," *Agronomy* 11 (2021): article 111, https://doi.org/10.3390/agronomy11010111.

18. On the enlistment of divine power against locusts in ancient Near Eastern culture, see A. R. George, "The Dogs of Ninkilim: Magic against Field Pests in Ancient Mesopotamia," in *Landwirtschaft im Alten Orient*, ed. Horst Klengel and Johannes Renger (Berlin: D. Reimer, 1999), 341–354; and Makale Bilgisi, "Locusts in the Hittite Culture," *TÜBA-AR: Türkiye Bilimler Akademisi Arkeoloji Dergisi* 25 (2019): 77–84. In the Greek world, Apollo played such an important role in combatting locusts that he was known by the title Parnopios (Of the Locusts). An episode where Apollo was thought to have driven locusts away was recorded by the Greek geographer Pausanias (*Description of Greece* 1.24.8).

19. See James Grehan, "The Legend of the Samarmar: Parades and Communal Identity in Syrian Towns, c. 1500–1800," *Past and Present* 204 (2009): 89–125.

20. This example is taken from Arnold van Huis, "Cultural Significance of Locusts, Grasshoppers, and Crickets in Sub-Saharan Africa," *Journal of Ethnobiology and Ethnomedicine* 18 (2022): 1–24, esp. 10.

21. See Shelomo Dov Goitein, *Jews and Arabs: A Concise History of Their Social and Cultural Relations* (Minneola, NY: Dover, 1955), 190; and Bat Zion Eraqi-Klorman, "Yemen: Religion, Magic and Jews," *Proceedings of the Seminar for Arabian Studies* 39 (2009): 125–134, esp. 130.

22. For more on Uvarov, see Michael Worboys, "Imperial Entomology: Boris P. Uvarov and Locusts, c. 1920–c. 1950," *British Journal for the History of Science* 55 (2022): 27–51. On the history of Great Britain's anti-locust efforts, see Athol Yates, "The British Military and the Anti-locust Campaign across the Arabian Peninsula, including the Emirates, 1942–1945," *Natural History* 29 (2019): 22–27. On French efforts, see Claude Peloquin, "Locust Swarms and the Spatial Temporal Politics of the French Resistance in World War II," *Geoforum* 49 (2013): 101–113. On Soviet interventions, see Etienne Forestier-Peyrat, "Fighting Locusts Together: Pest Control and the Birth of Soviet Development Aid, 1920–1939," *Global Environment* 7 (2014): 536–571.

23. John Whiting, "Jerusalem's Locust Plague," *National Geographic*, December 1915, 511–550, esp. 521.

24. Alexander Aaronsohn, *With the Turks in Palestine* (Boston: Houghton Mifflin, 1916), 50.

25. Roland Jennings, "The Locust Problem in Cyprus," *Bulletin of the School of African and Oriental Studies* 51 (1988): 295.

26. Colonial Office, *Report by His Britannic Majesty's Government to the Council of the League of Nations on the Administration of Iraq for the Year 1926* (London: His Majesty's Stationery Office, 1927), 65.

27. Jeanine Dagyeli, "The Fight against Heaven-Sent Insects: Dealing with Locust Plagues in the Emirate of Bukhara," *Environment and History* 26 (2020): 79–104.

28. Jama Mohamed, "The Evils of Locust Bait: Popular Nationalism during the 1945 Anti-locust Control Rebellion in Colonial Somaliland," *Past and Present* 174 (2002): 184–216.

29. See Gabriel Avecado, "Islamic Fatalism and the Clash of Civilizations: An Appraisal of a Contentious and Dubious Theory," *Social Forces* 86 (2008): 1711–1752.

30. Samuel Dolbee, "The Locust and the Starling: People, Insects and Disease in the Late Ottoman Jazira and After, 1860–1940" (PhD diss., New York University, 2017), 79–80. Since I consulted this work, Dolbee's dissertation has been published in expanded form as a monograph, *Locusts of Power: Borders, Empire, and Environment in the Modern Middle East* (Cambridge: Cambridge University Press, 2023).

31. For these examples, see Justin Stearns, *Infectious Ideas: Contagion in Premodern Islamic and Christian Thought in the Western Mediterranean* (Baltimore: Johns Hopkins University Press, 2011), 142. My thanks to my colleague Secil Yilmaz for calling my attention to Stearns's work and for discussing the issue of Islamic "fatalism" with me.

32. A. Kayani, M. J. King, and J. J. Fleiter, "Fatalism and Its Implications for Risky Road Use and Receptiveness to Safety Messages: A Qualitative Investigation in Pakistan," *Health Education Research* 27 (2010): 1043–1054; Hoda Baytiyeh and Mohamad Naja, "Can Education Reduce Middle Eastern Fatalistic Attitude regarding Earthquake Disasters?," *Disaster Prevention and Management* 23 (2014): 343–355; Mustafa Aykol, "Islam's Tragic Fatalism," *New York Times*, September 23, 2015.

33. As quoted in Hélène Carrère d'Encausse, *Islam and the Russian Empire: Reform and Revolution in Central Asia* (Berkeley: University of California Press, 1966), 51.

34. See Shounaz Mekky, "Tweeps Blame Egypt's Muslim Brotherhood for 'Curse of Locusts,'" *Alarabiya News*, March 6, 2013, https://english.alarabiya.net/articles/2013%2F03%2F06%2F269920.

35. Boris Uvarov, "The Locust Plague," *Journal of the Royal Society of Arts* 91 (1043): 109–118.

9. The Ninth Plague

1. G. Brooke Anderson and Michelle Bell, "Lights Out: Impact of the August 2003 Power Outage on Mortality in New York, NY," *Epidemiology* 23 (2012): 189–193.

2. For more on the history of darkness and its dangers in human experience, see A. Roger Ekirch, *At Day's Close: Night in Times Past* (New York: Norton, 2005); and Nina Edwards, *Darkness: A Cultural History* (London: Reaktion, 2018).

3. See Stella Lange, "The Wisdom of Solomon and Plato," *Journal of Biblical Literature* 55 (1936): 293–302.

4. R. E. Houser, "Philosophical Development through Metaphor: Light among the Greeks," *Proceedings of the American Catholic Association* 64 (1990): 75–85; Andrea Nightingale, "Cave Myths and the Metaphorics of Light: Plato, Aristotle, Lucretius," *Arion* 24 (2017): 39–70.

5. Hans Urs von Balthasar, *The Christian and Anxiety*, trans. Dennis Martin and Michael Miller (San Francisco: Ignatius, 1994), 39–79.

6. This manuscript can be viewed online, with relevant bibliography: "Vat.gr.747," DigiVatLib, accessed May 6, 2025, https://digi.vatlib.it/mss/detail/Vat.gr.747. Further references can also be found in Ioli Kalavruzou and Courtney Tomaselli, "The Study of Byzantine Illustrations since Kurt Weitzmann: Art Historical Methods and Approaches," in *A Companion to Byzantine Illustrated Manuscripts*, ed. Vasiliki Tsmakda (Boston: Brill, 2017), 23–34.

7. On the role of color and light in Byzantine art and the spiritual associations of gold and black, see Liz James, "Color and the Byzantine Rainbow," *Byzantine and Modern Greek Studies* 15 (1991): 66–95; and Liz James, *Light and Color in Byzantine Art* (Oxford: Clarendon, 1996).

8. On hell as a dark cave or cell-like place in Byzantine art, see Vasileios Marinis, *Death and the Afterlife in Byzantium* (Cambridge: Cambridge University Press, 2017), 60–66. For a recent

study of the depiction of hell in Byzantine art (which was visualized in many different ways), see Angeliki Lymberopoulou and Eirini Panou, eds., *Hell in the Byzantine World: A History of Art and Religion in Venetian Crete and the Eastern Mediterranean*, 2 vols. (Cambridge: Cambridge University Press, 2020).

9. Echoing Virgil, Jerome described hell as a place where "the horror and the silences terrified their souls" (Jerome, *Commentary on Ezekiel* 40.5).

10. The Bible in question, popularly known as *La Grande Bible de Tours*, was published as *La Sainte Bible: Traduction nouvelle selon la Vulgate*, ed. J.-J. Bourasse and P. Janvier (Tours: Alfred Mame, 1866). For more on Doré's biblical illustrations than I can offer here, see Sarah Schaeffer, *Gustave Doré and the Modern Biblical Imagination* (Oxford: Oxford University Press, 2021).

11. The full title of du Camp's publication is *Egypte, Nubie, Palestine et Syrie: Desssins photographiques recueillis pendant les années 1849, 1850 et 1851 accompagnés d'un texte explicatif* (Paris: Gide et J. Baudry, 1852). For more historical background, see Maria Golia, *Photography and Egypt* (Cairo: American University in Cairo Press, 2010).

12. James Ryan, "Hunting with a Camera: Photography, Wildlife, and Colonialism in Africa," in *Animal Spaces, Beastly Places: New Geographies of Animal-Human Relations*, ed. Chris Philo and Chris Wilbert (London: Routledge, 2000), 205–222. Doré was aware of people's interest in pictures of African wildlife, having provided illustrations for an African wildlife–centered book, Cecile Gerard's *Lion Hunting and Sporting Life in Algeria*, published in 1874.

13. Felicity Rash, "Lighting the 'Dark' Continent: Metaphors of Darkness and Light in the Writings of British and German Explorers and Missionaries 1865–1915," in *The Discourse of British and German Colonialism: Convergence and Competition*, ed. Felicity Rash and Geraldine Horan (London: Routledge, 2020), 107–123. For European colonization as an attempted extension of the Enlightenment, see Damien Tricoire, ed., *Enlightened Colonialism: Civilization Narratives and Imperial Politics in the Age of Reason* (Cham, Switzerland: Palgrave Macmillan, 2017).

14. Adrienne Childs and Susan Libby, eds., *Blacks and Blackness in European Art of the Long Nineteenth Century* (London: Routledge, 2014).

15. For more on this map, a Norwegian missionary map from 1890, see Ingie Hovland, *Mission Station Christianity: Norwegian Missionaries in Colonial Natal and Zululand, Southern Africa, 1850–1890* (Leiden: Brill, 2013), 175.

16. Kipling's poem, first published in the *London Times* in 1899, can be found online: Rudyard Kipling, "The White Man's Burden" (1899), Internet Modern History Sourcebook, https://sourcebooks.fordham.edu/mod/kipling.asp.

17. David O'Connor and Andrew Reid, introduction to *Ancient Egypt in Africa*, ed. David O'Connor and Andrew Reid (London: Routledge, 2007), 4–6. For more on the related race science debate over how to classify the ancient Egyptians in relation to later Black Africans, see Robert Bernasconi, "Black Skin, White Skulls: The Nineteenth Century Debate over the Racial Identity of the Ancient Egyptians," *Parallax* 13 (2007): 6–20.

18. John Emory Godbey and Allen Godbey, *Light in Darkness, or Missions and Missionary Heroes: An Illustrated History of the Missionary Work* (Kansas City, MO: Continental, 1887), 621.

19. Projit Mukharji, "The 'Cholera Cloud' in the Nineteenth-Century British World: History of an Object-without-an-Essence," *Bulletin of the History of Medicine* 86 (2012): 303–332.

20. Cf. Mukharji, "'Cholera Cloud,'" 329–331.

21. The lithograph is reproduced in Marie-France de Palacio, "Prendre la grippe comme on prend les eaux: Variations caricaturales sur un *mal à la mode* entre 1830 et 1848," *Quêtes littéraires* 10 (2020): 9–41, esp. 33, fig. 21.

22. Mukharji, "'Cholera Cloud,'" 326, quoting anonymous, "A Cholera Cloud," *Chicago Daily Tribune*, August 4, 1884, 8.

23. R. B. Medbery, *Memoir of William G. Crocker, Late Missionary in West Africa among the Bassas* (Boston: Gould and Lincoln, 1860), 90; Hollis Read, *Negro Problem Solved, or Africa as*

She Was, as She Is, and as She Shall Be: Her Curse and Her Cure (New York: Constantine, 1864), 378; J. E. Carlyle, *South Africa and the Mission Fields* (London: Nisbet, 1878), 324.

24. See, for example, Evans Lewin, "The Black Cloud of Africa," *Foreign Affairs* 4 (July 1926): 637–647.

25. From remarks given in 1962 on the installation of stained glass windows in the Hadassah Medical Center in Jerusalem, reprinted in Benjamin Harshav, ed., *Marc Chagall on Art and Culture* (Stanford, CA: Stanford University Press, 2003), 145.

26. For Chagall's account of his own life, see Marc Chagall, *My Life* (New York: Onion, 1960). For recent biographies, see Benjamin Harshav, *Marc Chagall and His Times: A Documentary Narrative* (Stanford, CA: Stanford University Press, 2004); and Jackie Wullschläger, *Chagall* (New York: Knopf, 2008).

27. The painting is included in Jean Rosensaft, *Chagall and the Bible* (New York: Universe, 1987), listed and illustrated as plate 31.

28. Ruth Mellinkoff, *The Horned Moses in Medieval Art and Thought* (Berkeley: University of California Press, 1970).

29. Marc Chagall, *The Biblical Message of Marc Chagall* (New York: Tudor, 1973), 15.

30. Wassily Kandinsky, *Concerning the Spiritual in Art*, trans. Michael Sadleir (London: Constable, 1914).

31. For the impact of war on Chagall's art, see the essays in the exhibit catalog by Susan Tamarkin, ed., *Chagall: Love, War, and Exile* (New York: Jewish Museum, 2013).

32. Quoted in Harshav, *Marc Chagall and His Times*, 155, my italics.

33. Fred Dallmayr, *Chagall as Peacemaker* (London: Routledge, 2020).

34. Compare Marc Chagall, *Moses and the Burning Bush* (1958), Jewish Museum, accessed November 11, 2022: https://thejewishmuseum.org/collection/18205-moses-and-the-burning-bush.

35. "Oral Interview with Miriam Beerman, 2009 December 28," Smithsonian Archives of American Art, https://www.aaa.si.edu/download_pdf_transcript/ajax?record_id=edanmdm-AAADCD_oh_287762.

36. From an interview quoted in Matthew Baigell, *Jewish American Artists and the Holocaust* (New Brunswick, NJ: Rutgers University Press, 1997), 54.

37. Miriam Beerman, "Artist's Statement," accessed November 11, 2022, http://www.miriambeerman.com/artists-statement/. For six of her seven paintings of the plagues, see Miriam Beerman, "Gallery 3," accessed May 6, 2025, http://www.miriambeerman.com/paintings-3/.

38. Beerman, "Artist's Statement."

10. The Tenth Plague

1. For Christian interpretations connecting "Passover" to "suffer," see Steve Reece, "Passover as 'Passion': A Folk Etymology in Luke 22, 15," *Biblica* 100 (2019): 601–610.

2. The biblical law allowing for monetary compensation inspired a Jewish ceremony practiced to this day known as the *pidyon haben*, in which the parents redeem a firstborn male child by making a payment to a member of the priestly caste.

3. For more on slavery as a model and metaphor in the New Testament, see Dale Martin, *Slavery as Salvation: The Metaphor of Slavery in Pauline Christianity* (New Haven, CT: Yale University Press, 1990).

4. Joshua Benjamins, "Slavery, Redemption, and Manumission as Structural Metaphors in Augustine's Theology," *Classical Antiquity* 40 (2021): 195–220.

5. A survey of early Christian interpretations of Exodus 12 can be found in Ruth Clements, "*Peri Pascha*: Passover and the Displacement of Jewish Interpretation within Origen's Exegesis" (ThD diss., Harvard Divinity School, 1997), 141–218.

6. On parallels with the Mishnaic description of the Passover Seder, see Stuart Hall, "Melito in Light of the Passover Haggadah," *Journal of Theological Studies* 22 (1971): 29–46; and W. C. van Unnik, "An Unusual Formulation of the Redemption in the Homily on the Passover by Melito of Sardis," *Sparsa Collecta* 3 (1983): 148–160. For text and translation, see Stuart Hall, ed., *Melito of Sardis: On Pascha and Fragments* (Oxford: Clarendon, 1979).

7. For a survey of how early Jews interpreted the purpose of the Passover sacrifice, see Frank Chan, "Baptismal Typology in Melito of Sardis' *Peri Pascha*: A Study in the Interpretation of Exodus 12 in the Second Century" (PhD diss., Westminster Theological Seminary, 2001), 251–391.

8. Caroline Walker Bynum, "The Power in the Blood Sacrifice, Satisfaction, and Substitution in Late Medieval Soteriology," in *The Redemption: An Interdisciplinary Symposium on Christ as the Redeemer*, ed. Stephen Davis, Daniel Kendall, and Gerald Collins (Oxford: Oxford University Press, 2004), 177–204.

9. There exists in German a history of the "lamb of God" as an artistic symbol: Saskia Lerdon, *Ecce Agnus Dei: Rezeptionsästhetische Untersuchung zum neutestamentlichen Gotteslamm in der bildenden Kunst* (Göttingen: Vandenhoeck & Ruprecht, 2020).

10. Quoting the blessing as translated by Gregory Dipippo, "The Rite of Blessing of the Agnus Dei," *New Liturgical Movement*, April 25, 2020, https://www.newliturgicalmovement.org/2020/04/the-rite-of-blessing-of-agnus-deis.html.

11. See Wrap Red Ribbons on Trees to Fight Covid 19, Facebook, https://www.facebook.com/RedribbonbloodofJesus/, created April 28, 2020. The account is anonymous and the source of its image, also found elsewhere online, is unclear.

12. See, for example, Andrew Gabriel, "Should I Declare the Blood of Jesus over My Home to Stop Covid-19?," *Andrew K. Gabriel* (blog), April 10, 2020, https://www.andrewkgabriel.com/2020/04/10/declare-jesus-blood-covid-19/.

13. Israel Yuval, "Easter and Passover as Early Jewish-Christian Dialogue," in *Passover and Easter: Origin and History to Modern Times*, ed. Paul F. Bradshaw and Lawrence A. Hoffman (Notre Dame, IN: University of Notre Dame Press, 1999), 98–124.

14. This is the verse, incidentally, that introduces the words "blood, fire, and pillars of smoke" into the Haggadah, a phrase given a different meaning in an interpretation discussed in the chapter on the plague of blood.

15. The first half of the midrash is attested detached from the rest of the midrash in an eleventh-century manuscript of the Haggadah known as the Dropsie Haggadah. See Ernest Daniel Goldschmidt, *Haggadah shel Pesach* (Jerusalem: Mossad Bialik, 1960), 80. For more on the early history of this part of the midrash, see David Henske, "'The Lord Brought Us Forth from Egypt': On the Absence of Moses in the Passover Haggadah," *AJS Review* 31, no. 1 (2007): 61–73, esp. 63–66.

16. See Rudolf Berliner, "Arma Christi," *Münchner Jahrbuch der bildenen Kunst* 3, no. 6 (1955): 35–116; and more recently Lisa H. Cooper and Andrea Denny-Brown, eds., *The Arma Christi in Medieval and Early Modern Material Culture* (Surrey, UK: Ashgate, 2014); and Heather Madar, "Iconography of Sign: A Semiotic Reading of the Arma Christi," in *ReVisioning: Critical Methods of Seeing Christianity in the History of Art*, ed. James Romaine and Linda Stratford (Cambridge: Lutterworth, 2014), 115–131. On the practice of writing out long descriptions of the Arma Christi on rolls, see Rossell Hope Robbis, "The 'Arma Christi' Rolls," *Modern Language Review* 34, no. 3 (1939): 415–421.

17. Mary Edsall, "The *Arma Christi* before the *Arma Christi*: Rhetorics of the Passion in Late Antiquity and the Early Middle Ages," in *The "Arma Christi" in Medieval and Early Modern Material Culture*, ed. Lisa H. Cooper and Andrea Denny-Brown (Surrey, UK: Ashgate, 2014), 21–51.

18. I rely here on the description of this sermon in John Hirsh, *The Boundaries of Faith: The Development and Transmission of Medieval Spirituality* (Leiden: Brill, 1996), 124–129.

19. For more on the veneration of holy weapons as relics in the Byzantine Empire, see Piotr Grotowski, *Arms and Armour of the Warrior Saints: Tradition and Innovation in Byzantine Iconography (843–1261)* (Leiden: Brill, 2009).

20. See Armin Bergmeier, "Volatile Images: The Empty Throne and Its Place in the Byzantine Last Judgement Iconography," in *Empires and Scriptural Authorities in Medieval Christian, Islamic and Buddhist Communities*, vol. 1 of *Cultures of Eschatology*, ed. Veronika Wieser, Vince Eltschinger, and Johann Heiss (Berlin: de Gruyter, 2020), 84–105 and fig. 2.

21. On the protective role ascribed to the Shekhinah in Jewish tradition, see Norman Cohen, "Shekhinta ba-Galuta: A Midrashic Response to Destruction and Persecution," *Journal for the Study of Judaism in the Persian, Hellenistic and Roman Periods* 13, nos. 1–2 (1982): 147–159. It seems worth noting that a *Zohar*, the Jewish mystical work, tells of how God entrusted his weapons to the Shekhinah, delivering to her "all the lances, all the swords, all the bows, all the arrows, all the spears, all the catapults, all the citadels, and all the weapons of war" (2.51a).

22. On the role of the Holy Spirit in Byzantine theology, including its association with visions and illumination, see Joost van Rossum, "The Experience of the Holy Spirit in Greek Patristic and Byzantine Theology," *Communio Viatorum* 53, no. 3 (2011): 25–39.

23. Esther Casier Quinn, *The Quest of Seth for the Oil of Life* (Chicago: University of Chicago Press, 1962); Thomas N. Hall, "The Cross as Green Tree in the *Vindicta Salvatoris* and the Green Rod of Moses in Exodus," *English Studies* 72, no. 4 (1991): 297–307.

24. The image is featured on the website of the Byzantine and Christian Museum, accessed May 24, 2025, https://www.byzantinemuseum.gr/en/permanentexhibition/byzantine_world/worship_art/?bxm=995#:~:text=Blood%20and%20water%20flow%20from,seen%20only%20in%20the%20sanctuary.

25. See Yuval, "Easter and Passover," 104–105.

26. For more on the anti-Jewish polemics woven into Byzantine liturgy, see Basilius Groen, "Anti-Judaism in the Present-Day Byzantine Liturgy," *Journal of Eastern Christian Studies* 60 (2008): 369–387.

27. For examples of the anti-Jewish imagery woven into literary accounts and visual depictions of the Arma Christi, see Anthony Bale, *The Jew in the Medieval Book: English Antisemitisms, 1350–1500* (Cambridge: Cambridge University Press, 2006), 145–168.

28. For these and other examples, see John Coffey, "England's Exodus: The Civil War as a War of Deliverance," in *England's Wars of Religion, Revisited*, ed. Charles Prior and Glenn Burgess (London: Routledge, 2016), 253–280.

29. Michael Walzer, *Exodus and Revolution* (New York: Basic Books, 1985).

30. The painting, along with bibliography, has been published in John Caldwell and Oswaldo Rodriguez Roque, *American Paintings in the Metropolitan Museum of Art*, 3 vols. (New York: Metropolitan Museum of Art, 1994), 1:502–503.

31. See, for example, Henry McNeal Turner, "The Plagues of This Country," *Christian Recorder*, July 12, 1862, #HMTProject, http://www.thehenrymcnealturnerproject.org/2017/05/plagues-of-this-country.html.

32. For the text of the Emancipation Memorial and Lincoln's response, see William Patton, *President Lincoln and the Chicago Memorial on Emancipation* (Baltimore: Maryland Historical Society, 1887). The quotation cited here appears on p. 12.

33. Patton, *President Lincoln and the Chicago Memorial on Emancipation*, 13. For more on this episode, see Richard Carwardine, "Whatever Shall Appear to Be God's Will, I Will Do: The Chicago Initiative and Lincoln's Proclamation," in *Lincoln's Proclamation: Emancipation Reconsidered*, ed. William Blair and Karen Fisher Younger (Chapel Hill: University of North Carolina Press, 2009), 75–102.

34. Quoted in Marion Miller, *Great Debates in American History*, 14 vols. (New York: Current Literature, 1913), 6:390.

35. John Stevens Cabot Abbott, *The History of the Civil War in America*, vol. 1 (Springfield, MA: Gurdon Bill, 1863), 235–236.

36. Sean Scott, "'Good Children Die Happy': Confronting Death during the Civil War," in *Children and Youth during the Civil War*, ed. James Marten (New York: New York University Press, 2012), 92–109.

37. On John Brown as an avenging angel, see "A Message to Pharaoh," as discussed in Joe Lockwood, "'Earth Feels the Time of Prophet Song': John Brown and Public Poetry," in *The Afterlife of John Brown*, ed. Andrew Taylor and Eldrid Herrington (New York: Palgrave Macmillan, 2005), 69–87, esp. 73–75.

38. Charles Denison, *Illustrated Life, Campaigns, and Public Services of Lieut. General Grant* (Philadelphia: Peterson, 1865), 245. Compare also P. V. Ferree, *The Heroes of the War for the Union and Their Accomplishments* (Cincinnati: Carroll, 1864), 402 (General George Henry Thomas as an "avenging angel"); and more caustically, the descriptions of marauding Union troops as "destroying angels," as noted in Walter Fleming, *Civil War and Reconstruction in Alabama* (New York: Columbia University Press, 1905), 120–121.

39. Eli Evans, *The Provincials: A Personal History of the Jews of Atlanta* (1973; repr., New York: Free Press, 1997), 240. I was not able to retrieve the account written by Mayer's descendant Ben Mayer of how his family commemorates the story during Passover, but an excerpt has been posted by Christopher Hodapp, "A Masonic Passover," *Freemasons for Dummies* (blog), April 18, 2011, https://freemasonsfordummies.blogspot.com/2011/04/masonic-passover.html.

40. I have learned from the historian Adam Mendelsohn that some Masons did use their fraternal connection to fellow Masons to try to transcend the division between North and South, but he and other historians I have asked doubt the veracity of the story recounted here—the reference to the Shriners, for example, is anachronistic since that particular Masonic fraternity was only founded after the war in 1872.

41. On the celebration of Sherman's campaign as a new exodus from Egypt, see Edmund Drago, "How Sherman's March through Georgia Affected the Slaves," *Georgia Historical Quarterly* 57 (1973): 361–375, esp. 364. For the hailing of Sherman as the angel of the Lord, see Lloyd Lewis, *Sherman: Fighting Prophet* (New York: Harcourt, Brace, 1932), 438.

42. Edward Lounsbery, *The Safe Refuge in the Day of Calamity* (Philadelphia: Ringwalt and Brown, 1862), 5.

43. Patton, *Chicago Memorial on Emancipation*, 15.

44. Morris Sutphen, *Discourse on the Occasion of the Death of Abraham Lincoln, Late President of the United States* (Philadelphia: Jas B. Rodgers, 1865), 5–6. Beecher's speech appears in John Gilmary Shea, ed., *The Lincoln Memorial: A Record of the Life, Assassination and Obsequies of the Martyred President* (New York: Bunce and Huntington, 1865), 101–108, esp. 104; and the relevant passage from the *New York Times* comes from the edition published on April 17, 1865, 4.

45. For more on Sharp's antislavery reading of the Exodus story, see Thomas Welch, "The Role of the Bible in the British Abolition of Slavery, 1671–1824," *Canadian Society of Church History: Historical Papers* 2000 (2000): 77–193. The passage cited here is from Granville Sharp, *The Law of Retribution: A Serious Warning to Great Britain and Her Colonies, Founded on Unquestionable Examples of God's Temporal Vengeance against Tyrants, Slave-holders, and Oppressors* (London: B. White, 1776), 16.

46. See John Coffey, "'Tremble Britannia': Fear, Providence and the Abolition of the Slave Trade 1758–1807," *English Historical Review* 127 (2012): 844–881.

47. *Genius of Universal Emancipation*, June 1828, 133.

48. Maria Stewart, "Religion and the Pure Principles, the Sure Foundation of Which We Must Build," reprinted in *Maria W. Stewart, America's First Black Woman Political Writer*, ed. Marilyn Richardson (Bloomington: Indiana University Press, 1987), 27–42, esp. 39–40.

49. The eulogy can be found online: Abraham Lincoln, "Eulogy on Henry Clay," July 16, 1852, Abraham Lincoln Online, https://www.abrahamlincolnonline.org/lincoln/speeches/clay.htm.

50. Henry Highland Garnet, "An Address to the Slaves of the United States," 1843, posted on BlackPast on January 25, 2007, https://www.blackpast.org/african-american-history/1843-henry-highland-garnet-address-slaves-united-states/.

51. For the text of Lincoln's speech, see Abraham Lincoln, "Second Inaugural Address" (Champaign, IL: Project Gutenberg, 1978), https://www.gutenberg.org/cache/epub/8/pg8-images.html.

52. Forbes's lecture was entitled "Covid-19: A Parable of Plagues of Deliverance" and was live streamed on September 14, 2020, by the Center for Social Justice and Reconciliation at the Union Theological Seminary. For an online recording, accessed on May 12, 2024, see https://www.youtube.com/watch?v=wJ91fRT1YfI.

Epilogue

1. As quoted in Kimberly Winston, "The Eleventh Plague: Passover in the Time of Coronavirus," Religion Unplugged, April 6, 2020, https://religionunplugged.com/news/2020/4/6/the-eleventh-plague-passover-in-the-time-of-coronavirus.

2. David Moss, *The Moss Haggadah: A Complete Reproduction of the Haggadah* (Rochester, NY: Bet Alpha Editions, 1990), folios 28b and 29a.

3. The story, translated by Orr Scharf, appears in *The Freedom Haggadah: A Story of Protest and Hope* (2023), n.p.

4. For more on the origin and development of the four sons midrash, see Fred Francis, "The Baraita of the Four Sons," *Journal of the American Academy of Religion* 42 (1974): 280–297; and, more recently, Joseph Tabory, "The Baraita of the Four Sons," *Tarbiz* 81 (2012): 165–189 (Hebrew).

INDEX

Note: Page numbers in *italics* indicate figures.

A NOTE ON THE TYPE

This book has been composed in Arno, an Old-style serif typeface in the classic Venetian tradition, designed by Robert Slimbach at Adobe.